On INTELLECTUALS

On
INTELLECTUALS
Theoretical Studies
Case Studies

Edited by Philip Rieff

Doubleday & Company, Inc.

Garden City, New York 1969

Acknowledgment is made to the following for permission to reprint their material:

Cambridge University Press: Comparative Studies in Society and History, Vol. 1, No. 1, Edward Shils. "The Intellectuals and the Powers: Some Perspectives for Comparative Analysis," © 1958 by Editorial Committee of Comparative Studies in Society and History.

Isaiah Berlin, "The Life and Opinions of Moses Hess," © 1959 by the Jewish Historical Society of England, for whom the essay was originally published by W. Heffer & Sons Limited, Cambridge, England.

Harold Matson Co., Inc.: Lines from *Dedicatory Stanzas to Stephen Spender* by C. Day Lewis; from *Where Are the War Poets?* by C. Day Lewis.

A. D. Peters & Company: Stephen Spender's four lines beginning "[I] who live under the shadows of war . . ." from *New Signatures,* Michael Roberts, Ed. (Hogarth, London, 1932, p. 91) reprinted by permission of A. D. Peters & Company.

Random House, Inc., and Faber and Faber Limited: Lines from "The Funeral," © 1934 and renewed 1962 by Stephen Spender. Reprinted from *Collected Poems 1928–1953,* by Stephen Spender. Lines from "Poem XVI" (retitled "1929"), © 1934 and renewed 1962 by W. H. Auden. Reprinted from *Collected Shorter Poems 1927–1957,* by W. H. Auden. Lines from "Letter to Lord Byron," from *Letters from Iceland,* by W. H. Auden and Louis MacNeice, © 1937 and renewed 1965 by W. H. Auden. Lines from "Spain 1937," © 1940 and renewed 1968 by W. H. Auden. Reprinted from *The Collected Poetry of W. H. Auden.* Lines from "Poem XXII," from *Poems,* by W. H. Auden, © 1934 and renewed 1962 by W. H. Auden. Lines from "Poem XXII," from *Poems,* by W. H. Auden, © 1934 and renewed 1962 by W. H. Auden.

Robert A. Nisbet, "Project Camelot: An Autopsy," © 1966 by Robert A. Nisbet.

CONTENTS

Preface vii

Contributors xi

Theoretical Studies:

"THE INTELLECTUAL": A SOCIAL ROLE
CATEGORY
  Talcott Parsons 3

THE INTELLECTUALS AND THE POWERS:
SOME PERSPECTIVES FOR COMPARATIVE
ANALYSIS
  Edward Shils 25

THE INTELLECTUAL AND SOCIETY: THE
SOCIAL FUNCTION OF THE "FOOL" IN THE
TWENTIETH CENTURY
  Ralf Dahrendorf 49

IDEAS, INTELLECTUALS, AND STRUCTURES OF
DISSENT
  J. P. Nettl 53

Case Studies:

THE LIFE AND OPINIONS OF MOSES HESS
Sir Isaiah Berlin 125

BARBARISM THE FIRST DANGER
Horace Bushnell 167

ENGLISH INTELLECTUALS AND POLITICS IN
THE 1930s
Stuart Samuels 196

PLAN OF THE SCIENTIFIC OPERATIONS
NECESSARY FOR REORGANIZING SOCIETY
Auguste Comte 248

PROJECT CAMELOT: AN AUTOPSY
Robert A. Nisbet 283

THE CASE OF DR OPPENHEIMER
Philip Rieff 314

Index 341

PREFACE

I have divided this book into a theoretical section and case studies. Part I contains four theoretical perspectives on the intellectual. The established view is offered first in historical perspective, with his customary magisterial amplitude, by the most influential sociological theorist of our time, Talcott Parsons. Edward Shils reviews the history and comparative structures of intellectual life in a masterly way, for the subject practically belongs to him; he, too, writes from the established sociological perspective. Ralf Dahrendorf sketches one pervasive view of the intellectual: as critic-jester, gadfly to men of power, and yet in Dahrendorf's later view someone far more powerful. J. P. Nettl's article concludes the first section: a brilliant move to formulate a theory of intellectuals in terms of their ideas rather than of their social roles. In this important and summative essay, Nettl edges the critical analysis of modern intellectuals beyond its present limits, sharpening the polemical edge of that analysis so to open to us fresh ways of thinking about ourselves.

No book on Western intellectuals can be instructive without catching the strangest case of all, that model of the modern intellectual: the intellectual Jew in the act of committing identity-suicide. Isaiah Berlin's essay on Hess presents such a case. Moses Hess was a dissenting intellectual, ever in search of a structure of dissent, who, having found the proletariat and young Dr. Marx, and sensing (as his untranslated letters to Herzen show) that

communist dissent might well prove a new barbarism, finally returned to the dissent eternally represented by the national existence
of the Jews.

In "Barbarism the First Danger," Horace Bushnell, a great
American Protestant intellectual, urges a missionary response upon
the Church, as an institution of civility, to those masses of nineteenth-century Americans who dissented with their feet and tried
to remove themselves westward from constraining surveillances.
Bushnell's lecture shows a clerical intellectual locked in combat
with an escaping laity and with the culture of violence, against
which only the shrewdest missionary spirit might prevail. In the
1840s religious intellectuals like Bushnell knew they were on the
defensive in the struggle over the shape and content of American
culture; they never recovered the initiative. Yet, in Bushnell's time,
that first culture elite of America (and the last), the clergy, still
knew what they were about; they had confidence enough in their
symbolic strength to mount counterattacks against our "bowie-
knife civilization," along the lines sketched by Bushnell. Nowadays,
and for many decades past, that confidence has been shattered.
The clergy has had no successor. America is without a culture elite.
There is no interdictory vanguard learned and convinced enough
to take the initiative in defense of culture against a barbarism more
powerful than ever Bushnell dreamt. On the contrary, both our
militarists and our militants are barbarians, in Bushnell's correct
usage. Both sides would enact therapies of violence that will destroy
all culture.

It is not surprising that both sides have recruited as their medicine men the social scientists, who have long aspired to succeed the
clergy as the American culture elite. Precisely these aspirants have
lost all memory of what culture must be about, despite the fact
that their original mentor, Comte, could teach them that the reconstruction of culture alone justifies their professional existence.
Comte knew that the main subject of sociology is the "grand crisis
now experienced by the most civilized nations" (p. 248). But who
among his brain children, the scientists of society, successful now
and affluent, reads Comte? Indeed, why should they? Few sociologists remain students of the grand crisis, or its successor crises;
rather, they are its walking symptoms. The selection from Comte

is intended to give the reader access to a document chartering the modern social scientist, heir apparent and opponent of the intellectual in any sense Bushnell would have understood.

In his autopsy of "Project Camelot," Robert A. Nisbet has dissected more than a special case. Here is the esteemed and profitable corruption to which Comte's "Spiritual Power," the social scientists, have blown up, for all to see and smell. Comte's savants have become project-managers, hands of the technological-military head, corrupting the intellectual life as it should be led, especially in the university. My own essay is on a memorable case of the modern scientist-intellectual who, though long emancipated from the surveillances of the Church, finds himself, half willingly, constrained by the state.

Samuels has written a case study of the fitful condition of British intellectuals in the thirties. Respect for British intellectuals is an old American habit, hard to break; but the habit is being broken. They are, more and more, only poor imitations of us. The destructive genius of modernity has passed from the Germans and the British to American intellectuals. Now ours is the ruling capacity to tease out of its concealments the one law modern intellectuals would piously obey, the law of creative catastrophe: that a culture in which everything can be said and shown will produce, as night follows day, a society in which everything, no matter how terrible, can be done.

Of the essays in Part I, those by Parsons and Nettl were written for this volume. Shils's essay first appeared in *Comparative Studies in Society and History,* Vol. 1, No. 1 (October 1958), published by the Cambridge University Press. Dahrendorf's short summary of a position he has developed at length elsewhere appeared in *Die Zeit,* Vol. 26, No. 13 (March 1953). It has been translated by Marianna Layer and revised by myself; the responsibility for this version is entirely my own. Of the essays in Part II, Berlin's "Moses Hess" was first delivered as his Lucien Wolf Memorial Lecture before the Jewish Historical Society, in London, December 1957. The essay appears here in a slightly abridged version; again, I am responsible for this version. Horace Bushnell delivered "Barbarism the First Danger" as a lecture in New York, Boston, and other civilized places between May and June 1847; it was published as "A Discourse for Home Missions" later that year, under the auspices of the American Home Missionary Society. Stuart Samuels' "English Intellectuals" was written for this volume. The selection from Comte is taken from the fourth volume (Third Part, May 1822) of his *System of Positive Polity*. Nisbet's "Project Camelot" was taken from *The Public Interest*, Vol. 1, No. 5 (Autumn 1966). My own essay, the last in the book, first appeared in *The Twentieth Century*, Vol. 156, Nos. 930 and 931 (1954).

Philip Rieff
University of Pennsylvania
May 1968

CONTRIBUTORS

Talcott Parsons is Professor of Sociology at Harvard University.

Edward Shils holds two major appointments: Professor of Social Thought, University of Chicago, and Fellow of Kings College, Cambridge.

Ralf Dahrendorf is Professor of Sociology at the University of Konstanz and an FDP deputy to the West German Parliament.

John Peter Nettl was Professor of Sociology and Political Science at the University of Pennsylvania. He was killed in an airplane crash in October 1968.

Professor Sir Isaiah Berlin is Warden of Wolfson College, Oxford.

Horace Bushnell (1802–76) was a leading Protestant theologian in the America of the mid-nineteenth century.

Stuart Samuels is Assistant Professor of History at the University of Pennsylvania.

Auguste Comte (1798–1857) called himself a positivist and has been called by many others the Father of Sociology.

Robert A. Nisbet is Professor of Sociology at the University of California, Riverside.

Philip Rieff is Benjamin Franklin Professor of Sociology at the University of Pennsylvania.

Theoretical Studies

"THE INTELLECTUAL":

A Social Role Category

Talcott Parsons

This essay will attempt a very general characterization of the category of "intellectual" in his place as a role type in social systems. It will treat the problem first in the most general terms, bringing to bear an overall analysis of the nature of human action systems and illustrations from a very broad sweep of comparative and evolutionary considerations. A second main part, however, will attempt to treat a few salient aspects of the characteristics and status of intellectuals in the modern world. In the final part I shall attempt to bring the analysis to focus on contemporary American society.

In theoretical terms the key reference point is the analytical independence (which, however, directly implies interdependence) between social and cultural systems. Social systems are organized about the exigencies of interaction among acting units, both individual persons and collective units. Cultural systems, on the other hand, are organized about the patterning of meaning in symbolic systems. Relative to action in the more usual senses, meaning systems are always in some respects and to some degree normative in their significance; they specify what in some sense *should* be done and evaluate the actual performance accordingly, rather than either describing what in fact is done or predicting what will be.

There is an immense diversity in the modes and levels at which this occurs, all the way from simple linguistic correctness, in pronunciation and grammar, through the simplest norms of logically correct reasoning and empirically correct statement of simple facts, correct observance of the norms of simple etiquette, such as saying "please" and "thank you" on the proper occasions, to the highest-order normative expectations in the fields of ethical or religious obligation.

In this setting I should like to speak of the intellectual as a person who, though as a member of a society in the nature of the case he performs a complex of social roles, is in his principal role-capacity expected—an expectation normally shared by himself—to put cultural considerations above social in defining the commitments by virtue of which his primary role and position are significant as contributions to valued outcomes of his action. In this respect he would be sharply distinguished from an organization executive, all the way from an absolute monarch on down, from the proprietor of an enterprise, from the "family man"—to say nothing of woman—all of whose primary responsibilities as defined in role terms are anchored primarily in functions for some social system as such. Of course the two foci are not entirely mutually exclusive because there are essential cultural conditions of the functioning of a social system. The best single, though by no means infallible, formula for drawing the line is that in the short run those with societal responsibilities are disposed to sacrifice cultural to societal interests.

Cultural systems are by no means monolithic undifferentiated unities but internally complex, and the more developed they are, the more complex they become. On this basis, though with evolutionary overtones, it is convenient to discriminate a number of foci of cultural interest and responsibility. Religion from the earliest phases of social evolution may be said to have been the matrix from which the other principal parts of cultural systems have differentiated.[1] Even when relatively little specifically "secular" culture can be said to exist, however, there have been signs of a process of differentiation between relatively "pure"

[1] This view was classically stated by Durkheim in *The Elementary Forms of the Religious Life* (London, 1915).

and "applied" religious functions. Among the most familiar of the latter are the administration of ritual in the *rites de passage* and in various kinds of cults and the "therapeutic" function in various forms, often classified by anthropologists as magical.[2] Relatively "pure" religious concern seems to make its earliest appearances in cults that are dissociated from the institutional religion of any whole society—e.g., those around the well-known "holy places" of early Semitic religion,[3] or even such phenomena as the Delphic oracle or the Eleusinian mysteries in Greece; in groups that engage in more or less "philosophical" speculation about problems of meaning, like the upper-class Indians—apparently not only the Brahmans—who produced the Brahmanas and the Upanishads; or "mystics" and "ascetics" who established patterns of orientation leading in the direction of monasticism, again probably earliest on a considerable scale in India.

There are two basic steps of cultural evolution, both of which were apparently extremely widespread over the historic world, that underlie any really extensive development of a more or less "pure" commitment to cultural over societal commitments and functions. These are the development of written language and the so-called "philosophic breakthrough."

Written language, of course, has a long and complex history, going back quite far, with many different levels and forms. There is, however, one essential set of considerations. These revolve around the fact that only with writing did it become possible for cultural content to become dissociated from the social context in which it originated or was used. By far the most important early "documents," then, are probably sacred writings, often in the form of inscriptions on stone—though, of course, chronicles of the exploits of kings and even commercial accounts occur quite early. In any case writing could emancipate tradition from dependence on oral communication and "fix" it independently of fallible memories. Indeed without it there could be no such

---

[2] The religion of the Navajo Indians is a classic case of religious ritual and health magic being almost indistinguishably fused. Cf. Clyde Kluckhohn, "Myths and Rituals: a General Theory," *Harvard Theological Review* (January 1942).

[3] Cf. Robertson Smith, *The Religion of the Semites* (New York, 1889).

thing as "history" in anything like the sense in which we understand the term.[4]

The second basic step is what is generally known as the "philosophic breakthrough," the process by which, at least partially independently and in very different forms in Greece, Israel, India, and China, in the first millennium B.C. there occurred a new level of explicit conceptualization of the nature of the cosmos as the setting of the human condition, and with it interpretation of the human condition itself and its larger meanings. In Greece this took the form of an explicitly philosophical conception of an order of nature in both its normative and its empirical meaning, which greatly reduced the element of capriciousness involved in the mythological conceptions of the anthropomorphic arbitrariness of the behavior of the traditional gods and, somewhat like them, the heroes. Greek philosophy in this sense, culminating in the figures of Socrates, Plato, and Aristotle, laid the main foundations of the rational cognitive culture of the whole of Western civilization, including both philosophy and science and penetrating far into theology.

In Israel, against the background of the early books of the Old Testament and the story of Moses, the main crystallization took place in the prophetic movement, which defined very sharply the universalistic conception of a personal creator God who had created the whole universe and man as His chosen instrument in the implementation of a divine plan, man being the only "creature" who was "made in the image of God." This conception of a transcendental God who ruled *all* human beings and the double conception of man's role, on the one hand as a wholly dependent "creature" of God, on the other as a responsible agent in doing God's will, underlay not only Judaism but Christianity as a whole and Islam. Its fusion with the Greek components in Christianity constituted the main cultural foundation of Western civilization.

In India the breakthrough produced the predominantly religious philosophy of the intellectual elite centering on the con-

---

[4] Though I am not completely sure of my ground here, it is my impression that anything that could be called genuine money—as distinguished from the protomoney of the famous stones of Yap—does not occur in any society that does not already possess written language.

ceptions of karma and transmigration, of the empirical and practical world as a special kind of "illusion" and the associated doctrines of radical salvation in Hindu and Buddhist forms. In China it was least radical, but here tradition was embodied in a collection of classics and itself systematized and canonized to yield an integrated conception of a cosmic order, a human society, and a physical world, which were all of a very distinctive pattern.

These philosophic breakthroughs seem to be the most salient features of a general process of differentiation between the social and the cultural systems. Two particularly conspicuous consequences of this can be distinguished in the social field itself. One of these is the increased prominence within particular societies of social groups and role types who constitute in different ways specialists in cultural matters. This takes the form of groups that are in some sense elite but still do not bear primary responsibility in the operative functions of their societies. It would, however, be rare to find as institutional role types any groups that were organized about the "pure" cultural functions noted above. The pure has rather tended to be fused with the applied. The main exception here is the prophet, who by definition stands outside the main social structure and always in important respects in opposition to it.[5]

The most important of the cultural specialist roles seems to be what is probably the oldest and in most senses the least changed, the administrator of ritual prescriptions—in a religious context the priest, the teacher, and the specialist in "law," i.e., some especially salient set of normative prescriptions for human and social conduct other than ritual as such.

Indeed, it can probably be said that the performer of ritual is the earliest cultural specialist and hence in some sense "intellectual." The "ideational" content has, however, tended to be taken for granted in the form of myth, and, though clear knowledge of it has been an essential qualification of the specialist, often involving prodigious feats of memory, critical evaluation, to say nothing of innovation, has not been so much tabooed as unheard of.

[5] On this and a number of other points in this part of the paper, see especially Max Weber, *The Sociology of Religion* (Boston, 1963).

The function of teaching is inherent at one level in the handing
down of oral ritual tradition, including its background of myth.
With written documents and further rationalization, however, it
could become increasingly differentiated, concerned with the mastery of the texts by the pupils and, in certain respects, with their
understanding of them as well as their capacity for reproducing
them by rote. To be sure, this would for a long time tend to be
organized socially in the form of a system of apprenticeship.
Similar considerations seem to apply to the function of "lawyer."
There is some form of culturally focused normative prescrip-
tion for conduct in all societies, however primitive. But with
written documents this function can become more independent
and more a matter for specialization, particularly in certain cultural systems in which the "legal" element is particularly prominent, such as the Hebrew and the Islamic.

It is perhaps from these two sources in particular, especially
the function of teaching, that a specialization in relatively pure
cultural concerns has tended to crystallize, because of the special
pressure on the teacher to *understand* the subject matter for the
transmission of which he is responsible. This tends in the first
instance to focus on textual criticism, the exegesis of texts, which
are in the nature of the case in many respects inherently unclear, ambiguous, and marked by many gaps, to say nothing
of the problem of their implications for situations unknown to
their authors, often arising long after the time of writing. Independent observation of phenomena in the environment of the
intellectual, in physical and biological nature and in his own
society, are, however, very important foci of independent intellectual concern, even in early times.

In Israel and China the most important foci of intellectualism,
crystallizing about law and teaching respectively, were those of
exegesis of a written tradition of scriptures and classics as they
have come to be called. In India there was a more independent
development of specifically philosophical innovation, and in
Greece a particularly well-rounded one, comprising fundamental
philosophy, science, especially in Aristotle, and a quite new level
of sophistication in highly self-conscious art, especially perhaps
the drama.

It is probably not fortuitous that, in the cultural traditions in which philosophic breakthroughs occurred, there was a marked tendency to organize the custody, and especially the teaching, of the more highly developed cultural tradition on a more elaborate basis, transcending the simplest form of apprenticeship. In China in particular, once the Confucian classics gained canonical status and became the basis of qualification for office, regular schools for their teaching were established. The academy established in Athens by Plato was the beginning of what, in Hellenistic and Roman times, became something approaching a university in the modern sense. Probably in India the system of apprenticeship through the role of guru was more the center of organization than in the other two cases. In post-exilic Judaism, command of the law became the primary focus of ethnic tradition. Not only was the law itself immensely elaborated in the Talmudic writings, but the rabbi, as the man learned in the law, became the principal type of Jewish intellectual—and certainly schools for rabbinical training were established. Finally it is a notable fact that in the Roman Empire, in both its western and eastern branches, there developed a tradition of learning in secular as distinguished from religious law, where regular schools became established for the training of a private legal profession, the jurisconsults.

In spite of the "Dark Ages," when most cultural activities were at a low ebb in the Western world, the development of the medieval synthesis brought together a number of otherwise diverse elements, notably those that were culturally Christian, including Hebrew, and components derived from Greco-Roman antiquity. Socially the Western Catholic Church and the state were authentically parts of the same society, differentiated from each other, but no longer separate in the sense in which the Early Church was separate from the world of "Caesar." On the one hand this provided the base for the most comprehensive development of cultural elements that any civilization had yet possessed, in theology, philosophy, art, science, and law. It did so under the aegis of Christian religious orientations, which provided a firm cultural base, independent of the structure of secular society (in medieval terms, "the state"), and a socially organized collectivity, which was the bearer of this cultural orientation.

In the earlier phases virtually the whole of culture was gathered into the fold of the Church. There was no philosophy independent of theology, no science at all outside a little in the monastery, and the only art was directly religious, in the illumination of manuscripts and the decoration of church and monastic buildings. Even so, the Church had built into her own structure crucial elements of the previous culture, notably Greek philosophy as an essential ingredient of her theology and Roman law as essential to her organization as a Church in the form of canon law.

Hence the stage was set for such great developments as scholastic philosophy, which was certainly far more than the simple handmaiden of theology and indeed, especially through Thomas Aquinas, made a major contribution to the reworking of theology and eventually extended the influence of philosophy beyond the Catholic range into the new theologies of the Reformation; in different ways both Luther and Calvin as well as others were philosophically trained and influenced. Western Christian theology from the high Middle Ages on has been explicitly philosophical, hence intellectual in something of a new sense. A movement reaching far back into the early Middle Ages but culminating in the Renaissance saw not only a very general revival of learning in the classics but above all developments in the arts, which, though still dealing largely with religious topics, achieved an independence for art as such that had not previously characterized it within a Christian framework.[6]

So it is not surprising that the later Renaissance saw the beginnings of truly modern science, first in Italy but extending rapidly to predominantly Protestant northern Europe, and also saw the notable revival of Roman law, this time secular rather than solely canon law. In literature the late Middle Ages and the Renaissance, with important involvements of Protestant culture, saw the emergence of the structure of the cultural world that constitutes the heritage of modern Western societies.

These great developments could not have taken place without an increasing number of people specializing in cultural concerns

[6] Thus the central symbol of Renaissance painting was the Madonna. With all its directly religious significance, it was certainly also a legitimizing symbolization, and the increasingly lifelike infants certainly fit in this context.

and being, relatively speaking, relieved of responsibility for current societal functions, even in the form of applied culture. A bewildering variety of social arrangements was involved, but in the earliest phases by far the most important location was the monastery, particularly with the development of the Dominican and Franciscan orders, which relaxed the relatively exclusive devotional emphasis of the earlier orders in favor of a larger place for both charitable and cultural pursuits. Most of the prominent schoolmen were members of the orders, conspicuously different from the secular clergy. So were many of the early artists, and presumably the architects of cathedrals as well as abbeys. The name of Roger Bacon is testimony to the fact that even science was not unknown to the medieval monastery. Indeed the ancestors of the modern university, in Paris, England, and Italy, were essentially offshoots of the monasteries, often standing in considerable tension with the administrative organization of the Church.

Increasingly, however, cultural specialists were to be found in lay statuses. During this period undoubtedly the most important organizational form was the patronage of princes and noblemen, including, of course, the princes of the Church, in the embellishment of churches and palaces and, increasingly, civic buildings. The urban nobles of Italy were particularly important in this respect, and the survival there of a special type of city-state organization may well have something to do with the flowering of the Renaissance in Italy, because the predominantly rural nobility farther north were much less disposed to value the developing secular culture until its importance had come to be fully established in Italy—despite the fact that the philosophical center of the later Middle Ages was Paris, not Italy.

Let us now take a drastic leap to the modern world. It does not seem to be wide of the truth to say that in no known society —or rather complex of societies—has there been such a widespread, intensive, and extensive specialization in cultural matters as in the modern West—West in the pre-cold war sense. This situation has a number of striking characteristics. One of the most salient is certainly the high relative prominence of the secular elements of the cultural world: secular philosophy, art,

science, law, etc. The explicitly religious elements have certainly
suffered an important *relative* decline—being confined more or
less to such fields as theology, as the applied functions of the
practicing clergy have been to church history and similar fields.
It is questionable, however, whether there has been an absolute decline—the contrary seems rather to be true. Still more
important, there has been a notable rise in the cultural standards
of the religious specialist through the integration of much secular
philosophy into theology and of the tradition of the critical historical disciplines, "higher criticism," and various elements of
this sort, into knowledge of the scriptures.

The big growth, however, has been in the secular fields. Relatively early on, law became an intellectual discipline as well as
an applied profession. Closely associated with it is history, which
may be said to be the "mother" of the social sciences. Then there
is the humanistic field centered on classical studies, particularly
language, literature, and the arts. Philosophy more and more declared its independence from theology and gradually came to be
affiliated with the impressive development of science, which has,
certainly in quantitative terms, become the most important part
of the immense complex of cultural specialization.

Several trends have marked the broad cultural development.
A major one has been the immense spread of subject matter
in which something on the order of professional concern and
performance has developed. This is true of the arts, in which
writers, sculptors, architects, painters, musicians, etc., have pro-
liferated. It is even truer of the fields with a primary cognitive
orientation with the development of humanistic scholarship, particularly the complex that can be called historical. Scholarly attention has been turned to wider and wider ranges of societies
and cultures, breaking outside the circle of the particular historical background of Western civilization to the oriental cultures. Science has spread from the physical to the biological
and the biological to the social. Techniques of study and analysis
have become immensely refined in a myriad of ways.

Let us now attempt to characterize some of the salient features of the modern, predominantly secular intellectual groups
with reference to three independent and cross-cutting dichotomies.
These are, respectively, that of primary social affiliation, namely

as to whether it is upper or lower in the system of stratification; that of the cultural subject matter itself, where the distinction between primarily humanistic and scientific seems to be most crucial; and that of the primarily pure in a cultural commitment or the primarily applied in defining the meaningfulness of command of cultural resources.

The first essential proposition concerns the broad historical fact that the primary societal center of gravity of cultural specialization has lain in the upper ranges of the scale of social stratification, though this proposition should not be understood in too simple a form. The important place of the monastery has been mentioned, and this has, in Western history, been the prototype of the elite group. With the high postmedieval development of an aristocratically dominated society, the typical "intellectuals" were, if not churchmen, not themselves aristocrats either, but definitely under the patronage of aristocrats, clerical and lay, monarchical and otherwise.

This situation is associated with the fact that the main outline of Western social structure down to perhaps the eighteenth century could, with however many qualifications, be characterized in terms of a "two-class system" as I have put it in several connections.[7] There were two primary cases of it in early modern society—the differentiation between the religious orders and the laity in the Church and that between the aristocracy and the common people in secular society. The main cultural impetus started in the monastery and was propagated, as a function of the increasing importance of secular elements of culture itself, to become a responsibility of the aristocratic elements of the secular order.

Here, however, one of the critical and in the long run creative conflicts of principle of society first came to a head in our own background—the conflict between the organization of the status of secular aristocracies in terms of status by ascription and the principle of competence in the mastery and innovative development of cultural systems. The cultural field is the most important locus of universalistic standards in the whole realm of action, whereas that of heredity of status is perhaps the most massively

[7] Cf., for example, Parsons et al., eds., *Theories of Society* (New York, 1961), Introduction to Part II, Vol. I, pp. 239ff.

ubiquitous of all particularistic standards. In addition, secular aristocracy was deeply involved in practical societal responsibilities, since it was the focus of political organization in the society.

The resolution of this conflict was, for a long time, the actual performance of most cultural functions by non-aristocratic personnel, drawn first from the monastery, then increasingly from a wide variety of social origins in secular society, but under the patronage of aristocracy, which took the responsibility for promoting cultural creativity. Of course, aristocratic patrons received important benefits—from the Medici family having their tombs designed by Michelangelo to the glory of supporting the famous Hobbes as a "family philosopher."

This division of labor between aristocrats and the intellectuals they patronized implied an important pattern of common values. We may look at their respective relations to this pattern in two lights. On the one hand it has meant a certain presumption on the part of intellectuals that the values of the aristocracy were indeed the "best" and, on the other hand, a certain tendency to define the parts of the intellectual universe that were both secular and relatively undifferentiated as the top of the relevant hierarchy. This may be said to have had something to do with the special prestige the "humanities" have come to have in the modern cultural world.

In more or less directly structural terms, a situation similar in this respect to that of the Renaissance has been by no means absent in many very recent cases. In England there has been a close connection between the special prestige position of the ancient universities, the special prestige of the humanities within them, particularly at Oxford, and the preservation in England of a social structure in which aristocracy has played a very special part. In modified forms similar things can be said about various countries of continental Europe, particularly France and Italy. Another striking case is the very pervasive one of Latin America, which seems to exhibit a remarkable uniformity over a very wide area in these respects.[8]

To be once more very schematic, as this whole analysis must be, it may be contended that the development of the modern

[8] Cf. Frank Tannenbaum, *Ten Keys to Latin America* (New York, 1962), Chapter VII.

university is the most important outcome in social structure of this inherent tension. The university may be said to have had two sociological "parents," on the one hand the Church and on the other aristocratic, including royal, patronage. It slowly and haltingly created an institutional framework within which scholarly pursuits could be followed on an *occupational* basis that was free from the bonds of hereditary ascription to the immediate controls of direct patronage, and at the same time from the restrictions of the monastery. That the progress was slow and halting is attested by the long periods of stagnation of European universities, and by the number of seminal intellectual movements that occurred outside the university setting, from the work of the *philosophes* of the French Enlightenment, through the English Utilitarians, to certain of the foundations of late nineteenth-century medical science through such figures as Pasteur and Freud.[9]

The keynote of the dichotomy just outlined is the famous association between a "scholar" and a "gentleman," when it is understood that "gentleman" is here meant in the class status sense, not in that of good character. A serious problem was posed, however, when the empirical sciences began to grow in relative significance: the experimental method necessitated technological operations, and the gentleman was not permitted, except for the use of arms, to "work with his hands." The difficulty extended into certain applied fields like medicine where even physical examination was taboo for the gentleman-physician. This, along with the sheer fact of greater antiquity, seems to be a main source of the prestige conflict between the humanities and the sciences, our second dichotomy, which is still going on. There has been a certain tendency to consider the scientist as not quite a "nice person," his calling as one not suitable for a gentleman. On the other hand the special virtue attributed in some scientific circles to willingness to "get one's hands dirty" smacks a good deal of reaction formation. In any case this complex may, along with deeper-lying factors, have something to do with the prominent part played in science by the more or less middle-class

9 On this last phase, see Joseph Ben-David, "Scientific Productivity and Academic Organization in 19th century Medicine," *American Sociological Review*, Vol. 25, No. 6 (December 1960).

Puritans rather than, e.g., in England, Anglican gentlemen. It helps to explain the hard struggle that the sciences underwent to gain high recognition, and hence the fact that their emergence at the very top is so recent.

This conflict between the humanities and the sciences has, of course, had an important bearing on the position of the social sciences. Almost in the nature of the case, they have been the latest of the three to emerge as genuine disciplines, and equally in the nature of the case, they have tended to be caught between the fires. In terms of subject matter they seem to belong to the humanities—a fact that underlay the late nineteenth-century German tendency to dissociate them from the sciences altogether as *Geistes*—or *Kulturwissenschaften*. But by virtue of method they belong to the sciences. History to this day has been slow to identify with the scientific tradition, and law has also tended to remain aloof from it. With the partial exception of economics, only well within our own century has a major crystallization of social or, to include psychology, behavioral science occurred, and this movement is still in its very early stages.

The third dichotomy is that between the concerns of the "pure" intellectual disciplines and the applied. The case of medicine has already been noted. The clinical aspect has been of such importance that a major conflict has been going on for a long time between the interests of clinical service to patients and the social setting of that service and the interests of developing the underlying body of scientific knowledge through research.[10]

Indeed, every science-based profession, and some, like law, that are not primarily so, has become involved in the conflicts over this problem. The problem is, of course, like the others, far from absolute. It seems, however, to be a sound historical generalization to say that the groups engaged in relatively pure research and analysis have made greater contributions to practical benefits than the practitioners have to scientifically general-

[10] That the resulting structural division within the American medical profession is important as underlying the apparently anomalous political conservatism of organized medicine in this country is a position I have argued in a recent paper. See John A. Clausen and Robert Strauss, eds., *Annals of the American Academy of Political and Social Science,* March 1963.

ized knowledge by processes of induction from *practical* as distinguished from empirical research. Thus the main source of physics as a science has not, with some important exceptions, lain in manufacturing technology, nor that of economic science in the practical experience of businessmen.[11] The history of medicine and engineering in these respects has been repeated by economics and psychology in our own time when the applied tail has tended to wag the more purely scientific dog.

The two most important institutional protections of the pure disciplines have, since the relative decline of the importance of the monastery, been the association of these disciplines with aristocracy on the one hand and with the university on the other. In the earlier phases, aristocracy alone could afford to support and legitimize cultural activity that was simultaneously culturally valued and "useless." With the growth of the intellectual disciplines and the relative decline of aristocracy, the university has become the main institutional trustee of the great cultural traditions, including incidentally, through theological faculties, their religious components.

A kind of "dialectic" process has been involved in this aspect of the development of universities. Three of the traditional faculties of the continental European university, those of theology, medicine, and law, were primarily "applied," with, in German terms, only the "philosophical" faculty devoted mainly to the purely cultural disciplines; and even this was compromised by its relation to the training of the teaching profession, especially at the secondary school level. Particularly in the United States, however, the recent phase has seen a new absorption by universities of the training and research functions of applied professions, notably law and medicine, so that the *university* law school and medical school have become pace setters, not only for the training of practitioners, but also for setting the primary *intellectual* standards of the respective professions. Accompanying this has been the establishment of schools associated with newly emerging professions, notably, in addition to public health as a close adjunct of medicine, business administration and education.

[11] Perhaps the most important specific piece of research supporting this generalization is the famous monograph of Merton on *Science Technology and Society in 17th Century England* (Bruges, 1938).

The primary measure of the ascendancy of the university as trustee of the relatively pure cultural tradition over the practical people whose functions are mainly applied is the value of a professional education in the applied professions. This has gone so far that, in most of these fields, professional training in a university setting has become the indispensable prerequisite of high standing in the practicing profession itself. There is no comparable respect in which "practical experience" has become a prerequisite of eligibility to teach or conduct research in the respective fields. In the light of these considerations the still common devaluation of "eggheadism" by practical men can fairly be interpreted as involving a generous component of reaction formation.

One further point needs attention before drawing a few conclusions about the present role and situation of the intellectuals. This concerns the well-known fact that, on the humanistic side of the arts, institutionalization in the framework of the university has been partial and one-sided. In the first instance it has been *scholarship,* especially historical scholarship, in these fields, that has found its place in the university. The "creative" artist and, in the appropriate fields, the "performing" artist have until recently remained outside. This is another basis of asymmetry between the humanities and the sciences. The academic humanist is to a particularly high degree engaged in studying, analyzing, and interpreting what other, non-academic people have done, particularly in a rather remote past. The scientist is far more the direct agent of the relevant creative process. Indeed the tendency to confine the term "creative" to the humanistic side of culture is indicative of what may be felt to be another reaction formation. Surely it is true that the highly original scientist typified by the Nobel Prize winner is creative in a sense in which the historian of literature as distinguished from the creator of his subject matter often is not. But the imperative of academic equality may operate to deny recognition of creativity to both the humanistic and the scientific members of the same faculty. Whether the increasing incorporation of the creative arts into the university setting is going to change this remains to be seen.

In this concluding section the first important point to make concerns the very high and, in the present century, rapidly increasing importance to modern societies of the intellectual disciplines and of the personnel trained in them. However greatly admired the relatively few greatest creative minds of the past may be, there seems to be little doubt that the proportions of populations with a high enough level of training and sophistication to be significantly creative is far higher today than ever before, with the exception of a very few historical cases like fifth-century Athens or the high Renaissance in Italy.[12] Particularly in the applied areas there has been an enormous spread of trained competence. Indeed, through universal education and in other ways the cultural competence of very large populations as a whole has been raised to previously unheard-of levels, however romantically picturesque the preliterate folk-culture elements that have been displaced may seem.

Secondly, through research, especially in the sciences, including the behavioral, but operating to some degree in nearly all fields, the development of cultural traditions has become an institutionalized dynamic factor in social change on a level that has not been true of earlier periods to any comparable extent—previous major cultural developments have been much more episodic, depending on special constellations of favorable circumstances.

It is probably not too much to say that, even in the pragmatic, "tough-minded" United States the groups with intellectual training, for most of their members to professional levels, have either actually become, or are rapidly approaching the position of being, strategically the most important in American society, possibly for its day-to-day functioning, certainly for its longer-run future. Furthermore, the university has become the source of the higher echelons of higher education, the training ground for its faculties' own successors in the teaching function, and, most important of all, the primary structural location of the all-important function of the advancement of knowledge in its broadest sense.

If it has not already happened, this combination of strategically important factors is rapidly bringing the university to the position of the centrally important social organization of our society,

---

[12] These great bursts of creative activity are surely not explained *only* by unusual concentrations of talented people. Another type of factor is that analyzed by Kroeber in his *Configurations of Culture Growth,* but there are certainly various others as well.

not, of course, totally displacing the big business corporation or the big trade union, and certainly not big government, but acquiring a previously unknown importance relative to them. None of these could now function effectively without a highly developed university system. The universities are in turn dependent on these agencies for many things, not only the elementary protection of academic freedom, but above all, financial support and general approval; the point is that they are also highly and increasingly dependent on the universities.[13] The contribution of the university is neither wealth nor political power, though it contributes heavily to the factors that are ingredients of both. It is, rather, a main fountainhead of the "non-material" factors of effective social action, normative ideas and standards, philosophical and scientific knowledge and understanding, and the types of competence based on these. These contributions are so significant that it becomes worth while, in the system of societal interchanges, to pay for them with considerable power and a great deal of wealth.

Let us go back to the conception of intellectuals as the social role category whose incumbents tend to give primacy to cultural considerations over societal in the definition of their expectations and the obligations applying to them. It then becomes evident that in the course of recent social developments the relative importance of intellectuals, in terms both of relative numbers and of spread of the subject-matter fields in which they can claim to be "authorities," has tended to increase greatly and rapidly.

The clarity of this cultural primacy is blurred by the very great and absolutely, but probably not *relatively,* increasing importance of the applied fields of the intellectual disciplines. Because of the essential fact of interpenetration, the society as a system can never be understood in concrete but only in analytical distinction from its institutionalized culture. Hence the society has been in the course of becoming progressively more importantly char-

[13] This growth in the importance of the university in the United States is the more notable in view of the fact that only a century ago, at the time of the Civil War, there was nothing that could be called a university, as distinguished from a college, on the North American continent. The establishment of the university system clearly dates from the last third of the nineteenth century.

acterized by the institutionalization of "high" culture, including being in the most directly pragmatic sense dependent on such culture, particularly science and law, for its functioning. Even the most parochial general practitioner of medicine in our society is educated in science in a sense in which only a tiny few in any occupation were a century ago.

In a sense that was scarcely true before the nineteenth century, the general trend of social development has come to be structured around the impact of systematic cultural innovation, by the strains and lags generated by the necessary slowness of the process of its full institutionalization and the unevenness of the impact in different sectors of the social structure. Hence it has become possible for an applied profession whose members are relatively highly "sophisticated" to take a political position that is in general terms identified with the least progressive in the society from the point of view of general trends—as in the case of "organized medicine."

In the broad situation just sketched, it is natural that the intellectual groups should tend to feel a growing sense of concern for the state of the society in which they live, a concern that is expressed both in a sense of responsibility and in the assertion of a "right to be heard," to exert "influence." In their own right, however, intellectuals, the more so the "purer" in our sense their cultural specialization, are necessarily *not* among the primary holders of political power or controllers of economic resources. Some to be sure seek positions of power in the large operative organizations, both private and governmental, though even here the main role of the applied intellectual expert is more in the "staff" than the "line" connection,[14] and exercising power is generally not their primary role.

It is through assertion of commitments to values on the one hand and the exertion of influence through the prestige of in-

[14] Thus, to take two examples of "eggheads" in government, W. W. Rostow is chairman of the planning section of the Department of State, not a primary "policy maker," and Jerome Wiesner is chairman of the President's Scientific *Advisory* Committee. In my technical terms these men work through the medium of influence much more than power. See my two complementary papers, "On the Concept of Influence," *Public Opinion Quarterly* (Spring 1963), and "On the Concept of Political Power," *Proceedings of the American Philosophical Society* (1963).

dividual, institutional, disciplinary, and other sources of "reputa-
tion" on the other that the intellectual in so far as he does not
control the more "material" means of having an impact must
try to exercise his responsibility and his right to be heard. Considerations such as these seem to have something to do with the
prominence of "ideologies" in our time.

I would define an ideology as a body of ideas that is at once
empirical and evaluative in reference to actual and potential
states of a social system.[15] An ideology thus includes an empirically grounded diagnosis whose degree of validity is, of course,
an open question of the state of the system, typically a society;
an estimate of possible directions of change; and a value-based
assertion of what the direction of change (or objection to change)
and measures to implement it should be.

Ideology here should be distinguished from the main cultural
content of a religion, which I would interpret to be the central
structure of the "grounding of meaning" of the human condition
that is characteristic of a cultural system. Ideology is concerned
rather with the value aspect of meaning for human societies,
hence its relation to the state of the social system. It thus has
special reference to the state of the behavioral science disciplines.
There is a sense in which ideology is a special "matrix" from
which various more strictly empirical and more specialized
branches of social science have tended to emerge, and it clearly
has a close relation to the role assigned above to history as the
"mother" of the social sciences. Ideology is in a sense history
grown self-conscious and socially responsible but at the same
time more selective relative to technical standards, more passionately partisan, more justificatory, and, under the pressure for
justification, more analytical and rationalistic.

That ideology as distinguished from religious thought should
have come to such relatively great prominence and that it is
concerned with the empirical state of secular societies reflects
the general process of differentiation of the cultural system with
which this analysis began. This process includes both differentiation of the cultural from the societal elements of action and in-

[15] See, on the concept, my paper, "An Approach to the Sociology of
Knowledge" in *Proceedings of the Fourth World Congress of Sociology*
(Stresa, Italy, 1959), Vol. IV.

ternal differentiation of the cultural system itself. It is not surprising that in some movements, like the Marxist, ideology should have been elevated to religious status, the "dialectic of history" coming to occupy the place of a strange secular god—or at least what Kenneth Burke refers to as the "god term" of the system.[16] At any rate I am arguing that ideology has become the primary instrument of the modern secular intellectual classes in their bid to be considered generally important, to have an impact on the affairs of the society commensurate with, or perhaps running somewhat ahead of, their actual position of strategic importance in it. Ideological propaganda as a way of exercising influence in a technical sense is for them the functional equivalent of power for the political and executive groups and of wealth for the "propertied" groups, which are now to a high degree corporate rather than individual.

This, of course, is a matter of generalized influence on the affairs of the society and should be carefully distinguished from influence exerted in the specific subfields of culture in which the detailed and more or less strictly technical competence of different intellectual subgroups rests. Very few scientists are considered to be "authorities" on science in general, but each has his special field of competence.

Indeed the general pattern of cultural development sketched above leads, among other things, more and more in the direction of pluralism, so that the intellectual world has come to be very highly differentiated within itself. This pluralism is one highly important source of protection against either religious or ideological rigidity of the sort familiar in some phases of religious development, such as early Calvinism or the early communist phase of Marxist ideology. It is perhaps the impact of this highly pluralistic differentiation of the cultural system, along with the increasing importance and level of sophistication of social science, that underlies Daniel Bell's contention that we have begun to experience the "end of ideology."[17]

The relation of social science to ideology, which cannot be discussed seriously here, is indeed coming to be a critical problem of our time. An inherent tension seems inevitable. There is no

[16] See Kenneth Burke, *The Rhetoric of Religion* (Boston, 1961).
[17] Daniel Bell, *The End of Ideology* (Glencoe, Illinois, 1960).

question that the origin of many of the most important problem statements of social science lies in ideological belief systems and the internal controversies that characterize them. Indeed every branch of or movement in social science has in the nature of the case important ideological elements. At the same time the urge for value-based practical solutions to the urgencies of the day comes into direct conflict with the double imperatives of the maximal (though always imperfect) objectivity of science and of seeking general theoretical and empirical solutions of problems regardless of their bearing on the immediate problems of action. Increasing differentiation is to be expected, but complete dissociation is clearly utopian.[18]

If sharp clarity of ideological orientation and conflict is, for the reasons just reviewed, blurred in North Amercan and Western European societies, it is a very conspicuous feature of societies at various levels of "underdevelopment." One of the reasons for this is the much greater approximation of most such societies to a structural "two-class" system in the sense suggested above. Where there is a conflict with "traditional" elites, the emerging elites are much more likely to be based on "intellectual" status than they are in highly differentiated societies, precisely because the broad base of more modern structures in the field of economic production, governmental administration, and the like is relatively so much weaker. The cultural base of their ideologies also tends to be much more diffuse and less differentiated, as, for example, in the strong aristocratic-humanistic trend of Latin American intellectuals' orientations as noted by Tannenbaum (op. cit.), which can on occasion incorporate an important element of Marxism or even tip radically into a communist pattern.

[18] On the tension, illustrated by certain problems of contemporary American ideology rooted in the orientations of humanistic intellectuals but extending well into social science, see Winston White, *Beyond Conformity*, (New York, 1961).

THE INTELLECTUALS AND THE POWERS:

Some Perspectives for Comparative Analysis

Edward Shils

LAITY AND INTELLECTUALS

In religion, in art, in all spheres of culture and politics, the mass of mankind in all hitherto known societies have not, except for transitory interludes, been preoccupied with the attainment of an immediate contact with the ultimate principles implicit in their beliefs and standards. The directly gratifying ends of particular actions, the exigencies of situations, considerations of individual and familial advantage, concrete moral maxims, concrete prescriptions and prohibitions, preponderate in the conduct of the majority of persons in most societies, large and small. The systemic coherence and the deeper and more general ground of beliefs and standards only intermittently hold their attention and touch on their passions. Ordinary life in every society is characterized by an unequal intensity of attachment to ultimate values, be they cognitive, moral, or aesthetic, and an unequal intensity of the need for coherence. Ordinary life shuns rigorous definition and consistent adherence to traditional or rational rules, and it has no need for continuous contact with the sacred. Ordinary life is slovenly, full of compromise and improvisation; it goes on in the "here and now".

In every society however there are some persons with an unusual sensitivity to the sacred, an uncommon reflectiveness about the nature of their universe, and the rules which govern their society. There is in every society a minority of persons who, more than the ordinary run of their fellow-men, are enquiring, and desirous of being in frequent communion with symbols which are more general than the immediate concrete situations of everyday life, and remote in their reference in both time and space. In this minority, there is a need to externalize this quest in oral and written discourse, in poetic or plastic expression, in historical reminiscence or writing, in ritual performance and acts of worship. This interior need to penetrate beyond the screen of immediate concrete experience marks the existence of the intellectuals in every society.

THE TASKS OF INTELLECTUALS

The personal need alone does not however create the body of intellectuals, nor does it determine its magnitude or its position within the structure of society. In every society, even among those sections of the population without the very pronounced sensitivity to remote symbols which characterizes the intellectuals, there is an intermittent need for contact with the sacred, and this gives rise to a demand for priests and theologians and to institutions or procedures for the education of these in the techniques and meanings of their functions. In every society, among those who cannot create images in the form of stories or pictures or statues or other works of art, there is still a considerable fraction which is receptive and indeed even demanding of the gratification provided by verbal images, colors, and forms. These persons provide the demand for art and literature, even though they themselves cannot create art or literature. Every society has a need for contact with its own past, and in more differentiated societies rulers seek to strengthen their claim to legitimacy by showing the continuity of their regimes with the great personalities of the past. Where this cannot be provided by the powers of individual memory within the kinship group, historical chroniclers and antiquarians are required. Correspondingly ecclesiastical and proto-ecclesiastical bodies must likewise show the spiritual wealth of their antecedents and their living relevance; this gives rise to hagiography and the activity of the hagiographer. In societies on larger than tribal scale, with complex tasks and traditions, the education, at least of those who are expected to become rulers or the associates, counsellors and aides of rulers, is called for; this requires teachers and a system of educational institutions. In any society which transcends the scale of a kinship group, in which the organs of authority acquire a more or less continuous existence, there is a need for administrators capable of keeping records and issuing rules and decrees. These activities require a certain fairly high level of education, which in turn requires institutions with teaching staffs, whether they be palace schools or privately or state-conducted academies or universities. The population of every society, and above all those who exercise authority in it, need to have at least intermittently some sense of the stability, coherence and orderliness of their society; they need therefore a body of symbols, such as songs, histories, poems, biographies, and constitutions, etc., which diffuse a sense of affinity among the members of the society.

The intellectuals' activities and their situation in society is the product of a compromise and an articulation of the intellectual disposition and the needs of society for those actions which can be performed only by persons who of necessity, by virtue of the actions they perform, are intellectuals. The larger the society and the more complex the tasks its rulers undertake, the greater the need therefore for a body of religious and secular intellectuals.

All these needs would exist even if there were no especially sensitive, enquiring, curious, creative minds in the society. There would be intellectuals in society even if there were no intellectuals by disposition.[1]

The moral and intellectual unity of a society, which in the size of its population and its territory goes beyond what any one man can know from his average first-hand experience, and which brings him into contact with persons outside his kinship group, depends on such intellectual institutions as schools, churches,

[1] The demand for intellectual services can sometimes exceed the supply of qualified persons; it will always exceed the supply of truly creative individuals. More frequently, however, modern societies have experienced an excess of the supply of technically qualified persons over the demand for their services.

newspapers, and similar structures. Through these, ordinary persons, in childhood, youth, or adulthood, enter into contact, however extensive, with those who are most familiar with the existing body of cultural values. By means of preaching, teaching, and writing, intellectuals infuse into sections of the population which are intellectual neither by inner vocation nor by social role, a perceptiveness and an imagery which they would otherwise lack. By the provision of such techniques as reading and writing and calculation, they enable the laity to enter into a wider universe. The creation of nations out of tribes, in early modern times in Europe and in contemporary Asia and Africa, is the work of intellectuals, just as the formation of the American nation out of diverse ethnic groups is the achievement of teachers, clergymen, and journalists. The legitimation of the reigning authority is naturally a function of many factors, including the tendencies within a population toward submission to and rejection of authority, the effectiveness of the authority in maintaining order, in showing strength and dispensing a semblance of justice. The legitimacy of authority is however a function of what its subjects believe about it; beliefs about authority are far from resting entirely on first-hand experience, and much of what is believed beyond first-hand experience is the product of traditions and teachings which are the gradually accumulated and attenuated product of the activities of intellectuals.

Through their provision of models and standards, by the presentation of symbols to be appreciated, intellectuals elicit, guide, and form the expressive dispositions within a society. Not that the expressive life of a society is under the exclusive dominion of its intellectuals. Indeed the situation has never existed—and in fact could never exist—in which the expressive life of a society, its aesthetic tastes, its artistic creations, or the ultimately aesthetic grounds of its ethical judgments fell entirely within the traditions espoused by the intellectuals of the society. Societies vary in the extent to which the expressive actions and orientations are in accordance with what is taught and represented by the dominant intellectuals. Within these variations much of the expressive life of a society, even what is most vulgar and tasteless, echoes some of the expressive elements in the central value system represented by the intellectuals.

The first two functions treated above show the intellectuals infusing into the laity attachments to more general symbols and providing for that section of the population a means of participation in the central value system. Intellectuals are not however concerned only to facilitate this wider participation in certain features of the central value system. They are above all concerned with its more intensive cultivation, with the elaboration and development of alternative potentialities. Where creativity and originality are emphatically acknowledged and prized, and where innovation is admitted and accepted, this is perceived as a primary obligation of intellectuals. However even in systems where individual creativity is not seen as a positive value, the labor of powerful minds and irrepressible individualities working on what has been received from the past, modifies the heritage by systematization and rationalization, and adapts it to new tasks and obstacles. In this process of elaboration, divergent potentialities of the system of cultural values are made explicit and conflicting positions are established. Each generation of intellectuals performs this elaborating function for its own and succeeding generations, and particularly for the next succeeding generation.

These specifically intellectual functions are performed not only for the intellectuals of a particular society but for the intellectuals of other societies as well. The intellectuals of different societies are ordered in a vague hierarchy, in which the lower learn from the higher. For South East Asia, the Indian intellectuals, in the Middle Ages and early modern times, performed this function. The intellectuals of Republican and Imperial Rome learned from Greek intellectuals. For Japan, for a time, Chinese intellectuals performed this function. In modern times, the British intellectuals through Oxford, Cambridge, and the London School of Economics, have formed the intellectuals of India, Africa, and for a long time the United States. In the nineteenth century German academic intellectuals provided a world-wide model, just as in the nineteenth and twentieth centuries, French artistic and literary intellectuals have provided models of development for aesthetically sensitive intellectuals all over the civilized world. In the eighteenth century, the intellectuals of the French Enlightenment inspired their confrères in Spain, Italy, Prussia, and Russia.

This function is performed for the intellectual community above all. The laity only comes to share in it at several removes and after a lapse of time.

The function of providing a model for intellectual activity, within and among societies, implies the acceptance of a general criterion of superior quality or achievement. The pattern of action of a certain group of intellectuals comes to be regarded as exemplary because it is thought to correspond more closely to certain ideal requirements of truth, beauty, or virtue. Such standards are never the objects of complete consensus, but they are often widely accepted over very extensive areas of the world at any given time.

The process of elaborating and developing further the potentialities inherent in a "system" of cultural values, entails also the possibility of "rejection" of the inherited set of values in varying degrees of comprehensiveness. In all societies, even those in which the intellectuals are notable for their conservatism, the diverse paths of creativity, as well as an inevitable tendency toward negativism, impel a partial rejection of the prevailing system of cultural values. The very process of elaboration and development involves a measure of rejection. The range of rejection of the inherited varies greatly; it can never be complete and all-embracing. Even where the rejecting intellectuals allege that they are "nihilistic" with respect to everything that is inherited, complete rejection without physical self-annihilation is impossible.

It is practically given by the nature of the intellectuals' orientation that there should be some tension between the intellectuals and the value-orientations embodied in the actual institutions of any society. This applies not only to the orientations of the ordinary members of the society, i.e., the laity, but to the value-orientations of those exercising authority in the society, since it is on them that the intellectuals' attention is most often focussed, they being the custodians of the central institutional system. It is not this particular form of "rejection" or alienation which interests us most at the moment. Rather it is the rejection by intellectuals of the inherited and prevailing values of those intellectuals who are already incorporated in ongoing social institutions. This intra-intellectual alienation or dissensus is a crucial part of the intellectual heritage of any society. Furthermore it supplies the important function of moulding and guiding the alienative tendencies which exist in any society. It provides an alternative pattern of integration for their own society, and for other societies the intellectuals of which come under their hegemony (e.g., the Fabian Socialists in Britain and the Indian intellectuals, or the French and British constitutional liberals of the early nineteenth century and the intellectuals of many countries in Southeastern Europe, in South America, Asia, etc.).

It is not only through the presentation of orientations toward general symbols which reaffirm, continue, modify or reject the society's traditional inheritance of beliefs and standards that intellectuals leave their mark on society. The intellectuals do not exhaust their functions through the establishment of a contact for the laity with the sacred values of their society. They fulfill authoritative, power-exercising functions over concrete actions as well. Intellectuals have played a great historical role on the higher levels of state administration, above all, in China, in British and independent India, in the Ottoman Empire and in modern Europe. Sovereigns have often considered a high standard of education, either humanistic or technical-legal, confirmed by diplomas and examinations, necessary for the satisfactory functioning of the state. The judiciary too has often been a domain of the intellectuals. In private economic organizations, the employment of intellectuals in administrative capacities has been uncommon to the point of rarity. Nor have intellectuals ever shown any inclination to become business enterprisers. It is only since the nineteenth century that business firms, first in Germany, then in America, and latterly in other industrialized countries, have taken to the large-scale employment of scientists in research departments and to a much smaller extent in executive capacities.

Equal in antiquity to the role of the highly educated in state administration is the role of the intellectual as personal agent, counsellor, tutor, or friend of the sovereign. Plato's experience in Syracuse, Aristotle's relations with Alexander, Alcuin's with Charlemagne, Hobbes and Charles II prior to the Restoration, Milton and Cromwell, Lord Keynes and the Treasury, and the "Brains Trust" under President F. D. Roosevelt, represent only a few of numerous instances in ancient and modern states,

Oriental and Occidental, in which intellectuals have been drawn into the entourage of rulers, their advice and aid sought, and their approval valued. Again there are many states and periods in which this has not been so. The Court of Wilhelm II for example drew relatively little on the educated classes of the time; important episodes of Chinese history are to be seen as a consequence of the intellectuals' reaction to the rulers' refusal to draw them into his most intimate and influential circle of counsellors; American administrative and political history from the time of Jacksonian Revolution until the New Liberalism of Woodrow Wilson, was characterized by the separation of intellectuals from the higher administrative and the legislative branches of government. Intellectuals have emerged occasionally in monarchies at the highest pinnacles of authority, through sheer accident or at least through no deliberate process of selection. Asoka, Marcus Aurelius, Akhnaton, are only a few of the scattered coincidences of sovereignty and the concern with the highest truths. In the last century and a half under conditions of liberal-democratic party politics, Benjamin Disraeli, William Gladstone, F. M. Guizot, Woodrow Wilson, Jawaharlal Nehru, Thomas Masaryk, etc., have provided impressive instances of intellectuals who have been able, by their own efforts and a wide appreciation for their gifts of civil politics enriched by an intensity of intellectual interest and exertion, to play a notable role in the exercise of great political authority. This has not been accidental; liberal and constitutional politics in great modern states and liberal and "progressive" nationalist movements in subject territories have to a large extent been "intellectuals' politics."

Indeed in modern times, first in the West, and then in the nineteenth and twentieth centuries at the peripheries of Western civilization and in the Orient, the major political vocation of the intellectuals has lain in the enunciation and pursuit of the ideal. Modern liberal and constitutional politics have largely been the creation of intellectuals with bourgeois affinities and sympathies, in societies dominated by land-owning and military aristocracies. This has been one major form of the pursuit of the ideal. Another has been the promulgation and inspiration of politics, i.e. revolutionary politics working outside the circle of constitutional traditions. Prior to the origins of ideological politics, which came into the open with the European Reformation, conspiracies, putsches, and the subversion of the existing regime, although they often involved intellectuals, were not the objects of a particular affinity between intellectuals and revolutionary tendencies. In modern times however, with the emergence of ideologically dominated political activities as a continuously constitutive part of public life, a genuine affinity has emerged.

Not by any means all intellectuals have been equally attracted by revolutionary politics. Moderates and partisans in civil politics, quiet apolitical concentration on their specialized intellectual preoccupations, cynical anti-political passivity, and faithful acceptance and service of the existing order, are all to be found in substantial proportions among modern intellectuals, as among intellectuals in antiquity. Nonetheless the function of modern intellectuals in furnishing the doctrine of revolutionary movements is to be considered as one of their most important accomplishments.

THE STRUCTURE OF THE INTELLECTUAL COMMUNITY

The performance of the functions enumerated above is possible only through a complex set of institutional arrangements. The institutional system in which intellectual objects are reproduced or created has varied markedly in history. Its variations have at least in part been affected by the nature of the intellectual tasks, the volume of the intellectual heritage, the material resources necessary and available for intellectual work, the modes of reproduction of intellectual achievements, and the scope of the audience.

The creation of imaginative works of literature and the production of works of analysis and meditation, at least since the end of the age of anonymity, has been a work of the individual creator, working under his own self-imposed discipline. As regards the actual work of creation, he has been free of the control imposed by corporate organization. Within the limits of what has been made available to him by his culture, he has chosen the tradition under which he was to work, the style, the attitude and the form. Considerations of flattering a prince or pleasing a patron or the reading public or a publisher have often entered extraneously—but not more than that—into the central process of creation; the process of creation itself has always been a process of free choice and adaptation. The avoidance of the strictures of the censor or the displeasure of a tyrant have also been only extraneous factors in a process of individual creation. For this reason the creation of literature has never been corporately organized. The literary man has always been a self-propelling entity. After the development of printing and the emergence of a large reading public, it became possible in the most advanced countries of the Western world for a small number of successful authors of both superior and inferior literature to earn substantial sums of money and for many to earn enough to maintain themselves. For this to have happened required not only a large public, sufficiently well-educated, and relatively inexpensive means of large-scale mechanical reproduction, but a well-organized system of book and periodical distribution (publishers, booksellers, editors), a means of giving publicity to new publications (reviews, bibliographies and literate convivial circles) and laws protecting rights to intellectual property (copyright laws). In the Western countries and in Japan, where the book trade is relatively well-organized, where there are many periodicals, and where there is a large reading public, there is room for thousands of free-lance intellectuals; in other countries in Asia and Africa, the small size of the literate public and the ineffective machinery of publication and distribution, confines to rather a small figure the number of free-lance intellectuals. But they exist there nonetheless and represent a genuine innovation in the cultural and social history of these countries.

Prior to these developments—which emerged only in the eighteenth century in Western Europe and later in other cultures— creative literary intellectuals were forced to depend on different sources of income. The minnesingers and troubadours who sought to sell their songs in return for hospitality, the Chinese philosopher-adventurers of the period of the Warring States who sought to enter the employment of princes as their counsellors, poets in Moghul courts, the Brahmin pandits at the courts of the Peshwa, and the European humanists, as stipendiaries of the ecclesiastical and secular princely courts at the beginning of the modern age, were approximations of the independent free-lance intellectual whose wares were supplied for payment. They were not genuinely free-lance since they were paid in pensions or stipends or in kind rather than through the sale of their products by contractual agreement. As intellectual clients rather than as autonomous agents, they constituted a patrimonial approximation to the free-lance intellectual. The patronage of princes, great noblemen and courtiers, financiers and merchants, has contributed greatly to the support of the intellectual activities of those who inherited no wealth, at a time and in fields of intellectual activity in which the sale of intellectual products could not find a large and wealthy enough public of purchasers. The creation of sinecures in government for literary men has been one form of patronage which shades off into gainful employment in the career of the civil servant. This latter means of maintenance, which was known in China over several millennia, has found many practitioners in the nineteenth and twentieth centuries in the West, above all in Great Britain. Diplomacy, military service, employment in commerce and even industry, have provided the livelihood of many authors for whom literature has been an avocation. Hence patronage, sinecures, and government service, together with the most fortunate of all, the independent position of the aristocratic, gentry, and rentier-intellectual who lived from inherited wealth, provided almost the sole means of maintenance for those who aspired to do intellectual work. These were appropriate not only to literary creation but to philosophy, science and scholarship. These were the ways in which the greatest poets and philosophers of antiquity lived—except for the Sophists who were free-lance intellectuals—as well as the great Chinese and Persian poets, the humanist scholars of the European Renaissance, and the leading scientists of early modern times.

Those intellectuals who took as their task the cultivation of the sacred symbols of religious life lived either in monasteries, endowed by wealthy patrons, or by begging for their daily needs and by occasional patronage. Merchants and bankers, tillers of the soil and handicraftsmen, and professional military men produced from their ranks very few intellectuals—the last, more than the first two groups. The secular and sacred officialdom, and the legal profession nearly monopolized the capacity to read and write, and they attracted to their ranks, within the limits imposed by the opportunities afforded by the prevailing system of social selection, the intellectually disposed, and provided them with the leisure and facilities to perform intellectual work as a full-time vocation or as an auxiliary activity. The nature of the tasks which these intellectuals assumed, the relative quantitative meagerness of the intellectual heritage, the restricted size of their audience and the small demand for intellectual services meant that intellectual activities required little corporate organization.

The development of the *modern* university—first in Germany, Holland, and Sweden, then in France, then in Great Britain and later in the United States, Russia and Japan, and more recently in Canada, Australia, India and other Commonwealth countries —has changed the structure of the intellectual community. Science which was once the work of amateurs—rentiers, civil servants, and noblemen, for the most part—and scholarship which was almost a monopoly of monks, secular officials, and rentiers, have now come into the almost exclusive jurisdiction of universities. The relationship between teacher and pupil through the laboratory, the research seminar, and the dissertation, has led to a great multiplication of the scientific and scholarly output and strengthened the continuity of intellectual development. In turn, the degree of specialization has been greatly increased as a result of the greater density of scientific and scholarly knowledge and the pursuit of the idol of originality. The independent intellectual and the intellectual living on the income from the sale of his works and from patronage, still exist and their creativity and productivity has not obviously diminished. The intellectual, however, who lives from a salary as a member of an institution devoted to the performance of intellectual work—teaching and scientific and scholarly research—has greatly increased in numbers, and his works make up a larger and larger proportion of the total intellectual product of every modern society.

The increased volume and complexity of the heritage of science and scholarship and the demand for continuity, as well as the wider insistence on diplomatization, has aggrandized the student body. This stratum of the intellectuals which in the nineteenth century already had acquired a special position in European public life, in the twentieth has greatly expanded. In every country where national sensibilities are very tender, and which has been in a state of political, economic or cultural dependency the university (and high school) student body has taken on a special role in political life. It has become the bearer of the idea of nationality.

Concomitantly the absorption of intellectuals into executive— "staff and line" posts within large corporate organizations concerned, not with intellectual matters, but with the exercise of authority, the production and sale of material objects, consumption goods, capital equipment, weapons of war, etc.—has greatly increased. Science, which was a profound toy of amateurs until the nineteenth century, became by the end of that century a vital component of economic life. It has spread from the chemical industry into agriculture and nearly every branch of industry and into important sectors of commerce. In the First and Second World Wars, scientists, and increasingly pure scientists, were drawn into involvement with the armed forces. Scientists have become increasingly involved in research closely connected with agriculture, supported and conducted within institutions conducted by public and private bodies concerned with the improvement of plant and animal strains, with ecology, etc.

The spread of literacy, leisure and material well-being, and the development of the mechanical means of reproduction and transmission of symbols in sounds and image, have also resulted in the creation of new corporate organizations in which intellectuals are employed. Whereas the creation of cultural objects for consumption by the educated was until nearly the end of the nineteenth century the work of the free-lance intellectual—at varying levels of quality—who sold his work to an enterpriser—a printer-bookseller—or who worked on the commission of the latter, recent developments bring the intellectual producer of this kind of cultural object within the framework of a corporate organization, e.g., a film studio, a radio or television network.

The trend in the present century therefore, in all countries of the world, liberal and totalitarian, has been toward an increasing incorporation of intellectuals into organized institutions. This represents a modification of the trend toward an increase in the proportion of institutionally independent intellectuals, which had

set in with the development of printing, and which in itself constituted—at least in numbers and in the quantity of intellectual
products—a new phase in world history.

This diversity and specialization of intellectuals in the twentieth century raises a question concerning the extent to which they
form a community, bound together by a sense of mutual affinity,
by attachment to a common set of rules and common identifying
symbols. They do not form such a community at present. There
are however numerous sub-communities within the larger intellectual universe which do meet these criteria. The particular
fields of the natural sciences and even science as a whole and
scholarship as a whole, do define actual communities bound together by the acceptance of a common body of standards—and
this, even though there are controversy and disagreement within
every field. These communities are only partially and very in-
adequately embodied in the professional and scientific societies.
The literary and artistic worlds too form such communities with
vague and indeterminate boundaries—even more vague and indeterminate than the boundaries of the scholarly and scientific
communities.

These communities are not mere figures of speech. Their common standards are continually being applied by each member
in his own work and in the institutions which assess and select
works and persons for appreciation or condemnation. They operate like a common-law system without formal enactment of their
rules but by the repeated and incessant application and clarifica-
tion of the rules. The editors of learned scientific, scholarly and
literary journals, the readers of publishing houses, the reviewers
of scientific, scholarly and literary works, and the appointments
committees which pass judgments on the candidates for posts in
universities or scientific research institutes, are the central institutions of these communities. The training of the oncoming generations in colleges and universities in the rules of the respective
intellectual communities, specify these rules by example and
transmit them by the identification of the research student with
his teacher, just as in ancient India, the disciple sitting at the
feet of his guru, acquired not only a knowledge of the concrete
subject matter but also the rules and the disposition for its interpretation and application. The award of prizes and distinctions

such as the Nobel Prize or election to membership in the Royal Society or to a famous continental academy, establishes models and affirms the rightness of certain patterns of thought. The most original scientists, the most profound thinkers, the most learned scholars, the greatest writers and artists provide the models, which embody the rules of the community, and teach by the example of their achievement.

The world-wide character of the community formed by mathematicians or physicists or other natural scientists approximates most closely to the ideal of a body, bound together by a universal devotion to a common set of standards derived from a common tradition and acknowledged by all who have passed through the discipline of scientific training. Even here however, specialization and considerations of military security impair the universality of the scientific community. In other fields of intellectual work, boundaries of language, national pride, and religious, political and ethical beliefs engender reluctance to accept the claims of standards of intellectual communities to universal observance. Technical specialization, the reduction of the general humanistic component in secondary and higher education, and the intensification of the ideological factor in politics, all resist the claims of the communities which, in the modern world, have, nonetheless, managed, despite enduring cleavages and intermittent crises, to command the allegiance of intellectuals.

Despite all impediments and counter-claims, the intellectual communities remain really effective systems of action. Whatever their distortions they transmit the traditions of intellectual life and maintain its standards in various special fields and as a whole.

THE TRADITIONS OF INTELLECTUALS

Intellectual work is sustained by and transmits a complex tradition which persists through changes in the structure of the intellectual class. In these traditions, the most vital ones are the standards and rules in the light of which achievement is striven for and assessed and the substantive beliefs and symbols which constitute the heritage of valid achievement. It is by the participation in these traditions of perception, appreciation, and expression, and the affirmation of the importance of performing in the modes, accredited by these traditions, that the intellectual is defined. One could almost say that if these traditions did not confront the intellectual as an ineluctable inheritance, they would be created anew in each generation by the passionate disposition of the "natural" intellectual to be in contact, by perception, ratiocination or expression, with symbols of general scope. They are traditions which are so to speak given by the nature of intellectual work. They are the immanent traditions of intellectual performance, the accepted body of rules of procedure, standards of judgment, criteria for the selection of subject-matters and problems, modes of presentation, canons for the assessment of excellence, models of previous achievement and prospective emulation. Every field of intellectual performance, more than any other craft or profession, possessing a long and acknowledged accumulation of achievements, has such a cultural tradition, always—though at varying rates—being added to and modified. What is called scientific method in each particular field of science or scholarship and the techniques of literary creation and of work in the plastic and other arts, each possess such a tradition, and without that tradition even the greatest and most creative geniuses who seek to discover and create in that domain could not be effective. Colleges and universities, scientific, scholarly, and artistic journals, museums, galleries—in short the whole system of intellectual institutions—exist to select those who are qualified to work within these traditions, and to train them in their appreciation, application and development. Even the most creative and rapidly developing domains of intellectual performance could disregard them only with very great loss.

These traditions, though they make neither direct nor logically implicit reference to the position of their adherents in relation to the surrounding society and the authorities which rule it, seem from their very structure to entail a measure of tension between themselves and the laity. The very intensity and concentration of commitment of these values, which are remote from the executive routines of daily life in family, firm, office, factory, church and civil service, from the pleasures of the ordinary man, and the obligations, compromises, and corruptions of those who exercise commanding authority in church, state, business, and army, entail an at least incipient sense, on each side, of the distance which separates these two trends of value-orientation.

Intellectual work arose from religious preoccupations. In the early history of the human race, it tended, in its concern with the ultimate or at least with what lies beyond the immediate concrete experience, to think with religious symbols. It continues to share with genuine religious experience the fascination with the sacred or the ultimate ground of thought and experience, and the aspiration to enter into intimate contact with it. In secular intellectual work, this involves the search for the truth, for the principles embedded in events and actions or for the establishment of a relationship between the self and the essential, whether the relationship be cognitive, appreciative, or expressive. The deeper religious attitude, the striving for contact and communion with the symbols of the ultimate powers which dominate human life, has a very intimate affinity with the profoundest scientific orientations, which seek to discern the most general and comprehensive laws of universal and human existence. Differently disciplined, both the religious and the scientific dispositions at their most creative, have in common the striving for contact with the most decisive and significant symbols and the realities underlying those symbols. It is therefore no stretching of the term to say that science and philosophy, even when they are not religious in a conventional sense, are as concerned with the sacred as religion itself. In consequence of this, in our enumeration of the traditions under which intellectual pursuits are carried on, we should say that the tradition of awesome respect and of serious striving for contact with the sacred, is perhaps the first, the most comprehensive and the most important of all the traditions of the intellectuals. In the great religious cultures of Islam, Buddhism, Taoism, and Hinduism, prior to the emergence of a differentiated modern intellectual class, the care of the sacred through the mastery, interpretation, and exposition of sacred writings, and the cultivation of the appropriate mental states or qualities were the first interests of the intellectuals. (In China, the development of a class of Confucian intellectual-civil servants produced its own tradition, more civil and aesthetic than religious in the conventional meaning.) In the West too, in antiquity, a substantial section of the philosophical intelligentsia bore this tradition, and on the higher reaches, even those who cut themselves off from the tribal and territorial religions, continued to be impelled by such considerations (e.g. Pythagoras, Euclid, Ptolemy, Aristotle, Plato, Socrates, Lucretius, Seneca). In modern times, although attracting a diminishing share of the creative capacities of the oncoming intellectual elite, religious orientations still remain a major preoccupation of a substantial fraction of the educated classes and not less of the most creative minds.

With this striving for contact with the ultimately important comes the self-esteem which always accompanies the performance of important activities. Any effort to understand the traditions of the intellectuals and their relations with the authorities who rule the other sections of society at any given time, must bear in mind the crucial significance of the self-regard which comes from preoccupation and contact with the most vital facts of human and cosmic existence, and the implied attitude of derogation towards those who act in more mundane or more routine capacities.[2]

When intellectuals ceased to be solely bearers of religiosity, the very act of separation, however gradual and unwitting and undeliberate, sets up a tension between the intellectuals and the religious authority of their society. Insofar as they were not merely civil servants and counsellors to princes—itself an unsettling, tension-generating relationship—there was created a tension between the public authorities and the intellectuals. Ecclesiastical and exemplary religious authority became an object of the distrust of intellectuals, and insofar as the authority of the government of earthly affairs associated itself with the religious powers, it too shared in that skepticism. The attitude is by no means universal nor need the distrust be aggressive. Confucian civil servants, disdainful towards Taoism or Buddhism, did not become rebels against their sovereigns as long as they themselves

[2] Naturally this sentiment is not equally shared by all intellectuals. Not all are equally involved in these "vital facts"—and therefore not all have the same feeling of the dignity of their activities. Intellectuals vary greatly in their sensitivity to their traditions—just as do the laity with respect to their traditions—but even in those who are relatively insensitive, there remains a considerable unconscious assimilation of many elements of these central traditions.

were treated respectfully. In the West where the separation of religious and other intellectual activities has become most pronounced, a more general feeling of distance from authority has been engendered and has become one of the strongest of the traditions of the intellectuals. First in the West, and then in the past half-century in Africa and Asia among intellectuals who have come under the Western traditions, the tradition of distrust of secular and ecclesiastical authority, and with these, of familial and communal authority, and in fact of tradition as such—has become the chief secondary tradition of the intellectuals. As such, it is nurtured by many of the subsidiary traditions such as scientism, revolutionism, progressivism, etc., which we shall treat below.

The tension between the intellectuals and the powers—their urge to submit to authority as the bearer of the highest good—whether it be order or progress or some other value—and to resist or condemn authority as a betrayer of the highest values—comes ultimately from the constitutive orientation of the intellectuals towards the sacred. Practically all the more concrete traditions in the light and shadows of which intellectuals have lived express this tension. We shall note, in brief, some of these traditions which, however diverse in their age and origins, have played a great part in forming the relations of the modern intellectuals to authority. They are a) the tradition of scientism, b) the romantic tradition, c) the apocalyptic tradition, d) the populistic tradition, and e) the tradition of anti-intellectual order.

All of these traditions are in conflict with other traditions of deference towards ecclesiastical and temporal authorities and the expectation of a career in their service. Even in those modern cultures where the traditions of the intellectuals' acceptance of authority are strongest, in modern Britain and modern Germany, they have by no means had the field to themselves. Similarly in modern Asia where variants of the traditions of devotion to the religiously sacred values and the service of temporal authority have, in ancient as well as modern times, had a powerful hold, anti-authoritarian and anti-civil traditions, diffused from the West and nurtured by related traditions derived from Taoism, Buddhism, and Hinduism, have found an eager and widespread reception.

The *tradition of scientism* is the tradition which denies the validity of tradition as such; it insists on the testing of everything which is received and on its rejection, if it does not correspond with the "facts of experience". It is the tradition which demands the avoidance of every extraneous impediment to the precise perception of reality, regardless of whether that impediment comes from tradition, from institutional authority, or internal passion or impulse. It is critical of the arbitrary and the irrational. In its emphasis on the indispensability of first-hand and direct experience, it sets itself in opposition to everything which comes between the mind of the knowing individual and "reality". It is easy to see how social convention and the traditional authority associated with institutions would fall prey to the ravages of this powerfully persuasive and corrosive tradition.

The *romantic tradition* appears at first sight to be in irreconcilable opposition to the tradition of scientism. At certain points, such as the estimation of the value of impulse and passion, there is a real and unbridgeable antagonism. In many important respects however they share fundamental features. Romanticism starts with the appreciation of the spontaneous manifestations of the essence of concrete individuality. Hence it values originality, i.e., the novel, that which is produced from the "genius" of the individual (or the folk), in contrast with the stereotyped and traditional actions of the philistine. Since ratiocination and detachment obstruct spontaneous expresson, they are thought to be life-destroying. Institutions which have rules and which prescribe the conduct of the individual members by conventions and commands are likewise viewed as life-destroying. The bourgeois family, mercantile activity, the market, indeed civil society in general, with its curb on enthusiasm and its sober acceptance of obligation, are repugnant to the romantic tradition—all are the enemies of spontaneity and genuineness, they impose a role on the individual and do not permit him to be himself. They kill what is living in the folk. Civil society has no place for the intellectual who is afflicted with a sense of his moral solitude within it. The affinities of the romantic tradition to the revolutionary criticism of the established order and to the bohemian refusal to have more part in it than is absolutely necessary are obvious. It too is one of the most explosively anti-authoritarian, and even anti-civil, powers of modern intellectual life.

The revolutionary tradition which has found so many of its leading recipients and exponents among intellectuals, draws much from scientism and romanticism, but essentially it rests on one much older, namely the *apocalyptic* or millenarian tradition. The belief that the evil world as we know it, so full of temptation and corruption, will come to an end one day and will be replaced by a purer and better world, originates in the apocalyptic outlook of the prophets of the Old Testament. It is promulgated in the Christian idea of the Kingdom of God, which the earlier Christians expected in their own time, and it lingers as a passionately turbulent stream, dammed up and hidden by the efforts of the Church, but recurrently appearing on the surface of history through the teaching and action of heretical sects. It received a powerful impetus from Manicheanism. In the Donatists, in the Bogomils, in the Albigensians and Waldensians, in the Hussites and Lollards, in the Anabaptists and in the Fifth Monarchy Men, in the belief that the evil world, the world of the Children of Darkness, would be destroyed and supplanted by the world of the Children of Light after a decisive judgment by the Sovereign of the universe, this tradition has lived on. It has come down to our own times in a transmuted form. Although it still exists in its religious form among numerous Christian and quasi-Christian sects in Europe, America, and Africa, its true recipients are the modern revolutionary movements and above all the Marxian movements. Marxian writers of the early part of this century acknowledged the Anabaptists, the Fifth Monarchy Men, the Levellers and the Diggers, as their forerunners, and although the Bolsheviks have been less willing to admit Russian sectarianism as an antecedent, there can be little doubt that the Russian sectarian image of the world and its cataclysmic history made it easier for the Marxian conception of society and its historical destiny to find acceptance in Russia. The disposition to distinguish sharply between good and evil and to refuse to admit the permissibility of any admixture, the insistence that justice be done though the heavens fall, the obstinate refusal to compromise or to tolerate compromise—all the features of doctrinaire politics, or the politics of the ideal—which are so common among modern intellectuals must be attributed in some measure at least to this tradition.

Another of the traditions which has everywhere in the world moved intellectuals in the last century and a half is the *populistic tradition*. Populism is a belief in the creativity and in the superior moral worth of the ordinary people, of the uneducated and un-intellectual; it perceives their virtue in their actual qualities or in their potentialities. In the simplicity and wisdom of their ways, the populist tradition alleges that it has discerned virtues which are morally superior to those found in the educated and in the higher social classes. Even where, as in Marxism, the actual state of the lower classes is not esteemed, they are alleged to be by destiny fitted to become the salvationary nucleus of their whole society. Romanticism with its distrust of the rational and calculating elements in bourgeois society, revolutionism with its hatred of the upper classes as the agents of wicked authority, the apocalyptic attitude which sees the last coming first and which alleges that official learning (religious and secular) has falsified the truths which the last judgment and the leap into freedom will validate—all these manifest a populistic disposition. German his-torical and philological scholarship in the nineteenth century, imbued with the romantic hatred of the rational, the economic, the analytic spirit, which it castigated as the source and product of the whole revolutionary, rationalistic trend of Western Euro-pean culture, discovered in the nameless masses, the folk, the fountain of linguistic and cultural creativity. French socialism went a step further and Marxism elevated this essentially roman-tic outlook into a systematic "scientific" theory.

In all countries peripheral to the most creative centers of Western culture at the height of its hegemony over the modern mind, intellectuals were both fascinated and rendered uneasy by the culture of Western Europe. Not only in early nineteenth-century Germany, but in Russia of the fifties, in the twentieth-century Middle-western United States, in Brazil (in the doctrine of "Indianism"), in the resentful and embittered Weimar Repub-lic, in India since the ascendancy of Gandhi and in the emerging intelligentsias of the new countries of Africa, populistic tendencies are massively at work. In all these countries the intellectuals have been or were educated either in foreign countries or in institutions within their own countries modelled on those at the center of the culture they sought or seek to emulate. In all these countries the intellectuals have developed anxiety about whether they have not allowed themselves to be corrupted by excessive permeation with the admired foreign culture. To identify themselves with the people, to praise the culture of the ordinary people as richer, truer, wiser and more relevant than the foreign culture in which they had themselves been educated, has been a way out of this distress. In most of these cases it is a protest against the "official" culture, the culture of the higher civil servants, of the universities and of the culture, political, literary, and philosophical, which has come out of them. As such it has fused easily with the other traditions of hostility to civil institutions and civil authority.

There is another tradition, closely connected with all of these and yet apparently their negation, which merits mention. This is the *anti-intellectual tradition of order*. Best known in the West in the form of French positivism (St. Simon and Comte), it has its roots in antiquity and in the belief that excessive intellectual analysis and discussion can disrupt the foundations of order. Plato's attitude towards poets had its parallel in the burning of the books by the former Confucian, Li-Ssu, at the origin of the Ch'in Dynasty; Hobbes' analysis of the role of intellectuals in bringing about the English civil war, Taine's interpretation of the significance of the *philosophes* in bringing on the French Revolution of 1789, and the ideas of Joseph de Maistre, all testify to the ambivalence in the traditional anti-authoritarianism of intellectuals.

IN CONCLUSION

Intellectuals are indispensable to any society, not just to industrial society, and the more complex the society, the more indispensable they are. An effective collaboration between intellectuals and the authorities which govern society is a requirement for order and continuity in public life and for the integration of the wider reaches of the laity into society. Yet, the original impetus to intellectual performance, and the traditions to which it has given rise and which are sustained by the institutions through which intellectual performance is made practicable generate a tension between intellectuals and the laity, high and low. This tension can never be eliminated, either by a complete consensus between the laity and the intellectuals or by the complete ascendancy of the intellectuals over the laity.

Within these two extreme and impossible alternatives, a wide variety of forms of consensus and dissensus in the relations of the intellectuals and the ruling powers of society have existed. The discovery and the achievement of the optimum balance of civility and intellectual creativity are the tasks of the statesman and the responsible intellectual. The study of these diverse patterns of consensus and dissensus, their institutional and cultural concomitants, and the conditions under which they have emerged and waned are the first items on the agenda of the comparative study of the intellectuals and the powers.

THE INTELLECTUAL AND SOCIETY:
The Social Function of the "Fool" in the Twentieth Century
Ralf Dahrendorf

Most people imagine their society as being composed of two unequal parts, one above and one below. This is true for all countries, and it has supposedly been true in all times. "Those above" are the ones who dictate to others the way they must act, who make all the important decisions, and who share to a higher degree than usual in the goods of this world. "Those below," on the other hand, must submit to the laws that "those above" make for them; they don't sit in back of the counter but stand in front of it, don't impose fines but pay them if they are caught. For many people there is also a middle rung on which stands everyone who neither only commands nor only obeys—that is, the man behind the counter, the accountant, the policeman, and the sergeant. Thus the picture of a social order emerges in which everyone has his place either above or below or somewhere in between; and even though today most people are no longer nailed to their positions forever, nevertheless they know at any given moment where they stand.

Such pictures of society have their justification. They describe in a rather simple manner the distance that social norms and traditions set up between man and man—distances no less real than those expressed in miles and kilometers. Yet these images have a serious limitation. They all lack an element that we are inclined to underestimate but that is as much a part of society as the three ranks—the men who stand outside of the "thermometer scale" of social ranks, who are not at all affected as it were by its gradations and careers, its privileges and petty quarrels. This is the special and unique position of the "fool," as I would like to call him for the time being. (Here I think first of the court jester and of Falstaff; however, even in the carnival figures of the fools' guilds there is an element of this same position.)

Everyone who stands above, in the middle, or at the bottom of the society plays his social role—but the fool is defined by the very fact that he always acts out of character. It is his role not to play any role: "what one does" and "how one behaves" are exactly what the fool does not do. The fool does not stand above, for he cannot dictate to others the laws of their actions. Neither does he stand below, for he acts as the critical conscience of the rulers, and takes liberties that would not go unpunished if they were done by "those below." He has no place at all among those who act as servants of "those above" and execute their orders.

The power of the fool lies in his freedom with respect to the hierarchy of the social order, that is, he speaks from outside as well as from inside it. The fool belongs to the social order and yet does not commit himself to it; he can without fear even speak uncomfortable truths about it.

Such characters are today either idiots or actors. We do not remember how important the fool once was for the politics of entire nations. "The monarchy and the most ideal monarch," Bismarck wrote in his *Thoughts and Memories,* "if in his idealism he is not to become a public danger, needs the critical sting with the help of which he is able to find his way when he is in danger of losing it."

Who exercises this criticism in a society of submissive courtiers? Who can afford to tell the monarchs the uncomfortable truths without endangering his own position? Here the fool was an indispensable instrument in correcting the errors of absolute masters. Certainly not always successful, and by no means always welcome, the fool nevertheless carried, in his person, the only hope of getting attention for the other side that everything and every political decision has. Lucky the king who had a wise and courageous fool!

All this is, however, by no means an excursion into medieval history. The task of the fool did not become superfluous in the French Revolution. Modern republics too need their fools as a critical sting—to use Bismarck's apt description—to help rulers find their way when they are in danger of losing it. This is not to say that the rulers must unconditionally follow the fools; rather, by listening to them they are forced to consider their decisions thoroughly and to go their way neither naïvely nor unscrupulously.

But the fools of modern society of whom I am speaking here, about whom all kinds of ingenious things have been said, are the intellectuals—now again much despised. Intellectuals in Germany are not only the members of "Group 47" or the editors of certain television programs. Some journalists, some professors, some painters, some architects also belong among them. Unfortunately, only too rarely in Germany does one find the "sometime intellectual," the man who, perhaps for the greater part of his life, occupies a quite unintellectual leadership position and yet functions at a certain distance from the role structure of the social hierarchy as a critic and court jester. Theodor Heuss was one of the very few who were able to combine the critical detachment of the intellectual and the public responsibility of the politician.

As the court jesters of modern society, all intellectuals have the duty to doubt everything that is obvious, to make relative all authority, to ask all those questions that no one else dares to ask. Certainly such questions are not comfortable: Do we really want German reunification? Is being a traitor a patriotic service under certain circumstances? Does religious education belong in the schools? Should abortion be made legal?

Such questions may be shocking. It is far from my purpose to approve of any answers that might appear implicit in the rather suggestive way they have been formulated. The great point, I am convinced, is that shocking questions must be asked: *each position whose opposite is not discussed is a weak position.* Thus, to strengthen accepted positions—political, moral, pedagogical, religious, or whatever—by questioning them and therefore finding solid ground for them is the social task of the court jesters of modern society, the intellectuals.

To put in question generally accepted values and conceptions is naturally neither a very comfortable nor, above all, a very popular undertaking. So it is almost inevitable that intellectuals are reviled in public. It has been so in all ages and in all countries. There is, however, a border between simple defamation and persecution. There is a difference between the calm, "Well, he is a liberal and therefore he should not be taken seriously in political things," and the malicious, "He is an enemy of the state, a destroyer of freedom, he endangers our security," and similar phrases. Here the self-confident, established society differs from the society that constantly fears for its own foundations and therefore suspects high treason in every criticism.

The truth of the fool is never quite serious, for it lacks the important mooring of responsibility (and also, of course, of power). This does not lessen its value; it makes it, however, all the more unreasonable to meet it with the heavy artillery of public suspicion and aspersions. Whether a society includes intellectual court jesters who critically question its institutions, and how it tolerates them, are a measure of its maturity and inner solidity.

IDEAS, INTELLECTUALS, AND
STRUCTURES OF DISSENT
J. P. Nettl

Long before the smooth-shaven face of Avis with its carefully creased kindliness stared at us from posters to announce its determination to try harder, the notion that it behooves those who are (relatively) small to claim universal competence was well established. In many waiting rooms of small, *arriviste* firms hangs a notice boldly declaring that the difficult will be performed immediately, only the impossible takes a little while. Johnny-come-lately sociology thrives on inversions and makes precisely the opposite claim—undertaking to tackle the impossible readily and at once. Thus we frequently find sociology attempting the impossible task of explaining *everything* with breath-taking panache; while in another sense it finds the difficulty of explaining *anything* almost insurmountable.

There can scarcely be a subject more diverse and hence more impossible to "explain" than the crucial but elusive problem of idea formation, and scarcely any group that lends itself less readily to classification than those who formulate them. The twin problems of ideology (in its widest ontological and epistemological sense) and of intellectuals are among the most frequently discussed themes in sociology—but also the most untidy, unsystematic, and controversial areas of inquiry. The temptation to clean up this jungle is great—not only because sociological theory hates pockets of obstinate randomness or even of diverse particularity, but also because the study of intellectuals belongs in a special sense to the internal history of modernity. "To the extent that the feudal order of medieval Christendom tumbles to its destruction, bourgeois society with its new principles of order and legitimation takes its place. The new form of legitimation of bourgeois society, which has reached up and brought down to earth the transcendental ideal of Christian theology, is in particular the work of the intellectuals."[1] These are large claims —for the subject as a whole as well as for the object, the intellectuals themselves, particularly when it turns out that the claim has to be qualified in all kinds of ways. Indeed most general analyses of intellectuals begin with a preface of all-embracingness for what follows—and follows it with a battery of limiting qualifications.[2] More important still is the fact that the largeness of the claims is perhaps due to professional self-interest; most analysts of intellectuals and of ideas consider themselves intellectuals or hope to become such. Preoccupation with such problems may be the sociologist's only recognized ticket—perhaps indeed the only ticket—with which to acquire the status of an intellectual.

Elsewhere in this volume Talcott Parsons reaches the predictable conclusion that if intellectuals are to be defined as primarily concerned with the articulation of cultural symbols, then indeed the last few centuries can be viewed as a period of increasing institutional differentiation of, and specialization in, such articulation. As functions and structures become differentiated in societies, so does the "ground of meaning" associated with them. This increasing relatedness of social function with corresponding cultural articulation and specificity is captured by highlighting the increasing role of universities. The problem of order is in

[1] Jacob Taubes, "Die Intellektuellen und die Universität," *Universitätstage* (1963), special number on University and Universality, p. 36. (My translation.)

[2] See for instance the much-cited collection edited by E. B. de Huszar, *The Intellectuals: A Controversial Portrait* (Glencoe, Illinois, 1960). Most of the views cited in this collection are in fact mutually exclusive. For "controversial" we must read (*anglice*) "contradictory," in other words an area of sociological randomness where no theory has yet succeeded in staking out any pre-emptive claims. An important recent attempt at a comprehensive and synthesizing analysis is Lewis A. Coser, *Men of Ideas: A Sociologist's View* (New York, 1965), which will be referred to several times below.

turn resolved by showing that there is indeed a place for intellectuals, and by making this place comfortable with all the mod. con. of role, structure, collectivity, values, and the rest of the paraphernalia of sociological interior decoration. The only problem that remains is that this type of analysis devitalizes the fundamental and necessary quality of intellect. The having and propagating of ideas, their acceptance, rejection, or transformation, tend to take on the quality of a uniform order and evolution that may or may not apply to the structures of society or the social system, but to which ideas can certainly be neither subordinated nor precisely matched by being shown to possess a conveniently parallel structural order of their own. As in the writing of Jules Verne, we are left with an analysis that predicates the impossible initial assumption; the sophisticated tale flows painlessly if, and only if, the necessary intellectual leap across a formidable barrier is made without reservation at the start.

The first problem is one of definition. Is the intellectual an institution, a collectivity, a role, a type of person, or what? The failure to surmount the definitional hurdle produces as many explanations as there are implied definitions. I shall argue here that any meaningful concept of intellectual must, at least initially, be free of all forms of institutional attachment. Moreover the problem of definition cannot in my view begin with roles or social structure or even, for that matter, with men at all, but can get off the ground only by looking first at ideas as such. It must be defined from inside out, *from* certain types of ideas *toward* certain categories of idea-articulators; only then can the related variable of institutionalization be added. Thus the problem of institutional location and significance depends, it seems to me, primarily on types of ideas rather than types of people. Empirical sociology and the scientism associated with it have undermined this particular hierarchy of priorities; in a field as wide open and as recognizably crucial as this the institutional and scientistic priorities of much American sociology have led to overemphasis of the priority of social structure as the locus of ideas instead of regarding idea-structures as *seeking* social "attachment." Only a few Europeans (Frenchmen, Germans) labor along with an equally one-sided attachment to the other priority, that of idea-systems as a means of analysis. We are always landed with the "pull" of acquired intellectual priorities; there are many areas of analysis where the identification of the relevant social structures must take precedence, but the study of intellectuals is, as I shall try to show, not one of them.

The attempt to marry intellectuals to institutionalization is a shotgun marriage of great therapeutic benefit to the priests but not to the doting couple. Of course the union exists (and not only in the minds of sociological analysts) in the form of a Hindu-type process of perpetual death in captivity and subsequent reincarnation. Again and again ideas have been institutionalized into ideologies, men of ideas encapsulated into a clergy or an academic establishment. It is a triumph of the capacity of human nature to survive even severe doses of social institutionalization, and of sociology too, that ideas should continue to break out with determined persistence at unexpected places somewhere along the smooth skin of the ever more institutionalized society. As soon as the styptic pencil has been applied, the plaster put on, the ideas and their bearers institutionalized or "structured," the breakout process repeats itself in an unexpected place somewhere else.

For one thing I do not readily accept the alleged total difference between the Christian universe of the Middle Ages and the secular universe of post-Renaissance modernity—at least as far as intellectuals are concerned. If anything, "bourgeois society with its new principles of order and legitimation" is proving a transitional phase, albeit long drawn out; however different in quality, technological modernity begins to resemble the Christian Middle Ages in terms of the twin demands of uniformity and universality. As one of the finest intuitive sociologists (professionally an economist, but every inch an intellectual) noted nearly thirty years ago, "unlike any other type of society, capitalism inevitably and by virtue of the very logic of its civilization creates, educates and subsidizes a vested interest in social unrest. . . . In capitalist society . . . any attack on the intellectuals must run up against the private fortresses of bourgeois business which, or some of which, will shelter the quarry. Moreover such an attack must proceed according to bourgeois principles of legislative and administrative practice which no doubt may be stretched or bent but will checkmate persecution beyond a certain point. Lawless violence the bourgeois stratum may accept or even applaud when thoroughly roused or frightened, but only temporarily . . . for the freedom it disapproves cannot be crushed without also crushing the freedom it approves. . . . From this follow both the unwillingness and the inability of the capitalist order to control its intellectual sector effectively. The unwillingness in question is unwillingness to use methods consistently uncongenial to the mentality shaped by the capitalist process, the inability is the inability to do so within the frame of institutions shaped by the capitalist process without submitting to non-bourgeois rule."[3]

This explains the social effectiveness of intellectuals *in* bourgeois society (as well as their effectiveness in transforming it radically), but hardly their allegedly unique emergence simultaneously *with* bourgeois society, or their dependence on it for their social and ideological existence. The reasons that have led some sociologists to begin their analysis of intellectuals with the seventeenth century are compounded from convenience—and the almost exclusive focus on social structure that proves such a severely limiting ideological factor of American sociology and its professional values.[4]

[3] Joseph Schumpeter, *Capitalism, Socialism and Democracy* (New York, 1942), pp. 145, 150. These remarkable ten pages on the sociology of intellectuals in my view still constitute the best short discussion of the socio-structural problem in existence.

[4] Cf. Coser's explanation in *Men of Ideas*, p. xf. A very similar but more strongly articulated self-limitation is evident with regard to the sociology of science. Here too the discussion of ideas, their attempted taxonomy and categorization, structural problem of change through time, and above all their relationship with social structure, is mainly noticeable through absence and careful abstention. One has only to read the work of Merton, Barber, Storer, and Hagstrom to be struck by the almost exclusive focus on social structure. In particular there is notable confusion in Merton and Barber between their emphasis on the *norms* of scientific endeavor and its *content*. Much of this tradition is formalized and legitimated by Parsons' discussion of science in *The Social System* (London, 1952). The field of systematizing the production of ideas, and their mutual collisions and interpenetrations, has been left to the historians and philosophers of science like N. R. Hanson, *Patterns of Discovery*

In the context of the production of ideas as such, however, the difference between a St. Augustine, a St. Jerome (or for that matter the preponderance of formidable heresies in the first few centuries of Christianity) on the one hand and the Luthers, Marxes, Freuds, Jaspers, and whoever else on the other strike one as significant primarily in terms of *content*. The fact that somebody always has systematic ideas about what is or what should be seems to be a given of the human race—even when it takes the form of a lament about the "idealessness" of an overly materialistic society. While it is perfectly legitimate and valuable to analyze and define both the ideas and their articulators in terms of the ideologies and the societies within which they take place, that is a very different order from suggesting that the very creation of ideas is itself a variable wholly dependent on ideological or social analysis. The crucial dependent variable here is the acceptance of ideas and the role-taking of their articulators by others rather than the production and articulation of the ideas themselves. Though the two aspects are, of course, related, they have to be rigorously separated and even contrasted for purposes of analysis.

We have in fact a problem of push—from ideas to social structure—and a problem of pull, from social structure toward suitable articulation of its values by intellectuals. If I deal here almost exclusively with push, it is because the pull side has received more than its due in the sociological literature, and because I am primarily concerned with intellectuals as such rather than with societies and their structure.[5]

(Cambridge, 1958) and Thomas S. Kuhn, *The Structure of Scientific Revolutions* (Chicago, 1962). I have discussed the problem of abstention from, and demarcation of, legitimate "fields" of inquiry in the social sciences in J. P. Nettl, "Center and Periphery in Social Science," *American Behavioral Scientist*, Vol. IX, No. 10 (1966), pp. 39–46.

[5] Of course this mechanistic push-pull idea is grossly oversimple. Even the substantial literature on pull is lopsided in one sense—it is almost purely the history of intellectuals. "The discontented intellectual with his sane searchings has attracted attention wholly out of proportion to his political importance, partly because these searchings leave behind them written records and also because those who write history are themselves intellectuals." J. Barrington Moore, Jr., *Social Origins of Dictatorship and Democracy: Lord and Peasant in the Making of the Modern*

There have been a sufficient number of later discoveries of unknown or neglected geniuses of the past to underline the fallibility of the social process of selection. To measure the existence and interest (or even importance) of ideas by the written and processual evidence of the past, let alone by the diffusion and acceptance of these ideas and their structural encapsulation through movements or schools, is highly inefficient as an indicator of all that has been thought, said, or written. It tells us more about the acceptability of ideas—hence about the societies that accept or reject them—than about the nature of the ideas and the total intellectualism of past ages. If total recall were available we might well find, alongside lost symphonies or poems, a surprising range of ideas that have either been physically lost or to which contemporary societies and accepted belief systems proved resistant. The need to tailor the scope of new ideas to what is socially acceptable, in the context of both qualitative content and the scope or range of subject matter incorporated, imposes far greater limits than is usually recognized. We like to think of the receptivity to ideas as total, especially today—yet the need to measure the capacity for receiving ideas remains greater than ever.[6] "A man who wants to found a school must know when to stop; in his function, more than in any other, *principia non sunt multiplicanda praeter necessitatem*. The fact that Plato would not stop was certainly one of the factors in the curious lack of continuity we see in the history of the Academy."[7]

Let us therefore start with the assumption that the production of ideas, if not a constant, is at least a given, and treat the capacity to absorb, accept, and diffuse as a variable. I am not competent to arrange this given in any systematic way; nor apparently is or has been anyone else. There have been a few attempts at a systematic typology that correlates types of society,

World (Boston, 1966), p. 480. This great gritty book implicitly accepts the distinction between idea formation and articulating social structure by determinedly digging out the latter without the often misleading barnacles and accretions of the former.

[6] See for instance the recent discussion and categorization of scientific "reception" systems in Alfred de Grazia, ed., *The Velikovsky Affair* (New York, 1966), Chap. 5, pp. 171–232.

[7] Florian Znaniecki, *The Social Role of the Man of Knowledge* (New York, 1940), p. 123.

and/or particular social structures, with particular systems of cognition and ideas—attempts that are more in the nature of personal typologies by luminous minds than historical classification tested or validated over time.[8] Better known and more directly influential is the work of the sociologists of knowledge, especially the evolutionary perspectives of Mannheim with their gradually crystallizing strata of mediating and ultimately dominating intellectuals "floating free" from any partial ideology of particular social structure or interest. I shall have more to say on this later in the context of a technology-suffused and industrial definition of modernity.

There is, of course, a substantial literature on intellectuals, men of ideas, and so on, as well as an entirely separate body of work on the creation and diffusion of scientific knowledge. I do not propose to plow my way critically through references to this literature in order to justify a (hopefully) different approach. In general the literature on intellectuals suffers from a basic failure to define or delineate the object of analysis in such a way as to make it possible to generate any rigorous or comparative analysis. Apart from Gurvitch and Mannheim, most discussions either embark on a general voyage of exploration concerned with men who have ideas, or else attempt to identify and discuss a sociologically meaningful stratum of intellectuals. The societal context dominates, with the result that there is little attempt to differentiate between ideas as opposed to the social context of those who articulate them.

This means one of two things. On the one hand, in so far as focus on an over-inclusive stratum of men of ideas does not lead simply to descriptions and a sort of anecdotal form of historical sociology, it produces unhelpful dichotomies like men of action versus men of ideas, bureaucrats versus intellectuals, which have

[8] See most recently and impressively Georges Gurvitch, *Les Cadres sociaux de la connaissance* (Paris, 1966). Like so much else, the work of Gurvitch is ultimately rooted in the cognitive relativism of Marx. Parsons did of course incorporate the problem of idea-systems into his first systematic formulation of action theory and returned to it in *Essays in Sociological Theory* (rev. ed., New York, 1966). But "this classification schema of idea systems seems much too closely governed by the ideal-typical demands of a socio-scientific conceptualization, to be empirically usable according to the demands of a functional theory of knowledge." Wolfram Burisch, *Ideologie und Sachzwang* (Tübingen, 1967) p. 72.

then to be mediated by pointing up the historical exceptions (Reformation, French Revolution, Marxism).[9] Indeed the perhaps most percipient recent discussion of intellectuals finds it easier to isolate and analyze the phenomenon by focusing initially on its enemies, the anti-intellectuals. The definition and role of intellectuals is thus a sort of analytical residue based on the view that particular societies happen to take of their men of ideas.[10] Moreover this analysis, too, focuses on the opposition between practical and speculative men, on ideas versus action.

The other alternative leads to what might be called the sociologists' occupational disease and its consequences for analysis. The more naturally "sociological" the mind of a sociologist, the sharper his vision of the roles of his subjects. It is accordingly ironic that some of the best and sharpest minds in the business

[9] The classic and most comprehensive example of such a definition of intellectuals is probably that given by Julien Benda in his famous *La Trahison des clercs:* "clerks are all those whose activity essentially is not the pursuit of practical aims, but those who seek their joy in the practice of an art or a science or of metaphysical speculation, in short in the possession of non-material advantages, and hence in a certain manner say: 'my kingdom is not of this world.'" Note how this definition anticipates the contrast with men of action spelled out later by e.g., Merton in "The Role of the Intellectual in Public Bureaucracy," *Social Theory and Social Structure* (2nd rev. ed., New York, 1957), pp. 207–24. Benda himself of course deplored the tendency of what he called *clercs* or intellectuals to descend increasingly into the arena of action or politics, in other words to seek a socio-structural context. Cf. also Coser's definition in *Men of Ideas*, p. viii: "Those who exhibit in their activities a pronounced concern with the core values of society ... the men who seek to provide moral standards and to maintain meaningful general symbols. In the tasks they perform, modern intellectuals are descendants of the upholders of sacred tradition, but they are also and at the same time descendants of the biblical prophets, all those inspired madmen who preached in the wilderness far removed from the institutionalized pieties of court and synagogue, castigating the men of power for the wickedness of their ways. Intellectuals are men who never seem satisfied with things as they are, with appeals to custom and usage. They question the truth of the moment in terms of higher and wider truth. They counter appeals to factuality by invoking the 'impractical ought.' They consider themselves special custodians of abstract ideas like reason and justice and truth, jealous guardians of moral standards that are too often ignored in the market place of the houses of power."

[10] See Richard Hofstadter, *Anti-Intellectualism in American Life* (New York, 1963). For Hofstadter's own definition of intellectuals and a brief critical contrast of it with the present approach, see below, note 23.

should have concentrated on throwing into the sharpest relief the social role of intellectuals. The focus is thus on role definition and contrast with other roles, often by analogy; the result, an emphasis on the free or unattached nature of intellectuals as a social role which entirely ignores the very attached or *engagé* nature of the ideas they articulate.[11] As in the case of the more amorphous category of men of ideas, focus on role can scarcely take the matter beyond a sociological exegesis of what a society itself chooses to make of its own intellectuals. For role analysis can never attempt to be objective, but must take as its point of departure the view of A and all A's taken by all B's or indeed by everyone other than A. Valuable though it often is, it distorts the analysis of intellectuals.

The present analysis departs from this tradition in two ways: first, by attempting a much closer and tighter definition of intellectuals, which differentiates them from men of ideas as a whole, and from scientists in particular; second, the initial approach is not through any types of men who have ideas, but with types of ideas as such. The usual order of priorities is thus reversed; instead of starting with certain types of men and differentiating them according to social role and context, I start with the assumption that types of ideas can be differentially classified and that it is this differentiation that ultimately governs roles and social contexts.

I propose to divide the relevant types of ideas produced into dimensions that focus on the relationship of new ideas to the existing stock of knowledge they seek to effect, and go on from there to the manner as well as structural channels through which they become diffused. These dimensions can be labeled respec-

---

[11] For instance Florian Znaniecki, op. cit.; Joseph Schumpeter, op. cit. (See particularly the mention of Pietro Aretino on pp. 147–48). This leads directly to Ralf Dahrendorf's emphasis on the analogy of the intellectual with the medieval court jester as representing the relatively uninhibited and unattached "mirror of conscience," a role of free-floating permissiveness. (Dahrendorf, "Der Intellektuelle und die Gesellschaft," *Zeit*, Vol. XIII [March 29, 1963] and see p. 51 in this volume.) Cf. also intellectuals as free-ranging "players of the mind" in Johan Huizinga, *homo Ludens* (Boston, 1955), p. 8ff. It will be obvious how this in turn relates to the crucial role specification of free-floatingness for intellectuals which is the core of Mannheim's work, though as already mentioned he does of course deal both with the problem of social stratum and role as well as with types of ideas.

tively that of quality and that of scope. Quality in this context will be defined as acceptance or rejection of the axio-normative (or value and norm) structures of given systems of thought, a re-arrangement of the significance and interrelationship of known components.[12] Scope, on the other hand, deals with the broadening of the area of discussion through the addition of genuinely new or at least newly relevant knowledge. If and when we are suddenly asked to accept a totally new order of facts as salient and relevant to our concerns, or when we are faced by a new corpus of knowledge altogether, the problem created is obviously different from one in which an argument, however bitter and hectic, takes place along agreed or at least recognized and known dimensions.

As I shall try to show, the difference between these two analytical categories of ideas and systems of thought is not absolute. When new areas are imposed on an existing state of knowledge the process of incorporation and acceptance is not exclusively one of substitution but must also and *in addition* be one of rearranging existing components. Conversely there are often new elements as well as emphasis in the propagation of qualitative change. It is in the main a question of saliency; either the new dominates and controls the qualitative rearrangements that follow from it, or the new is incidental to the reshuffling of known and accepted components. These respective emphases may not in fact bear much resemblance to any "objective" relationship between the new and the rearranged such as might be discovered or postulated by a much later and almost completely uninvolved analyst—in the sort of analysis provided by recent work in the history and the philosophy of science. As a recent work has emphasized, the difference between looking back at a scientific revolution and evaluating it from the view of the participants is almost unbridgeable.[13] What matters here is the

---

[12] The term "axio-normative" as used first by Florian Znaniecki designates the interrelated component area of values and norms. For a recent critique of the tendency especially of action theory to overseparate values and norms and also correlate them wrongly, see Nettl and Martins, "Values and Norms in Sociology" (forthcoming); Charles Bidwell, "Values, Norms and the Integration of Complex Social System," *Sociological Quarterly*, Vol. VII, No. 2 (Spring 1966), pp. 119–36.

[13] Thomas S. Kuhn, op. cit.

manner in which different ideas (new as well as rearranged) are put forward and accepted or rejected at the time—in other words the relationship between ideas and their environment. I shall treat as qualitative or scope ideas those that "objectively" fit into each respective category as qualified by the extent to which the recipients themselves treat them as such.

This limitation naturally also has its problematic and fuzzy boundaries. The discovery of the genuinely new and its scientific validation must necessarily be limited in range and confined to particular rather than universal means of application—even though the implications that can be drawn from it may be much greater in terms of reordering the secondary and tertiary effects. Initially scientific discovery, indeed any discovery of the genuinely new or newly relevant, is always *particular;* "though the scientist's concern with nature may be global in its extent, the problems on which he works must be problems of detail."[14] Ideas and systems of ideas concerned primarily with the rearrangement of an accepted hierarchy of components are already by definition much broader and more universal. Any systematic formulation of social ideas, for instance, must of necessity cover a broad area of interrelationships. A convergent, though I think less accurate and clear, way of stating this difference is in terms of social or humanistic concerns (*Geistes*—or *Kulturwissenschaften*) versus the exact sciences (*Naturwissenschaften*); the former disciplines encompassing larger areas of interrelationships and covering more components than the latter. This formulation, however, impinges on the arid debates about the status of science versus *Wissenschaft,* which I would like to avoid here.

There is thus a double classification here. On the first dimension are types of ideas: the new, which has been conceptualized here as concerned with scope, versus the rearranged, conceptualized as concerned with quality. The second dimension is concerned with intellectual context and relevance: the particularistic sciences versus the universalistic humanities.[15]

14 Ibid., p. 167.
15 This classification does not of course exhaust the range of ideas or their formation; ideas related to art and artistic creativity would almost certainly provide another distinct category, but one with which we are not here concerned. There is a considerable literature on the formation and articulation of artistic ideas or "vision." For a recent analysis that suggests a

To these dichotomies must be added yet a third: the type of social structure best suited to the diffusion of new ideas of scope as opposed to those qualitative ones concerned with the restructuring of components. Obviously the nature and efficiency of these channels affect not only the influence of ideas but their very existence in historical terms: even if there were means of discovering them all, history has little or no interest in ideas *in vacuo*. The fact that Aristarchus of Samos anticipated Copernicus' overthrow of Ptolemaic astronomy by eighteen hundred years can, of course, be explained, but adds little to the importance of the Copernican heliocentric revolution when it did come.[16] Moreover the greater the extent of universalistic restructuring of the accepted, the more definitely ideas fall within the category of quality, and in turn the greater their dependence on clearly articulated socio-political structures for recognition and diffusion.

The acceptance of a discovery of something genuinely new, of an exploration of particularistic scope, initially requires a limited number of highly skilled "peers" who eventually diffuse the new by application or teaching. Though the discoveries of a Newton or a Mendel may affect the lives of every one of us, the vast majority accept the validity of their discoveries only as a given, backed by the say-so of reputable scientists, and by a corpus of authoritative teaching texts, which act as bibles for new recruits to the profession. It will accordingly be suggested that an academic environment (not necessarily, except under certain conditions to be further explored, a *university* environment) is, broadly speaking, the most suitable structure for diffusing scientific ideas of scope—for formulating, testing, validating, and spreading them. The choice of problems to be tackled is dictated

process of creation or artistic thinking made up of elements of our two present polarities, and thus outlines a category halfway between those analyzed here, see Anton Ehrenzweig, *The Hidden Order of Art* (London, 1967). Ehrenzweig's previous *The Psychoanalysis of Artistic Vision and Hearing* (London, 1953) suggested the need for a paradigm-based unconscious that alone enables us to order, and hence to confront, the chaotic and incoherent conscious perception of works of art. It thus lays the groundwork for the later book, which outlines a theory of creative thought.
[16] See T. L. Heath, *Aristarchus of Samos: The Ancient Copernicus* (Oxford, 1913); Arthur Koestler, *The Sleepwalkers: A History of Man's Changing Vision of the Universe* (London, 1959), pp. 50f.

by internal, professional considerations. Qualitative ideas, on the other hand, seem to predicate socio-political movements and environments for their manner of formulation, acceptance, and diffusion. Without such movements they become academic curiosities in the history of ideas or may be lost altogether. The choice of problems to be tackled is almost invariably influenced, if not governed, by criteria of social relevance and importance. This type of strenuously argued, qualitative rearrangement of known components, strongly oriented toward the socio-political environment, is well captured by the notion of dissent, which I shall use here.

This implies that the clash of ideas takes a somewhat different form according to whether the ideas themselves are concerned with scope or quality. By focussing on the notion of dissent I hope to add to the argument another, fourth factor of differentiation between the two analytical categories of ideas—a factor concerned with the different type of structure of their conflict. The articulation of new ideas almost invariably takes the form of conflict—if not always directly in the vision of those who originally formulate them, then at least indirectly as applied and extended by others. This simply means that, whether the "new" is particularistic and adds to scope or universalistic and changes quality, it is structured primarily in contrast to the old that preceded it. But from then on our two types of new ideas go their different ways.

Obviously the addition of totally new knowledge or relevance either adds to or replaces the old—at least it is treated that way. Quantum theory in physics adds something new but replaces nothing; subatomic units with which it significantly deals simply did not exist in science before this century. Cartesian and other modern systems of geometry both enlarge the scope and thus partially replace Euclidean geometry: Newtonian physics broaden and replace Copernican and are in turn displaced by still more inclusive relativity theories; oxygen replaces phlogiston, and since the invention of antibiotics other treatments for the relevant infections have become marginal. The qualitative restructuring of components, on the other hand, contains a much greater element of preference: there are no *certainties* as between Keynes and Pigou, between Lévy-Bruhl and Lévy-Strauss, not even between Marx, Feuerbach, and Hegel. Dissent as used here is implicit in the structured opposition of preferences in idea-systems rather than in the sense of commitment to new scientific knowledge replacing older, now partially or wholly invalidated knowledge.

Again this is not a matter of absoluteness. On the one hand "there is hardly a scientific theory that is not questioned by some scientists of repute"[17]—which means that even scientific truths are not final; on the other hand, as Marx and Comte showed so clearly, even the most determined preferences for a particular hierarchy or arrangement of socio-political components can be presented and accepted as scientific truth. But the issue here is not merely the innate quality of ideas and hence the quality of conflict between them in the abstract, but the ideological and socio-structural manner of their conflict. And here we find that disagreement over scientific truth is primarily, or at least initially, individual, and attempts to politicize it openly are as a rule depreciated. As against this, dissent over quality is oriented toward the collective, and individual, abstruse discussions are not so much deviant as irrelevant.[18]

In drawing this distinction between new scientific or scope ideas on one hand, and new forms of qualitative dissent on the other, I may have aligned myself with a tradition in the history and philosophy of science that has recently been persuasively challenged. Instead of regarding science as an endless accretion and incorporation of new discoveries, moving deterministically toward the present mature truths, its progress is rather divided into normal science, which accords with this unilinear evolution, and abnormal revolutions, which restructure fundamental "para-

---

[17] For this statement about scientific theory, see Laurence J. Lafleur, "Cranks and Scientists," *Scientific Monthly,* Vol. LXXIII (November 1951), p. 285.

[18] Cf. the debate over the ethics of participation by popular journals in the discussion of the theories of Dr. Velikovsky as set out in his *Worlds in Collision* (New York, 1950). This debate is summarized and some important sociological conclusions are drawn by Alfred de Grazia, ed., op. cit. On the other side we need only remember Lenin's contempt for the purely theoretical debates over Marxist "truth," which formed a large part of his disillusion with, and attacks on, the major Marxist theorist of his day, Karl Kautsky. See, for instance, J. P. Nettl, *Rosa Luxemburg* (London, 1966), for this problem generally among Marxist intellectuals.

digms" or ideologies of epistemology.[19] But I do not think the distinction between types of ideas put forward here is invalidated even if one accepts the notion of fundamental restructurings. For one thing, Kuhn's examples of revolution start with "minuscule" detail, with particularistic discoveries that do not fit the old paradigm (what he calls anomaly). Admittedly there may often be an atmosphere of crisis in the profession already. Secondly, the fundamental substitution of one major or minor paradigm by another is a historian's categorization rather than a participant's recognition of cataclysmic change. Finally, the end of a scientific revolution is characterized by the enthronement and (more important) internalization of a new paradigm, which provides the only suitable structure for normal or particularistic science to continue on its way. In fact the world of qualitative dissent, with its permanent conflict of paradigms proffered and thrust forward by structural movements in competition or combat with each other, can be compared only with what Kuhn calls pre-paradigm or immature science. In science "truth emerges more readily from error than from confusion."[20]

Moreover the articulation of qualitatively new ideas conflicts not so much with what is, as with what the dissenter says it is. That is to say, a new scientific truth conflicts with its predecessor within an arena of understanding as to what constitutes the old and hence the new; the new does not generally exist merely by virtue of the external or objective collapse of the old, as a result of a special demonstration of its failures which entails an ad hoc respecification as a consequence. "The act of judgment that leads scientists to reject a previously accepted theory is always based upon more than a comparison of that theory with the world (i.e., anomaly). The decision to reject one paradigm is always simul-

[19] The most recent case for the cumulative theory of evolutionary improvement in science is C. C. Gillespie, *The Edge of Objectivity: An Essay in the History of Scientific Ideas* (Princeton, 1960). The case for opposed types of normal and revolutionary science is argued in Kuhn, op. cit. This author stresses the analogy between revolution in science and in politics on grounds of similar breakdown (p. 91f.). It is interesting to compare this analogy equating scientific revolutions and political ones with the precisely opposite analogy of Merton, who compares the "minimal logical conformity" with the procedures of mature, functioning science (*Social Theory and Social Structure* [Glencoe, Illinois, 1957 2nd revised edition], p. 484).

[20] Francis Bacon, *Novum Organum,* cited in Kuhn, op. cit., p. 18.

taneously the decision to accept another, and the judgment leading to that decision involves the comparison of *both paradigms* with nature *and* with each other."[21] A qualitative dissent, however, defines the new or differently rearranged precisely by virtue of such a special respecification of the old. This has, as it were, to be demolished and shown wanting on account of its own internal failures or insufficiencies, which are in a sense independent of the new that supplants it. Scientific discoveries imply a "no" contingent upon a prior "yes," while dissent implies a "yes" contingent upon a prior "no."[22] Hence dissent involves a special and summary statement of the ideas dissented from—an ideology. And the opponents of this dissent in turn dissent from it; their defensive formulation of the status quo, which they uphold, is not made from mere affect but negatively stimulated by the respecification of the old, the "no" involved in the original dissent. The notion of dissent will accordingly be used here not merely in its oppositional sense but to signify an articulated response: intellectuals as dissenters are not always trying to change a status quo (though more often they are) but may also be defending it by arguing for a different arrangement of components than the original dissenters. The outcome of the debate is not, of course, involved in the definition but is theoretically random; old or new dissenters may come out on top.[23]

[21] Kuhn, op. cit., p. 77. (Original italics.)

[22] This formulation differs obliquely from that of Gerald Holton, "Modern Science and the International Tradition," in De Huszar, ed., op. cit., p. 186, to the effect that "each change necessarily encompasses previous knowledge. Science grows ring by ring, like a tree . . . providing a larger setting within which some contradictions and asymmetries in the earlier work disappear." This, indeed Holton's whole discussion, implies that scientific discoveries are originally (instead of derivatively) qualitative and wide rather than focused on scope and particularistic, but that they nonetheless represent a "no" contingent upon a prior "yes" rather than a "yes" contingent upon a prior "no."

[23] The foregoing attempt to distinguish between categories of ideas with a view to assigning one category specifically to intellectuals as prime articulators might be critically compared with the distinction between intellect and intelligence put forward by Richard Hofstadter, op. cit., p. 25. "Intellect is the critical, creative and contemplative side of mind. Whereas intelligence seeks to grasp, manipulate, re-order, adjust, intellect examines, ponders, wonders, theorises, criticises, imagines." (Cf. above, note 10.) A recent scientific discussion of these problems may be found in Sylvan S. Tomkins, "Affect and the Psychology of Knowledge," in Tomkins and Carroll E. Izard, eds., *Affect, Cognition and Personality* (New York, 1965).

We thus have a set of our classifications that can be schematically arranged as follows:

Idea type	Scope	Quality
Intellectual context	Particular/ Scientific	Universal/ Humanistic
Social structure	Peer group. Academic institutionalization	Stratum, group or class. Socio-political institutionalization
Structure of articulation	Replacement contingent on discovery	Replacement contingent on negation
Type of conflict	Acceptance of new paradigm as basis of work by limited community	Extended conflict between unlimited structures professing alternative ideologies

As we shall see, these categories crosscut awkwardly. Ideas of a very particularistic kind can be swept into a universal social context, often against the wish of the originator (i.e., Freud; see below, p. 75). Systems of universal rearrangement of the components of social life claim the status of science (i.e., Marx; see below, p. 76). A crucial feature of the present argument will be that the very idea of social science uneasily straddles the fulcrum of these categories and pulls the natural habitat of universal-qualitative systems of ideas in their sociological context away from the socio-political arena and into the universe of science and the universities (below, p. 89). Above all these classifications become dichotomies; acting like sharp rotor blades on a set of turbines, they chew up the concept of intellectual into its constituent elements, turning social congruence into role contradictions and conflicts. "For a century more or less science has been the [one of the three] chief enemies of Intellect among Intellectuals."[24] The next section of this essay uses these categories of ideas in order to formulate a definition of what constitutes an intellectual, to discover what the term should mean, and briefly to analyze his historical role.

[24] Jacques Barzun, *The House of Intellect* (New York, 1959), p. 22.

The process of disintegration of this composite but historically important role is the concern of the last section.

If Athens provides us with the first clearly differentiated stratum of intellectuals, the Reformation in its broadest temporal sense was probably the first appearance of such a stratum whose activities still directly influence the modern world of today. In accordance with the classification adopted here, this was clearly an instance of qualitative dissent, which became structured by religious-political movements of great durability. Yet the undermining of the intellectual foundations of medieval cosmology was less a product of the qualitative Reformation than of the so-called Renaissance of knowledge and science, which added new dimensions of scope and relevance but which itself left much less, and anyhow less obvious, structural evidence of its existence. The acceptance of the new knowledge in the revolution of the physical and astronomical sciences is often identified with the work of the universities of Italy, Paris, Germany, and Poland. It can certainly be argued that the rise of such institutions, and the strengthening of their role and function within their contemporary societies, are directly related to changes in the basis of existing epistemology—changes in the scope of ideas. Thus the strength and socio-cultural importance of universities vary with the development and discovery of knowledge or lack of it; the mere diffusion of existing knowledge through teaching would lead to a decline in their importance—possibly to such an extent as to facilitate the future location of discoveries outside the universities altogether. But instead of institutional facilitation of "new" ideas, of encouraging the enlargement of existing scope, it may in fact be the independent explosion of new ideas outside academic institutions that *in turn* brings about a compensating expansion in the role and importance of universities—an order of priorities that reformers of higher education, especially in England, may do well to remember!

The eighteenth- and nineteenth-century articulation of ideas in France was by contrast mainly qualitative; the work of the *philosophes* in France was significantly unconnected with universities. Instead, as so many writers have thundered at us in the last few years, their ideas were directly related to the latent socio-political movements that finally led to the French Revolution, and that in turn crystallized, highlighted, and above all simplified these ideas for purposes of effective socio-political action.[25]

European universities as a whole stagnated during these otherwise exciting years; the best work in both science and the humanities was done outside them. "The famous salon of Madame Helvétius, where the ideological movement was born, was of special importance. During the life-time of her husband it had been a major nursery for the ideas of the Encyclopaedists, where Condillac, Diderot and D'Alembert had often gathered to discuss with passion the philosophy of the Enlightenment. . . . A new group of younger intellectuals also began to make its appearance. Morellet, Volney, Turgot, Condorcet, the elderly Benjamin Franklin along with Pierre Cabanis, the young physiologist and moral philosopher, Destutt de Tracy, the former cavalry officer turned philosopher, and a whole group of young men in the process of developing that particular philosophical doctrine which in later years was to be named the 'ideological movement' . . . Auteuil allowed the young intellectuals to form close and enduring contacts with one another while remaining conscious of the pre-eminence of their elders. This drawing together in Madame Helvétius' salon counterbalanced the disruptive tendencies of Parisian intellectual life and helped to give the doctrine the character of a collective enterprise. For many of the ideologists Auteuil came to mean more than a salon to which one repaired from time to time. Cabanis lived there for many years, so did Destutt de Tracy. Condorcet stayed here before he was forced to go into hiding. A considerable number of other *idéologues* lived at Auteuil for shorter or longer periods."[26]

On the more directly scientific side there was the so-called Society of Arcueil. This, too, provided an extra-institutional and spontaneous setting for the congregation of learned men, on which in turn the Institut National, one of the formal new

[25] See the analysis in Daniel Mornet, *Les Origines intellectuelles de la révolution française 1715–1787* (new edition, Paris, Armand Colin, 1967).
[26] Lewis A. Coser, op. cit., pp. 191–92.

Thermidorian institutions of higher learning, was to be based.[27] The process of institutionalization of higher learning in Thermidorian and Napoleonic France was initially the result of a deliberate political decision by scientists and "men of ideas" who attained positions of power after 1789, but especially after 1795. Out of the informal congeries and clusterings of such men throughout the second half of the eighteenth century the Revolution created new institutions rather than attempting to draw them into the old existing ones. That is partly why it was a revolution.

But if the period 1795–1800 witnessed a general access to power on the part of what have been called men of ideas, scientists as well as intellectuals, the era of Napoleon sharply reasserted the effective distinction between them in terms of political and social status and influence. The intellectuals or *idéologues* with their universal, humanistic perspectives and above all their qualitative dissent were soon evicted into a powerless wilderness of irrelevance. Napoleon came to refer to them as "metaphysicians who swarm like vermin around me . . . a band of imbeciles who sigh from the bottom of their souls for liberty of the press and of speech, and believe in the omnipotence of public opinion."[28]

Lest it be thought that these were personal antipathies, let us look at the even more forthright condemnation Napoleon reserved for their ideas: "this gloomy metaphysics which subtly looks for first causes . . . instead of making the laws attune to knowledge of the human heart and to the lessons of history, to this all the misfortune of our beautiful France must be attributed."[29] There was no room for qualitative dissent, only for affect (knowledge of the human heart) and science (the lessons of history).

The qualitative dissenters spent the Napoleonic era in a political wilderness, some even in exile. The scientists, however, did

[27] See the excellent recent account in Maurice Crosland, *The Society of Arcueil: A Review of French Science at the Time of Napoleon I* (London, 1967).

[28] These quotations are from Charles H. Van Duzen, *The Contribution of the Idéologues to French Revolutionary Thought* (Baltimore, 1935), p. 151, and *Cambridge Modern History*, Vol. IX (Cambridge, 1906), p. 132.

[29] Hippolyte Taine, *Les Origines de la France contemporaine*, Vol. II (Paris, Hachette, 1898), pp. 219–20.

very well under Napoleon. They completed the reform of higher education, which the intellectuals had begun a decade earlier. Berthollet and Monge became senators, and Monge became a count. In short the indiscriminate association of the ambitious man of power with the men of ideas, which had still made General Bonaparte proudly join the title of his command with mention of his membership of the Institute below his signature to official documents in 1798, now decomposed into a clear distinction by Consul and Emperor Napoleon between the particularistic scientists and the universalistic ideologists. History shows several instances of this distinction being forcibly and instrumentally made by men of power. I would argue that it is based on the different nature of types of ideas rather than on any sociological differences between types or groups of men. It is worth noting that history has been more perceptive of this distinction than sociology.[30]

Though history has on several occasions helped to keep sociologically tidy the two categories of ideas and their bearers, the distinction between the two suggested types of innovation or dissent in ideas is not always kept so neatly, especially as far as their identification with two different structural channels of diffusion is concerned. It has, for instance, been suggested that the strength of institutionalized science was such in seventeenth-century England that the foundation of the Royal Society immediately after the Restoration in 1660–63, and its subsequent vigor and influence, may have helped to give English philosophy its two hundred years of empirical if not downright utilitarian cast. A potentially dissenting profession was thus pulled into the orbit of scientific particularism and academic institutionalization by the strength of universities at a time when intellectually dominated socio-political dissent was on the verge of exhaustion. As against this, the decline of universities in the eighteenth and early nineteenth centuries in much of Europe made it at least probable that innovations of *all* kinds, including the most particularistic sciences, would most likely come from outside them.

[30] Cf. the discussion in Chapter 15 of Coser, op. cit., pp. 189–205. Another case history discussed by Coser is that of Gomulka and the Polish intellectuals in 1956. The distinction has in fact always been strongly in evidence in Communist countries, but has not been drawn by Coser. Cf. below, pp. 106–107.

The "natural" propensity for each of our category of ideas to seek particular structures for diffusion may well be tempered by such considerations. Philosophy is capable of formulating ideas on either of our two dimensions. In the first case it was pulled into scientific particularism; in Wittgenstein's words, "the problems are solved, not by giving new information, but by arranging what we have always known. Philosophy is a battle against the bewitchment of our intelligence by means of language." In the second, the fact that even strongly scope-oriented scientific research or discovery takes place outside an academic environment might cause it to have more obvious socio-political connotations and to find readier echos of socio-structural dissent than could otherwise be the case.

One wonders in this connection whether the history of Darwinism or Utilitarianism would have been different and more purely intellectual if Darwin, Bentham, and Mill had been fully institutionalized professors. In any case the dispersed or uninstitutionalized location of some of the best ideas of the nineteenth and early twentieth centuries is highlighted by the fact that in the field of medicine many of the significant discoveries of the period were made outside—and indeed against—the institutionalized teaching of medicine in universities and teaching hospitals. Both Pasteur and Freud, to cite only two distinguished figures, were essentially private, "free-floating" citizens and found it almost impossible, as well as to some extent undesirable, to obtain institutional affiliation.[81] But significantly the development of the work of both these men, whose dissent was contingent on discovery rather than negation, was eventually encapsulated in universities and in the "technological" application of medical practice as taught there. Freud has given rise to no social movement and little socio-political ideology, but he has fathered a powerful movement of professional and academic psychoanalysis, and this in turn has provided a central component of the modern American culture of egocentric and remissive self-indulgence in revolt against the interdicts of its collectivist predecessors. Indeed Freud himself was quite determined to prevent

[81] See the discussion in Joseph Ben David, "Scientific Productivity and Academic Organization in Nineteenth Century Medicine," *American Sociological Review,* Vol. XXV, No. 6 (December 1960), pp. 828–43.

the articulation of his ideas in any but clinical terms, and beyond the range of a strictly personal epistemological commitment. He fought bitterly with the most distinguished of his students who attempted to generalize and apply his ideas in the arena of stipulative culture and ideology, let alone politics. And all these attempts failed in the end. As an intellectual system Freud's teaching boiled down to a purely personal commitment to stoic rationality.[82] It would thus be quite wrong to regard the analytical distinction between types of ideas and their "ideal" or differentiated structural accommodation discussed earlier as necessarily adhered to in the history of ideas. To this extent these ideal types of congruence or correspondence reflect in part a modern perspective of differentiation applied retroactively to the past.

The most comprehensive qualitative dissent of modern times has been Marxism. Nearly everyone who writes on intellectuals ascribes special significance to this phenomenon since it is so crucial in the history of the species. If the present suggestion of dividing the production of knowledge, the formulation of ideas, into two analytical categories is valid, it certainly opens up some very suggestive possibilities in relation to Marxism. We know that Marx's system was a specific and detailed rearrangement and systematization of other people's ideas: Saint-Simon, Proudhon, Blanqui, and others in France on a socio-political dimension; Hegel and Feuerbach in Germany on a more philosophical and epistemological dimension. Marx was above all a rearranger, an "inverter" *par excellence* and of excellence, whose radicalism consisted not so much of the new but of the different. The deliberate removal of social thinking from an academic context to a political, the projection of ideas beyond the possibilities of their present socio-structural realization in anticipation of a future when society would catch up with these ideas, all this was not merely the consequence of official refusal to have intellectual radicals in the universities (though, of course, Marx

[82] For the history of this see Philip Rieff, *Freud: The Mind of the Moralist* (New York, 1961 [rev. ed.]), and *The Triumph of the Therapeutic: Uses of Faith after Freud* (New York, 1967). Cf. also Peter L. Berger, "Towards a Sociological Understanding of Psychoanalysis," *Social Research*, Vol. XXXII, No. 1 (1965), pp. 26–41.

himself, as well as some of his immediate sources of ideas and attitudes like Feuerbach, Ruge, Bruno Bauer, and David Strauss, were all in trouble with their university authorities). It was the nature of the *ideas* that made them ultimately less relevant to academic transmission than to socio-political diffusion.

At another level there is, of course, in Marx a personal resentment against academicization. He would not let the grip of his analysis be lost in arid academic speculation, or *praxis* to be sacrificed to *logos:* "the philosophers have only interpreted the world differently, what counts is to change it." Or, more forcefully still: "Philosophy stands in the same relation to the study of the actual world as onanism to sexual love." This, it is suggested, provides a key to the fairly fundamental psychological contrast, even conflict, between the intellectual and the academic, which can be only obscured if they are lumped together in the indiscriminate category of "men of ideas" and such similar strata. I shall have more to say later on this psychological reflection among individuals and groups of the distinction between types of ideas put forward here.

Thus one may legitimately ask whether Marx's determination to thrust his system of ideas into the crucible of the real world for the purpose of its eventual transformation is not in the last resort functionally related to the specific type of thinking at issue here. Hegel provided much of the "new" for Marx; he was a typical, perhaps the archetypal, university philosopher. There is no logical reason why his ideas should not have led directly to a political movement of *étatiste* revitalization. They did not. His disciples, the so-called young or radical Hegelians, were deprived of or threatened in their academic positions on political grounds. (The border line between intellectually and socio-politically dangerous doctrines is never easy to draw, as the history of Galileo and much more recently of Scopes with his evolutionary teaching in Dayton, Tennessee, has shown. The world does not necessarily accept the sociologists' categories, and any conflict over ideas that takes place within an institutional setting and that leads to institutional reprisals becomes ipso facto political in the broadest sense.) Yet it was only through Marxism and the Marxist movement that Hegel and the young Hegelians ever achieved any direct political importance. "No German ever escapes Hegel,

[even] a German Marxist is suspect of saying Marx when he means Hegel."[33]

The partially Hegelian perspective of the early Lukacs shows clearly how the socio-political implications of Hegel's ideas had to be sewn onto and transmitted through the Marxist movement, and how difficult (and personally venturesome) this grafting could be. In a sense Lukacs' whole intellectual history is a struggle for synthesis between the radical tradition of German philosophy, with its strongly marked search for new scope, and the increasing squeeze on permitted areas of relevance applied by the Stalinist political system of "mere" vulgarized paradox or component-reversal.[34] Other non-German intellectual and academic disciples of Hegel could, in so far as they were politically motivated at all, find refuge only in a diffusely liberal do-goodism as did T. H. Green in England. Dissent within the framework of basic givens may thus be interpreted primarily as a socio-political phenomenon; the colonization of new areas and their integration into the existing stock of thought may be considered as an academic function most suitable for institutionalization in universities. In this sense Marx was an intellectual, Hegel was not. The former postulated change based on negation, the latter articulated a new philosophy of history based on a "discovered" dialectic of change. Though Hegel's ideas were capable of socio-political application, they needed interpretation and application by others. *Over and above this,* however, Marx was also a revolutionary, while Hegel was also a professor.

One should perhaps not generalize too much from a particular case. In such a brief outline of an enormously complex subject it is not possible to test enough cases to support a theory—or even a theoretical classification, which is all that is attempted here. We are left with a hypothesis. In general, however, the idea that the problem of intellectuals might be best tackled through an analytical dichotomy of types of idea-systems seems attractive. It may perhaps even be possible to go further than this. The relationship between the appearance of ideas on the

[33] Philip Rieff, *The Triumph of the Therapeutic,* p. 153.
[34] This difficulty is well pointed up in the excellent analysis by George Lichtheim, "The Concept of Ideology," *History and Theory,* Vol. IV, No. 2 (1965), pp. 164–95.

scope dimension and on the dimension of quality may not be random or arbitrary, as has in a sense been implied here, but may have to be mutually reinforcing if it is to be effective; new ideas involving scope produced in academic institutions often need "outside" support in the form of dissent before they can be diffused and institutionalized in a social context. In other words, the diffusion of *either* of the two types of ideas becomes most effective if *both* their respective loci of production are separately and adequately institutionalized. Only at this stage, then, does the problem of institutionalization reappear to affect the discussion of ideas.

Such may also be the real implication of the history of differentiation and institutional specifications of universities of which Parsons has made so much elsewhere in this volume. As long as almost the entire area of possible ideas was encapsulated in an undifferentiatedly religious context (in a sort of Parsonian regression from ancient Greco-Roman specificity to medieval diffuseness), the *social* context of dissent and the relationship of intellectuals to it is far harder to disentangle. Otherwise we finish up once more with an analysis of an undifferentiated stratum of "men of ideas" or—worse still—"discover" intellectuals by virtue of historical evidence of social conflict. The real problem of the Middle Ages in this regard is the impossibility of separating scope from qualitative forms of dissent; everything was part of the faith, of the basic order of society. Hence everyone who thought was an intellectual, or no one.

The time has come to dismiss the scope dimension from the present discussion for the time being. The reason why so much has been made of the problem of intellectuals, and why there are as many ideas about them as there are writers on the subject, is precisely because no attempt has been made to provide categories within which choices about types of ideas can be made and then to relate these categories differentially to particular social institutions and channels of diffusion. If nothing else, the suggested categories and their institutional correlates provide a form of *latent* structure that enables us to test out certain hypotheses of similarity and contrast with regard to particular ideas and historical periods.

If we assume for present purposes that the problem is primarily one of contrast between ideas and societies and add the relationship between the bearers of ideas and the social structure in which they operate as an additional variable, then the whole area of the search for new knowledge in universities can provisionally be left out. It must, of course, be reintroduced if we discover, as I think we shall, that the development of the differentiated institution of universities has in fact burst out of the narrow confines of its "ideal" specificity, of concern with problems of scope. Academic institutions are currently posing difficult questions once more as a result of the reintegration of *both* types of idea formation within a single institutional form. In many countries, especially in the United States, universities have today become loci of institutionalized dissent; we shall later try to see how and why.

What then is an intellectual? Someone who merely articulates qualitatively new ideas, who dissents on a qualitative dimension? Hardly. The rearrangement of the known, which I have stressed as being an essential prerequisite for any intellectual projection into socially structured movements, is a very common form of thinking. It does not necessarily lead to any social consequences of dissent; while intellectual influence on social dissent presupposes rearrangement if not inversion of known epistemological components, mere rearrangement or inversion by itself predicates nothing other than paradox. In fact the reversal of the obvious has become an accepted form of philosophical discourse, sociological depiction, and even of poetic expression, so that the extremity of contrast or contradiction sometimes represents a measure of the intellectual depth of the writer. The Germans were way ahead on this dimension: the philosophers Husserl and Heidegger on the one hand—with their repeated obeisances toward Hegel—and romantic poets like Hölderlin and Novalis on the other. Hölderlin's statement of ultimate contradiction— that life is death, and death too is a form of life—in his poem *In lieblicher Bläue,* and Novalis' claim that the obliteration of the principle of contradiction is perhaps the highest task of superior logic, both relate directly to the very different and entirely unromantic galvanization of the reader's credulity in Orwell's famous depiction of ultimate totalitarian awfulness—war is peace and peace war.[35]

The actual definition of an intellectual must accordingly include not only a certain type of thinking but also a relationship to socio-structural dissent, at least potentially. The ideas must be predicated on the assumption that they are capable of being put into effect in society. Moreover the ideas must have universality; though identified with a particular social collectivity or set of institutions, they must not express a particular interest but relate the bearers of the ideas or ideology with a type of society, if not indeed any and all societies as a whole. Finally the ideas must have a cultural base or form of validation in that they are ultimately concerned with the quality of *life in general*.[36] The most useful definition of the intellectual for our purposes so far put forward is by Edgar Morin. "The intellectual emerges from a cultural base and with a socio-political role (cultural in this context is defined as a self-conscious concern with cultural dimensions). . . . Thus the intellectual can be defined from a triple set of dimensions: (1) a profession that is culturally validated, (2) a role that is socio-political, (3) a consciousness that relates to universals."[37]

An intellectual is thus defined relatively narrowly, involving criteria that have to be met on three different dimensions. Emphasis on a culturally validated profession stipulates the arena of idea-articulation and, it should be emphasized, of the audience as well. An intellectual must therefore be someone qualified,

[35] The poem's attribution to Hölderlin is uncertain, since it only exists in the form of a reprint by his friend Waiblinger. It is reprinted (in prose only) in the recent Stuttgart edition of Hölderin's works (*Grosse Stuttgarter Ausgabe*, Vol. II, Part 1, p. 372. See also notes in Vol. II, Part 2, pp. 991–92).

[36] This is the dimension particularly emphasized by Edward Shils, "The Intellectuals and the Powers," *Comparative Studies in Society and History*, Vol. I (October 1958), p. 5, where he speaks of "unusual sensitivity to the sacred, an uncommon reflectiveness about the nature of their universe and the rules which govern their society."

[37] Edgar Morin, "Intellectuels: critique du mythe et mythe de la critique," *Arguments*, Vol. IV, No. 20 (October 1960), special number on intellectuals, p. 35. The French original has been altered slightly in translation, especially in the definition of culture.

and accepted as qualified, to speak on matters of cultural concern. This is, of course, the issue that has led many sociologists like Shils and Lipset to enumerate certain recognized professions in society that qualify automatically.[38] But such cultural validation should in my view neither be considered as a professional constant, nor indeed be deduced from the English word "profession" at all. Rather it comes from what the person concerned "professes"—in other words self-conscious preoccupation or concern with cultural problems. It thus surpasses and encompasses the notion of profession as such and is subject to variation through time and space. The notion of a culturally validated profession also implies a hierarchy, in that some professions appear more directly validated than others at different times. Thus, as will be argued later, science is currently and contradictorily a strong locus of cultural validation.[39]

Little need be said about the meaning of a socio-political role: the earlier emphasis on the relation of intellectual dissent to socio-political structure anticipates this dimension of the present definition. It merely reinforces the distinction between intellectuals and academics whose focus is on seminal diffusion of ideas to students, without any predicate for societal action.

Universality is also already implicit in the foregoing discussion: indeed it constituted one of the categories of ideas from which were deduced a particular type of dissent and its articulators. Tocqueville in his analysis of the causes of the French Revolution more than a hundred years ago emphasized the extent to which the French intellectuals of the eighteenth century increasingly concentrated on a single overriding and universal idea. This, he

[38] Seymour Martin Lipset, "American Intellectuals: Their Politics and Status," in *Political Man* (Doubleday Anchor ed., New York, 1963), pp. 332–71, originally in *Daedalus*, Vol. LXXXVIII, No. 3 (Spring 1959), pp. 460–86. Edward Shils's work is widely scattered. Representative statements include "The Intellectuals and the Powers: Some Perspectives for Comparative Analysis," *Comparative Studies in Society and History*, Vol. I (1958–59), pp. 5–22; "Mass Society and Its Culture," *Daedalus*, Vol. LXXXIX (Spring 1960).

[39] There should be no need to define the meaning of culture in this context. For present purposes it may simply be taken as the area of concern of qualitative dissent. Though somewhat self-defining, this is perfectly adequate for the present discussion.

felt, was one of the major causes for the intensity and intransigence of the French Revolution.[40] The French word for consciousness is *conscience,* which suggests a universalization of awareness as well as of feeling, thus covering both values and cognition. *Conscience* is therefore to be contrasted not only with particularism as a system of thought but also with professionalism as a social category.

This definition of the intellectual encompasses the discussion of ideas that preceded it and also places the relevant category of ideas on a sociological dimension that locates intellectuals in a profession, a role, and an area of concern. With this definition it is possible to proceed to a brief discussion of the historical relationship between intellectuals and movements of dissent in different societies.

If it were possible to imagine a world or even an individual society without conflict, hermetically sealed and fully integrated, there would be no intellectuals—though there might still be new ideas and men to formulate them. It is sometimes claimed that industrialization (at least the cultural and ideological commitment to it), and the seven-league strides toward an all-embracing and dominating technology, will eventually create such a world —or at least the preconditions for it. The only conflicts that remain from now on would then be between developed and relatively underdeveloped countries, and between and within the latter. This, it is claimed, is the cause of the intellectuals' death agony in developed or highly industrialized countries at the present time. That this problem will be the subject of my conclusion is not so much fitting as inevitable.

In the past, as long as there have been people who have tried to alter values by rearranging the priority of its components, there has always been a conflict between ideas, and such conflict has found some structural echo—whether this took the form of an intellectual transformation of ideal belief systems into sociopolitical movements in Greece, heresies and orthodoxies in early or medieval Christendom, nascent secular movements during the

[40] See *The Old Regime and the French Revolution* (English translation, New York, 1955).

Reformation, or finally the more typical post-Reformation dissent of the last three hundred years.[41] There have, of course, been long periods of relative "smoothness" in which dissent never got beyond words spoken or written without biting into the texture of society. In so far as there was social or generally collective conflict in Western Europe during the later Roman Empire, the late Middle Ages, the first fifty years of the eighteenth century, it had little benefit of intellectual validation or influence. Outside Europe these periods of "smoothness" were often longer and more complete. Then again there were periods of total upheaval, of near disaster to civilization, when dissent was irrelevant and meaningless. Hence the historical periods in which, and for the emergence of which, intellectuals were significant are capable of specification and were always limited in time.

These are the periods of at least latent socio-political dissent and innovation; even amid great diversity they demonstrate certain invariant features. For instance, we know a great deal about the relationship between the innovators and the executors, between intellectuals and bureaucrats in different periods. From our knowledge has emerged the thesis that the socio-political structuring of qualitative innovation leads with seeming inevitability to the later *Gleichschaltung* or isolation of intellectuals by bureaucrats who take over and implement the very ideas of those whom they now seek to isolate from all positions of power and influence. The particularly salient example of the Napoleonic era has already been mentioned (above, p. 82). Mannheim has characterized it in his usual "utopian dialect-dynamic" manner: "The situation [of the intellectuals] always becomes critical when the [social] stratum supportively standing behind them has forced its way into the control of its contemporary situation; when the course of historical development releases the utopia based on political action, and at the same time lets loose the stratum

[41] On Greece in this context see Alvin W. Gouldner, *Enter Plato: Classical Greece and the Origins of Social Theory* (New York, 1966), which is very illuminating. A specific discussion of Pythagoreanism as one of the first social movements of "culture revitalization" is by A. F. Wallace, "Revitalization Movements," in S. M. Lipset and Neil J. Smelser, eds., *Sociology: The Progress of a Decade* (New York, 1961), pp. 206–20.

tied up with it, through the bonds of its own ascent based on the demand for that same utopia."[42]

Whether it is the Papal Curia hurling condemnation at Catholic intellectuals—some of whose pressing demands it will adopt piecemeal in course of time—or Napoleon rounding on certain selected ex-fellow members of the Institute, or even Stalin clamping down on the cosmic explosion of innovation in the Soviet Union in the 1920s, the story carries the sort of irony that historians, if not indeed history itself, love to fondle. Merton's dictum that those who innovate are not heard, while those who are heard do not innovate, is really a teasing falsehood, since the very tragedy of innovation is that it *is* heard but that those who innovate do not usually act, while those who act borrow their ideas from others.

There are, of course, exceptions. At least twice in fairly recent history the qualitative innovators, the intellectuals, have precipitated and actually led a breakaway social movement. Oddly enough, the similarity between Marxism and the Reformation has usually been pointed up on the quite different grounds of total encapsulation and commitment to internal ideological consistency, to historicism and determinism, in short on grounds of intellectual similarity. I have always assumed that this particular manner of identifying the two movements is a search for intellectual comfort; if Marxism is only the philosophy of a secular church, then we have been through all this before and survived intact. In actual fact the similarities, such as they are, become much more significant in terms of the relationship between intellectual dissent and the relevant socio-political structures.

The Reformation in its various forms took over existing collectivities and removed them wholesale out of the control of the Universal Church, while Marxism first stipulated and then also took over a ready-made collectivity, the working class, by simply cutting it off from its objective dependence on capitalism. In both cases the "theft" and removal of existing social structures and collectivities (states, towns, and communities in the Refor-

42 Karl Mannheim, *Ideologie und Utopie* (3rd German ed., Frankfurt, 1952), p. 221; cf. also "Historismus," in *Archiv für Sozialwissenschaft und Sozialpolitik*, Vol. LII (1924) p. 44.

mation—*cujus regio ejus religio* is quite literally true; trade unions, workers' organizations, and finally the Russian state in the Communist case) required a sustained and often bitter campaign ideologically to justify the separateness and distinctiveness of the stolen institutions. The difference is that this justification followed the actual separation in the Reformation, preceded it in the case of Marxist dissent. Hence the emphasis on lay and civic factors in the Reformation, the articulation of "class for itself" by Marxists. In both cases the intellectuals provided the theoretical depiction of reality as well as the *praxis* that created it.

Once created and institutionalized, however, the new reality soon becomes relatively static. If conservatism is the maintenance of the status quo, it applies indifferently to the prevention as well as, in case of success, to the making permanent of institutionalized dissent. To this extent non-innovating bureaucrats are always the logical successors of the intellectuals—and especially in cases where the latter have been successful, where former dissent, which has become the new orthodoxy, has in turn to be defended against reaction, the former orthodoxy, which may constitute the current dissent. The word "mandarin" has occasionally been used for both the articulate bureaucrat and the supportive intellectual in a non-revolutionary as well as a post-revolutionary situation. Since "mandarin" comes from what has possibly been the most stable and conservative regime and society in history, the Chinese Empire, it is peculiarly apt in this context.[43] There is after all some similarity of process between the inhibition of articulated dissent and its successful defense against reaction or yet further manifestations of dissent.

All this confirms the view that if intellectuals are to be defined along the three dimensions mentioned earlier, and regarded as being concerned essentially with the rearrangement of known components (dissent), then their actual appearance in terms of socio-political structure, the effectiveness of their political role, can be only an occasional phenomenon in history. The intellectual phenomenon is not a necessary component of all mobilizing situations, but only a special case. As understanding of the im-

[43] See particularly Jacob Taubes, op. cit., pp. 41–42.

portance of socio-political mobilization increases and we learn more about the different manner in which it is brought about, it becomes more important to distinguish between the type of dissent-structures in which intellectuals play a special role and other more general forms of collectivity mobilization—such as bureaucratic, interest-based, military, and national-constitutional.

There have been some recent attempts to treat problems of social change primarily in such terms of mobilization or societal guidance, the latter notion entailing the need to "activate" societies deliberately by facilitating the mobilization of weaker collectivities by stronger ones.[44] The isolated individual with his purely personal intellectual dissent has little meaning or interest except in some notional form of universal and all-embracing history (or indeed in the now happily disappearing discipline of so-called intellectual or literary history in universities). The extent to which dissenters require a suitable social structure to fulfill the role of a social stratum of intellectuals, let alone become effective for purposes of self-identification and action, cannot be overemphasized. Whether it be the Reformation, the French Revolution, the Marxist phenomenon, or even the first institutionalized stratum—partly academic, partly political—actually to call itself "intellectuals" in *fin-de-siècle* France, in each case the intellectuals concerned have created or joined onto a dissenting social structure and themselves crystallized as a self-conscious group through such attachment.[45]

The archetypal case of intellectual dissent in search of suitable socio-political reinforcement in the last hundred years is no doubt that of Russia. The word "intelligentsia" comes from the Russian

[44] See J. P. Nettl, *Political Mobilization* (London/New York, 1967); Amitai Etzioni, *The Active Society: A Theory of Societal and Political Processes* (New York, 1968).

[45] The term "intellectual" appears to originate from the pen of Clemenceau in an article in *L'Aurore* of January 23, 1898, as a collective description of the most prominent *Dreyfusards*. The new term was promptly taken up in a pejorative sense of unscrupulousness and irresponsible disloyalty to the nation by Maurice Barrès in *Scènes et doctrines du nationalisme* (Paris, 1902), p. 46 (where incidentally even the un-French quality of the word itself becomes part of the accusation). Cf. also Barrès, *Les Déracinés* (Paris, E. Fasquelle, 1897), where the stratum of disloyal (because deliberately unattached) intellectuals is analyzed and attached at greater length.

and captures the subtle increase in exacerbation over the word "intellectual": while the latter may develop from a social stratum into a collectivity under certain favorable circumstances, an intelligentsia is more of a self-conscious collectivity *ab ovo*. In other words, in the Russian context the relationship between dissent in ideas and a socio-political role is historically much more strongly marked. In Yevtushenko's words:

> in Russia the poet is more than a poet.
> There only those are born poets
> in whom a proud civic spirit dwells
> For whom there is no comfort, no peace.
> The poet is the image of his own age
> and the phantom herald of the future.

Alexander Blok made the same point more than fifty years earlier: "Nowhere is literature so intimately bound up with life as in Russia, and nowhere does the writer give away his individual vision so completely to the crowd." The last hundred and fifty years in Russia were a period of brilliant effusion and collision of dissenting ideas with a plethora of structural dissent; like an atom-bombarding machine, a stream of ideas was injected under pressure into a society receptive to their explosive impact. As we shall see, this phenomenon was so strongly marked as to underpin and partially justify the later Communist claim that the history of intellectuals must necessarily and always be one of *revolutionary* dissent. In any case the Russian example provides the clearest ideal-typical evidence for the positive relationship between dissenting intellectuals and a corresponding social structure of dissent.

The case of Third Republic France is in many ways a turning point in the arrival of what I shall here call modernity with regard to the situation of the intellectuals. It represents the beginning of the reintegration of qualitative or intellectual dissent into the universities as institutions of higher learning, which threatened the structural separation of the "optimal" or ideal-typical settings for the production and diffusion of the two types of ideas that formed the base line of the present discussion. The *république des professeurs* was a mandarinate of scribblers—victorious dissenters become comfortably institutionalized—and represented the political triumph of the *parti intellectuel,* a combination of political collectivity and institutionalized intellectual stratum hitherto unique.[46]

If it is true that France often antedates not only the political *problems* but also the political *forms* of the modern world, then we may see in the Third and Fourth Republics an embryonic version of some of the fundamental problems posed for intellectuals in the United States and the Soviet Union today. The combination in one and the same stratum of an institutionally powerful mandarinate and an intellectual *fronde* seems to require a constant assertion of insecurity, a self-conscious refusal to accept the fact that the political kingdom of the intellectuals is safely established, and above all an incessant appeal to arms against an exaggeratedly menacing right whose aim continues to be the destruction of enlightenment. And there have always been enough "know-nothing" thrusts—anti-Dreyfusards, McCarthyites, Zhdanovites—to justify the vigilance, the *appel aux armes.* The established intellectuals of Third Republic France in particular, the purest version of politically established intellectuals, came to represent a counter-clergy possessing the culturally validated profession of *enseignement,* a socio-political role, and a pronounced appeal to universal values. The old cry of "the faith in danger" was now raised against the clergy by a counter-clergy equally ready to cry wolf with its tocsin of "the Republic in danger." Like the clergy that opposed and at the same time mirrored, these intellectuals appealed constantly to the danger of total perdition represented by the ever present forces of darkness.

But such a combination of academic institutionalization and intellectual leadership of a socio-political movement was likely, according to the canon of this analysis, to prove unstable. Mandarins and intellectuals live uneasily together and dislike each other intensely. Already in the nineteenth century there had been occasional outbursts of feeling among intellectuals against what were regarded as traitors, men claiming the culturally validated profession of intellectuals who had turned into a self-satisfied mandarinate in universities. We need only recall the onslaughts on the contemporary (and contemptible) "professor" of their

[46] Cf. Albert Thibaudet, "Pour l'histoire du parti intellectuel," *Nouvelle Revue française,* Vol. XXV (1932), pp. 265–72.

time by such writers as Schopenhauer, Kierkegaard, and Nietzsche. In the later nineteenth century dissenting intellectuals were especially strongly represented by non-institutionalized philosophers; the professorial formulations of a Hegel with their latent capacity for institutionalized dissent by others had given way to unattached dissenting intellectuals formulating ideas that subordinated innovation in scope to the deliberate aim of, and above all the *form* of, qualitative dissent.

Whether the ideas of Kierkegaard and Nietzsche belong more properly on one dimension or another is arguable, but their very lack of institutional attachment certainly facilitated the pull toward the dimension of qualitative dissent. There is nothing like lack of recognition, debt, and a seedy boardinghouse to stimulate this emphasis. And though it took many years for Nietzsche's ideas to be taken up and reflected by any social structure of dissent, this, too, came about in the late nineteenth and triumphantly in the early twentieth century in Italy, Germany, and France. In any case the evidence suggests that those who claim membership in intellectual professions, who combine a cultural orientation with an appeal to universality, and who have become academically institutionalized, are subject to attacks from new "outside" groups of intellectuals, often aided by breakaway "professional" allies from within. This is especially likely to be the case where such a mandarinate successfully exercises political influence. This inherent intellectual instability in the *république des professeurs* may explain the savagery and irony of anti-establishment attitudes on the part of intellectuals in France, often themselves institutionalized, far better than all the popular emphasis on the bloody-mindedness of the French character.

In France the break between the professional mandarinate of ex-intellectuals, which made up the *république des professeurs,* and the new group of dissenting intellectuals began to take place openly after the Second World War.[47] A powerful group among the established intellectuals moved sharply against the *république*

[47] For the final break in the arts, and the new tone of this anti-establishment orientation after 1946, see the ex-surrealist magazine *Arts,* which flourished from 1948–49 for a few years. A very skillful satire on the comforts of established and institutionalized dissent in all directions is Marcel Aymé, *Le Confort intellectuel* (Paris, 1949).

des professeurs and into, or close to, the increasingly bolshevized embrace of the Communist party in spite of its solid ouvrierist tradition.[48] This leap to a new and further left, however, proved only a brief and possibly final flowering of socio-political dissent, lasting from the 1920s to the mid-1950s—and over all declining in numbers and intensity the while. As Lichtheim has shown, the intellectual integration of even this last large-scale movement of dissent into "modern" French society had at this time of writing been more or less accomplished.[49] Until 1968, all that remained of fundamentalist dissent were a number of intellectually as well as demographically youthful splinter groups, whose main institutional *attachment* appeared to be a group of Left Bank bookshops and a few small journals—and, of course, the universities themselves, since most of them were students.[50]

More and more frustrated by the growing tentacles of integration of French society, the remaining intellectuals focused on what might be called extra-societal structures of dissent; in one case abroad, in the other "below" society. I shall later discuss briefly the search for an ideologically sympathetic environment in transitional, preferably revolutionary societies (like Latin America with its guerrilla movements), rather than in those

[48] See David Caute, *Communism and the French Intellectuals 1914–1960* (London, 1964).

[49] See George Lichtheim, *Marxism in Modern France* (London/New York, 1966). Cf. Michelle Perrot and Annie Kriegel, *Le Socialisme français et le pouvoir* (Paris, EDI, 1966).

[50] It is difficult to summarize accurately the intellectual or ideological orientation of these groups. Among them were hard-core activists professing attachment variously to Trotskyism, to Maoism, and to a distillation of the revolutionary ideology of Castro. These groups often engaged in strongly sectarian polemics of differentiation between each other. However there was also a much larger body of democratic anarchists, in some cases with revolutionary commitment, who approximated much more closely to similar student groups in the United States and Germany, and whose intellectual legitimation was much more eclectic. Their main focus was on *praxis*. This important feature of recent student activism will be discussed at greater length below. Of particular *intellectual* interest is the group of students and friends of Louis Althusser (among them Régis Debray), *normalien* and rigorous structuralist Marxist philosopher, which again demonstrates the typical French combination of impeccable intellectual qualifications and extreme socio-political dissent. In the words of Henry Miller, "the insane have a terrific obsession for logic and order, as have the French."

reluctantly accepted as modern—the escape abroad.[51] The other, even more remarkable case of French intellectual extremism in dissent is that of escape downward—into the region of crime. This obviously involves the *bouleversement* or reversal *par excellence* of the accepted, conventional hierarchy of social priorities. The writings of Jean Genet and Georges Bataille represent the clearest effort to justify, indeed sanctify, crime and criminals as a structure of social dissent with which intellectuals can identify and for which they can speak. Crime becomes the epitome of deed without benefit of words; a *sacred* world of disorder, violence, and above all excess—of criminality—contrasted with the *profane* world of order, reason, and abstinence. "Born as we are out of chaos, why can we never establish contact with it? No sooner do we look at it than order, pattern, shape is born under our eyes," as a Polish novelist of the absurd has recently put it.[52] Sartre has given this identification of profanity with order and reason the official stamp of his philosophical approval.[53] A similar reversal is apparent in the work of existential psychiatrists like Laing and Cooper in England, who regard schizophrenics as "normal" victims of a corrupt family or hospital environment, a taken role of madness imposed from the outside.[54] To resist integration, French intellectuals have thus tended toward physical or intellectual escapism—perhaps the ex-

[51] This is not of course a new or even recent phenomenon among intellectuals. Coser, op. cit., pp. 227–46, devotes a chapter entitled "Salvation Abroad" to two instances, the eighteenth-century *philosophes'* love affair with China and Russia as "orderly" and intelligently ruled societies, and the preoccupation of intellectuals in the 1930s with the revolutionary society of the future, the USSR.

[52] Witold Gombrowicz, *Kosmos* (Warsaw, 1965), p. 189.

[53] Much of Genet's writing is concerned with this problem, but nowhere more clearly than in the early and little-known play *Haute Surveillance* (*Death Watch*). See also Georges Bataille, *La Littérature et le mal* (Paris, 1957); *Histoire de l'oeil* (Paris, 1928, under the name of Lord Auch); *Le Mort*, new edition (Paris, 1967). On Genet, see Jean Paul Sartre, *Saint Genet, comédien et martyr* (Paris, 1952). The tradition of course goes back two hundred years to Sade, who, according to Bataille, "linked violence to consciousness."

[54] See, for instance, R. D. Laing, *The Divided Self: A Study of Sanity and Madness* (London, 1959); *The Self and Others: Further Studies in Sanity and Madness* (London, 1961); Laing and D. E. Cooper, eds., *Reason and Violence: A Decade of Sartre's Philosophy* (London, 1964).

treme form of rejection of modern society. When, quite suddenly and unexpectedly, the system came to be challenged by student activists in May 1968, the intellectuals were left mutely on the sidelines.

From the Soviet Union in the 1930s came an alternative challenge of integration to the dissenting role of the intellectual. Though it chose to regard itself as the clarion call for a new and revolutionary version of modernity the Soviet attitude to intellectuals in practice and in theory provided, as we shall see, merely a link between the *république des professeurs* and the industrial-technological modernity that the United States and the Soviet Union today share somewhat indifferently. There was no room here for qualitative dissent. Indeed the very concept of qualitative dissent—and with it the *raison d'être* of intellectuals —had disappeared into the graded limbos of madness, reaction, and treachery. This claim for political-revolutionary achievement leading directly and necessarily to ultimate social achievability, in which dissent and therefore intellectuals had become historically unnecessary, was, of course, based retrospectively on the Bolshevik definition of intellectuals as not merely dissenters but of necessity revolutionaries. From Marx himself came the notion of *praxis,* which supcrimposed the mandate of social action on the formulation of social dissent.[55] But once the Revolution had been attained this role naturally collapsed, at least within the new society; one could still be revolutionary at a distance by attacking reaction abroad and denouncing those whom the regime flushed out as its allies at home. This, however, was not enough by itself; a search for a post-Revolutionary definition of intellectuals or intelligentsia began forthwith. And it is here that the convergence with the other great center of modernity, the United States, becomes important.

But if the end result appeared to be the same, the Soviet point of departure in the search for such a definition of the intellectual's role differed radically from the bourgeois conception of their place in a modern society. Instead of differentiation and

[55] *"Ainsi se précise la conception marxiste de l'intellectuel: alliance naturelle de l'idéologie révolutionnaire et de la classe révolutionnaire, renversement du logos pur en praxis."* Michel Mazzola, "Marx, le marxism, et les intellectuals", *Arguments,* Vol. V, No. 20 (October 1960), p. 24.

institutionalization in the optimal location of universities, the
Soviet emphasis was on dispersion of intellect throughout society,
every man his own intellectual—diffuseness instead of specificity.[56] Soviet society denied (at least analytically, if not in practice) any version of differentiated modernity and asserted a projection of liberated and all-capable man for its vanguard or
elite—at least during the process of transit to full Communism.
Accordingly the successfully modernizing Soviet Union of the
Five-Year Plans now evolved a definition of intellectuals or intelligentsia that refused to distinguish qualitatively between science and culture, to accept any difference between the dimensions of scope and quality. The notion of an intelligentsia came
to be identified with a stratum that possessed a given level of
cerebral skill of almost any literate or numerate kind and nothing
more. The Moscow Dictionary of Philosophy of the early 1950s
states that "the intellectuals constitute an intermediary social
stratum made up of men who devote themselves to work with
their minds. It includes engineers, technicians, lawyers, artists,
teachers, scientific workers. . . . Intellectuals have never been,
nor can ever be, a separate class, for they do not have an independent position in the system of social production."[57] With
the problem of dissent no longer relevant, only the search for
scope was left. Hence it was logical and inevitable that scientists
should have priority, while writers should make the applied scientific product culturally available. Their task was to share in the
application of scientific discovery by filling it out with the tools
of their own cultural dimension, rather than attempt themselves
to cleave new tasks of discovery outside of the areas already
staked out by social science in practice—this last being after
all no more than the essential self-definition of revolutionary
Marxism. It was the party that now combined social *logos* and
social *praxis*.

The history of the Soviet Union is in one sense no more

[56] For a discussion of the original Soviet, and especially the more recent
and intense Chinese, version of a deliberately diffuse or dedifferentiated
modernity see J. P. Nettl and Roland Robertson, *International Systems and
the Modernization of Societies: The Formation of National Goals and
Attitudes* (London/New York, 1968), Part I.
[57] See also in general Richard Pipes, ed., *The Russian Intelligentsia* (New
York, 1961).

than the history of the attempt to teach the intellectuals their new place in a cosmos of socialist modernity. Some of the strongest words on this subject were spoken by "party-oriented" intellectuals themselves. Here is Maxim Gorky:

"Real life is splendid and magnificent. Literature must attain to the level of real life. That is the point. The ability with which the offending writers pronounced lengthy and vague speeches revealed the anaemia of their minds. Some of them demonstratively strolled past the groups engaged in conversation, seemingly admiring the wretched weather, and apparently convinced that geniuses they were and geniuses they would remain under all conditions. Not one of them regretted that he had not found time to visit the work on the White Sea and Baltic Canal—not one of them was acquainted with the results of the two years' work done by Angelo Omedo, one of the greatest hydrographers and hydro-electric engineers living, in Transcaucasia, the Caucasus, Central Asia, and Siberia: not one of them was interested in the state of the huge project for an Institute of Experimental Medicine; and, in general, the progress of the new culture is something that apparently lies beyond their field of vision, and that whatever knowledge they may have of it is derived solely from newspapers—not very wholesome fare for literary artists. For example, just now huts are being built outside Moscow for thousands of workers engaged in the construction of the Volga–Moscow canal. These thousands of people of various types constitute splendid study material. I am not certain that any of my 'colleagues of the pen' will devote the slightest attention to this rich material.

"I have not forgotten that during these fifteen years our young literature has produced scores of very valuable books. But I have also not forgotten that the number of themes dealt with in these books is by no means very large, and that many of the themes, treated hastily and superficially, have been compromised or to be more direct, spoilt.

"One cannot help noting the fact that, with the exception of . . . a very few, our writers have not produced a single valuable book on children—for fathers and mothers—not to speak of books *for* children, which are evidently considered to be unworthy of 'high art.' Nobody has dealt with the theme of the regeneration of the peasant in the factory, or of the intellectual and emotional transformation of members of the national minorities into Communist internationalists. We have not had a clear portrait of the woman-administrator, nobody has given us portraits of the scientific worker, the inventor, the artist—portraits of people many of whom were born in remote villages or in the filthy back streets of the cities, or brought up in chimneyless huts together with the calves, or on city outskirts together with beggars and thieves. Yet many of them are already known to Europe as people of the highest talent. But in our country they are unknown—or else have been forgotten."[58]

It will be apparent that the Soviet view of intellectuals in a socialist society on the one hand, and the priority given to the scope dimension of ideas in the context of scientific discovery and application on the other, also contains an implicit conflict. The definition of an intelligentsia as merely a stratum in society, having no sociological meaning in terms of self-consciousness or action but merely possessing certain skills treated as neutral indices like red hair or size, cannot account for the effective preference accorded from the period of forced industrialization onward to those with ideas of scope—the scientific innovators. The diffuseness postulated by the ideology was in fact undermined by a new form of differentiation that effectively institutionalized this preference with according it any overt recognition. Many studies of scientific organization in the Soviet Union clearly point to the greater access to *power* (as opposed to income and status) that scientists have compared to writers or artists. Even during the height of Stalinist control, research institutes in practice retained a great deal of initiative and autonomy.[59] Informal attacks on the status of those not producing original work within the scientific community certainly exist as well. "The overwhelm-

[58] Maxim Gorky, Speech to Writers Congress, Moscow, 1932, reprinted in *Culture and the People* (New York, 1939), pp. 196–98.
[59] R. W. Davies, "Science and the Soviet Economy," *Inaugural Lecture in the University of Birmingham,* delivered January 18, 1967, p. 9. See also Norman Kaplan's findings on the comparative autonomy of Soviet, as compared to American, medical research from bureaucratic control, in B. Barker and W. Hirsch, eds., *The Sociology of Science* (New York, 1962), pp. 370–87. Cf. Professor P. L. Kapitsa's statement on this point in *Teoriya, Eksperiment, Praktika* (Moscow, 1966), pp. 31–32.

ing majority of our professors cannot be counted among the leading scientists of our country; one cannot rely on them to pick out creative talent from among their students because they prefer the man who knows the most to the man who understands the most."[60] Clearly the stratum of the intelligentsia is by no means amorphous and undifferentiated but bubbles with internal conflict and stress between and within the "professions" of scientists and the literati. We shall see later that on the other, apparently more lowly, dimension of culture, which Stalin and Zhdanov worked so hard to integrate by force, there is today renewed evidence of qualitative dissent. As yet, however, the socio-political means of structuring such dissent are no greater than those achieved by corresponding groups in France—journals like *Novy Mir* and a few others.

It would be quite wrong to regard these determined attempts to integrate the intellectuals and shut them off from potentially deviant social collectivities as peculiar to the Soviet version of modernity or even to just one depressing period of Soviet history. It is merely that the Soviet formulation was particularly crass. Though the tone is utterly different and the social self-image no doubt a polar opposite, the substance of what Gorky and Zhdanov were telling the Soviet intelligentsia curiously resembles the analysis by, for instance, Talcott Parsons in this volume and Lipset elsewhere of what constitutes the role and function of intellectuals in a modern society. (In modern sociology, group or even quasi-group *depiction* almost invariably involves role assignment and/or functional specification.)[61] Even the internal differentiation between "hack" members of the academic profession and genuine "scholars" (or original scientific researchers) adumbrated by Kapitsa finds its reflection in the United States, especi-

---

[60] Kapitsa, op. cit., p. 35. The statement was made in 1943 (!) with reference to the Physics Faculty of Moscow University.

[61] Lipset's analysis is in "American Intellectuals, Their Politics and Status," op. cit. On p. 311 he defines intellectuals as "all those who create, distribute and apply culture, that is the symbolic world of man, including art, science and religion. Within this group there are two main levels: the hard core of creators of culture—scholars, artists, philosophers, authors, some editors of newspapers and some journalists; and the distributors—performers in the various arts, most teachers, most reporters. A peripheral group is composed of those who apply culture as part of their jobs— professionals like physicians and lawyers."

ally in the forlorn attempt to define intellectuals as disinterested, austere, and somewhat withdrawn scholars—who are then contrasted with academic bureaucrats and wheeler-dealers generally.[62] In both definitions the self-conscious cohesiveness of a collectivity is noticeably missing—let alone any inherent identification with socio-structural dissent (in the Soviet version the latter has, of course, itself been obliterated out of existence). There is no relationship between intellectuals or intelligentsia and the formulation of ideas, or any attempt to classify ideas. Instead we have a neutral stratum (not even a quasi-group) consisting of certain professions and possessing certain skills. In both cases the significant functional location and specification are no longer ideas at all but culture, in its broadest social science sense. Though there is no American tradition of intelligentsia in the Russian (or any other) sense, and it may epigrammatically but not inaccurately be asserted that the rise and sociological history of the American intellectual is in large part that of a butt and target of prevalent anti-intellectualism, yet the modern social situation of intellectuals is, and is depicted as, very similar to that in the Soviet Union. How has this strange convergence come about?

The intellectual and historical origin of assigning to science and scientists a distinct place in the intellectual stratum, from which the indiscriminate amalgamation of intellectuals with scientists into a cultural stratum of the learned and skilled is but a mere step, dates back fairly and squarely to the development of social science in the early nineteenth century. If Montesquieu was aware of the social underpinnings of constitutional politics, Saint-Simon was the first to draw an analogy between the scientific solution of physical and social problems. The concept of social science itself suggests an amalgam of society and science. According to the way the terms have been employed here, social science suggests a fusion between scope and quality; it collapses (at least intellectually) the two dimensions into one. Social life too can be understood as well as engineered, it is suggested, by incorporating and applying new areas of scientific knowledge.

[62] See most recently Robert A. Nisbet, "What Is an Intellectual?" *Commentary*, December 1965.

Social change accordingly need no longer be the result of a socio-political power struggle based on conflict over the arrangement about known components and priorities. Only ignorance may require a socio-political fillip to be administered to the diffusion of truth by eliminating obscurantist obstacles. But this is a concession to human weakness, no longer a *conditia sine qua non*. Bentham, for instance, reluctantly turned to intellectual dissent and political radicalism only because his lengthy and voluminous (and how lengthy and voluminous) articulation of truth with its new areas of scope and relevance failed to convince or find application.

Evolution or revolution, the acceptance that man is by nature destined to improve or that there will always be vested interests opposed to the new truth, these become different approaches to the same end based on psychological make-up, temperament, and idiosyncratic preferences; they do not in themselves affect the new linkage between science and society. The left-right dichotomy accordingly disappears; we are left with the revolutionary millennium or with Comte's "revolutionary" social engineering in a distinctly conservative cast, as alternative means. This is surely the clue for the ultimately trite discovery of a bigamous marriage between Comtean positivism and Marxist revolution that a few "pure" Marxists like Lichtheim have so long and so strenuously pointed up.[63] For this marriage is no more than the fusion of scope-directed science with component-reversing, qualitative intellectualism which, to the guardians of good order in the history of ideas, instinctively becomes a notorious miscegenation and a scandal (even though they are not always able to see precisely why).

The consequences of this bigamous marriage and its implications for the modern world are rather important. The claim for scientific justification in social matters, the even more dominating replacement of social logic for purposes of action by the logic of machinery and the acceptance of the concomitant priorities of technological needs over social action, finally the replacement of the classical intellectual by the scientist on the intellectual's own particular ground, all these abort the very social basis and

[63] See George Lichtheim, *Marxism: An Historical and Critical Study* (London, 1961).

raison d'être of the intellectual. Accordingly he shouts "cultural crisis" and calls for a restoration of the previous position, an alliance between subordinate technology and dominant intellectual creativity. "Only such an alliance between creative imagination and scientific vigor can help us get through the present crisis of cultural democracy. The most miraculous progress in the social sciences will never replace the need for a choice among values."[64] We have here three distinct but interconnected processes linking up to erode the structurally latent but sometimes highly salient phenomenon of intellectual impact on three hundred years of Western socio-political history.

Often this process of erosion is identified, if at all, as part of the much more general societal phenomenon of totalitarianism. Leaving aside any one-sided emphasis on its extreme forms that, according to popular though culture-bound analysis, "could not happen here" (in "democratic" societies), it has been fashionable to point up the process by which democracy and totalitarianism have, as it were, joined furtive hands behind the original sibling of the former, liberalism; an often unconscious betrayal, which took place to a greater or lesser extent in *all* Western countries.[65] The *Gesamtverapperatisierung* of life, which Adolf Weber already lamented in the First World War—that lurid first genuinely totalitarian event of modern history—is ironically related to the attempt by Max Weber to create a value-free social science to go with it, in which a strict distinction between social analysis and political preferences is made mandatory. If this *Verapperatisierung* is combined with "irrational" appeals to national aggrandizement, racial prejudice, or arbitrary acts of willful tyranny, if the political decision-making process is left to the free-for-all of an institutional Darwinism under the aegis of unrestrained *personalismo,* then we speak, in the words of Lukacs, of the

---

[64] Joffre Dumazedier, *Vers une civilisation du loisir?* (Paris, Seuil, 1967), p. 294.

[65] This is what I have elsewhere (*Political Mobilization,* pp. 164ff.) called the pessimistic Tocqueville tradition, exemplified by Hannah Arendt, *The Origins of Totalitarianism* (2nd ed., Cleveland/New York, 1962), and J. L. Talmon, *The Origins of Democratic Totalitarianism* (Vol. I: London, 1952; Vol. II: London, 1960). Marxist analysis ascribes the decline of liberalism to the replacement of *haut bourgeois* control by the emergent *petit bourgeoisie.*

Zerstörung der Vernunft, the destruction of reason, or *anglice* of all good sense.

But, as Wolfgang Rothe has shown in a recent book, this increasingly irrational aspect is at most an addition, a matter of degree; from the point of view of the intellectual *Verapperatisierung* itself, the growing bureaucratization of life and even nature was the real totalitarian factor that swept him to the very margin of validity and survival. "The spirit stands on the left, nature on the right."[66] But social science at the same time failed to connect the two. For this often subcutaneous but irresistible bureaucratizing and technological influence has all the sheen and gleam of scientific rationality to accompany it. And the task of social science (in its carefully differentiated and enthusiastically ascribed role) became that of translating the new rationality into human and social terms, of ensuring that the gap between technology and society appeared small and painless—and above all temporary.[67]

[66] Wolfgang Rothe, *Schriftsteller und totalitäre Welt* (Zurich, 1966), pp. 242–43. The point he makes is that writers like Kafka, Broch, and Musil already saw during and after the First World War not only the violence but the creaseless surface of totalitarianism, which left no structural or intellectual niches to hide in or exploit. Nineteen thirty-three was thus not something new but a *terminus ad quem.* Karl Kraus, the most prolific prophet of doom, had by this time run out of things to say; the first sentence of *Die Dritte Walpurgisnacht,* his last major work two years before his death, opens with the astonishing sentence: *"Zu Hitler fällt mir nichts ein."* Quite a lot did occur to him in the book itself, but the remark conveys something of the exhaustion of the European intellectual after twenty *mouvementés* years even when faced by so horrendous a phenomenon as Adolf Hitler.

[67] The interesting thing about the origins and early demise of Project Camelot (the Pentagon's 1964–65 multimillion-dollar project to find the cause and possible cure for social revolution with Chile as guinea pig) was not so much its failure even to get started, but the fact that its sponsors and most of the invited social science participants thought it an entirely reasonable undertaking, given the situation or role of sociology and political science as "policy sciences." Reaction against it came initially from a Norwegian sociologist and the collapse of the project was finally due to outraged Chilean reactions and subsequent State Department protests to the President. Many people thought the project had been mishandled rather than that it was wrong or illegitimate. One of the causes of its initial acceptability to social scientists (apart from the chance to undertake well-financed fundamental research in depth) was the "value-free," pseudo-scientific language in which the original invitation was couched—"a study whose objective is to determine the feasibility of developing a general

In value-free analysis the manipulation of the components of a logically ordered and in any case science-dominated society makes dissent into something obscurantist and irrational. What should it focus on? The interrelationship of modern society is total, everything hinges on everything else, and dissent over any one or number of components automatically questions society as a whole, if not indeed rational modernity itself.[68] All this gives the intellectual seeking to structure himself in a crevice of disagreement the appearance of a man sliding helplessly down a glass-smooth surface, crying but not gripping. The three tools of his existence—cultural validation, socio-political role, universal reference—become brittle and break in his hand. With culture linked functionally to the social system, his profession ceases to be culturally validated as soon as he "unscientifically" reflects or articulates inner-directed and dissenting values; he no longer contributes to "culture." His socio-political role has disappeared, for as a social scientist he is almost invariably back in a science-dominated university, from which the leap into socio-structural dissent is barred by an almost completely unbridgeable institutional chasm. And if he is not an academic and not institutionalized at all, he has even less chance of making an impact. Pragmatic politics assign him little or no role in the political

social systems model which would make it possible to predict and influence politically significant aspects of social change in the developing countries of the world . . . to analyse the predisposing conditions and precipitants of the potential for internal war." The scientistic language blots out the value-laden aims and creates an instant community of research for research's sake between sponsors and executants. This aspect largely escaped notice in the subsequent post-mortem. But the affair did raise an extensive and highly individual discussion of the role and ethics of sociology.

For a collection of participant and professional opinions, see I. L. Horowitz, "The Life and Death of Project Camelot," *Trans-Action*, 3–4 (November–December 1965); *The American Sociologist* (issues from Vol. I, No. 1, November 1965, to Vol. I, No. 5, November 1966); A. de Grazia, "Project Camelot," *Behavioral Scientist*, September 1965; *Science Magazine*, September 10, 1965; *American Psychologist*, May 1966. The most recent overview is Irving Louis Horowitz, *The Rise and Fall of Project Camelot* (Cambridge, Mass., 1967), and cf. "Project Camelot: An Autopsy" by Robert A. Nisbet, pp. 283–313 in this volume.

[68] For this argument, see above all R. K. Merton, op. cit.

process. At most, as we have seen, he may expect to hook onto a journal, a film company, or even an art gallery. Only his conscience can continue to commune with the universal; he is left to bay at the moon in total rejection of everything or at least in lament for the destruction of an *acceptable* totality. "Radical criticism has abandoned the attempt to rethink the world or to change it; it is content to condemn," gloats a recent self-styled pragmatist, who regards modern society as characterized by its scientific nature.[69] Since he is generally middle-aged,

[69] Raymond Aron, *The Industrial Society: Three Essays on Ideology and Development* (New York, 1967), p. 179. A good example of this total, almost valedictory lament is Herbert Marcuse, *One-Dimensional Man: Studies in the Ideology of Advanced Industrial Society* (London, 1964). Much German writing has focused on this problem of the oppressive totality of modern society. See, for instance, Theodor W. Adorno, *Negative Dialektik* (Frankfurt, 1966), which puts a philosophical case (or rather a case based on philosophical categories and traditions) for this position. Cf. also the extremely acute analysis by Jurgen Habermas, *Strukturwandel der Offenlichkeit* (Neuwied, 1962), which contains *inter alia* the following statement: "The whole is now nowhere in the picture, much less in the mind; it has disintegrated into the visibility immediate, into 'facts.' Instead of ideologies we have opinions, which do not commit those who express them" (p. 156). The same diagnosis of modernity, but from a much more welcoming or favorable point of view, may be found in Helmut Schelsky, "Man in a Scientific Civilization," *Auf der Suche nach Wirklichkeit* (Düsseldorf-Cologne, 1965), and the older *Ortsbestimmung der Deutschen Soziologie* (Düsseldorf-Cologne, 1959). Schelsky takes approximately the same line as Aron, but his analysis of "scientific" society is much more explicit. Cf. most recently Ralf Dahrendorf, *Die Soziologie und der Soziologe—Zur Fragen von Theorie und Praxis* (Inaugural lecture at University of Konstanz, Konstanz, 1967).

For the argument that the present universe of modernity has in fact destroyed the old totality in which subject and object were identical, in which man's production kept pace with his moral awareness, see most recently Ernst Fischer, *Kunst und Koexistenz: Beitrag zu einer modernen marxistischen Asthetik* (Hamburg, 1967). Although a Communist today, Ernst Fischer partially duplicates the arguments of the neo-Marxist theorists of mass society in America (see below, pp. 104–5). The problem of modern *universals* as against critical Marxist totality as a form of intellectual liberation in man also arises in the work of many of the French structuralists like Roland Barthes, Lucien Goldman, and Pierre Macherey. (See the latter's recent *Pour une théorie de la production littéraire* [Paris, 1967].

In general the recent upsurge of structuralism in any case poses vital questions in connection with universality and culture. Structuralism necessar-

married, with children and benefits from a not ungenerous academic salary, the intellectual watches enviously the offensive of the only stratum of effective dissent in modern society that threatens to replace him on all the dimensions of cultural profession, social role, and universal reference. This is the generation of kids that, at the end of the 1950s, was to opt out almost entirely, that "dissented" not in wordy laments or even acutely probing analyses but by the action of withdrawal and indifference, and that (with the help of self-interested entrepreneurs) also produced its own culture. And they in turn gave way to a more politically radical form of dissent of an almost revolutionary character, still firmly based on youth but overtaking, isolating, and forcing the "mere" withdrawers into the quaint irrelevance of hippies with their "flower power". They regard the latter as clients of the system, penetrated by the benefits of the subeconomy that has been specially created around them.

This is not the place to evaluate the students' revolution of the last two years, in Europe, America, and Japan, whose end and consequences are not yet in sight. The two relevantly significant points about it are that it is a non-intellectual movement (though not at all anti-intellectual) and that it firmly subordinates *logos* to *praxis*. There is no visible intellectual system of ideas to which

---

ily dissolves man in units of "wholes" whose agent he becomes; as such the totality composed of universal structural relations is both inhuman and ahistorical—anti-intellectual, too, since at the very least man is in no sense the self-conscious agent of change. Predictably therefore Sartre has attacked the structuralists as the last-ditch defenders of a decaying bourgeois ideology. Yet structuralist philosophers like Althusser (*Pour Marx; Lire le Kapital*), and even structuralist psychoanalysts like Jacques Lacan (*Ecrits* [Paris, 1967]) have tried to influence and at the same time adopt Marxism more successfully in many ways than Sartre, at least on the intellectual level if not on that of political action. Most structuralists implicitly reject technological modernity (Aron's scientific society) and its scientism, modern sociology—though for widely differing reasons; Althusser as part of his explicit Marxism, Lévy-Strauss by default inasmuch as his work focuses on so-called primitive and almost extinct societies, Lacan (*L'Agressivité en psychoanalyse*) through the connection between ideology of freedom and the ideology of free enterprise which leads to unrestrained capitalism and colonialism, finally because, as Freud said, psychoanalysis is "the plague" for Americans, and Americans have, according to Lacan, ruined Freud in return.

this dissent structure could attach itself; the facts cited by the students themselves divide into three distinct categories of successful revolutionaries of the past (Lenin, Mao, Castro), intellectual critics of capitalist democracy (Marcuse, Rosa Luxemburg), and the disciplinarians of Marxism turned into a handbook for guerrilla warfare (Debray). The students know what they do not want, but its destruction must by itself provide the positive forms of the future. There is moreover a latent conflict between the impact of institutional power through the "capture" of universities, within which the student movement has proved almost irresistible, and the attempt to carry this victory over into a wider societal context by linking up with the workers, whose attitude has been ambivalent (and as far as organized labor is concerned directly hostile). The European students were thus enmeshed in the trappings of a traditional Marxism that still identified the industrial working class with the "proletarian" or "universal" class who were the agents of Marx's philosophy of social regeneration. The student spokesmen have all refused to envisage students as a class or even anything more than an occupational or institutional group. For a potentially effective structure of dissent, this is a self-denying ordinance. Moreover the reliance on the working class as essential ally and revolutionary agent throws the students back into the reluctant arms of a Marxism that is neither able to provide a sufficiently universal form of intellectual system, nor activist enough to merge its structures of sociopolitical dissent with that of the students, based on the institutions of higher education. Hence the attempts by the students themselves to provide their effective *praxis* with a wider societal meaning have not been very successful so far, but nonetheless reinforce the failure of the intellectuals to cope with, much less to "pull" toward themselves, the activist dissent in the universities.

In the United States this entrapment by a Marxist tradition did not exist to anything like the same extent. Hence a more pragmatic search for theory was possible, either from the past or, more important, in conjunction with the evaluation of *praxis*. The students did not feel committed to the workers in either theory or activist *praxis*. The process of intellectualizing student dissent has therefore gone somewhat further. Also they have had some intellectual support. Only in the United States have a few intellectuals openly recognized the echoless chamber of their own isolation in a modern society and searched for means of breaking out. In the absence of any socio-political structures of dissent to marry into, they have instead championed (and inevitably verbalized) the dissent-by-withdrawal of youth, and more recently the student protest in universities. Susan Sontag's defense of Camp and her more recent book of essays against the intellectualization of current modes of dissent are symptomatic. Her rejection of "modernity" is positive and uncompromising rather than sad, apologetic, and valedictory.[70] Something similar if much more cautious is taking place in the Soviet Union. Though youthful deviance cannot receive open intellectual support some writers, especially poets like Yevtushenko, Voznessensky, and Essenin-Volpin, identify with youth openly enough to underline the existence of a self-conscious stratum and even of a severe structural disjunction between them and their ruling elders. In China, of course, the position has been completely and deliberately reversed; the carefully nurtured conflict between youth and adults in the cultural revolution suggests that the former is regarded as the orthodoxy of the future and the latter as the deviance of the past. But then China is self-consciously *not* a "modern" conflictless society.[71]

But these cases are exceptions. In the self-consciously advanced societies of the West such alignments by intellectuals are isolated and are characterized as deviant. Even the few intellectuals who approve of and articulate such protest can nevertheless scarcely ever "move in on it" in the classical Mannheimian sense, but at best only translate its meaning into terms comprehensible to the dominant culture of modernity. The youthful dissenters—both the withdrawers and the radicals—are suspicious of intellectual support and often promptly test it in terms of support for specific action (as did the Berlin students with Marcuse and Habermas during a teach-in in 1967). Except in the form of evaluating an experience that has already taken place, the process of verbalization can itself represent a blunting edge of conformity and a

---

[70] Susan Sontag, *Against Interpretation and Other Essays* (New York, 1966).
[71] See J. P. Nettl, "Permanent Revolution," *New Society*, No. 246 (June 15, 1967), pp. 876–79.

concomitant reduction of action potential. Many of the students are activists in the purist sense, without and against articulate ideological umbrellas; they discuss experience, not results; above all, they do not argue about the future.[72] The way that the liberal intellectual opposition against the "cartelization" of German politics (the socialist betrayal inherent in the Grand Coalition of SPD and CDU, which rescued the latter from bankruptcy and disintegration) has simply been by-passed into irrelevance by the action of the Berlin students is symptomatic. "What we are faced with today [in Germany] is not communism but revolution. . . . It was not the writers who narrowed the alternative down to such an extreme . . . it was not the writers but the students who first faced up to the alternative and who bear its scars. In the Berlin police pogroms in the summer of this year [1967] the first nuclei of a revolutionary-minded opposition were formed, and it is the students who have begun to build up a political underground press. . . . As for the intellectuals, who for the past twenty years have felt themselves to be the exponents of a radical opposition, the majority of them have a long way to go before they realize the extent either of their defeat *or* of the political demands which will be made on them in the years to come."[73] Though American intellectual dissent has been more articulate and certainly more radical than in Germany, these harsh words obviously apply here with equal force; since Berkeley and especially the long hot summers of 1966–67, culminating in the national convention of the new politics in Chicago in the summer of 1968, the Black Power Conference in Newark, and the virtual "liberation" of the Columbia campus in spring 1968, the intellectuals have been left a long way behind. The race problem in particular is simply beyond them. At the time

[72] Even before the student revolt in Paris in May 1968 there was a large and growing literature on student protest in the United States, Germany, and, limpingly, Britain, much of it liberally benevolent in a political sense, but conservatively apprehensive in the academic context. See recently, e.g., Nathan Glazer, "Student Politics in a Democratic Society," *American Scholar,* Spring 1967; Julius Gould, "Politics and the Academy," *Government and Opposition,* Vol. III, No. 1, pp. 23–48; Kurt Sontheimer, "Student Opposition in Western Germany," ibid., pp. 49–68.

[73] Hans Magnus Enzensberger, "The Writer and Politics," *Times Literary Supplement,* September 28, 1967 (special Frankfurt issue), p. 858.

these words are being written, the typical document of the movement is Régis Debray's *Revolution in the Revolution,* whose significant aspect is its hardheaded practicality, its refusal to justify or even attempt the typical or traditional intellectual task of providing a theoretical link between the old doctrines of revolution and the new. As one of the very few persuasive statements of the rationality of this "total" position has pointed out, revolutionaries in the past had alternatives; "today there is no alternative. The world is a single unit, and it has become intolerable . . . because the possibility of transforming may exist but is denied." Death is the only possible act of individual dissociation. "Provided that the revolutionary makes no transcendental appeal and provided that he acts out of the maximum possible consciousness of what is knowable to him, his envisaged death has become the measure of the parity which can now exist between the self and the world: it is the measure of his total independence."[74]

It is in the nature of protest-by-withdrawal and of the new radicalism that, like quarter, no explanation be asked or given. One ironic result is that in some ways social scientists accordingly do better "explanation-wise" than intellectuals. As Lasswell has shown, sociology has no difficulty in enmeshing the withdrawal type of deviance in the flails of its analysis, even though the new radicalism has so far escaped sociological explanation as well.[75]

It should already be clear that if modern industrial society and the type of student activism that arises to protest against it in its entirety create special problems for intellectuals, social science is the pin that has pried them out of position after position in their "natural" field of activity. We have seen how their socio-political role has collapsed, or rather disintegrated—on the one hand into socio-political withdrawal centered around a youth subculture that is developing specific institutions of its own, and on the other hand into a mandarinate of social scientists

---

[74] John Berger, "The Death of Heroes," *New Society,* No. 277 (January 18, 1968), p. 94.

[75] See, for instance, Harold D. Lasswell, *Psychology and Politics* (New York, 1930), and the recent retrospect in "Political Constitution and Character," *Psychoanalysis and Psychoanalytical Review,* Vol. XLVI (1959), pp. 3–18; "The Garrison-State Hypothesis Today" in S. P. Huntington, ed., *Changing Patterns of Military Politics* (Glencoe, Illinois, 1962).

who self-consciously confine themselves to, and service, the means pole of the means-ends axis. This self-limitation to means would leave, it might be thought, at least the articulation of values—centrally integrated or otherwise—to intellectuals; much has been made of the basic difference between fact and value. But no: "the systematic explication and analysis of values as causes and consequences of social action is an essential part of the *urgent task* of *purposive, objective diagnosis of societal functioning . . .* in order to bring systematic knowledge of operative value standards *directly into major societal diagnosis and planning . . .* as part of systematic self appraisal." The self-limitations to means turns out to be a mask hiding a determination to influence ends.[76] European continental sociologists are acutely aware of this problem and are determined to distinguish between American sociology (with its "conformity," its depiction of a "purely functional man in a social sense," its "social reformation which makes society into a purposive self-sufficiency and man into a mere social beast of burden") and their own more critical profession.[77] With ultimate irony, European sociology regards itself in this context as decidedly *more* empirical than American, and lampoons the latter's growing admission of social planning purpose and its determination to diffuse truth and facts about values *as* values. The European stance (together with that of American-European critics of sociology like Marcuse and Fromm) thus distinguishes between articulation and value analysis while Amer-

[76] Robin M. Williams, Jr., "Individual and Group Values," *Annals of the American Academy of Political and Social Science,* Vol. CCCLXXI (May 1967), p. 37. (My italics.)

This is a random choice from among recent literature; similar statements can be gouged out of much modern social science. In my (as yet tentative) view, this follows from the very notion of separating facts and values as antipodes which has been one of sociological structure-functionalism's most widespread and influential aspects. Can one really say, in a century of almost magical technological and scientific advance, that values have *nothing* to do with cognition? Note also the ideologically simplistic and empirically false implication that, if means are found for discovering and summating shared values and aggregating marginally competitive ones, leadership will simply plan and act to secure such values. This is where social science finally invades the field of value speculation, with Iago-modest pretense of concern with means while secretly pursuing ends.

[77] Kurt Sontheimer, "Sociology as Instrument of Conformism," *Frankfurter Hefte* (1956), pp. 538, 540. (My translation.)

ican social science integrates them (or differentiates them according to taste) into the institutional concern of social scientists.[78]

The intellectual cultural grounding has also been eroded by popular demand for and supply of an "appropriate" industrial culture on tap. Social science has lopped off great chunks from the cultural preserve of the intellectuals and has broken up the intellectuals' concept of cultural unity and totality into suitably scientific particular and relativistic surrounds for problems of social action and process.[79] In short, as culture has increasingly become capable of both technological supply and sociological analysis, the intellectuals have had to cede ground on both fronts. Not, of course, without a struggle. The onslaught of mass culture on its intellectual parent has been a primary topic of intellectual concern in recent years. It is significant, however, that the very form of the discussion has itself tended to take place more and more within the context and according to the concepts of sociology, so that the intellectuals fought under the, for them, false colors of social science. Their battle was thus half lost from the start. Nothing shows more clearly the inherent contradiction in the position of the left-wing intellectuals fighting a losing battle within the confines of an ideologically hostile sociology than the way in which the proponents of left-wing democracy and humanism have dug themselves in along the last ditch of an elitist defense of high culture.[80]

[78] Cf. Isaiah Berlin's statement that "our time" has substituted "a mounting wave of hostility to all ideas as such" for a previous conflict of ideas. ("Political Ideas in the Twentieth Century," *Foreign Affairs*, Vol. XXVIII, No. 3 [1950], p. 379.)

[79] For the industrialization of popular culture see Eric Hobshawm, "Pop Goes the Artist," *Times Literary Supplement*, December 17, 1964, and of course the technological exegesis of culture that spills out from the increasingly rebarbative writings of Marshall McLuhan. For culture as a surround, see J. P. Nettl, "Center and Periphery in Social Science," *American Behavioral Scientist*, Vol. IX, No. 10 (1966), pp. 39–46, and works cited there. I emphasize that I am not here concerned with the problem of *quality* as between high and mass industrialized culture. The issue is the economics of provision and method of diffusion rather than the quality itself.

[80] As Leon Bramson in *The Political Context of Sociology* (Princeton, 1961) has shown, this paradox illuminates (or rather obscures) the works of Marcuse, Erich Fromm, Sebastian de Grazia, Hannah Arendt, and finally

The sociological critics of the mass society concept have, of course, had to make one or two concessions. Some have re-created the same contradiction in reverse. Shils, for instance, has no difficulty in pinpointing the elitist and anti-American predilections of the mass society theorists. But he cannot make any sort of case for an adequate role for the intellectual in mass culture except as a useful and moderately well-read hack; with the label "sociology" and the absolute commitment to analyzing what is rather than what will, might, or should be, the problem simply dissolves into dust. Shils accordingly accepts the "modern" definition of intellectuals—that of an academic or even literate establishment, which includes sociologists as being the direct heirs of the "old" intellectuals' universality and culture orientation. Criticism, yes—but constructive, supportive of the system, and concerned with the near, predictable, above all attainable future, please, not with some distant utopia. Ideology, maybe—one that "colors the moral tone of its time and heightens sensibility to the imperfections of society. It might be effective through pointing out deficiencies, and by exaggerating them make sensitive people aware of the defects of their society and cause them to try to find remedies." In sum, "an ideology of diminished intensity . . . without its more Manichean phases . . . engaged in a continuing dialogue with the protagonists of the central institutional and value systems in a way in which Marxism was only very infrequently and yet not entirely ineffective." Oh, toothless Marxist bulldog in amiable retirement! And this American intellectual-sociologist's charge is "the critical and solicitous care for the whole of the proximate future, if American society is not to be-

---

of course even Karl Mannheim. The attempt to transpose the canon of these highfalutin European thinkers, with their lofty meta-theoretical approach, to respectably empirical American dimensions, but without forgoing the *substance* of their disdain for mass society, resulted in studies like *The Authoritarian Personality* (T. W. Adorno and others, New York, 1950) and, more recently, William Kornhauser's *The Politics of Mass Society* (New York, 1959). See also the compendium edited by Norman Jacobs, *Culture for the Millions?* (Princeton, 1961). The problem has recently been surveyed by Herbert J. Ganz, "Popular Culture in America: Social Problems in a Mass Society or Social Asset in a Pluralist Society," in Herbert S. Becker, ed., *Social Problems: A Modern Approach* (New York, 1966), pp. 549–620.

come the victim of the parochial preoccupations of specialized technological experts," etc., etc.[81]

This new type of sensitive and restrained intellectual-sociologist is left facing a disagreeable-looking Third World at which he preaches humaneness and civility for all those within it who can read, write, and rule by virtue of their education. But Shils, the archetype of the contemporary intellectual he describes, is himself "transitional" in so far as he still recognizes an identifiable, possibly self-conscious stratum of intellectuals, while Lipset has abandoned any product orientation or qualitative analysis altogether, and simply appropriates (in the best Parsonian manner) the concept of intellectual for certain professions who work with their brains—especially in matters directly affecting culture and social control.[82]

We need not concern ourselves at too great length with the relative poverty of modern sociology in its analysis of its defeated intellectual predecessors—though it is important to understand the extent to which sociology has itself pared down the role of

[81] Edward Shils, "The Intellectuals and the Future," *Bulletin of the Atomic Scientists,* October 1967, p. 13 and passim.

[82] Shils's main statements are: on mass culture, "Daydreams and Nightmares: Reflections on the Criticism of Mass Culture," *Sewannee Review,* Vol. LXV, No. 4, October/December 1957; cf. Coser's reply, "Daydreams, Nightmares, Professor Shils," *Dissent,* Summer 1958 "Mass Society and Its Culture," op. cit. "The Intellectuals and the Future," op. cit., pp. 7–14. On the Third World, see Shils, "The Intellectuals and the Powers," *Comparative Studies in Society and History,* Vol. I (1958), pp. 5–22; "The Intellectuals in the Political Development of the New States," *World Politics,* Vol. XII, No. 3 (April 1960), pp. 329–68; and the study of Indian intellectuals, *The Intellectual between Tradition and Modernity* (The Hague, 1961). It is interesting to note the contributions of C. P. Snow (*The Two Cultures; The Two Cultures Revisited*) in this context. Mistaking professional differentiation for social and intellectual disjunction, he sees a regrettable gulf between scientists and humanists (intellectuals) that he would like to eliminate. Far from recreating a genuine quasi-group of intellectuals in the Mannheim sense, his wishes are more likely to lead to the total victory of what we have here described as technological modernity. In any case, as many of his critics have pointed out, modern *culture* is not so handily divisible anyway; his problem is probably an unreal one, postulated mainly to usher in a pet solution. A more rigorous inquiry into the nature of *ideas* might have suggested our present distinction between quality and scope, and led him to understand the real fate of the intellectual instead of bewailing an artificial distinction between two types of *professional* academic activity or culture.

the intellectual and replaced him.[83] But perhaps the worst blow to their situation in modern times has been an institutional rather than an ideological or cultural factor: the development of higher education as such, which Parsons celebrates elsewhere in this volume. Again this is closely related to the development of social science, though they are of course separate and not logically connected phenomena. The development of sociology shrinks the cultural validation of the intellectuals' concerns: the institutionalization of social science teaching lops off the universal dimension and particularizes it in an increasingly differentiated academic environment into distinct disciplinary "fields" with carefully guarded frontiers. The scope-oriented teaching—and of course learning—function separates both subject matter and those who produce it from their socio-political environment; we are all too familiar with theorists who can be defined as being *remote* from facts instead of *explaining* them. It is the same distinction as that between writers and professional Eng. Lit. critics. The American proliferation of universities and the growing differentiation of disciplines within them thus completes in its transatlantic setting the early tendency toward institutionalization we noted in the France of the *république des professeurs* and the Soviet Union of the *piatiletky*.

There remains the problem of whether this very growth of higher education, this proliferation of universities and their almost complete capture of social science thinking, could in fact lead to a new form of institutionalized dissent based on universities. Instead of comforting each other, students and the bulk of faculty would entrench themselves in "their" institutions and use these as a power base for dissent within but against society. As long as the Continental European reliance on the working class with its Marxist "trappings" dominates the intellectual per-

[83] The question of the possible superfluousness of the intellectual in modern society has of course been posed *ipsis verbis*, but not as a rule by sociologists, who have preferred, as I have noted, to redefine him. For overt discussion of the question of supercession, see, for instance, H. Stuart Hughes, "Is the Intellectual Obsolete?" *Commentary*, October 1956 (a bad time to ask in view of Hungary); Merle Kling, "The Intellectual: Will He Wither Away?" *New Republic*, April 8, 1957; Irving Howe, "The Age of Conformity," *Partisan Review*, Vol. XXI (January/February 1954), pp. 7–33.

spectives of student dissent, the process of institutional crystallization of dissent in, or rather of, the universities must remain
somewhat inhibited; the universities themselves will be divided
along lines that mirror the students' view of class disjunctions
in society. But here American traditions of radical pragmatism
and institutional autonomy may provide a lead, not only in
crystallizing the social institutions of dissent, but also in providing
a theoretical grounding for this process. This might be the next
task of American intellectuals, and provide them with a new
lease of group life against their all-embracing modern society.

If such a development is to take place, the role of social
scientists within universities is crucial. The students may become
increasingly committed, but the institutional realignment of universities as dissent structures depends heavily on the faculty and
especially on the social scientists who have taken over in the
form of roles those broader societal functions that in the past
were carried out by intellectuals. In any case these roles represent a narrowing of the broad functions of intellectuals, as I have
tried to show. But even within these narrower roles the influence
of social scientists is pivotal in such a situation. What about these
savants and institutionalized intellectuals of academe? Many of
them are putative intellectuals disguised as professors in the
humanities and social sciences, even as social *scientists;* their
dense concentration and intense institutional interaction would
presumably tend to facilitate the communication of dissent, should
it arise. One of the most interesting aspects of the work of
C. Wright Mills was his sustained (though at the time unsuccess-
ful) attempt to provide for his fellow social scientists an ideology
of dissent that was not merely a fashionable version of Marxism,
nor yet a philosophical-cultural critique of modernity, but that
implied full acceptance of the methods of modern social science
without their anti-intellectual *Problematik* or intentions. In other
words, a role of critical dissent based on their institutional position. So far there has certainly been considerable evidence that
the locus of much current American protest is firmly located in
academic establishments—at least as far as its universalization
and mediating role of exposition is concerned. This is particularly true of the civil rights movement (though here the legal
profession was initially the most important institutional structure)

and more recently of the protest against the Vietnam war. In many instances dissenting positions were taken by universities as institutional collectivities, for instance over government defense contracts at the University of Pennsylvania and in opposition to the disclosure of student grades for purposes of the draft at Columbia University. By 1968 this movement of dissent became directed with increasingly specific purpose toward the securing of the institutional base within individual universities; hence the takeover of Columbia and elsewhere and the creation of "liberated zones." A visitor from Europe to the United States in 1967 could not have helped being surprised by the general atmosphere of institutionalized dissent almost certainly approximating a structured form of social opposition. By 1968 this had crystallized into attempts all over the Western world to take over universities altogether.

Against this, however, are ranged powerful factors pulling the other way. Far from being able to choose or influence the issues or areas of dissent, universities often merely get the "leftovers" of the political process—especially in the Anglo-Saxon countries with their consensually restricted form of party politics. It is often only those issues that cannot surmount the threshold of official party or trade union politics that capture the interest and imagination of academic dissenters—a sort of last-ditch residue that may nonetheless prove the basis of future societal concerns. And student activism may in turn prove instrumentally useful to such groups in order to obtain from the regime concessions that their own demands hitherto had failed to achieve—such as substantially higher wages in France.

But more important perhaps is the problem of role. Dissent based on a universalistic rearrangement of known components combines badly with the limited or parochial concerns of the professional scientist. When scientists are also socio-political dissenters it is easy to drive a wedge between the two conflicting roles. In the best traditions of sociological analysis, role conflicts are pointed up and are sometimes even interpreted or at least publicly characterized as a form of character weakness if not mental instability. The case of Robert Oppenheimer with its suggestions of fundamental defects of character (and illness) clearly shows the extent to which scientists are not additionally permitted the composite role of intellectuals by society, and how one-sidedly institutional latitude is interpreted by government research establishments.[84]

Yet the denial of such composite roles and their carving up into stable but humbler constituent roles perhaps carry their own boomerang for "modern" society. For the dissenting scientist may himself in time come to represent just such an irreducible, specific constituent role—once his propensity to dissent becomes accepted as an integral part *of* his scientific role and not merely an unstable intellectual graft *onto* it. As deferent to science as modernity is, a scientist speaking intellectually on matters of universal concern ironically commands far more attention than a self-defined intellectual from New York's West Side or a social scientist from a university. This is a direct consequence of the improved status of science and of its broad institutionalization as an elite within modern society. But at the same time the effectiveness of what he has to say is usually low—as yet; a classic example of dissonance between source and content of message.[85] But one thing the dissenting scientist *can* do authoritatively is to challenge the scientific status of the mandarinate's articulation, especially its social science sector; thus credibly and professionally under-

[84] It will be obvious that in the present context I regard Oppenheimer as a scientist with intellectual tendencies rather than as an intellectual who happens to be a professional physicist. The difference is crucial: on the one hand a role category assigned by society, on the other a reliance for defining an intellectual upon a personality type or status assigned by an area of intellectual concern. It is here that the earlier distinction between scope and quality dimensions in the production and diffusion of ideas becomes very salient. The present analysis therefore differs tangentially from the suggestion that the condemnation of Oppenheimer represents a defeat for the position of the intellectuals, put forward by Philip Rieff in "The Case of Dr. Oppenheimer," pp. 314–40, in this volume, originally in *The Twentieth Century*, Vol. CLVI (1954). Why should Oppenheimer be rated as an intellectual in this context, and Teller not? As far as I am concerned, there is no evidence that the intellectuals had, or indeed can have, the sort of position in a modern society to which the Oppenheimer case could represent a defeat. Thus one might categorize Oppenheimer as a semi-intellectual without any access to suitable socio-political structures of dissent, and hence without claim to a socio-political role, no acceptable *claim* to universality, and only limited chance of culture validation.

[85] For this problem as a general factor in socio-political communication, see the brief overview in Robert E. Lane and David Sears, *Public Opinion* (Englewood Cliffs, 1964).

mining the ideological "scientism" on which the "modern" displacement of intellectuals by social scientists is based and by which it is justified.[86] All that can be said at present is that some form of generalized dissent by scientists, and especially the acceptance of such dissent as part of the scientists' function and role, may provide one possible recreation of structured dissent even within a technologically modern society. And this possibility will be greatly enhanced if such a change in attitudes on the part of a crucial professional group in modern society is combined with an institutionalized location in universities self-consciously crystallizing as structures of dissent.

None of this is of course intended to suggest for one moment that as an individual or as a personality type the intellectual is ceasing to exist in modern society. He is being and will continue to be studied as a type of person, with particular attention to his ideas and their influence—in other words a series of intellectual biographies, of greater or lesser import.[87] The problem of personality structure has deliberately been avoided here. Instead I have concentrated on the three-cornered relationship between certain types of ideas, their articulators, and the social structure of their environment. From a societal or social-theory point of view the meaningfulness of intellectuals can be gauged only in their social setting, and "measured" only in accordance with some hypothesis about what constitutes each of the three components of the relationship as well as about the types of relationship that make the function and role of intellectuals more or less favorable in a historical context. Hence the conclusion that modern society inhibits the existence of intellectuals is based on their societal situation and not on their existence as individual men or women with dissenting ideas. Since ideas are never entirely independent of their social setting, however, the inhibition of social function has in this analysis been of necessity closely

---

[86] See, for instance, the article by Dr. Noam Chomsky, "The Responsibility of Intellectuals," *New York Review of Books,* Vol. VIII, No. 3 (February 23, 1967), pp. 16–26.

[87] A good example of this approach is Christopher Lasch, *The New Radicalism in America 1889–1963: The Intellectual as a Social Type* (New York, 1965). The subtitle is a misnomer for a fascinating string of individual and group portraits.

linked to the ideological constraint of qualitative dissent in a scientific age; to paraphrase Marx, the intellectuals have sought to change the world, the point now is to explain it. Changes are acceptable only if they can be scientifically justified.

As a "type," the dissenter continues to exist and probably always will—until every paradox, every contradiction, can be socially and ideologically accommodated in advance. But in the West at present he is "particularized" into choices *between* the components of intellectualism rather than combinations of them. He has thus the choice of universality of concern, which means forgoing the badge of science and the possibility of a socio-political connection. Or again he may choose to guide or inspire collectivities by going into politics but these will be based on the mere articulation of interests; arguing for justice for Negroes in America, Old Age Pensioners in Britain, or students in France. Here he trades the possibility of impact on the socio-political structure for universality. Yet again he may stress cultural valida-tion, but must in that case come to terms with an elitist isolation that in fact ignores and turns its back on the effective culture of modern society. He may of course choose to live from the inter-pretation of the "real meaning" of contemporary culture by reinterpreting it for the benefit of his elite colleagues and the more masochistic elements among diffusers of popular culture (a very American phenomenon this).[88] But in this case there can also be no socio-political role.

I have already hinted at the reason why in some ways the situation of the intellectual as a personality type is somewhat easier in the Soviet Union than in America—in spite of the latter's much-vaunted freedom of expression. Everything in this analysis leads to the conclusion that freedom of expression, in which control is objective, ideological, and based on the prior-ity of mute machines, is less conducive to intellectualism than the demand for commitment where a subjective, purposive con-trol spells out its position more or less clearly. The notion that writers should be *engagé* in their work is backed up by a very

[88] A recent example of this is George Steiner, *Language and Silence* (New York, 1967), with its widely hailed claim that modern culture is in fact destroying language. McLuhan of course does best of all at explaining the awfulness of modern culture, and making a major academic career on the strength of these scientific explanations.

powerful Russian socio-cultural tradition of a hundred years of great "realist" literature, and by the existence of a mass audience to whom literature and cultural problems really matter. By definition as well as tradition Russian intellectuals may be more readily identified with writers than anywhere else except perhaps in France. This traditional differentiation between the articulation of scope and quality ideas among readily distinguishable professions has largely survived the "severe years" of Zhdanovism and the purges; "it is shameful to hide from your time: you must make it," says Yevtushenko.[89] The problem of whose task it is to evaluate, qualify, and perhaps to dissent thus conjures up a ready and widely acceptable answer out of an internalized cultural tradition—the writers, the poets. Even the Party appears to accept this position, however much the boundaries of freedom to dissent are subject to ordeal by battle, by trial and error. Hence the definition (and self-definition) of who is entitled to qualify and to evaluate, who constitute the intellectuals, actually presents far less of a problem in the Soviet Union than in the United States and most of Western Europe. It is significant that today in the Soviet Union and France (and partly in Germany and Italy) the intellectual's case is still put primarily by self-defined but accepted intellectuals, while in the United States and Britain it is sociology and sociologists who in large measure claim to speak for them. Yet even so the problem of structural "echo," of the relationship between intellectuals and dissenting collectivities, of mobilization for dissent, remains obscure. As elsewhere the intellectuals in the Soviet Union focus on youth, whose lot it is to "re-evaluate everything," who know that "it falls to them to carry time forward."[90] But youth, like the intellectuals themselves, is by itself at best an amorphous stratum and lacks an institutionalized or structural base.

In sum the Soviet version of modernity currently admits or rather readmits the functional allocation of universality, of qualitative concerns, to *individual* members of a certain stratum of the

[89] "Bratskges" (Bratsk Station), Yunost IV (1965).
[90] Venyamin Kaverin, in *Novy Mir*, Vol. IX (1965), p. 163. These reflections follow on a reported meeting Kaverin had with Fadeev, who told Kaverin about a book he had in mind but would never write. Fadeev committed suicide in 1956 and a chapter of the book was in fact published in *Ogonyok* under the title "Ferrous Metal Industry."

intelligentsia, the writers. But the admission of this traditional functional specification also sets relatively severe limits on the extent to which dissent is possible, and above all to the collective-structural form such dissent may take. The social role of the intellectual is inhibited even more strongly and much more directly than in the United States, though his personal self-definition and identity are relatively facilitated.

In Europe there is perhaps one area where the intellectual personality type is especially strong, and where no widespread view of "modernity" has yet eroded the traditional status and function of the intellectual. It is now clear that the imposition of the Soviet socio-political experience in terms of contemporary Communist rule on Eastern Europe has not transformed these societies as the Soviet Union itself was transformed; the changes, though fundamental, have left large pockets of traditional high-status groups, among them the intellectuals. These have thus been in large measure responsible for the common onslaught of dissent against the Stalinist system, and the varied changes that have resulted. Unlike the West or the Soviet Union, the status quo is less universal, less rational, these countries do not regard themselves as modern in the same sense; there is therefore much greater faith in the capacity of self-induced change, and the outcomes are regarded as much more random. All this results in a faith in experimentation, a capacity to match action to fundamental ideas, a willingness finally to ask fundamental questions as a normal process of intellectual activity—a "typical" intellectual environment in other words. This places Eastern Europe in a special category different from both the West and the Soviet Union—a category that is not without challenge from some of the established parties (in Poland and East Germany) and may prove merely a temporary stage in the establishment of control by either Western or Soviet versions of modernity. But whatever the outcome of the ferment that in the last twelve years has broken out in Poland, Hungary, Yugoslavia, and Czechoslovakia, the situation of the intellectuals in these countries—in terms of role, status, group identity, and influence—differs radically from that of both West and East, perhaps resembling an earlier period of history long since gone. Any attempt to universalize the situation of the intellectuals in these countries, to confuse their con-

temporary role there with their general situation in the *modern* world, merely leads to confusion between intelligentsia and intellectuals, and presents a peculiarly lopsided view of the modern world as a whole.[91]

As already mentioned, the intellectual as a personality type had in part accepted the decline of his role and function in modern Western societies and had accordingly transferred his attention and services to the developing world. The French intellectuals sallied out *en petite masse* toward Algeria, Cuba, even China (rebuffed there, of course). The attraction was not only the existence there of articulate, indeed revolutionary, dissent in the form of collectivities and social structure. In Latin countries, particularly Spain, Portugal, and Latin America, intellectuals have traditionally formed an ascribed status group, whose individual members were readily identifiable *inter se* and above all from below. The modern dominant Western dichotomy, intellectual man of action, hardly exists; Castro and his colleagues and the guerrilla leaders elsewhere (as well as more orthodox political figures like Betancourt and Haya de la Torre) are readily identified as politicians *as well as* intellectuals without any of the agonies of social scientists obsessed with role specification. Hence *confort intellectuel* is more readily obtainable there—quite apart from the structural facilitation for dissent.[92]

[91] See, for instance, Wolfgang Kraus, *Der Fünfte Stand: Aufbruch der Intellektuellen in West und Ost* (Berlin/Munich/Vienna, 1967), for the claim that the needs of modern society for a highly skilled intelligentsia on the one hand, and the successful challenges by intellectuals of the established systems in Eastern Europe, *together* demonstrate the application of the unprecedented power of intellectuals in the modern world. This book has a curious ethnocentric flavor in its alignment with an established tradition of blithely universalizing the exceptionally parochial intellectual experience of Vienna and its former intellectual dependencies.

[92] Cf. also Hugh Seton-Watson, *The Patterns of Communist Revolution* (London, 1955), for the more general argument that intellectuals constitute a high ascribed status group in *all* agrarian societies as compared to industrial countries. Hence frustrated intellectuals (status without power— what Lenski has called an uneven or broken rank profile) are one of the prime sources of revolution in such countries, as they were in Russia. I believe this explanation to be too broad, as regards agrarian societies in general, as well as in the implicit catch-all definition of intellectuals already referred to earlier.

Elsewhere, in countries with a less developed tradition of dissent *par principe,* social science and intellectual interest in and concern for developing countries has grown apace in recent years. And one of the most encouraging signs has been that the nostalgic search for an admittedly temporary recreation abroad of one's own "pre-modern" past, in which intellectuals had a definite place, is itself being shouldered aside by the assertion, partly even in social-scientific terms, that a different version of modernity may be emerging there, neither dissentless nor scientific, but distinctly conflictful and human. Once more Russians vie with Americans in making the same point in different ways and from different base lines. Recent American emphasis on the specifics of the socio-politics of development in different areas of the Third World, the notion of multiple modernities, ultimately converges with Russian emphasis on the so-called National Democratic State and the existence of different national paths to socialism.[93]

These few pointers to the survival or even resurgence of intellectuals as a role category do not make a summer in the gloom of modernity. In the modern world over all things look bleak for intellectuals. But we cannot really predict the future (seeing that we cannot change and scarcely even explain the present). For therapeutic reasons if nothing else, personal dissent, however socially ineffective and unstructured, is better than none. And as the students have shown, the need as well as the capacity for social dissent of a very activist kind certainly exist; the problem is its capacity or willingness to be intellectually articulated in a meaningful and not merely hung-over Marxist manner.

[93] For the former, see J. P. Nettl, *Political Mobilization,* and Nettl and Roland Robertson, op. cit. For the latter, T. P. Thornton, ed., *The Third World in Soviet Perspective* (Princeton, 1964); more recently, Herbert S. Dinerstein, "Soviet Policy in Latin America," *American Political Science Review,* Vol. LXI, No. 1 (March 1967), pp. 80–90.

Case Studies

THE LIFE AND OPINIONS OF
MOSES HESS

Sir Isaiah Berlin

I cannot deny that Moses Hess was both a Communist and a Zionist. He played a decisive role in the history of the first movement, he virtually invented the second. Indeed this remarkable fact is his chief, perhaps his sole, claim to fame.

Nevertheless, in the course of his troubled and dedicated life, Moses Hess uttered some highly original and telling judgments that have not, even now, obtained the recognition that they seem to me to deserve. He was a prophet without much honour in his own generation, certainly none in his own country. Yet much of what he said was new and, as it has turned out, both important and true. In particular he detected in the life both of European society in general, and of the European Jews in particular, symptoms of what, he feared, was a fatal disease; or, if not fatal, at any rate dangerous. Against it he offered remedies which, whether or not they were effective, were at any rate specific proposals capable of being realized, and not cries of self-pity, or empty forms of words, or vague and idle dreams. His theses were indeed dismissed at the time of their utterance, as being some, or all, of these things. But this verdict seems to me wholly unjust. The counter-thesis that I should like to put before you is that Hess was, at any rate after 1848, an exceptionally penetrating and independent thinker who understood and formulated the problems with which he was dealing more clearly than the majority of his critics, whose rival diagnoses, admired for their wisdom in their own day, have stood up badly to the test of time. But even if I am mistaken about this, the questions that Hess raised, in the form in which he raised them, are exceedingly live issues today, and have become, if anything, more critical than they were in his own lifetime. Even if he had no other claim on our attention, this would, I think, be sufficient in itself.

Moses Hess was born in 1812, in the city of Bonn, into a Jewish family whose forebears may have come from Poland. His parents belonged to that generation of German Jews which had been freed by the French wars of liberation. Between 1795 and 1814 Bonn was under French rule; the gates of the Jewish ghetto were flung wide open, and its inmates, after centuries of being driven in upon themselves, were permitted to emerge into the light of day. Personal freedom (or at any rate an enlarged measure of it), economic opportunity, secular knowledge, liberal ideas, acted like a heady wine upon the children of the newly emancipated Jews. When, in 1815, after the final defeat of Napoleon, the Rhineland was annexed to Prussia, and King Frederick William III made an attempt to return to ancient ways, the reimposition of most of the old restrictions on the Jews of his kingdom produced a crisis among the newly liberated. Some among them could not bear the thought of a return to their former degraded status, and accepted baptism with varying degrees of sincere conviction. The radical journalist, Ludwig Börne, changed his name and his faith on the same day; so too did Heinrich Marx, the father of Karl Marx. The poet Heine, the jurist Eduard Gans, Ludwig Stahl (who later founded the Christian Social Party), the children of the philosopher Moses Mendelssohn, were the best known converts to Christianity. Others reacted in the opposite direction. For reasons both of genuine piety and of pride, they became even more fiercely attached to their ancient religion. Amongst these were the members of Hess's family. In 1817 his father moved to Cologne, where he established a sugar refinery, soon grew prosperous, and in due course became head of the Jewish community of the city. The boy, aged five, was left behind in Bonn, where his devoutly religious maternal grandfather gave him a traditional Jewish up-bringing, and a solid knowledge of the Bible, the Talmud and the mediaeval commentaries. Almost half a century later Hess gave a moving account of this single-minded old merchant, who could not hold back his tears when he spoke of the destruction of the temple in Jerusalem and the dispersion of the Jews. There is no doubt that his early education affected Hess indelibly: images and symbols drawn from the history of the Jews remained with him to the end of his life. One may, perhaps, permit oneself to wonder about the consequences to the world, had Karl Marx, the grandson of a rabbi, been brought up in this fashion, and not (as in fact he was) on a diet of eighteenth-century rational-ism by a father who was a mild follower of Voltaire.

Hess's mother died when he was fourteen, and he then went to live in his father's house in Cologne. When he was eighteen, he was reluctantly allowed by his father to go to the university of Bonn. There is no evidence of what happened to him there. In-deed, it is dubious whether he even matriculated. At any rate, the experience seems to have left no impression upon him. We know little about him at this time; only that, in common with a good many other idealistic young men in Germany, he was deeply affected by the mystical nationalism and romanticism which then was sweeping over the German intelligentsia. His father wished him to enter his own expanding business. Moritz Hess, as he was called at this time, flatly declined. He appears to have had no clear idea of what he wanted to do. He wished only to serve mankind, help the destitute, liberate the oppressed and, above all, not make money, since this appeared to him *bourgeois* egotism in its most repulsive form. He quarrelled with his father, and left his parent's house with a very small sum of money in his pocket, to see the world, or at any rate Europe. He went to England, where he starved miserably, then to Holland and France. He was in Paris in 1832, and it was perhaps among the poor German *émigrés*—mostly left-wing exiles—that he im-bibed the radical ideas then in vogue in that relatively free capital.[1] The revolution of 1830 had created immense hopes

[1] Doubt is thrown upon this by Professor E. Silberner, "Der Junge Moses Hess," in the *International Review of Social History* (Assen, Holland), Vol. III, Pt. 2, pp. 238–68.

among the liberals of Europe, and Paris was fermenting with socialist sects and ideas, especially those affected by Saint-Simonian and Fourierist doctrines, which, by and large, called upon men to recognize and fight the evils of cut-throat competition and individual enterprise and the strife and destruction of both the bodies and the souls of men inevitably entailed by them, and instead to co-operate in collective undertakings that would release the great productive energies of mankind in a planned and harmonious manner, and create universal prosperity, justice and happiness on earth. Some of these men were confused dreamers. Others were acute and highly practical organizers who understood the revolutionary consequences of technological progress. Idealistic and short-lived communist colonies in America and elsewhere sprang from the former strain. From the latter grew the Suez and Panama canals, the new railway system of France, and novel technocratic notions and institutions of many sorts, from the industrial monopolies to the New Deal, from vast cartels and state-owned enterprises to five-year plans and the welfare state. The most radical of these trends was the continuing underground tradition of out-and-out communism, preached by the proscribed followers of the executed revolutionary Babeuf, who declared that not merely the love, but the possession, of private property was the root of all evil, and that justice or liberty were not possible without complete social and economic equality which, in its turn, depended upon the total abolition of inheritance and of virtually all private ownership. Hess accepted these doctrines fervently, adding to them his own enthusiastic faith in the romantic irrationalism preached by the disciples of Fichte and Schelling, together with what he understood of Spinoza, whom the romantics affected to admire; and, like other radical young intellectuals of his generation, tried to cast this amalgam into the mould of the great dominant philosophy of that time—the Hegelian system. Totally destitute, he returned to Cologne on foot, made his peace with his father, and was appointed a clerk in the family sugar refinery. This, as might have been foreseen, ended in complete failure. He finally abandoned his father's house, scraped together a sum of money sufficient to keep him alive for a few months, and, anxious to say his own, personal word in the metaphysical debates that (partly as a result of government censorship) took the place of political discussion in Germany in his day, composed a treatise embodying his entire *Weltanschauung*. This pretentious, tedious, badly written metaphysics of history, full of Hegelian clichés, was published in 1837, was called *The Sacred History of Mankind by a Young Disciple of Spinoza,* and today is virtually unreadable. Although the title claims the inspiration of Spinoza, apart from a vague rationalism, and belief in the unity of all creation, the text has little to do with the great seventeenth-century master; its inspiration is more that of romantic Protestant theology: the spirit is that of Schleiermacher. The central thesis is that in the beginning men lived in an undifferentiated unity of spirit and matter—a condition of primitive communism that preceded the invention of property. This period is carefully divided by the author into fourteen sub-periods each dominated by a great leader. This original unity was broken by Christianity, which began by reconciling spirit with matter, but, in its distorted mediaeval form, exaggerated the spirit, and led to a one-sided mysticism. The dynamic process of the Hegelian historical dialectic will, however, set this right. It is the task of modern man, armed with consciousness of his historic mission, to create a rational harmony of matter and spirit, as preached by Schelling in Germany—though, in the author's view, with too much emphasis on spirit; and by Saint-Simon in France—though with too much emphasis on matter. This harmony is to be embodied in a new dispensation—"social humanity"—in which the evil institution of private property—the social form of covetous greed—together with competition and the division of labour by which men are brutalized and dehumanized into the semblance of mere animate property—so much raw material to be exploited by an *élite* of capitalists, will at long last be abolished. Thus the Hebrew prophets—the truest heralds of the new world —will at last be vindicated. To achieve this ideal men must (in the spirit of Fichte) obey the moral imperative of seeking after the holy life of reciprocal self-sacrifice. The Jews are mentioned by Hess only to be dismissed as embodying a preliminary stage superseded by Christianity. The ancient Jewish state is to be admired, indeed, as representing a unity—a fusion of state, church, religion, and political and social life—a single set of

principles regulating the whole of human life. Men have wandered from God, but they will return to Him, and "the ancient
law will rise again, transfigured. . . ." In this way the Jews will
disappear as a people, but not before they have conquered the
world spiritually. Thereby their special mission will be fulfilled.
Indeed their part is over already, for they have been rendered
obsolete by Christianity, and they are counselled to leave the
stage of history. "The people chosen by their God must disappear forever, that out of its death might spring a new, more
precious life."

All this was no worse, but certainly no better, than the farrago
of metaphysics, social messianism, and personal ardour that
constituted the normal matter of the innumerable historico-theo-
logical systems with which German universities were at this time
flooding the philosophical public. Most of these treatises were
deeply religious in spirit and purpose, being attempts to find in
art or science the path to individual or national salvation which
the orthodox Christian churches seemed no longer capable of
providing for critical minds. Some sought substitutes for religion
in literature, in music, in varieties of mystical experience. Others,
perhaps the majority of such spiritually *désoeuvrés,* at any rate
in countries under German influence, sought for the answer in
history as the progressive revelation of the ways of God or the
Absolute Spirit, and this led to the schools of what is best called
historiosophy—the attempt to make history do the work of theology or speculative metaphysics—of which the most celebrated
are the movements associated with the names of Schelling, Hegel, Comte, Spengler, and to some degree, Marx and the disciples
of Darwin. Dr. Arnold Toynbee is the leading, it may be the
last, representative of this type of secular messianism in our day.

The Sacred History of Mankind found no readers, and is
today deservedly forgotten. It is of interest only because it
shows that, even in this early phase, Hess was a full-fledged
Socialist, indeed the earliest German Socialist—the first faithful
German disciple of the French egalitarians—a belated, somewhat idealistic, German Babouvist. Moreover, it established Hess
as a member of the avant-garde philosophical Left—the Young
Hegelians of extreme radical views. All the disciples of Hegel
believed that their master had discovered the true pattern of

human history, which lay in perpetual movement towards increasing rationality and freedom, that is to say, a state in which more and more men would comprehend more and more clearly what the logically inevitable purposes of the Universal Spirit must be—whither history, revealing its nature and direction to itself, in the form of the critical and creative human spirit, was developing. This growth of self awareness on the part of the universe conceived as an active subject—a spirit or organism—takes the form of the increase of rational knowledge among men, and therefore of their power over nature and over themselves, that is, their freedom, and thereby brings the millennium nearer. According to Hegelians of all shades of opinion this process consisted in the perpetual struggle and collision of forces at every "level"—social, intellectual, economic, political, physical—leading to crises (that sometimes took the form of social revolutions), each of which marked a stage in the ascent of "the World Spirit." The left-wing Hegelians interpreted this as meaning that the essential function of the most advanced elements in society—the most rational, the most conscious of what they were, what stage they had reached, and whither the next inevitable step in the ascent of the Spirit must lead—was essentially destructive, destructive of whatever was static, dead, literally stupid, frozen, irrational, whatever obstructed self-criticism and thereby the progress of humanity towards its goal. In their view absolute rationality meant the attainment by humanity of absolute freedom over itself and over its environment; and this could be achieved only by actively removing the obstacles to such emancipation—a view that carried plainly revolutionary implications. Some young Hegelians confined their radicalism to the realms of theory, and spent their energies on subverting traditional beliefs—mainly religious and metaphysical, like David Friedrich Strauss with his boldly iconoclastic *Life of Jesus,* or Feuerbach and the brothers Bauer who, in their different ways, interpreted religion in terms of social mythology. Others went farther, and, like the eighteenth-century materialists, held that unless the social and psychological conditions which had kept men in ignorance, and given birth to the religious or social or political illusions that had reconciled humanity to its helplessness and misery, were themselves destroyed, no true progress could be made. Among these were such young philosophical amateurs as Arnold Ruge, Friedrich Engels and, the best known of all, Karl Marx. Hess felt it craven to be anywhere but in the forefront of this battle for the soul of mankind. He was twenty-five years old, a generous, high-minded, kindly, touchingly pure-hearted, enthusiastic, not over astute young man, ready, indeed eager, to suffer for his ideas, filled with love of humanity, optimism, a passion for abstractions, and aversion from the world of practical affairs towards which the more hard-headed members of his family were trying to steer him. His marriage tells us more of his character and temperament than anything else. He met in Cologne, and married, a prostitute, not, apparently, because he had fallen in love with her, but in order to redress the injustice perpetrated by society; he wished to perform an act expressive of the need for love among men and for equality between them. So far as we know he lived in complete harmony and happiness with his wife for the rest of his days. Sibylle Hess, who was a gentile, worshipped him to the end of his life, occasionally deceived him (against which he protested, but not very strongly), and shared his poverty with the greatest devotion. It was perhaps this child-like quality—Hess's unworldliness and purity of character, rising at moments to genuine saintliness[2]—that so deeply irritated the tough-minded "realists" among his fellow Socialists, who looked on him as a benevolent ass. Yet even Marx, who utterly despised him, could discover no moral vice or fault to cast in his teeth.

Hess spent the next four years in intensive reading of books about philosophy and social theory, still supported, we must surmise, by his irritated, but far from heartless, family. His next volume, which appeared in 1841, attracted more attention. *The European Triarchy* is a primarily political treatise, an answer to a now even more forgotten work called *The European Pentarchy* that advocated the parcelling out of Europe between the five great powers; and it represents an advance in its author's social and political views. The only salvation of mankind lies, we are told, in the universal adoption of socialism, in particular in the

[2] Hess's moral character has a strong affinity with Dostoevsky's ideal of the "positively good man" embodied in the heroes of *The Idiot* and *The Brothers Karamazov*. A Jewish communist is the last human type in which Dostoevsky would have looked for any semblance to his ideal.

abolition of private property.[3] The reason for this is not the need for economic efficiency, nor the inexorable demands of history, nor the emergence of a particular class—the proletariat —at war with other classes, which is destined inevitably to destroy or supersede all its rivals, but quite simply that socialism alone is just. Hess, in sharp contrast to Marx and his school, even while he fully accepts the analysis of society into social-economic classes, does not believe that class conflict is either desirable or inevitable. He is a socialist, indeed a communist, because he thinks that all egoism—like all domination—is destructive of the human personality and frustrates master and slave alike, inasmuch as individual faculties can never be developed fully in conditions of competition, but only in harmonious collaboration with others, as the French socialist—Saint-Simon and Fourier—had conclusively shown. Communism for Hess was the sole form of social altruism realizable in the historical conditions of the age. (In 1843 he describes it as being simply "practical ethics.") He did not attempt to give a detailed analysis of the structure or needs of the proletariat, largely because (like his fellow Radicals, Marx, Ruge, Engels, Grün, Feuerbach and the brothers Bauer) he had personally met too few members of this class, and was a good deal more honest than most of his allies. History for him is a struggle of self-assertive egoism (of individuals or classes or nations) with the opposite principles of altruism, love and social justice. The fact that the belief in equality, solidarity and justice had always represented, at any rate, the professed aspirations of men, proves that these qualities flow from man's true nature. Rational and harmonious co-operation between men is possible (sometimes appeal is made to the authority of Spinoza or Hegel, sometimes to the theses of the French *philosophes*) but it must always

[3] Professor E. Silberner in his very illuminating article on Moses Hess (*Historia Judaica,* Vol. 13 [April 1951], Pt. 1) describes the doctrine of this book, despite its advocacy of the abolition of private inheritance and the community of ownership, as not quite tantamount to socialism. I am not sure that I understand what, in his opinion, distinguishes Hess's doctrine from, at any rate, the stock French socialism of his time. Hess does not, it is true, go so far as Cabet, but he is certainly at least as socialist as, say, Louis Blanc, and more so than the Fourierists or Proudhon. Perhaps in his forthcoming biography of Hess Professor Silberner will clarify this issue.

be fought for. Human happiness lies in human hands, and if enough individuals can be convinced of the truth of the propositions advanced by the author, human beings will be enabled to create their own happiness. The "scientific" socialists—Marx and his tough-minded followers—later poured derision on this "utopian," "rose water," "humanitarian" doctrine as an absurdly idealistic, ineffective kind of socialism, suspended in a timeless void, abstract, unhistorical; not evolved out of insight into concrete social conditions, and represented their own brand of socialism as superior, if only in virtue of the fact that it was "deduced" from the concrete facts—that it was not something the realization of which turned on luck or accident, on what might or might not happen, that depended upon the precarious good will of this or that group of men, or on this or that set unpredictable of circumstances. Marx genuinely believed (as in a sense Hegel believed before him) that what alone made a cause worth fighting for, was that it represented the inevitable next stage in the social evolution of mankind, a stage that could be determined accurately only by means of scientific analysis and prediction. The social revolution—the expropriation of the owners of property and their replacement by public ownership, and the victory of the property-less class—was, on this view, in any case inevitable; for this reason it was what rational men would pursue simply because they know that to seek after anything else, to identify themselves with any other group of persons, was automatically to ignore the social "reality" by which any individual, and his ideas, were determined, and consequently to court destruction by the forces of history—something that only fools or madmen could want.

Hess would have none of this. He believed that justice was but desirable, not because it was inevitable; nor was it to be identified with whatever was bound, in any case, to emerge from the womb of time. All kinds of bad and irrational conditions had been produced before now, and persisted. Nothing was to be accepted merely because it had occurred—but solely because it was objectively good. Hegelian historicism had evidently not struck so deep in him after all; heretical as this was, he stoutly maintained that the only way to achieve social justice, the abolition of poverty and the equitable distribution of the ever more plentiful goods (which, owing to maldistribution, were breeding more misery than happiness) was by the conscious will of men convinced of the moral necessity of their action. One could, and one had a duty to, convince men by rational argument that if they turned their resources into productive and harmonious channels, they would be better off both materially and morally; this was Hess's "True Socialism"—the utopian sentimentalism for which Marx and Engels mocked him so bitterly.[4] They called him Rabbi Moses and Rabbi Hess, and laughed his theses to scorn.

And yet, in the light of our later experience, it almost seems as if Hess, with his naïveté, his traditional Jewish morality, his pleas for justice and his quotations from Spinoza and the Bible, may not, after all, have been as profoundly mistaken as the more celebrated founders of "scientific" socialism. The exacerbation of the class war, as predicted and encouraged by Marx and Engels, has in due course occurred. The revolution for which they worked has, in one form or another, transformed the lives of large portions of the human race. But it seems clear that where this occurred in accordance with Marxist principles and tactics, that is to say by means of the violent expropriation of the property owning classes, the mere fact of the abolition of private property and the creation of the dictatorship of the communist party (or a committee of it) claiming to represent the proletariat, have not, by themselves, brought about internal or external harmony, or economic equality, or personal liberty or social justice. And, on the other hand, wherever these ideals have been realized or, at any rate, approached, this seems to have been, almost invariably, the result of the conscious effort of individuals working for them as ends in themselves, under no illusion that they embodied the inexorable forces of history or any other agency; least of all the work of men disposed to deceive themselves or others by systematically representing what would normally be recognized as acts of cruelty, exploitation, injustice and oppression as being mysteriously transformed into virtuous actions, or

4 His views at this time (1843) are very clearly set out in two articles, *Sozialismus und Kommunismus* and *Philosophie der That*, in an *émigré* anthology called *Einundzwanzig Bogen aus der Schweiz*, as well as in his articles in the Paris *Vorwärts*, the *Deutsch-Französische Jahrbücher*, and *Der Sprecher* edited by Karl Grün in Wesel.

at least means to virtue, by the sanctifying process of historical necessity—the inexorable march of "God in history"—the historical dialectic.

Throughout his life Hess's socialism remains founded on purely moral premises. In this respect his opinions resemble those of the nineteenth-century Christian socialists, or the Russian Socialist-Revolutionaries, or the British and Scandinavian socialists of our time, far more than those of Marxists and other "realists." Hess wants the abolition of private property because he thinks that men will not cease to fight and oppress one another, and will not cease to be themselves poisoned by the injustice they breed, unless they live a social or communal life; and to this type of life he thinks private property to be a fatal obstacle. Private property must be abolished. But unless the reform is carried out with full moral realization of what its purpose is, it will achieve nothing. Mere mechanical abolition of private property is certainly not enough. There must be a change of heart. But this cannot happen until the material and institutional conditions which have hardened men's hearts are themselves altered. Yet the mere alteration of this framework will not by itself produce the required spiritual transformation, unless the moral principles which alone are worthy of free men are understood and consciously applied.

These moral principles belong to all men as such, and are recognized even if they are not acted upon by all men in some degree, but most clearly by the best and wisest. These principles are not necessarily those of only one given class, even though the demands of an oppressed class embody them more genuinely than the demands of those who gain by such oppression. This is the notion of "abstract humanity" with which Marxists charge Hess and the other utopians; as if the concept of the "class of the exploited" is any less abstract. Hess's creed derived from these principles from first to last. His socialism, and later his Zionism, are direct consequences of it. Those who find the concept of class rights more real than that of human rights, as well as those who find comfort in believing men to be agents of impersonal forces that will secure the victory for their own group soon or late, whatever their opponents may wish or think, that is to say, all natural Hegelians, Marxists, Calvinists, and other extreme determinists, particularly in the fields of politics or social life, will inevitably find Hess both unrealistic and unsympathetic.

The European Triarchy in particular advocated the union of the three civilized powers in Europe: Germany the home of ideas and the champion of religious liberty; France the battlefield on which effective social reform and political independence had been won; and England the home of economic freedom, and moreover itself the synthesis of the French and German spirit—neither "over-speculative" like Germany, nor "vulgarly" materialistic like France. These three powers must unite against Russia, the reservoir of reaction, the home of barbarian repression threatening to engulf Europe and trample upon its liberties. Appeals for union against Russia as an enemy of the West were, by then, common enough in Germany and, indeed, elsewhere in Europe. The only originality of Hess's book consisted in the fact that it tied this familiar proposal to the necessity for radical social reform, and of "peaceful revolution" (he believed that violence bred violence and destroyed the soil for peaceful reconstruction), as being alone likely to save Europe from collapsing under the weight of the contradictions of its capitalist system of production and distribution.

The book attracted some attention. Hess was revealed to the German intellectual world as an eloquent left-wing agitator, and in the course of the next two years was offered, and accepted, various journalistic posts, which brought him into close contact with other like minded young men, notably Engels, Marx and Ruge. The first and fieriest German Hegelian to turn communist, Hess converted the young Friedrich Engels to his creed.[5] He met Marx in 1841, and although the latter had had some inkling of current communist doctrines from the book published in Germany by Lorenz Stein which gave an account of the views of the leaders of the French communist sects, it was most probably Hess's hot eloquence that first shook the foundations of his faith in Hegelian political theory with its deification of the bureaucratic state as the expression of human reason and discipline, and turned him on to the path of militant social collectivism. There were of course passages in Hess's book which cannot have

---

[5] In an article in the Owenite journal The New Moral World, Engels says that Hess was the first young Hegelian to become a communist, and to declare that "competition was robbery." (New Moral World, No. 21, 1843.)

satisfied Marx even then. The ethical tone, but, even more, the
frequent references to the Hebrew prophets, and the prevalence
of Hebraic motifs generally, had never been to his taste. Marx
himself, as is only too plain, decided to eliminate this particular
source of embarrassment once and for all from his life. He had
no intention of going through the torments of an ambivalent status such as afflicted more sensitive and less ruthless natures,
such Jews as Börne, for instance, or Heine or Lassalle or Disraeli,
throughout their mature lives. All his bitter and exasperated
feeling against the discrimination practised against himself he
transferred by a bold, if not altogether conscious, stroke to a
much vaster field: by identifying his own grievances with those
of the insulted and the oppressed everywhere, and in particular
with those of the proletariat, he achieved his own psychological
emancipation. It was in the name of the oppressed workers that
he thundered, of a great, symbolic multitude—impersonal, remote from his own world and his own wounds—not of his own
painful humiliation as a Jew denied a professorial chair; it was
for them alone that he demanded and prophesied justice, revenge, destruction. As for the Jews, in an essay written two
years after he met Hess, he declared them simply to be a repel-
lent symptom of a social malaise of the time, an excrescence
upon the social body—not a race, or a nation, or even a religion
to be saved by conversion to some other faith or way of life, but
a collection of parasites, a gang of money-lenders rendered inevitable by the economically self-contradictory and unjust society
that had generated them—to be eliminated as a group by the
final solution to all social ills—the coming, inescapable, universal,
social revolution. The violently anti-Semitic tone of this essay,
which Engels more feebly echoes (anti-Semitism was not uncommon among socialists of that, or indeed later, time), became
more and more characteristic of Marx in his later years. It affected the attitudes of communists—particularly Jewish communists, towards the Jews, and is one of the most neurotic and re-
volting aspects of his masterful but vulgar personality. The tone
adopted by Hess was profoundly different. His actual opinions
were not very different from those of Marx or any other young
Hegelian radical of this time. But he did not suffer from a self-
hatred that made him wish to commit acts of violence against

his nature. He did not try to cut the traces of his origins out of himself, because he did not, like Marx, feel it as a malignant growth that was suffocating him and of which he was ashamed. In *The European Triarchy* he merely repeated what he had said some four years earlier—that the task of the Jews was to disperse and assimilate—they had served their turn in making first Christianity, and after that (inasmuch as Judaism stresses social ties more than Christianity) social regeneration by communism possible; they had acted as a "goad" and a "ferment" that has promoted the "mobility" of the West and prevented it from stagnating like China, but this function was now over. Because they had rejected Christianity, they were now a mere ghostly presence "unable either to die or to come to life," a mere skeleton, a fossil, and it was time that they married gentiles and disappeared. The "Triarchy" of the civilized great powers would emancipate them fully, and give them the rights of men and citizens; but their real emancipation would occur only when all hatred and contempt for them on the part of others disappeared. In short he repeated the noble commonplaces that have formed the staple doctrine of liberal assimilationists everywhere and at all times.

The act of apostasy constituted by this creed precipitated the final rupture between him and his devotedly Jewish father. Yet this is not the whole story of Hess's feelings about the Jews even at this time. In 1840, in Damascus, a Jew was accused and convicted of committing an act of ritual murder. Anti-Jewish disorders followed. The repercussions of this terrible and ancient slander led to agitation by the horrified Jews of France and England, scandalized their sympathisers everywhere, and ended in some redress for this injustice obtained by the Montefiore-Crémieux mission. Hess reacted painfully to this incident, and for the first time, so he tells us later, began to wonder whether the general solution that he advocated for all human ills would, in fact, automatically cure those of the Jews also. In the same year, during the great wave of anti-French chauvinism which passed over Germany at that time, he came across a Francophobe hymn by the poet Becker, and in a burst of patriotic feeling set it to music and sent his composition to the author. Becker sent a polite reply with an anti-Semitic scribble[6] in a

6 *"Du bist ein Jid."*

disguised, but still recognizable, hand, on the back of the en-
velope. Hess was dreadfully upset; but as a rationalist and
socialist, decided to conquer his feelings both about Damascus
and about Becker. These, he tried to say to himself, were the
aberrations of a society in its death throes. The social regeneration of mankind would make them forever impossible. There was
no room in the universal society of the future for sectional religions or interests. The Jews must scatter and vanish as a historical entity. A universal religion must replace a purely national
one. If the Jews could not bring themselves to accept baptism
for themselves, at least they must baptize their children; in this
way the "Judaeo-Christian tradesmen's world" would end in dignified dissolution. In any case the sufferings of the proletariat
were surely a greater and more urgent cause than those of the
Jews, however painful and undeserved. Hess repressed his
wounded feelings, at any rate for the time being. Doctrine—
helped out with special pleading—triumphed over the direct evidence of experience.[7] This is the prototype of the story of many
a Jewish socialist and communist since his day. It is to Hess's
eternal credit that he was among the few to recognize, before
his life was done, that this comforting theory rested on a fallacy;
not an ignoble fallacy, perhaps, but still delusive. Twenty years
later, having diagnosed it as such, he proclaimed his results to the
world, with great simplicity and courage. At no moment in his
life did he have anything to hide. He made mistakes, since he
was often naïve and uncritical. He was saved by his moral in-

[7] But not entirely. In *Rome and Jerusalem,* Hess mentions a manuscript
composed at this time proclaiming the need for self-determination as a
solution for the Jewish problem. The fate of this *esquisse* is unknown: most
probably Hess incorporated it in *Rome and Jerusalem.* But there does
survive a fragment of this early period, which, as Professor E. Silberner, its
discoverer, has been good enough to tell me, declared the need for a Jewish
nationhood. This demonstrates that Hess did not, as might otherwise have
been suspected, unconsciously antedate the moment at which he first
conceived the idea of the Jewish state. But at this stage it was probably no
more than a bold fantasy. The young Lassalle, too, toyed with the notion of
a new Judea at this time. The 1830s and '40s are rich in extravagant political
schemes. Nevertheless, despite occasional moods of this kind, Hess was
wholly anti-nationalist at this period, and consciously rejected the Zionist
ideas which had suggested themselves insistently to him, and to which he
was later to return.

sight which remained uncontaminated by personal vanity or dogma. And his conscience was always clear.

The time of disenchantment was still to come. In 1841 Hess fell under the spell of the brilliance and boldness of Karl Marx's views. He met Marx in August of that year, preached communism to him, and early in September wrote to his sceptical friend Auerbach, "He is the greatest, perhaps the only true philosopher actually now alive. Doctor Marx—that is the name of my idol—is still a very young man. He is only twenty-four and will strike the final death blow at mediaeval religion and politics. He combines philosophical depth with a most biting wit: imagine Rousseau, Voltaire, Holbach, Lessing, Heine and Hegel —not thrown together anyhow, but fused into a single personality, and you will have Doctor Marx." With Marx he collaborated on the radical *Rheinische Zeitung,* until things became too hot for him in the Rhineland. Accused—justly enough—of being the original fountainhead of violent communist agitation in Germany (a strange historical responsibility to bear for a peace loving idealist deeply opposed to the use of force) he was sent off to the security of Paris as a correspondent for his journal. In Paris he took a hand in the conversion of the celebrated Russian revolutionary, Michael Bakunin, to the revolutionary communism that preceded the anarchism of his later life, and for a time became an enthusiastic supporter of Proudhon. He admired Proudhon and Cabet—the most fanatical of all the socialists of that time—for making their appeal directly to the poor and the oppressed, and not waiting, like Saint-Simon or Fourier, for some enlightened despot or millionaire to put through their social schemes for them. In 1843 he returned to Cologne, agitated among the workers, published routine left-wing articles attacking private property, religion, and the tyranny of the state; he seems to have occupied a political position intermediate between communism and anarchism.[8] He was at this time an active member of a faithful band of brothers, which included Proudhon, Bruno Bauer, Karl Grün, Max Stirner, all afterwards condemned by Marx as mere abstract moralists—men who denounced capitalism for no better reason than that they believed it to be evil— which was mere subjectivism disguised as objective judgment.

[8] See footnote 4.

Marx maintained that since all men were in fact conditioned by the position of their class, and their position in their class, and since their moral and political opinions were a rationalization of their interests (that is to say, of what their class at a given stage of its evolution needed and desired, or was endangered by and feared) to suppose that one could praise or condemn from some neutral vantage point, above the battle, above the class struggle, was to fall into a fatal "metaphysical" illusion. The only truly objective ground from which one could rationally attack, or act to destroy, a given view, institution, regime, was that of the new dialectical science of historical development. Rational politics was the support of what history—the class struggle—would bring forth, and the condemnation of what it could not but destroy; to resist the movement of history, operating through objective material factors and their effects on—and reflections in—human consciousness, was therefore arbitrary, irrational, literally suicidal. Proudhon, Cabet, Hess, were in this sense "idealists" and utopians, and had condemned themselves to impotence, to what Trotsky was later to call "the rubbish heap of history."

Nevertheless, despite their contempt for their former mentor (and perhaps their jealousy of a forerunner), Marx, and especially Engels, preserved relatively good relations with Hess, made some use of his draft (if only to condemn it) for the *Communist Manifesto* which they composed late in 1847,[9] and treated him with a mixture of patronizing irony and ill-tempered impatience that was due to what all Marxists were later in a chorus to describe as "sentimental and idealistic communism." Hess was too simple and free from amour-propre to react to, or even notice this insulting attitude. He tended to return good for evil, and treated the fathers of "scientific" socialism with deep respect and even loyalty to the end of his life. He saw in them, whatever their faults, indefatigable workers in the cause of justice for the oppressed workers. That was enough for him. Whoever resisted injustice and fought for a freer and better life for all men was his friend and ally.

[9] As also, somewhat earlier, in their *German Ideology*, unpublished in their lifetime, of which with his customary disinterestedness, Hess, who was reviled in other parts of the work, actually seems to have written a section.

After a precarious existence in Paris, eked out by hack work in various German *émigré* journals, he went to Brussels in 1845 and stayed there, on and off, until 1848. He paid visits to Germany, helped Engels to edit a left-wing journal, *Der Gesellschaftsspiegel,* in Elberfeld, and to agitate (they won converts everywhere except among the workers), wrote on the evils inherent in capitalism as the cause of overproduction and misery in the midst of plenty, condemned money as itself a factor in the process of *Entmenschlichung*—turning human beings into goods bought and sold for a price—and was finally dismissed by Marx as a "feeble echo of French socialism and communism with a slight philosophical flavour."

The revolution of 1848 broke out while he was in Germany. His widow later maintained that he had been condemned to death for his part in it, but this is probably a pious invention. The defeat of the revolution did not break his spirit or diminish his faith in mankind. Unlike most of his radical allies in France and Germany, whom the easy victories of Bismarck, the Emperor of Austria and Prince Napoleon, over the forces of democracy left morally and intellectually bankrupt, he neither crossed over to the enemy, nor retreated into the typically *émigré* condition of resentful inactivity broken by occasional efforts to justify one's own conduct and condemn that of everyone else. He wandered over, and starved, in Switzerland, Belgium, Holland, opened a brush shop in Marseilles, and finally returned to Paris in 1854, where after more than twenty years of nomadic life, he finally settled. Living in poverty (alleviated for a short while by an inheritance left him by his father who died in 1851) and supporting himself by casual journalism, the father of German communism continued to believe unswervingly in the classless society, the perfectibility of all mankind, and the part to be played in this by the progress of empirical discovery and invention. He studied anthropology, physiology and the natural sciences in general—for he was convinced that mankind would be regenerated by scientific knowledge applied by men of skill and public spirit. Politically he sympathized with whatever seemed to him to move towards the light. He won the friendship and respect of Ferdinand Lassalle—"the man with the head of Goethe on Jewish shoulders"—and co-operated with him in the creation of his new General Federation of German Workers —the foundation of all organized social democracy in Europe. At the same period he ardently acclaimed the Italian struggle for unity and independence. The Italians, especially Mazzini and his friends, represented the principle of nationalism as he had always understood and believed in it. Hess did not accept the Marxist doctrine of the unreality of nationalism as a basic factor in history. He condemned cosmopolitanism as the deliberate and unnatural suppression of real historical differences which enriched mankind. But he did not see what right any nation had to regard itself as superior to another, and he sharply rejected the Hegelian distinction between the "historic" nations, and those unfortunate "submerged" nationalities, which the more bellicose nations, chosen to "play a historic role" in virtue of their superiority, had a "historic" right to absorb and dominate. Like the eighteenth-century humanist Herder, he believed in the natural differentiation of mankind into separate races or nations. He did not bother to define these concepts, since he thought that they signified something that all sane men recognized, and which had only acquired disreputable associations because of the brutal acts that had been, and still were, committed in their names. He condemned Prussian chauvinism without reserve. He detested Russian expansionism and tyranny. But the desire of the Italians to establish themselves as a free nation in their own land evoked his warmest sympathy. He saw in the Papacy, rather than in foreign invasions, the major cause of Italian backwardness, disunity and economic and spiritual misery, echoing, in this respect, the views of Italian patriots from Machiavelli to our own day. As he reflected about the problems of Italian nationalism, and followed the career of the Italian patriotic movement with the devoted sympathy and admiration that every liberal in Europe (and particularly in England) felt for the followers of Garibaldi and Mazzini, the nature and destiny of his own scattered and "submerged" people—the Jews—once again began to preoccupy his thought. In 1861 he returned to Cologne under a political amnesty granted by the King of Prussia. In 1862 he there published his best and most famous book, *Rome and Jerusalem,* in which his new doctrine was expounded.

Whether Lassalle's national brand of socialism—he was collaborating closely with Lassalle at this time—had influenced him, or whether his ideas grew according to some inner pattern of their own, there is no doubt that he spoke and wrote thereafter like a man who had had a transfiguring experience.[10] Scarcely any notice of his book was taken then, or subsequently, by political specialists or the general European reader. It remained, like Hess himself, outside the central currents of its time. Upon the educated German Jews, however, it fell like a bombshell, as, indeed, it was intended to do. Even today, almost a hundred years after its publication, when much of it is necessarily obsolete, and a great deal that must once have seemed wildly utopian and fanciful, has in fact, sometimes by scarcely perceptible steps, come to pass, it still impresses one as a bold and original masterpiece of social analysis. It is a clear, penetrating, candid, uncompromising book, at once a collection of disturbing home truths calculated to cause acute discomfort to liberal assimilationists among Jews everywhere, and at the same time, and despite its occasional rhetoric, a direct, simple and exceedingly moving profession of faith. It contains a description of the condition of the Jews in the West, a diagnosis of their ills, and a programme for the future. The pinpricks of his cosmopolitan socialist friends evidently no longer affected Hess. He gave expression to a dominant conviction which he had for many years repressed, and which finally proved too strong to stifle, and felt at peace.

Rome and Jerusalem consists of a preface, twelve letters written to a bereaved lady,[11] an epilogue, and ten supplementary notes. It deals with a wide variety of aspects of the same central subject—the Jews, what they are, and what they should be. The

[10] So far as is known at present no single event or experience precipitated Hess's full conversion. In a sense the fate of the Jews was always close to his thoughts, so that perhaps there is no problem here. Yet one feels that something must have caused this crystallization of his beliefs and feelings. Perhaps the eagerly awaited full edition of Hess's letters, when it is published by Professor Silberner, will shed light on this decisive moment in Hess's life.

[11] The lady was, in fact (as Professor Silberner has established), a genuine friend of Hess, but the *genre* is a common vehicle in the nineteenth century for political *pensées*.

essential tone is given near the beginning of the book, in the first letter, in which the author says, "Here I am again, after twenty years of estrangement, in the midst of my people. I take part in its days of joy and sorrow, in its memories and hopes, its spiritual struggles within its own house, and among the civilized peoples in whose midst it lives, but with which, despite two thousand years of common life and effort, it cannot achieve complete unity. One thought which I believed I had extinguished forever within my breast is again vividly present to me: the thought of my nationality, inseparable from the heritage of my fathers and from the Holy land—the eternal city, the birthplace of the belief in the divine unity of life and in the future brotherhood of all men." Hess goes on to assert that nationality is real. Nations are a natural historical growth, like families, like physical types. To deny this is merely to falsify the facts, and springs from unworthy motives of fear and cowardice. In the case of the Jews the ringing phrases that some among them use against nationalism and mediaeval prejudice, are only an attempt to conceal their desire to dissociate themselves from their "unhappy, persecuted, ridiculed people." "The modern liberal Jew is to be despised with his fine words about humanity and enlightenment, intended only to disguise his disloyalty to his brothers." This create a false situation that becomes increasingly unbearable to everyone. Europeans have always regarded the existence of Jews as an anomaly. It may well be that the progress of justice and humanity will one day lead to justice for the Jews: they will perhaps be emancipated, but they will never be respected so long as they act on the principle of *"Ubi bene, ibi patria."*[12] Denial of nationality forfeits everyone's respect. Assimilation is no solution: "It is not the pious old Jew, who would rather have his tongue cut out than misuse it by denying his nationality: it is the modern Jew who is despicable for disowning his race because the heavy hand of fate oppresses it." The banner of enlightenment will not save him from the stern verdict of public opinion. "It is no use pleading various geographical or philosophical alibis." The modern Jew is merely despised for trying to leave what he thinks to be a sinking ship. "You may don a thousand masks, change your name and your religion and your

[12] "Where I do well, there is my country."

mode of life, creep through the world incognito so that nobody
notices that you are a Jew. Yet every insult to the Jewish name
will wound you more than a man of honour who remains loyal
to his family and defends his good name." Some Jews in Germany think that they can save themselves by modernizing their
religion, or, finally, by conversion. But this will not help them.
"Neither reform, nor baptism, neither education nor emancipation, will completely open before the Jews of Germany the doors
of social life." He says again and again that the Germans are
anti-Jewish racially. The tall, blond Germans are much too conscious of the small, dark Jews as being something intrinsically
different from themselves. What the Germans hate is not so
much the Jewish religion or Jewish names as the Jewish noses;
change of faith or name evidently does not help: consequently
what the Jews are tempted to deny is not so much their religion
as their race. But their noses will not vanish, their hair will remain curly, their type has, after all, remained unaltered since
the ancient Egyptian bas-reliefs in which the Semitic type, as we
know it, is quite unmistakable. They are "a race, a brotherhood,
a nation, whose own existence is unfortunately denied by its own
children, and one which every street urchin considers it his duty
to despise, so long as it is homeless." Homelessness is the heart
of this problem: for without soil "a man sinks to the status of
a parasite, feeding on others." All betrayal is base as such. "If it
is true that Jewish emancipation is not compatible with adherence
to the Jewish nation, a Jew ought to give up the former for the
latter." And, still more violently: "Jews are not a religious group,
but a separate nation, a special race, and the modern Jew who
denies this is not only an apostate, a religious renegade, but
a traitor to his people, his tribe, his race." Racial chauvinism—
nationalism in any form—is condemned by Hess in the most
passionate terms, then and later. But to deny one's nation or
race is at least as repulsive as to proclaim its superior rights or
powers. The German Jews cannot understand this. They are
genuinely puzzled by German anti-Semitism. They feel that they
are true patriots, soldiers who have fought for Germany, "Teuto-
maniacs" as fiercely hostile to the French as other Germans.
They sing popular patriotic German songs as fervently as any
Germans; yet when Becker, the author of one of these, insulted

him, Hess, for attempting to set it to music, this was a brutal and deplorable act, as he declares he now realizes, but, in a sense almost instinctive—a natural reaction. Intolerant nationalism is certainly a vice, but one must realize that it is a racial vice; for races exist, and Jews belong to a race which is not that of the Germans. To deny this is to falsify the facts. To be a race or a nation is not to desire racial or national mastery. It is a disease of nationalism to seek to dominate others: but Jews, like other peoples, need a normal national life. Hess goes on to say that the great French historian Augustin Thierry at the beginning of the nineteenth century rightly maintained that history is dominated by the struggles not only of classes, but also of races and na-tionalities. "Semites" and "Teutons" are not mere linguistic cate-gories, although they carry no titles to superiority in themselves. Each race has different and incommensurable gifts, and they can all contribute to the enrichment of mankind. The Aryan race, according to Hess, has the gift of explanation—that of sci-ence, and the gift of creating beauty, a capacity for art. The Semites' genius lies elsewhere—in their ethical insight and in their sense of holiness—in the sanctifying of the world by religion. There are no superior and inferior races. All races must be made free, and then only they will co-operate as equals. Like others, like many Christian and Moslem peoples, the Jews have "slept a deep sleep under gravestones upon which various preach-ers have inscribed their soporific formulae," but the crowing of the Gallic cock "has awakened the kingdom of the sleepers, and the French, the soldiers of progress, will break the grave-stones, and the peoples will begin to rise from their graves. Just as Rome, which since Innocent the Third has been the city of eternal sleep, is today gradually being resurrected as the city of eternal life by the stout hearted patriots who fight for Italian freedom, so Jerusalem too will awake." "The waters of the Tiber —the sound of the victories in North Italy—awake the Jews from their slumbers, and resound in the hills of Zion." He de-clares that he too had been living his life in a dream. It was only in 1840, when the charge of ritual murder was made against the Jews in Damascus, that he himself suddenly realized where the truth lay. "It dawned on me for the first time in the midst of my socialist activities, that I belonged to my unfortunate, slandered, despised and dispersed people," and he goes on to say that he stifled his cry of pain, because of the greater sufferings of the European proletariat to which he thought that he ought to devote his life.

Polish nationalism had evidently made little impression on Hess, since it was bound up with Roman Catholicism, and Rome has been an "inexhaustible well" of anti-Semitic poison. But the awakening of Italy—secular and humanist—had made him realize that the last of all the great national questions, the Jewish question, must finally obtain its solution too. He declares that this question has too long been concealed behind the "fantastic illusions" of rationalists and philanthropists who deny the national character of the Jewish religion. The religious reform movement among the German Jews has done nothing but "bring emptiness into Jewish life, and break off boughs from the Jewish tree." With a shameful lack of pride its leaders tell the Jews to conceal themselves among the other nations. With what result? They change their names, only so that the anti-Semites might dig up their original Jewish names, and fling them in their faces; so that poor Meyerbeer, the composer, is now always called by them Jacob Meyer Lippmann Beer; and Ludwig Börne is always called Baruch, which is, indeed, his real name. Socialists in Germany[13] indulge in this pastime no less than others. This situation is deeply humiliating. Jews have been persecuted and massacred, but in the Middle Ages, by remaining steadfast and faithful to their ancestral values, they at least avoided degradation. Modern Jews, especially those who have changed their names, deserve the contumely which openly or secretly is heaped upon them.

Hess proceeded to be as good as his word. He declared that his first name was henceforth not Moritz but his Hebrew name, Moses.[14] He said that he regretted that he was not called Itzig; nothing was worse than flying under false colours. In a moving passage, early in the book, he says that Moses was not buried in the Holy Land, whereas the bones of Joseph were carried there, because, according to the Rabbis,[15] when Moses presented

---

[13] And, he might have added, France, Russia, and a good many other countries.

[14] His works continued to appear under the non-committal "M. Hess."

[15] He gives as his source the Midrash *Rabba* on Deuteronomy 2.

himself before his future father-in-law, Jethro the priest of Midian, to sue for his daughter's hand, he did not reveal his true origin: he allowed it to be assumed that he was an Egyptian; whereas Joseph revealed himself to his brethren, and never disavowed anyone or anything. One moment of weakness deprived Moses of his right to burial in the land of the ancestors whom he had by his silence denied; so that, according to the Scriptures, no man knows the place of his grave.

What, then, are the Jews to do if they are not to remain sorry hypocrites or worthless nonentities among the nations? Hess affirms that Jews are made Palestinian patriots by their very religion. When his grandfather wept as he read to him Jeremiah's vision of Rachel, in her tomb in Ramah, lamenting over her children as they were carried off before her eyes to the Babylonish captivity; and when he showed him olives and dates, saying with shining eyes, "These come from *Eretz Yisróel*," he was many miles from his native Rhineland. Jews buy Palestine earth, he goes on to say, on which to rest their head when they are buried; they carry sprigs of palm bound in myrtle during the Feast of the Tabernacles; and, he might have added, they pray for rain or dew at the seasons at which their forefathers did so in the Holy land. This is more than a superstition or a dogma. Everything that comes from Palestine, everything that reminds them of it, moves them and is dear to them as nothing else. If the Germans are prepared to accept them only at the price of denying their race, their religion, their temperament, their historical memories, their essential character—then the price is not only morally too high, but not capable of being paid at all: the proposal is both disgusting and impracticable.

Nor is the solution to be found among those fanatical fundamentalists who, with their heads buried in the sand, denounce all science, all aspects of modern secular life. How, he asks, are the Jews to build a bridge between the "nihilism of the reform Rabbis who have learned nothing" and the "conservatism of the orthodox who have forgotten nothing"? There is only one solution, and it awaits the Jews upon the banks of the Jordan. The French nation will aid them. France the great liberator, the first to break the ancient shackles and herald the civil liberties of the Jews like those of other peoples—France must, once she

has built the Suez canal, make it possible for the Jews to establish
colonies on its shores, for without soil (Hess repeats this over
and over again) there is no national life. But who will go to this
barren Eastern country? Not, it is certain, the Jews of the West.
They will stay in the various European lands in which they have
gained education, culture, honourable positions in society. They
are too deeply bound up with Western civilization. They have
lost their vitality as Jews. They will not wish to emigrate to a
remote and barren land. They may place their knowledge, their
wealth, their influence, at the disposal of the immigrants, but they
will not go themselves. For them Palestine will be at best what
Hess calls "a spiritual nerve centre." Universities will arise there,
and a common language which all these immigrants will speak.
Who, then, will go? There can be no doubt of that. The Jews
of Eastern Europe and the other lands where the ancient faith
has kept them solid and insulated from their environment, it is
these and only these that will move.[16] Their vitality is like that
of the corn seeds sometimes found in the graves of Egyptian
mummies: given soil and light and air, they grow and become
fertile again. "Western Jewry is encrusted by the dead residues
of the obsolete products of a decayed rationalism which no inner
force—only a shock from without—can remove; but the rigid
crust of orthodoxy that stunts the progress of Eastern Jewry will
be melted when the sparks of national feeling that smoulder
beneath it are kindled into the sacred fire which heralds the new
spring, and the resurrection of our nation into a new life." The
Jewish assimilationists who detest what they call religious ob-
scurantism desire to root out these superstitions. But to crush
the rabbinical shell in which Judaism is contained is to crush
the seed within. It needs not destruction but earth to grow in.

There follows an extraordinary excursus[17] on the Hassidic
movement. Whereas the Reform movement inspired by Moses
Mendelssohn is an attempt to dilute Judaism and to free the
Jewish people on foreign soil—which is patently impossible—
the great revivalist sect of the Hassidim is a genuine development of the Jewish religion, a response to the authentic need

[16] This surely constitutes one of the most exact true prophecies ever made
about events three quarters of a century later.
[17] Letter VI, note 5.

for life on the part of the devout masses, for fresh significance for old symbols, and therefore destined to a great future. Unlike the Reformers who are using the timber of Judaism for non-Jewish ends, and secretly share Heine's view that the Jewish religion is a misfortune rather than a religion, forgetting that even converted Jews, whether they want it or not, are painfully affected by the condition of the Jewish masses, the Hassidim are a living spiritual force. It is true that Hess confuses the name of the founder of the *Chabad* Hassidim, and speaks of an apocryphal Samuel of Wilno instead of Shneur Zalman. But what is remarkable is that an *émigré* communist agitator should have heard of this movement at all, and have realized at so early a date that the founder of this movement—the Baal Shem—was destined, in the end, to triumph over Moses Mendelssohn. For Hassidism and Zionism were, and are, living forces, as the Reform movement, with all its humanity, civilization, and learning, is not.

It is the benighted beings of whom there are millions in the dominions of the Russian, Prussian, Austrian and Turkish empires, the Jews of these backward provinces, that will, according to Hess, immigrate to Palestine and create the new state. There the existence of Jewish self-identity will neither "need to be demonstrated, nor to be demonstrated away." As for the other Jews, they will, if they wish it, assimilate to the countries of their birth; and in this way, as men who recognize themselves to be of foreign origin and have, by an act of free choice, decided to change their nationality, will obtain more respect than those who pretend that they have no nationality to exchange. Even the Germans who today (that is to say, in the sixties of the last century) despise all "the painstaking efforts of their Jewish fellow citizens to Germanize themselves," and care nothing for all their "cultural achievements" the catalogue of which the latter are forever reciting, will, once the Jews are a nation on their own ancestral soil, give them as a nation that which they refuse to give them as individuals.

But that day may not be near: and in the meanwhile religion is the great preservative of Judaism, and must on no account be diluted or "brought up to date." For Hess the Jewish religion is, in its secular aspect, the foundation of all egalitarianism and socialism: for it recognizes no castes or classes, and assumes the unity of all creation. It allows no feudalism, no social hierarchy, it is just and equal and the true source of the noblest social movements of modern times. It does recognize the principle of nationality, but (so Hess maintained) it excludes chauvinistic nationalism, such as that of Prussia, as morally wrong; yet equally it leaves no room for its contrary—empty and artificial cosmopolitanism which, by denying even the just claims of nationality, falsifies the facts, sets up illusory ideals, and with its bogus prospectus lures innocent men to their doom. The first condition of true internationalism is that there should be nationalities. Internationalism is a movement not to abolish, but to unite, nations. Consequently Hess welcomes the renaissance of Jewish historiography among the German Jews and quotes with approval the names of Weill, Kompert, Bernstein, Wihl, and, above all, Graetz, who became his friend, and from whose history of the Jewish people—"people, let it be noted, not Church or religion"—he copiously and happily quotes.

Everything that had been suppressed by Hess for over twenty years now came welling up. He constantly returns to beliefs instilled in him by his father and grandfather. "I myself, had I a family, would, in spite of my dogmatic heterodoxy, not only join an orthodox synagogue, but would also observe in my home all the feast and fast days, so as to keep alive in my heart, and in the hearts of my children, the traditions of my people."[18] He denounces all forms of adulteration and compromise, all forms of adaptation "to meet the needs of modern times." Prayers must on no account be shortened, nor German versions used instead of Hebrew; Jewish preachers must be held in the greatest honour. What he fears above everything is what he calls "nihilism." The Reform movement he regards as thin and unconvincing, a pathetic and vulgar imitation of Christianity, a counterfeit modern substitute for something ancient and unique. If he must choose, he would rather keep all the six hundred and thirteen rules of the *Shulchan Aruch;* one day a new Sanhedrin, meeting in Jerusalem, may change or abrogate them; until then, the Jews must preserve what they possess—their authentic spiritual heritage, unmodified. He mocks at the fictitious "missions"

18 Letter VII.

which some Jews persuade themselves that they have been called
to perform among the nations—to teach toleration to other
religions, or propagate the doctrine of "pure theism," or even
the arts of commerce. "It is better for the Jew who does not believe in a national regeneration of his people to labour, like an
enlightened Christian of today, for the dissolution of his religion.
I can understand how one can hold this view; what I do not
understand is how one can believe simultaneously in "enlightenment" and in the Jewish mission in exile, that is to say, in the
ultimate dissolution and the continued existence of Judaism at
one and the same time." Do the Jews who wish to sacrifice their
historical past to such abstractions as "Liberty" and "Progress"
really imagine that anyone will be taken in? Does Meyerbeer
really think that anyone besides himself is deceived because he
so carefully avoids Biblical themes in his operas?

Having settled his account with the German Jews, Hess turned
to the practical problem of the colonization of Palestine. He
noted that Rabbi Hirsch Kalischer of Thorn had already drafted
a plan for precisely such a movement[19]; he noted, too, that a
Monsieur Ernest Laharanne, in a book called the *New Oriental
Question,* supported this view. Laharanne, who was employed in
the private office of the Emperor Napoleon III, was a Christian
and a passionate advocate of Zionism. He denounced the rich
emancipated Jews for their indifference, the pious Jews for de-
featism, and declared a state in Palestine to be the only solution
of the Jewish problem; the Sultan and the Pope would doubtless
resist this plan, but he felt sure that free French democracy would
ultimately prevail against both. He spoke of the fundamental
right of the Jews to a historic home, and believed, too optimis-
tically, that the Turks would, for a handful of gold tossed them
by Jewish bankers (or, perhaps, obtained by the nobler expedient
of a democratic subscription from the entire Jewish people), admit large Jewish colonization. He spoke lyrically of the infinite
mystery of Jewish survival, of the fact unparalleled in the history
of mankind, that faced by enemies in every age—Alexandrian
Greeks, Romans, Asiatics, Africans, barbarians, feudal kings,

[19] Kalischer's *Drishat Tsion* appeared a few months before *Rome and
Jerusalem;* like Newton and Leibniz, the two authors knew little of one
another's lines of thought.

grand inquisitors, Jesuits, modern tyrants—they yet survived and multiplied. The French and the Jews must march together, together they must revitalize the parched land of Palestine and rescue it from the terrible Turk. French democracy, Jewish genius, modern science, that was to be the new triple alliance that would at once save an ancient people and revive an ancient land.

Hess, as may be imagined, welcomed this with great enthusiasm. In a characteristically apocalyptic mood, he prophesied that the national solidarity and unity that was the basis of Jewish religion, would gradually make all men one. Natural science would liberate the workers, racial struggles would come to an end, and so, too, would those of classes. Jewish religion and Jewish history (a vast amalgam in which he included the teachings of the Old Testament and the Talmud, the Essenes and Jesus) said to men: "Be of the oppressed and not of the oppressors; receive abuse and return it not; let the motive of all your actions be the love of God, and rejoice in suffering."[20] By this gospel the world would be regenerated; but the first requirement was the establishment of the Jewish state in Palestine. The rich Jews must buy the land and train agricultural experts. The *Alliance Israélite*—a philanthropic body of French Jews—must help Rabbi Natonek of Stuhl-Weissenburg in Hungary, who was ready to interview the Sultan about this plan, armed with a letter of recommendation from the Turkish Ambassador in Vienna. Jewish colonists must be led by men trained in modern methods of thought and action and not by "obscurantist rabbis." The plan was capable of being realized; it must be realized; nothing stood in the way but bigotry and artificial cosmopolitanism, from both of which the majority of the Jews recoiled instinctively. Hess ends his extraordinary sermon on a note of high enthusiasm.

The language of *Rome and Jerusalem*, after a hundred years, seems antiquated. The style is by turns sentimental, rhetorical, and at times merely flat; there are a good many digressions and references to issues now totally forgotten. And yet it is a masterpiece. It lives because of its shining honesty, its fearlessness,

[20] He refers to the passages in the Tractates *Sabbath* 88B; *Yoma* 23A; *Gittin* 36B; as cited in Graetz, Vol. III, Pt. 2, P. 216.

the concreteness of its imagination and the reality of the problem that it reveals. The morbid condition that Hess seeks to diagnose and cure has not vanished; on the contrary, it is as widespread now as in his day, but its symptoms are better known. Consequently the book is, despite its lack of literary talent, not dated. And because it is simple, and not encumbered by the dead formulae and the (by now often meaningless) Hegelian patter that mars some of the most original pages of Marx and his followers, its impact is still exceedingly fresh and direct: it can still provoke sympathy or violent opposition; it remains an analytic and polemical essay of the first order. No one concerned with its central theme can read it with indifference.

Hess had travelled a long way from the violently anti-religious communism and anti-nationalism of his younger days. The fierce attack upon the assimilationist reformers was in part, of course, an attack on his own dead self. The solution consisting in a dignified national dissolution by means of systematic inter-marriage and the education of children in a faith different from one's own, which he now so ferociously denounced, was the very conduct that he himself had earlier advocated. The conscientious internationalism of his young Hegelian days was replaced by the realization (it seems destined to come, late or soon, to almost every Jewish social thinker, whatever his views) that the Jewish problem is something *sui generis,* and seems to need a specific solution of its own, since it resists the solvent of even the most powerful universal panaceas. Nor was this in Hess's case the final reaction of a persecuted and exhausted old socialist, who, tired of waiting for the realization of his universalist dreams, settles for a more limited national solution as a temporary expedient, or returns to the happy, conformist days of his youth as an escape from the excessive burden of the universal social struggle. To think this is to misunderstand Hess profoundly. He was a man who abandoned no belief unless he had convinced himself by rational methods that it was false. His Zionism did not cause him to abandon socialism. He evidently felt no incompatibility between communist ideals and belief in a Jewish national *Risorgimento.* Hess was not, like Hegel or Marx, a historical thinker of genius who broke with previous tradition, perceived relationships hitherto unnoticed (or at least not clearly described), imposed his vision on mankind, and transformed the categories in terms of which human beings think of their situation, their past, and their destiny. But neither did he suffer from the defects of these despotic system builders. He was intellectually (as indeed in every other respect) a man of complete integrity and did not, for any psychological or tactical reason, try to force the facts into some preconceived dogmatic pattern. The strongest single characteristic of his writings, especially of his later works, is a pure-hearted devotion to the truth, expressed with candid, at times childlike, simplicity. It is this that makes his words often devastating, and causes them to linger in the memory longer than the richer and weightier sentences of the more celebrated prophets of the age.

Hess abandoned neither socialism nor Zionism because he saw no incompatibility between them. His socialism—which was nothing but desire for social justice and a harmonious life—did not, any more than Lassalle's, preclude nationality. He could conceive of no inevitable collision between purposes or policies that seemed true, responded to genuine needs, and were morally good. It did not so much as occur to him that modern Jews should be prevented or even dissuaded from, let us say, the celebration of the Feast of the Passover, or the fulfilment of other religious duties, because these were obsolete survivals or superstitions that had nothing in common with an enlightened scientific outlook. He took it for granted that one truth and one value could not require the suppression of another: hence the moral values of socialism, and the truths embodied in a sense of one's individual social national human past, could not possibly, if correctly conceived, ever clash. Life would be sadly and quite gratuitously, impoverished by the sacrifice of anything good or true or beautiful. It is this "idealism," this "naïveté," that the tougher-minded revolutionaries derided in his day much as they do in ours.

After being Lassalle's representative in Cologne, and five years after publishing *Rome and Jerusalem*—to the theses of which he remained unwaveringly faithful to the end of his days—in 1867 Hess joined the International Working Men's Association, founded, as everyone knows, by his old comrade in arms and

remorseless denigrator, Karl Marx. He represented the workers
of Berlin in the First International, and in 1868 and 1869, as a
Marxist delegate, fought the representatives of Proudhon and of
Bakunin, old friends whom he deeply admired, because he
thought that their doctrines would disrupt working class unity.
He never became an orthodox Marxist. He still did not believe
in violence or class warfare as an inescapable historical category;
and he was a full-fledged Zionist *avant la parole*. But he was a
socialist, and when he spoke of the Jewish state in Palestine, he
declared that the soil of that country must be acquired by the
Jews acting as a single national whole in order to prevent private
exploitation. Similarly he regarded full legal protection of labor
among the future colonists as a *sine qua non,* and declared that
the organization of industry, agriculture and trade must follow
Mosaic—which for him was synonymous with socialistic—principles. He wanted to see in the new Jewish state workers' co-
operatives of the type organized by Lassalle in Germany, state-
aided until such time as the proletarians formed a majority of the
inhabitants of Palestine, when the state would automatically,
peacefully, and without revolution, become a socialist commonwealth.

All these ideas met, it may well be imagined, with an exceedingly hostile reception among educated Jews, particularly
those German Liberal Jews against whom Hess's sharpest sallies
were directed. Such words had certainly never before been addressed to them. Jews in Germany had for almost a century
been much adjured and much discussed. Mendelssohn and his
followers had accused them of clinging senselessly to the ghetto
for its own sake, of blind avoidance of the magnificent opportunity of entering the world of Western culture that was at last
open to receive them. The orthodox charged them with godless-
ness, with heresy and sin. They were told to cling to their
ancient faith; to abandon it; to adjust it to modern life; to dilute
it; to emulate German culture by critical examination of their
own antiquities; to be historians, scholars, higher critics; to enter
Western civilization by their own door; by doors already built by
others; not to enter it at all. But in this great babel of voices, no
one had yet proposed to them to recognize themselves for what
they were—a nation: odd, *sui generis,* but still a nation; and

therefore to give up nothing, avoid self-deception, not to seek to persuade themselves that what was not theirs and had never been theirs, was dearer to them than what was truly their own, not to offer up, with pain and an unbearable sense of shame, what alone they could truly love, their own habits, outlook, memories, traditions, their history, their pride, their sense of identity as a nation, all that they, like other peoples, were and lived by, everything indeed, that they could respect in themselves or others respected in them. Others—Englishmen, Frenchmen, Italians—probably understood this better than the emancipated Jews to whom Hess spoke. "No people struggling for its country can deny the Jewish people the right to its own land without the most fatal inconsistency," he wrote. And so, in the twentieth century, it duly and honourably turned out. But in the circumstances of the time his words were wounding to many, not least because they were true. "Educated parvenus in Christian society" he called his opponents with more bitterness than justice. He poured vinegar in their wounds with the bitter zeal of a convert turning upon the blind mass from which he is sprung. Their reaction may well be imagined. The most eminent German Jewish scholar of the day, Steinschneider, expressed himself with comparative moderation, and called Hess a repentant sinner,[21] adding the hope that the book would not be exploited by the enemies of the Jews already in Palestine. The celebrated scholar, and publicist, the advocate of Reform Judaism, Abraham Geiger, whose disavowal of nationality and intense efforts to feel and think like a Hegelian German of Jewish persuasion Hess had pilloried in telling language, reacted with understandable hostility: "An old romantic with new reactionary plans," he called the author, and condemned his book root and branch. "An almost complete outsider," he went on to say in his anonymous review, "who, after bankruptcy as a socialist, and all kinds of swindles, wants to make a hit with nationalism . . . and along with the questions of restoring Czech and Montenegrin nationality, etc. . . . wants to revive that of the Jews." *Die Allgemeine Zeitung des Judenthums* said, "We are first and foremost Germans, Frenchmen, Englishmen, Americans—only then Jews. . . . The growth of

21 *"Ein Baal Teschuva."*

civilization will cause desire for Palestine to evaporate among the Eastern Jews."[22] So the debate—which even now is by no means closed—began, more than thirty years before the word Zionism had been so much as heard of. The *Alliance Israélite Universelle* cautiously opened its journal, the *Archives Israélites,* to Hess, and offered tepid support. The *Alliance* was attracted by the notion of having so well known a publicist on its side, but was frightened of the notion of organized immigration to Palestine, although it was prepared to support such Jews as had already found their way there as the result of such minor efforts to colonize Palestine as were already, at that time, beginning to be made.

The scandal caused by the book duly died down. Like Hess's earlier works, it had, as far as can be determined, no influence at all. The return of the Jews to Palestine had, after all, been spoken of not only by pious Jews or Christian visionaries, but by the great Napoleon himself at the time of his Egyptian campaign, by Fichte, by the Russian revolutionary Decembrist Pestel, who, like Fichte, wished to rid Europe of the Jews, by the French-Jewish publicist Joseph Salvador, by the eccentric English traveller Laurence Oliphant, by Rabbi Kalischer, and other obscurer figures. It is possible that George Henry Lewes, who had met Hess in Paris, had spoken of his views to George Eliot and so inspired her novel *Daniel Deronda,* with its Jewish nationalist hero. But all this was of no account in a world where no one except, perhaps, a few groups of Jews scattered in Eastern Europe (and, oddly enough, Australia) took such matters seriously. Hess was not destined to see in his own lifetime even the beginning of the fulfillment of his ideals.

The rest of his life is characteristic enough. Like other impoverished *émigré* journalists, he acted as correspondent of various German and Swiss journals, as well as the Chicago German weekly *Die Illinois Staats-Zeitung,* for which he wrote from 1865 a series of despatches which show a grasp of European affairs scarcely inferior to those of the *New York Tribune's* European

[22] I owe these quotations to a valuable article by Mr. Israel Cohen, entitled "Moses Hess, Rebel and Prophet," published in *The Zionist Quarterly* (New York), Fall 1951.

correspondent—Karl Marx—and far greater powers of accurate prediction of events.[23] He was dismissed from it in 1870 ostensibly for excessive interest in politics in which his German-American readers were held to have too little interest. In the same year, on the outbreak of the Franco-Prussian war he was expelled from Paris as a Prussian citizen, although, as may be imagined, he denounced Bismarck's aggression with all his might, and called upon the Jews to give their sympathies to France— the cradle of liberty and fraternity, the home of revolution and all humane ideals. He went to Brussels where he called for an alliance of all free peoples against "Prussianized Germany," a country intent on destroying France, only because France wanted to make humanity happier. In 1875 he died, as for the most part he had lived, in obscurity and poverty, an unworldly isolated figure, and by his own wish was buried in the Jewish cemetery in Deutz by the side of his parents. His posthumous work, *Die Dynamische Stofflehre*, was published by his devoted wife in 1877 as a pious monument to his memory. She declared it to be his life's work, but it is a confused, half philosophical half scientific, speculation of no interest or value today.[24] His real life's work is the simple and moving book which still contains more truth about the Jews, both in the nineteenth century and in our own, than any comparable work. Like its author, it was all but forgotten until events themselves rescued both from unjust oblivion. Today streets are called after him in the two principal cities of the State of Israel: nothing would have surprised or delighted him more greatly. After 1862 he was a Jew first and a Marxist second; he would, I suspect, have considered the systematic disparagement of his ideas and personality by Engels and his imitators as more than made up for by the recognition given him by the Jewish state in which he believed with his whole being. Yet nothing seemed less likely during his lifetime.

[23] The evidence for Hess's gifts as a political prophet, as well as much else of interest, may be found in *"Tribun und Prophet"* by Dr. Helmut Hirsch, *International Review of Social History*, Vol. 2, Pt. 2. (Assen, Netherlands, 1957). See also the admirable *Denker und Kämpfer* by the same author.
[24] Hess's only biographer, Dr. Theodor Zlocisti, in *Moses Hess, Der Vorkämpfer des Sozialismus und Zionismus* (Berlin, 1921) thinks otherwise, and calls him a forerunner of modern atomic theory.

Like other intellectually honest, morally sensitive and un-
frightened men, Moses Hess turned out to have a deeper understanding of some essential matters than more gifted and
sophisticated social thinkers. In his socialist days—and they only
ceased with his death—he said that the abolition of property
and the destruction of the middle classes did not necessarily and
automatically lead to paradise; for they did not necessarily
cure injustice or guarantee social or individual equality. This was
a bold and original view for a socialist of those days. His allies
were, for the most part, men dominated by a desire for a clear-
cut social structure, and a rationalist, rather than rational, desire
to solve social problems in almost geometrical, black and white
terms. Like their forerunners in the eighteenth century, but
armed with different hypotheses, they tried to treat history as an
exact science, and to deduce from the study of it some unique
plan of action guaranteed to make men forever free, equal,
happy and good. In this dogmatic and intolerant milieu Hess
permitted himself to doubt whether any solution could, in principle, achieve this, unless and until the men who built the new
world themselves lived by the principles of justice, and felt
benevolence and love towards individual human beings and not
merely humanity at large, that is to say, were endowed with a
character and an outlook which no amount of social and political
reform could of itself secure. It is surely a sign of immaturity
(even though it may be evidence of a noble and disinterested
nature) to stake everything on any one final solution to social
problems. When to such immaturity there is added a ruthless will,
and a genius for organization which enables its possessor to
force human beings into patterns unrelated to their nature and
their own wishes, then what starts as pure and disinterested
idealism inevitably ends in oppression, cruelty and blood. A
sense of symmetry and regularity, and a gift for vigorous deduction, that are pre-requisites of aptitude for some natural sciences,
will, in the field of social organization, unless they are modified
by a great deal of sensibility, understanding and humanity, inevitably lead to appalling bullying on the one side and untold
suffering on the other. Even though he knew that he would be
mercilessly denounced for stupidity, ignorance and irresponsible
utopianism by his admired, tyrannical comrades in arms, Marx

and Engels, Hess could not bring himself to view the world through their distorting spectacles. He did not accept their view of man's nature. He believed in the permanent and universal validity of certain general human values. To the end of his days he firmly believed that human feeling, natural affections, the desire for social justice, individual freedom and solidarity within historically continuous groups—families or religious associations or nationalities—were to be valued as being good in themselves. He did not think that these deep human interests, however they might be modified in space or time, were necessarily altered by historical evolution or conditioned by class consciousness or by any other relatively transient phenomenon to anything like the decisive extent of which the so-called scientific Marxists spoke. As for the relative value and importance of the desire for national independence, it is perhaps enough to point to recent events in Hungary, in Poland and elsewhere[25] for evidence that the orthodox Marxist interpretation of national feeling and its lack of influence upon the working classes of a nation conspicuously no longer capitalist, contains fallacies that have proved tragic enough to many of those involved in them. These are merely the latest and most spectacular examples of truths which Hess saw more clearly than his comrades, without the slightest trace of chauvinism or morbid nationalism, and, let it be added, in the context of the extreme left-wing socialism of which he was one of the purest and most eloquent proponents. This alone seems to me to establish that his claims, even as a social theorist, as against his critics, are not too difficult to sustain, and that his significance has been for many years systematically underestimated by faithful Marxists[26] to the

[25] This was spoken in 1957.
[26] E.g., by Monsieur Auguste Cornu, in his scholarly and lucid *Moses Hess et la gauche Hégélienne* (Paris, 1934), who treats Hess as a minor and somewhat slow-witted precursor of Marx, whose views had been rendered obsolete by Marxism. Monsieur Cornu's later works go even further in this respect. This is in effect also the view of Georg Lukács in his article *"M. Hess und die Probleme der Idealistichen Dialektik," Archiv für die Geschichte des Sozialismus und der Arbeiterbewegung,* Jahrgang XII (Leipzig, 1926). I. Goitein in his contribution to the same volume, *"Probleme der Gesellschaft und des Staates bei M. Hess,"* shows far more insight.

greater glory of their own creed, but at the expense of the facts of history.

In his view of the Jewish question (as it used to be called) Hess's predictions have proved to be almost uncannily accurate. Thus, in one of his more sibylline passages, he declares that the liberal Jews of Germany will one day suffer a cataclysm the extent of which they cannot begin to conceive. Nobody will deny that, at any rate, this prophecy has proved to be only too horribly verified. Similarly Hess preached against assimilation in its hey-day, and all that he said about the false position into which the assimilators had put both themselves and their victims, seems to me to have been wholly vindicated by the events that followed. No one can today pretend not to know what Hess had meant by his references to "philosophical or geographical or historical alibis" behind which Jews (or other human beings) try to make out that they are not what they most conspicuously are because they cannot face embarrassing truths about themselves; thereby deceiving only themselves, causing discomfort or shame to their friends, and amusement or contempt, and, in the end, hatred, on the part of their enemies. Hess had observed that the Jews were in fact a nation, however skilfully definitions were juggled to prove that they were not, and he said so in simple, and, to some, startling and even shocking language. Yet it seems clear that the State of Israel, whatever attitude may be adopted towards it, could not have come into being if the Jews had in fact been not such as he, but as his opponents supposed them to be, whether they were orthodox rabbis, or liberal assimilationists, or doctrinaire communists. He has, furthermore, proved to be right in supposing that the Western Jews would not, of their own volition, choose to emigrate, whatever the difficulties they encountered in their various communities, because, in the end, they were too happy, too comfortable, too well integrated in them. Although, like his friend Heine, he had to some degree anticipated the development of German barbarism, yet Hitler was far beyond anything that either had imagined; and Hess had, therefore, on the evidence available in his day, correctly assumed that it was the Eastern and not the German Jews who would be driven both by their internal solidarity and by economic desperation to new worlds, and in particular to the creation of an autonomous community in Palestine. He believed in natural science applied to create social welfare; he believed in co-operatives, communal endeavour, state ownership, or, at any rate, public ownership. A large degree—larger than is pleasing to those who favor other forms of social organization—of these principles have today been realized in the State of Israel. He believed deeply in the faithful preservation of historical tradition. He spoke about this in language scarcely less fervent, but a good deal less biased and irrational, than Burke or Fitchte. He did so not because he feared change—he was after all a radical and a revolutionary—but because through his most extreme and radical beliefs there persists a conviction that there is never any duty to maim or impoverish oneself for the sake of an abstract ideal; that nobody can, or should be required to vivisect himself, to throw away that which affords him the deepest spiritual satisfaction known to human beings—the right to self-expression, to personal relationships, to the love of familiar places or forms of life, of beautiful things, or the roots and symbols of one's own, or one's family's, or one's nation's past. He believed that nobody should be made to sacrifice his own individual pattern of the unanalysable relationships—the central emotional or intellectual experiences—of which human lives are compounded, to offer them up, even as a temporary expedient, for the sake of some tidy solution, deduced from abstract and impersonal premises, some form of life derived from an alien source, imposed upon men by artificial means, and felt to be the mechanical application of some general rule to a concrete situation for which it was not made. All that Hess, towards the end of his life, wrote or said, rests on the assumption that to deny what inwardly one knows to be true, to do violence to the facts for whatever tactical or doctrinal motive, is at once degrading and doomed to futility. The foundations of his beliefs, both socialist and Zionist, were unashamedly moral. He was convinced, moreover, as a matter of empirical knowledge, that moral beliefs played a major role in human affairs.

The socialist morality that he so pure-heartedly preached, as well as the type of nationalism that he idealized, have, on the whole, proved more enduring and productive of human freedom and happiness than the more "realistic" solutions of his more Machiavellian rivals, both on the right and on the left. For this reason he is to be counted among the genuine prophets of our own day who said much that was novel, true, and of still the first importance. This is the title to immortality of "the communist Rabbi," the friend of Heine and Michelet, the man whom Karl Marx, in his rare moments of high good humour, used to call "the donkey, Moses Hess."

BARBARISM THE FIRST DANGER

Horace Bushnell

JUDGES XVII. 13.

THEN SAID MICAH, NOW KNOW I THAT THE
LORD WILL DO NO GOOD, SEEING I HAVE A
LEVITE TO MY PRIEST.

A very unimportant chapter of biography is here preserved to
us—save that if we take the subject as an exponent of his
times, we shall find a serious and momentous truth illustrated
in his conduct. He lives in the time of the Judges, that is, in the
emigrant age of Israel. It is the time, when his nation are passing
through the struggles incident to a new settlement, a time therefore of decline towards barbarism. Public security is gone. The
people have run wild. Superstition has dislodged the clear sovereignty of reason. Forms are more sacred than duties, and a
costly church furniture is taken as synonymous with a godly life.
It is at just such times that we are to look for the union of great
crimes and scrupulous acts of devotion. The villain and the
saint coalesce, without difficulty, in one and the same character;
and superstition, which delights in absurdities, hides the im-
posture from him who suffers it. Thus Micah enters on the stage
of history as a thief, having stolen eleven hundred shekels of
silver from his mother; but before the scene closes, he becomes,
at least in his own view, quite a saint; and that too, if we may
judge, without any great detriment to his former character.

Finding that his mother has invoked a solemn curse upon the thief, whoever he may be, that has stolen her money; and also, which is more frightful still, that she had actually dedicated the money, before it was stolen, to a religious use, even to make a molten image for himself, the superstitious fancy of the barbarian begins to worry his peace. To have stolen the money was nothing specially dreadful, but to have a parent's curse hanging over his head, and sacred money hid in his house—both considered to involve the certainty of some impending mischief that is fatal—is more than he has courage to support. Moved, of course, by no ingenuous and dignified spirit of repentance, but only by a drivelling superstition, he goes to his mother and chokes out his confession, saying: "The silver is with me, I took it"! And what a beautiful evidence of piety, thinks the glad mother, that her Micah was afraid to keep the sacred money! So she pours out her dear blessing on him, saying: "Blessed be thou of the Lord, my son"! Then she takes the silver and from it has a molten image cast for her worthy and hopeful son, which he sets up in "the house of his gods," among the teraphim and other trumpery there collected. And as Micah is now growing religious, he must also have a priest. First, he consecrates his own son; but his son not being a Levite, it was difficult for so pious a man to be satisfied. Fortunately, a young Levite—a strolling mendicant probably—comes that way, and he promptly engages the youth to remain and act the padre for him, saying: "Dwell with me and be a *father* unto me." Having thus got up a religion, the thief is content, and his mental troubles are quieted. Becoming a Romanist before Rome is founded, he says: "Now know I that the Lord will do me good, seeing I have a Levite to my priest." That it would do him any good to be a better man, does not appear to have occurred to him. Religion, to him, consisted rather in a fine silver apparatus of gods and a priest in regular succession!

Set now the picture in its frame, the man in connection with his times, and you have in exhibition a great practical truth, which demands your earnest study. Nothing is more certain, as you may see in this example of Micah and his times, than that *emigration, or a new settlement of the social state, involves a tendency to social decline.* There must, in every such case, be a relapse towards barbarism, more or less protracted, more or less complete. Commonly, nothing but extraordinary efforts in behalf of education and religion, will suffice to prevent a fatal lapse of social order. Apart from this great truth, clearly seen as enveloped in the practical struggles of our American history, no one can understand its real import, the problem it involves, or the position at which we have now arrived. Least of all can he understand the sublime relation of home missions, and other like enterprises, to the unknown future of our great nation. He must know that we are a people trying out the perils incident to a new settlement of the social state; he must behold religion passing out into the wilds of nature with us, to fortify law, industry and good manners, and bear up our otherwise declining fortunes, till we become an established and fully cultivated people. Just here, hang all the struggles of our history for the two centuries now past, and for at least another century to come.

We shall also discover, in pursuing our subject, in what manner we are to apprehend danger from the spread of Romanism. If you seem to struggle, in this matter of Romanism, with contrary convictions; to see reason in the alarms urged upon you so frequently, and yet feel it to be the greatest unreason to fear the prevalence here of a religion so distinctively opposite to our character and institutions; if you waver between a feeling of panic and a feeling of derision; if you are half frighted by the cry of Romanism, and half scorn it as a bugbear; you will be able to settle yourself into a sober and fixed opinion of the subject, when you perceive that we are in danger, first, of something far worse than Romanism, and through that of Romanism itself. OUR FIRST DANGER IS BARBARISM—Romanism next; for before we can think it a religion, to have a Levite to our priest, we must bring back the times of the Judges. Let us empty ourselves of our character, let us fall into superstition, through the ignorance, wildness and social confusion incident to a migratory habit and a rapid succession of new settlements, and Romanism will find us just where character leaves us. The real danger is the prior. Taking care of that we are safe. Sleeping over that, nothing ought to save us; for if we must have a wild race of nomads roaming over the vast western territories of our land—a race without education, law, manners or religion—we need not trouble ourselves farther on account of Romanism; for to such a people, Romanism, bad as it is, will come as a blessing.

I shall recur to this question of Romanism again. I only name it here as a preliminary, that may assist you to apprehend the true import of my subject. Let us now proceed to the question itself: How far emigration and a continual re-settlement, as in this country, involves a tendency to moral and social disorganization? In the discussion of this question, I shall draw principally on the facts of history; I only suggest here, as a preparative and key to the facts that may be cited, a few of the reasons why such a decline is likely to appear.

First of all, the society transplanted, in a case of emigration, cannot carry its roots with it; for society is a vital creature, having roots of antiquity, which inhere in the very soil—in the spots consecrated by valor, by genius and by religion. Transplanted to a new field, the emigrant race lose, of necessity, a considerable portion of that vital force which is the organific and conserving power of society. All the old roots of local love and historic feeling—the joints and bands that minister nourishment—are left behind; and nothing remains to organize a living growth, but the two unimportant incidents, proximity and a common interest.

Education must, for a long time, be imperfect in degree and partial in extent. There is no literary atmosphere breathing through the forests or across the prairies. The colleges, if any they have, are only rudimental beginnings, and the youth a raw company of woodsmen. Hurried into life, at the bar, or in the pulpit, when as yet they are only half educated, their performances are crude in the matter and rough in the form. No matter how cultivated the professional men of the first age, those of the second, third and fourth will mix up extravagance and cant in all their demonstrations, and will be acceptable to the people partly for that reason. For the immense labors and rough hardships necessary to be encountered, in the way of providing the means of living, will ordinarily create in them a rough and partially wild habit.

Then, as their tastes grow wild, their resentments will grow violent and their enjoyments coarse. The salutary restraints of society being, to a great extent, removed, they will think it no degradation to do before the woods and wild animals, what, in the presence of a cultivated social state, they would blush to perpetrate. They are likely even to look upon the indulgence of low vices and brutal pleasures, as the necessary garnish of their life of adventure.

In religion, their views will, of course, be narrow and crude, and their animosities bitter. Sometimes the very life of religion will seem about to die, as it actually would, save that some occasional outburst of over-wrought feeling or fanatical zeal kindles a temporary fire. Probably it will be found that low superstitions begin to creep in, a regarding of dreams, a faith in the presentation of scripture texts, in apparitions and visions, perhaps also in necromancy.

Mean time, if we speak of civil order, it will probably be found that the old common law of the race is not transplanted as a vital power, but only as a recollection that refuses to live, because of the newness of the soil, and the varied circumstances which, in so many ways, render it inapplicable. It asks for loyalty where there is no demesne, offers a jury before there is a court, and sanctifies a magna charta where no plain of Runnymede is ever to be known. Hence, the need of much new legislation, consequently much of confusion and a considerable lapse of time, before the new body of law, with its tribunals and uses, can erect its trunk and grow up into life from a native root. Mean time, it is well if the social wildness and the violent resentments of the people do not break over all the barriers of legal restraint, and dissolve the very bonds of order.

If now, beside all the causes here enumerated, the emigrants are much involved in war to maintain their possessions, or if they are gathered from many nations having different languages, laws, manners, and religions, the tendency to social decline is, of course, greatly aggravated. Indeed, where all the forms of habit, prejudice and opinion are found to impinge upon each other, and every recollection of the past, every peculiar trait of national feeling and personal character requires to be obliterated, before it is possible for the new elements to coalesce, what can save a people, we are tempted to ask, from being precipitated downward even below society itself!

Having glanced, in this rapid manner, at the causes of decline theoretically involved in emigration, (for emigration works no mischief by itself, but only as it provokes the malignant action of other causes,) let us now pass to some historic illustrations. And I begin with the emigration headed by Abraham, where the facts are already familiar, so that when you are engaged in tracing their import as illustrations of my subject, your minds will be distracted by no effort of attention to conceive the facts themselves.

There was never an emigration conducted under better auspices. As in the original settlement of New England, the aim and purpose of the movement were strictly religious. The emigrants, too, were shepherds in their habit, never attached to the soil, but accustomed to movement. They came out also as a family, for Lot appears to have been only a ward of Abraham; and in the family state—which is itself a patriarchate, the simplest and most unquestionable of all governments, as it is closest to nature—they had a complete frame of social order already provided. Though trained as a nomad and manifestly ignorant of certain moral distinctions familiar to us, Abraham yet evinces, in his character, a degree of beauty and princely dignity, such as seldom can be found under the politer forms of civilization. In his heroic pursuit and slaughter of the kings to rescue Lot, in the singular dignity of his meeting with Melchisedec on his return, in the generous and conciliatory terms by which he sought to avoid the quarrel already begun between Lot's herdsmen and his own, in his hospitality at the tent door in Mamre, in his burial of Sarah, in the whole manner of his life in short there is a grand, massive nobility of character, which, if we cannot call it civilization or refinement, is yet only so much higher and more charming, as it is closer to nature, more original and older than the days of accomplished heartlessness and drawing-room pretence. It is the pure, virgin character of a great and primitive manhood, which, in the simple, godly life of the east country, was not yet spent.

See now what a mass of barbarism is shortly developed out of this fair beginning. The character of Lot is not strongly fortified by religious principle, and the restraints of society being now removed, he soon falls into loose habits of virtue and, in the end, brings himself and his family to a very sorry figure. Thus out of Lot springs the wild race of the Moabites, a race as degraded in character, as the abominable and filthy rites of their god Baal Peor require them to be—enemies, of course, to Jehovah and the kindred stock of Israel, in all after times. The Ammonites are a branch of the same stock.

Mean time, Abraham himself is throwing off upon the world, in his son Ishmael, another stock of barbarians. Driven out with his mother, to seek his fortune as he may, among the wild tribes of idolaters that infest the country, the lad, we are told, grows up in the wilderness and becomes an archer. By which it appears that he betook himself to some secret cave or fastness, in the south, and there, by the use of his bow as a hunter and robber, maintained himself, and became the father of the Bedouin race. There he trained up the young Ishmaelites, otherwise called Arabs—a name which, according to some, signifies *westerners*—a prolific, talented, and powerful race of men, whose nature it has been to this hour to live by plunder, whose hand is against every man and every man's hand against them. Thus you have another wild people, a cruel, treacherous, lying stock of thieves and idolaters developed out of the emigration.

One generation later, viz.:—out of the family of Isaac, comes another. I speak of the persecuted Esau and the Idumeans or Edomites descended of him. These were a warlike and ferocious race, governed by dukes or great captains, and for long ages the sturdiest of all the enemies of Israel.

It is remarkable too that, when David is giving the roll, in one of his Psalms, of the great league of nations that were conspiring, at that time, against his country, he puts at the head of all precisely these three fierce and barbarous people, descended of Terah, the common ancestor both of them and of his countrymen. "For they have consulted together with one consent, they are confederate against thee, the tabernacles of Edom and the Ishmaelites, of Moab and the Hagarenes." Then follow the other nations who are led by these.

Mean time, if we consider the dastardly conduct of the ten brothers of Joseph, who for jealousy sell him into slavery, and then, by a solemn lie, convince their father that he is dead— remembering also and holding in comparison Abraham's noble and magnanimous treatment of Lot—we shall see that there has certainly been a very great falling off towards barbarism, in the chosen family itself.

But we must follow them further, even into this book of Judges, where they come to make their final settlement in the land. In Egypt they had become acquainted with agriculture, with cities and the settled modes of life; though degraded, to some extent, by their temporary subjection to slavery. But their freedom, connected with their strong legal discipline under Moses, the new sentiments and new social capacities, which had been formed under this protracted discipline of forty years, during which the old generation of slavery had become extinct, had prepared them to enter the country appointed and make a fair beginning. They took their places; for a time all was well. Still they were a people without roots, and they began, ere long, to fall into social anarchy. They served the Lord all the days of Joshua, and all the days of the elders that had overlived Joshua and had seen all the great works of the Lord that he did for Israel, and when that generation were gathered unto their fathers—so says the history—there arose another generation, which knew not the Lord, nor yet the works which he had done for Israel. Now came the dark time; for in every emigration, the moral and social trial commonly falls, not on the first generation, but more frequently on the second, third and fourth. So it was here, and it really seemed that the nation must utterly die, before it could get root. Three times it is said in the history, that "there was no king in Israel and that every man did what was right in his own eyes." By which we are to understand, not that royalty was discontinued, for it had not existed; but that there was no civil head, that government was utterly dissolved. It was, in truth, the paradisaic age of no government; a day when they had it, not for a theory, but for a fact. Wrongs were redressed by uprisings of popular impatience, by assassination or private revenge. In one case of outrage, which may be taken doubtless as a good specimen of the barbarity of the times, the tribes were roused to vengeance, in the manner of a riot, by sending round, as a proclamation, the pieces of a murdered woman's body! If at any time they had a government, it was commonly the government of a usurper, who butchered, as he

came into power, after the method of the Turks, all the families
that had any semblance of right to civil precedence, or any
possible hope of succession. The roads were destroyed, and there
was no passage through the country, save in by-ways, or across
the fields and mountains. The arts perished; there was not even
a smith left in the land, and they were obliged to go down to
the Philistines to get an axe or a mattock sharpened. In one
case, they fought a battle with ox goads, because they had no
better implements. Their religion being all one with the laws,
fell of course into the same confusion with them. As we see in
the case of Micah, Jehovah and the gods, all stand upon a par!
They have their molten images set up together in "the house of
the gods," to be smoked by the same incense; and Micah's
Levite probably has it for his duty to practice before them all!
Such is the decline suffered by this emigrant nation, in the
process of colonizing a new region and building up a new social
fabric. But dismal as the picture is to which they have descended,
we have it for our comfort, that they are not utterly lost. After
they have sounded the lowest notes of misery and social de-
basement, a Samuel appears, collects the scattered elements,
works them gradually towards order, and the new nation, taking
root, begins to rise.

Passing over now the instructive lessons that might be drawn
from the Egyptian, Grecian, Carthaginian and Roman colonies,
we descend to the great American question itself. That the Mexican and the South American States have actually lost ground,
since the emigration; that they have been descending steadily
towards barbarism, in the loss of the old Castilian dignity, in the
decay of society and manners, and the general prostration of
order, is well understood. But it is commonly supposed, I believe, that our North American settlements, especially those of
New England, have never suffered any similar retrogradation;
that they have, on the contrary, steadily advanced or ascended
to their present state. No impression could be more opposite to
the real facts of history. Probably never before did any emigrant
people resist, with so great promptitude and effect, the inherent
causes of decline involved in a new state of society. Nor can it
be said that the issue was ever doubtful. Indeed I am not sure
that, if we consider the *rough amount* of character in the whole

community, any real diminution was ever suffered. For if much was lost in the complete finish of the higher class, something was also gained in the sharpness, vigor, and capacity of the lower. And if there was even a decay of virtue and good manners in all classes, there was yet a gain in all, as regards spirit, self-reliance, physical endurance, and other like traits, which are essential as the staple of a perfect manhood. If there was more coarseness, so possibly there was more volume. If there was less of learning, there was also a more perfect deliverance from the restraints of learning. If they had less of society, they had as much more of action. If they finished nothing, they created more. But in taking such a view as this, which is the most favorable permitted us, it is implied, as will be observed by all, that there was, in certain very important respects, a marked decline.

This decline was most evident in the higher class, and in the cultivated manners and tastes, brought over by the emigrant families. The leading spirits of the first age were truly great and cultivated men—cedars of Lebanon, nay, the topmost branches of the cedars, that God had brought over to plant by the waters of the new world. They were many of them scholars, who had received at the English universities, the highest advantages of culture furnished in that age. Their minds were matured and polished by severe study. They knew society. Some of them were persons who had travelled in foreign countries, who had figured in civil stations and were not unskilled even as courtiers. They were fellow disciples and compatriots with such men as Owen, Howe, Milton, John Hampden, Oliver Cromwell and the other great spirits, who were struggling in that age for the civil and religious emancipation of their country. But they came into the wilderness, as it were to be tempted of the devil, throwing themselves and their families, for a whole century to come, upon the severest struggles of toil and warfare, to provide and fortify their new home. For a long time, they had no market. In their modes of dress, their residences and their furniture, they were many of them restricted to supplies that were coarse and rude. Their means of education for the youth were defective, in that which is necessary to a finished and really accomplished character, though sufficient to give a good degree of rudimental force. And, more than all, society, that indefinable but powerful something, which gives a tone of refinement to literary tastes, and without which, feeling cannot rise to its highest dignity—this was a want, which no industry or care could supply. The trials and exposures were rough, the great world was far away, petty strifes and bickerings—always enveloped in the ill nature of the race, but restrained among a great people under the established forms of cultivated life—broke out and raged in their little communities. A painful subsidence of manners soon began to appear. In many families, a certain flavor of refinement passed, by tradition, and in fact was never wholly spent. Still it was evident, after the first race was gone, and the second and third had come into their places, that character had fallen to a lower type. The educated men were, in comparison, a rude or, at least, partially cultivated race. Their English style is loose. Elegance, well chastened thought, dignity of feeling do not appear. The spelling is even more irregular and capricious than it had been. And the public proceedings of courts and churches, if the records are referred to, exhibit a certain rawness, that is quite characteristic. We feel, in short, that we have descended to an inferior race. It is somewhat as if a nest of eagles had been filled with a brood of owls.

The decline of manners and mental cultivation, consequent on a life in the woods, carried with it a correspondent decline of morals and religion. And the natural downward tendency was aggravated, by the wars in which they were compelled to engage. Thus, after the bloody war with Philip, the synod of Massachusetts, convened to deliberate on the state of virtue and religion, set forth the following mournful particulars: "a decay of godliness and secret apostasy among professors"; "pride and contention"; a "want of truth and promise breaking"; a "neglect of family prayer"; "profane swearing"; "intemperance"; "a common practice of traveling on the Sabbath day"; "inordinate passions and breaches of the seventh commandment." Allowing all that may be necessary for exaggeration in this picture, we are still obliged, when they speak of a *common practice* of travelling on the Sabbath day, to acknowledge that there must have been a very marked decline in their moral habit. Following too into the war the four companies, for example, of Connecticut Rangers, we find them quite at home in the woods, displaying, in their modes of warfare and their wild, rough spirit, the full-grown Texan habit. On going to the church and court records of this period and onward, for the next fifty or seventy years, we discover mournful evidences of incontinence, even in the respectable families. As if, being cut off from the more refined pleasures of society, their baser passions had burnt away the restraints of delicacy, and the growing coarseness of manners had allowed them finally to seek, in these baser passions, the spring of their enjoyments. Shortly after this war, the wretched scenes of infatuation enacted at Salem, furnish us the proof that religion is dwindling towards superstitition. Not that a belief in witchcraft was peculiar to New England, or to that age of the world, but only that a want of thorough mental discipline in the ministry and the courts, connected with a general taint of superstition contracted in the woods by the whole people, aggravated the public delusion and finally suffered the whole body of society to go mad, in scenes which it is even horrible to contemplate.

Still the way is downward till we come to the "great revival," so called, and the times of the French wars. And here we find a period of thirty or forty years, where the dregs of decline and the seeds of new life are so intermixed, and the signs so crossed, one by another, that we hardly know what judgment to hold. Over and above all patriotic motives that may be conceived, there was a readiness to enlist in these wars, that indicates an adventurous and partially wild habit. The little State of Connecticut, containing at that time probably about 75,000 people, raised and equipped over 5,000 men, for three years in succession. As might be expected, when these two wars were over, the people were found to be reduced to a miserable state of poverty, and, what was yet worse, it was also discovered that their habits of industry and virtuous thrift had received a fatal shock. Then it was, that the people of New England seemed, for once, to want a spur to their creative activity, and a society was organized "For the Promotion of Industry"—a society which brought out three hundred women with their spinning-wheels on Boston common, to give an example to the other sex, of a virtue which they had so nearly forgotten. Mean time, the whole community, I may almost say, was unconsciously steeping itself in drink; and this also conspired with the wars, to break down the thrift of the people. In Massachusetts alone, when she had only 150,000 people, fifteen thousand hogsheads of rum were distilled every year, and a very large share of it was consumed by her own citizens; a fact in which you will see—what the living men of that day did not—a certain doom of decline, towards social misery and brutality.

At the same time, when it even seems, in one view, that all the foundations are dissolved, and that every hope of a new American civilization has perished, there begin to rise symptoms of order, and possibly of a new era. If the masses have been unsettled, they have also been made conscious of power. Or if they have been corrupted, in the same wars which have robbed them of their virtuous habits, certain great men, afterwards to be distinguished as leaders in our history, have also had their apprenticeship—learned to be leaders, felt the elevation of power, received new impulses, prepared themselves to act with address and vigor in scenes of yet higher moment. Religion, too, has been reviving, and re-asserting its power, not of course in demonstrations the most unexceptionable or respectable, but in such as the times of the Judges will suffer. It is the wild chant of Deborah, or better still, it is the nail that was driven by Jael's hammer—not the ointment ministered by the graceful hand of Mary. This new quickening accomplished, in fact, for religion, what the French wars accomplished for liberty; it broke up the age of frost, and brought in a new era of power. We begin, therefore, shortly to discover that a new spring has been given to character. An upward motion is visible, which upward motion has continued even to the present time, save as the war of the Revolution produced a temporary decline.

Pardon me now, if I venture to fill out the view of my subject, by saying that New England society is still in the transition state. Compared with some portions of the old world, and in certain points of view, we are still in the rough—presenting to the eye a healthy living aspect, such as the old world cannot any where offer, but still a raw, unfinished aspect, which it remains for the next century to civilize and bring into full ornamental perfection. For as our history now begins to live on its own root, and to send up a vitalizing power into the social body; as wealth is unfolded; as schools and colleges are perfecting their standards of learning; as literature and art advance to maturity, we are rising steadily into noon, as a people socially complete.

But the great problem of American society is not solved, however much it may be illustrated, by the history of New England. Still we are rolling on from east to west, plunging into the wilderness, scouring across the great inland deserts and mountains, to plant our habitations on the western ocean. Here again the natural tendencies of emigration towards barbarism, or social decline, are displayed, in signs that cannot be mistaken. The struggle through which we have passed, is continually repeating itself, under new modifications. We see the same experiment involving similar jeopardies; and we draw out of our own experience warnings to make us anxious, and encouragements to make us hopeful for our country—a double argument of fear and hope, to make us doubly faithful in our Christian efforts for its welfare.

In some respects, this westward emigration is secured by advantages which our own colonial emigration had not; in others, it is beset by disadvantages quite as decided. Among the advantages are these—First, a better and more available market for the sale of its products, and hence, a much greater facility in rising to a state of outward comfort. Secondly, a good and well established government, able to protect the beginnings made, exerting also an important moral constraint over all tendencies to lawlessness and public disorder. Thirdly, a connection with the eastern and older portions of the country, by which they are made to feel the moral effect of association with a more advanced state of manners, of social culture and religious virtue. Fourthly, a history; for it is not as when our fathers forsook a history to plant themselves in this new world; but the emigrant, whenever he strays, remembers that he is an American still. He looks out from his hut of logs on the western border, and feels the warmth of a distinct nationality glowing round him, like the clear warm light of day itself. On the other hand, these manifest advantages are counterbalanced by disadvantages. First, the western emigration is not religious, but is instigated by mere personal interest and adventure. Secondly, it does not carry with it a homogeneous or a well educated people. Together with a portion of enterprising, well qualified young men, who are rushing westward after their fortune, it gathers in the rude minded and ignorant masses of western Pennsylvania; the luckless and impoverished families flying from slavery in Virginia, Kentucky and Tennessee; together with such hordes of foreigners, as the over-populated countries of Europe are obliged to spare—men of all habits, characters and religions—and these it pours along in a promiscuous flood, to people the new world, and settle into social order as best they may. Then, thirdly, a considerable portion of the new west, has a social and historical connexion with slavery, which is continually doubling the inherent perils of emigration itself.

And here, since this institution of slavery, entering into the fortunes of our history, complicates, in so many ways, the disorders we suffer, I must pause a few moments to sketch its characteristics. Slavery, it is not to be denied, is an essentially barbarous institution. It gives us too that sign, which is the perpetual distinction of barbarism, that it has no law of progress. The highest level it reaches, is the level at which it begins. Indeed, we need not scruple to allow that it has yielded us one considerable advantage, in virtue of the fact, that it produces its best condition first. For while the northern people were generally delving in labor, for many generations, to create a condition of comfort, slavery set the masters at once on a footing of ease, gave them leisure for elegant intercourse, for unprofessional studies, and seasoned their character thus with that kind of cultivation which distinguishes men of society. A class of statesmen were thus raised up, who were prepared to figure as leaders in scenes of public life, where so much depends on manners and social address. But now the scale is changing. Free labor is rising, at length, into a state of wealth and comfort, to take the lead of American society. Meanwhile, the foster sons of slavery—the high families, the statesmen—gradually receding in character, as they must under this vicious institution, are receding also in power and influence, and have been ever since the revolution. Slavery is a condition against nature; the curse of nature therefore is on it, and it bows to its doom, by a law as irresistible as gravity. It produces a condition of ease which is not the reward of labor, and a state of degradation which is not the curse of idleness. Therefore the ease it enjoys cannot but end in a curse, and the degradation it suffers cannot rise into a blessing. It nourishes imperious and violent passions. It makes the masters solitary sheiks on their estate, forbidding thus the possibility of public schools, and preventing also that condensed form of society, which is necessary to the vigorous maintenance of churches. Education and religion thus displaced, the dinner table only remains, and on this hangs, in great part, the keeping of the social state. But however highly we may estimate the humanizing power of hospitality, it cannot be regarded as any sufficient spring of character. It is neither a school, nor a gospel. And when it comes of self-indulgence, or only seeks relief for the tedium of an idle life, scarcely does it bring with it the blessings of a virtue. The accomplishments it yields are of a mock quality, rather than of a real, having about the same relation to a substantial and finished culture, that honor has to character. This kind of currency will pass no longer; for it is not expense without comfort, or splendor set in disorder, as diamonds in pewter; it is not airs in place of elegance, or assurance substituted for ease; neither is it to be master of a fluent speech, or to garnish the same with stale quotations from the classics; much less is it to live in the Don Juan vein, accepting barbarism by poetic inspiration—the same which a late noble poet, drawing out of Turks and pirates, became the chosen laureate of slavery —not any or all of these can make up such a style of man, or of life, as we in this age demand. We have come up now to a point, where we look for true intellectual refinement, and a ripe state of personal culture. But how clearly is it seen to be a violation of its own laws, for slavery to produce a genuine scholar, or a man, who, in any department of excellence, unless it be in politics, is not a full century behind his time. And if we ask for what is dearer and better still, for a pure Christian morality, the youth of slavery are trained in no such habits, as are most congenial to virtue. The point of honor is the only principle many of them know. Violence and dissipation bring down every succeeding generation to a state continually lower; so that now, after a hundred and fifty years are passed, the slave-holding territory may be described as a vast missionary ground, and one so uncomfortable to the faithful ministry of Christ, by reason of its jealous tempers, and the known repugnance it has to many of the first maxims of the gospel, that scarcely a missionary can be found to enter it. Connected with this moral decay, the resources of nature also are exhausted, and her fertile territories changed to a desert, by the uncreating power of a spendthrift institution. And then, having made a waste where God had made a garden, slavery gathers up the relics of bankruptcy, and the baser relics still of virtue and all-manly enterprise, and goes forth to renew, on a virgin soil, its dismal and forlorn history. Thus, at length, has been produced what may be called the bowie-knife style of civilization, and the new West of the South is overrun by it—a spirit of blood which defies all laws of God and man; honorable but not honest; prompt to resent an injury, slack to discharge a debt; educated to ease, and readier, of course, when the means of living fail, to find them at the gambling-table or the race-ground, than in any work of industry—probably squandering the means of living there, to relieve the tedium of ease itself.

Such is the influence of slavery, as it enters into our American social state, and imparts its moral type of barbarism, through emigration, to the new west. Hence, the Mexican war, which has its beginning and birth in what I have called the bowie-knife style of civilization—a war in the nineteenth century, which, if it was not purposely begun, many are visibly determined shall be, a war for the extension of slavery. It was no one political party, as some pretend, who made this war, but it was the whole southwest and west rather of all parties, instigated by a wild and riotous spirit of adventure, which no terms of reason or of Christian prudence and humanity could check. And if this war results, as probably it may, in the acquisition of a vast western territory, then is our great pasture ground of barbarism so much to be enlarged, the room to run wild extended, the chances of final anarchy and confusion multiplied.

We are now prepared to complete our view, by passing directly to the subject of western emigration itself. And what are the moral and social results here preparing? That I can draw a picture of western society, which will be universally approved, is more than I have any right to expect. I can only give such a sketch as the facts seem to require, and without exaggeration; observing, however, that if any western man should be dissatisfied, it will, by no means, convince me that I am wrong; for to conceive a people rightly it is not sufficient to know them; they must be viewed from a stand point without. And just as the character of New England cannot be rightly drawn, save as it is viewed from abroad, so no western or westernized man, coming directly out from the scenes of western life, is qualified, on that account, to estimate their social standing and prospects. On the contrary, he may even be partially disqualified, by the experience under which he has fallen. At the same time, let it be understood, that in what I may say, however the public may receive it, I do not consider myself as reflecting any necessary dishonor on the west, or on western society. It is no dishonor in them, any more than it was to New England, to suffer what they must, from the very laws of society itself. On the contrary, if the west puts forth a manly struggle to breast the laws of decline involved in a new social state, it may even display the more heroic qualities, because of the adverse elements it has the spirit to master. Much the same allowances, too, are to be made here, that were supposed to hold in reference to the decline of New England. It is not general or universal. It includes only a portion of western society, and this portion only in regard to certain particulars. Probably there is no decline, but an improvement rather, if we take in all, and regard what I have called the total amount of character. Many of the emigrants from Pennsylvania, Virginia, and yet further south, were at a very low point of character when they removed, and these, brought within the reach even partially of schools and churches, are rapidly improving. If the emigrants from New England lose ground, in manners, piety and habits of intelligence, they also gain in spirit, freedom, self-reliance, and other qualities that are certainly desirable. Besides, we are making strenuous efforts to save the west from the decline that would otherwise appear; so that, while there is a certain tendency to barbarism in their new condition of society, that tendency, we may believe, is held in check and, in many cases, displaced, even from the beginning, by signs of improvement.

Western character has many powerful and promising qualities, but it wants the salt of religious virtue, the sobriety of discipline, and the modesty of true intelligence. It is frank, bold, earnest and positive, but somewhat rude and extravagant, and specially destitute of the genial sentiments which enrich the more settled and cultivated forms of society. A very large portion of the western community, it is well known, are already so far gone in ignorance, as to make a pride of it, and even to decry education as an over-genteel accomplishment. They hold, of course, their manhood in their will, not in their understanding; which is the same as to say that law is weak, and passion violent. Hence, the many public murders, committed in the newer states of the west and south, which are never legally investigated. Or, perhaps you will even see an ambitious young city, mustering itself in a military mob, to murder an inoffensive Christian minister and citizen; and when it is done, when the fit of passion is over, the law, instead of rising up to re-assert its rights, as we see it do in older and less barbarous communities, still sleeping in its violated majesty. Or, if you will discover how near it is possible to come, and within how short a time, to a complete dissolution of civil order, you may see the executive power of a sovereign state standing by, for six months, to look on, as a spectator, while two organized military parties of its own citizens are prosecuting an open war, one to defend, the other to capture an American city! Where shall such disorders stop? And what is the limit towards which they run? If, in the days of the Judges, Pennsylvania rebelled against the excise of whiskey, and now Illinois substitutes the camp and the siege, in place of justice itself and the ordinary methods of legal redress, what shall by and by appear, in some new state as far west of Illinois, as that is of Pennsylvania? What are we to expect as this reign of passion, spreading onward across the vast regions yet unoccupied, grows yet more violent as it is deeper in ignorance, and wilder still, as it is more remote from the haunts of Christian civilization? Is it not well understood that a partially wild race of men, such as cannot any longer be properly included in the terms of civilization, is already formed? I speak of what is sometimes called the pioneer race. They roll on, like a prairie fire, before the advance of regular emigration; they have no fixed habits, and do not care to appropriate the soil, consequently have no education or religion. They live mainly by hunting and pasture; and, when a regular settlement begins within an hour's ride, they feel the proximity too close, quit their hut of logs, which is in fact only their tent, and start on, by another long remove, into the wild regions beyond them. These semi-barbarians too, are continually multiplying in numbers, and becoming more distinct in their habits. Ere long, there is reason to fear, they will be scouring in populous bands, over the vast territories of Oregon and California, to be known as the pasturing tribes—the wild hunters and robber clans of the western hemisphere—American Moabites, Arabs and Edomites!

Or if it seem extravagant to speak of any such result, let it not be forgotten that one emigrant family of the Saxon race has already sunk into barbarism, since our history began. I speak of the Dutch Boers in South Africa. They are Calvinistic Protestants; they began their settlement at Cape Town, in the year 1651. And now they are virtually barbarians; for they are scarcely less wild in their habits than the Hottentots themselves. They subsist by pasture, roving from place to place. Lynch law and private revenge are the principal methods of redressing injuries. Their habits are filthy. Their women do the work. Education is forgotten, and the cruelties they practice in their sanguinary wars, are such as resemble them to beasts of prey. They are now a race of nominally Christian barbarians—barbarians under the synod of Dort, a standing proof that Protestants, and they too of the Saxon blood, may drop out of civilization, and take their place on the same level of ignorance and social brutality with the barbarous tribes of the earth. Let no American that loves his country refuse to heed the example.

Many are accustomed to regard the exposure of our western country to Romanism with extreme horror, regarding a possible lapse into this corrupt form of religion as the climax of all possible disasters. In that opinion there is quite as little to approve, as there is in the over-confident opinion of those who declare that Romanism cannot spread in this country. Nothing is necessary to make room for Romanism, but to empty us of all opposing qualities; and it will not take a long period of ignorance and religious anarchy to do that. Nor do I mean to imply, in thus speaking, that Romanism can co-exist only with barbarism, much less to sharpen a point of satire against the Romish church. Under this we know are gathered many great and accomplished men, and many nations farther advanced, in some respects, than we. I only mean, that while it is possible for a people brought up in Romanism to become socially advanced under it, a free minded people, brought up in mental and moral habits wholly opposite, never can be led into it, save through the gate of superstition; which gate of superstition never can be opened, save by a loss of knowledge, social order and religion, such as approximates to barbarism. There may be cases where a cultivated man, wearied out and lost in the mazes of fantastic speculation, throws up suddenly the prerogatives of reason, and takes it for certain that God will do him good, if he has a Levite to his priest. There may be truly godly men—men, so to speak, of an overgrown religious sentiment, who see no consistent issue short of Romanism to assumptions already made, and whose nerves are too weak to go back and manfully sift these assumptions— there may be such, who fall a prey to their own delicate illusions, and drop into the Romish church to settle their peace. But these are only caprices, accidents, idiosyncrasies, which support no general conclusion, save that between opposite superlatives, the sublimities and follies of mankind, there is often a natural brotherhood. Thus, over-cultivation may sometimes join hands at the church door with barbarism, both entering as fellow proselytes together. Thus over-speculation will sometimes throw up private judgment in disgust, and place itself on a par, with those who have no private judgment to lose. But the great danger of Romanism, the only danger of any moment, is from the multiplication of the latter class—those who have no private judgment to lose; and it is a real danger. Man is a religious being, and if he cannot come to God through his intelligence, he will come to what sort of God his superstitions offer him. When, therefore, I consider how certainly an ignorant soul is prepared to superstition, remembering also the vast amount of ignorance that prevails among the western people, I want no other proof that superstition has already a wide and terrible sway over the western mind. Or if I suffer a doubt, the great Mormon city and temple rise as proof visible before me—proof, however, that does not accrue as against the west alone, save that it shows how all fantastic errors and absurdities will assuredly congregate there. Who could have thought it possible that a wretched and silly delusion, like that of the Mormons, could gather in its thousands of disciples in this enlightened age, build a populous city, and erect a temple, rivalling in grandeur, even that of the false prophet at Mecca? And when we see, in facts like these, how readily material may be gathered to represent the times of the Judges, it is vain to imagine that Romanism can find no affinities prepared among us, or that none can be found, who will think it a religion, to have a Levite to their priest. Romanism can do any thing in this country which we will help it to do, and we ought not to complain if it does no more. Or if we persist in training a barbarous people for its use, let us indulge no regrets that Romanism gives them such a religion as they are capable of receiving.

I have led you thus over a wide field, and yet the subject is not exhausted. But I can pursue the argument no farther. If now you ask what is to be the conclusion of the great problem we have on hand; shall we go clear, at last, of all these perils; shall we rise into order, law, intelligence and religion; or will parts of the nation go down, at last, below the capacity to rise? I care not to answer that question. Indeed it is a question to be answered, not in speeches or conjectures, but by our works! The answer hangs, not on what we may think or reason, but on what we shall do! We can make it what we desire; we can make it as bad as we have power even to fear! Enough that we understand the magnificence of the problem, and the tremendous perils incident thereto, viz: that we have it on hand to struggle up, for a half century or a century to come, against the downward currents of decline, and bear up the nation with us, into a settled condition of Christian culture and virtue; which, if we do, the critical point of our destiny is turned. We are then to be the most august and happiest nation that has ever appeared on earth, the leading power of the world's history. Was there ever a struggle offered to the good and great of mankind, so fit to kindle enthusiasm, or nerve the soul to patient sacrifices!

WHAT, THEN, SHALL WE DO!

First of all, we must not despair. There is no cause for despair. Dark as the picture is that I have given, I do not, for one, suffer a misgiving thought. In many portions of the field, the crisis is already past. In others, it soon will be. And every new state, or section added to the parts already secure, brings an accession of aid and a more preponderant weight of influence. Of the new regions, we may say that Vermont, Western New York, and a part of Ohio, are already gained, and are now side by side with us, helping us to support the downward pressure of the emigrant masses. We have only to make sure, in like manner, of all the States this side of the Mississippi, and then the critical point is, in my estimation, past. Much will remain to be done; but the result will be sure. For when once the vast region this side of the Mississippi is seen to be ascending with us into order and Christian refinement, the regions beyond will scarcely be able to drag themselves down into anarchy. The die of our destiny is cast. Seeing then the momentous perils that hang about us, let them only quicken us to a more fixed and heroic devotion. It must be a faint heart that cannot bear up, in a struggle so evidently temporary. Nothing is more certain than that, if we deserve to triumph, we shall triumph; and if that be not enough to sustain our courage, we are worthy of no such cause as this.

And what next? We must get rid, if possible, I answer, of slavery. It aggravates every bad tendency we suffer. We cannot, as American Christians, be at peace with it longer. Not forgetting the moderation that belongs to every just cause, we must lift our voices against it, and must not desist from all proper means to secure its removal, till the work is done.

We must also return, as soon as possible, to a condition of peace, and maintain it, as the only hope of moral and social progress in our country. War is the proper work only of barbarians—the bane, therefore, of all social order and virtue. Even New England itself, as I have shown you, came near sinking into a fatal debauchery of character in the wars she encountered.

For a war exasperates all the evils incident to emigration, post-pones all settled habits, and turns all sobriety to madness.

If something could be done to civilize the manner of American politics, to abate the rudeness of political animosities, to establish candor and courtesy and dignity of feeling between opposing parties and their leaders, it would greatly expedite the progress of refinement in our people. And I know of no more ready or proper expedient, than for every Christian man to look at the most interior merits of every cause or question, and stand ready to support the right, bear what name it may.

Be it also understood, that the sooner we have railroads and telegraphs spinning into the wilderness, and setting the remotest hamlets in connexion and close proximity with the east, the more certain it is that light, good manners and Christian refinement, will become universally diffused. For when the emigrant settle-ments of Minnesota or of Oregon feel that they are just in the suburb of Boston, it is nearly the same thing, in fact, as if they actually were.

Education, too, is another and yet more sacred interest which we are to favor and promote by every reasonable means. Colleges are a great and pressing want; but we want only a few. Indeed, we have enough already for the next twenty years, if only they were fully organized and sufficiently endowed. Subordinate schools, and especially rudimental schools, are a much more press-ing want; but these, in order to have any value, must be created and supported principally by the people for whose benefit they exist. The most, therefore, which can be done is to stimulate the demand for such schools, in every convenient manner.

This brings me to speak, last of all, of that which is really the chief, the all-important work, viz: to provide a talented and educated body of Christian teachers, and keep them pressing into the wilderness, as far as emigration itself can go. These mixing with the families, and entering into their new struggles, will stimulate the demand for instruction, assist in the founding of schools and academies, and become the guardians of every good interest. We must throw ourselves out, therefore, upon HOME MISSIONS as the first and sublimest Christian duty which the age lays upon us.

Religion is the only prop on which we can lean with any

confidence; and Home Missions are the vehicle of religion. In no form of human society is there any law of self-support and self-conservation. There is no shape of society, least of all any shape of new society, that will not rot itself down and dissolve, unless there descend upon it from above, a conserving power which it has not in itself. Nothing but religion, a ligature binding society to God, can save it. No light, save that which is celestial, no virtue but that which is born of God, no power of motivity, but that which is drawn from other worlds, can suffice to preserve, compact and edify a new social state. It was religion that sustained and finally turned the crisis of New England. It was religion, dispensed by the old Missionary Society of Connecticut, and other sister institutions of a later date, which finally turned the crisis of Vermont, Western New York, and Eastern Ohio. Among these later institutions, and as the most vigorous and powerful too of all, we are to class the Home Missionary Society, for which I now speak—a Society which is now hovering over Michigan, Indiana, Illinois, Wisconsin, Iowa, and other new regions beyond, as once it did over the regions just named. It has now a spiritual army six hundred strong, in these fields, and waits to make its hundreds, thousands. For it has undertaken the most magnificent work ever yet appropriated to any human institution, with a zeal proportioned to its grandeur. In this institution, for I speak this evening only to its friends, we are enlisted, as I trust, with whatever of Christian determination God permits us to exercise. Here we feel that we have the future in our charge, and we mean to see the trust faithfully fulfilled. To save this mighty nation; to make it the leading power of the earth; to present to mankind the spectacle of a nation stretching from ocean to ocean, across this broad continent; a nation of free men, self-governed, governed by simple law, without soldiers or a police; a nation of a hundred millions of people, covering the sea with their fleets, the land with cities, roads and harvests; first in learning and art, and all the fruits of genius, and, what is highest and best of all, a religious nation, blooming in all the Christian virtues, the protector of the poor; the scourge of oppression; the dispenser of light, and the symbol to mankind, of the ennobling genial power of righteous laws, and a simple Christian faith—this is the charge God lays upon us, this we accept and this, by

God's blessing, we mean to perform, with a spirit worthy of its magnitude. I say not that we must forsake other and more distant fields of duty. God will never call us to that. I only say that there can be no other duty at all comparable to the duty of saving our country; none that God so manifestly imposes. What less than a romantic folly could it seem, to any sober mind, if such indeed were the alternative, to be pouring out our mercies into the obscure outposts of heathenism, and leaving this great nation, this brightest hope of the ages, to go down as a frustrated and broken experiment!

It is time also to understand, that if we are to fill this great field with Christian churches and a Christian people, we must have a spirit of life in our breasts, and a tone of Christian devotion such as we have not hitherto exhibited. Here is the only real cause of discouragement I know. It is not money, it is not men, it is no mere human outlay that can bear up such a work as this. We want the unworldly spirit; that which knits us, and through us knits our great country to God. And then also, we want that intense and Christ-like humanity, which will attract the feeling of our whole country towards us. For it is not in oppositions, it is not in raising a crusade against Romanism, or filling the air with outcries of any sort, that we are to save our country. We must rise upon it as the morning, in the tranquillity of love. We must rain righteousness upon it, as a genial shower.

It is beautiful also to see that God designs, by the very work we undertake, to fill out and finish our own Christian type of character and society. In the case of our fathers, it seems probable that nothing but the strong pillars of high Calvinism held them up, or could have held them up, till the critical point of their history was passed. There were no missionaries coming over unto them. Nothing could hold them up but an internal force, such as they had in these doctrines—doctrines that were incorporated in their souls, as the spinal column in their bodies. Thus, when their manners were grown wild, their sentiments coarse, and their ill-trained understandings generally incapable of nice speculation, still the tough questions of their theology kept them always in action; still they could grasp hold of the great iron pillars of election, reprobation and decrees, and their clumsy-handed thoughts were able to feel them distinctly. Whoever could dis-

tinguish a thunderbolt could surely think of these, and it mattered
not so much, whether they thought exactly right, as that they kept
thinking, and in their thinking brought down God upon their
souls. So they took hold of the iron pillars that held up the
theologic heavens, and climbed and heaved in huge surges of
might, and kept their gross faculties in exercise, till the critical
hour of their trial was passed. The themes they handled kept them
too before God. They dwelt in the summits of divine government.
They looked upon the throne, they heard the thunders roll
below, and felt the empyrean shake above, at the going forth of
God's decrees. Such a religion as they had could not be distant,
or feeble. It had power to invest the coarse mind with a divine
presence, and make Jehovah felt as an element of experience.
Never was there a better foundation for a grand, massive
character in religion; and now God means to finish out this
character, by uniting in it the softer shades of feeling, and the
broader compass of a more catholic and genial spirit. We go
forth now to a people, who unite all manner of opinions, and
we go in company with Christians of other names and other
creeds, who are undertakers also in the same great work. We
cannot, therefore, spend our strength now upon exclusive and
distinctive dogmas, but we must proceed in a catholic and comprehensive spirit. Otherwise we shall be at war with each other
and shall only spend our force, in demolishing all the force we
have. Thus, the Methodists, for example, have a ministry ad-
mirably adapted, as regards their mode of action, to the new
west—a kind of light artillery that God has organized, to pursue
and overtake the fugitives that flee into the wilderness from his
presence. They are prompt and effective in action, ready for all
service, and omnipresent, as it were, in the field. The new settler
reaches the ground to be occupied, and, by the next week, he
is likely to find the circuit crossing by his door, and to hear the
voice of one crying in the wilderness, "The kingdom of God is
come nigh unto you!" Our Methodist brethren have put on their
armor too against the enemies of learning among themselves.
They are building colleges, and one among the number, which
they mean to make the most complete and best endowed university in the west. If sometimes their demonstrations are rude,
and their spirit of rivalry violent, still it is good to have such

rivals, for their labor is still ours, and when they have reached the state of intelligence they are after, they are sure to become effectually, if not formally, one with us. Therefore let there be, if possible, no controversy with them; but let us rather encourage ourselves in a work so vast, by the fact that we have so vast an army of helpers in the field with us. So of all the other Christian families, who are going into the field to do a work for their Master. There should be not only concord of spirit, but also an actual understanding; so that we may cover together as much ground as possible. And then we should all go forth together, to calm the angry divisions of controversy and sweeten the bitter prejudices of sectarian strife. Earnest for the truth, we must also remember, that truth itself is catholic and comprehensive. We must shun that vapid liberalism, which instead of attracting us into unity, will only dissolve us into indifference, and yet we must be willing to stretch our forbearance and charity even to Romanists themselves, when we clearly find the spirit of Jesus in their life. In this manner, God will instruct us by our work, and make our work itself our reward. Engaging with our utmost ardor to save the wilder portions of our country, we shall carry on thus our own noble beginnings to completion, and finish out a character, as earnest in its sacrifices and catholic in its charities, as it is firm in its original elements. May we not also hope to draw down from the skies, upon us and upon all the regions for which we labor, such a baptism of love as will melt both us and them, and all the families of Christ in our land, into one Christian fraternity.

Thus will we go on and give it to our sons and daughters to come after us. We will measure our strength by the grandeur of our object. The wilderness shall bud and blossom as the rose before us; and we will not cease, till a Christian nation throws up its temples of worship on every hill and plain; till knowledge, virtue and religion, blending their dignity and their healthful power, have filled our great country with a manly and a happy race of people, and the bands of a complete Christian commonwealth are seen to span the continent.

And now, Jehovah God, thou who by long ages of watch and discipline, didst make of thy servant Abraham a people, be thou the God also of this great nation. Remember still its holy beginnings, and for the fathers' sakes, still cherish and sanctify it. Fill it with thy Light and thy Potent Influence, till the glory of thy Son breaks out on the western sea, as now upon the eastern, and these uttermost parts, given to Christ for a possession, become the bounds of a new Christian Empire, whose name the believing and the good of all people shall hail as the name of hope and blessing!

ENGLISH INTELLECTUALS AND POLITICS IN THE 1930s

Stuart Samuels

The English Left Intelligentsia of the 1930s emerged from a definite political and economic situation and not from any previously existing left-wing literary or philosophical tradition. Although there had been a long-established history of individual British writers' and poets' involvement in politics, represented best in the public imagination by Milton, Bryon, Shelley, William Morris, and Shaw, the drive toward political commitment in the thirties resulted in the formation, for the first time to any great extent, of a radical intelligentsia in England—a body of creative people who, as a group, openly criticized the existing form of society and who established institutions and intellectual pressure groups to mount a campaign to alter that society. Never before had so large and so varied a group of intellectuals felt sufficient ideological and common concern, enough communal self-awareness, to speak of themselves as WE.

If the most outstanding characteristic of English intellectual life in the thirties was the development of political consciousness, then the most agonizing dilemma for the young and sensitive intellectual was not so much the problem of choosing between the appeals of left-wing communism and right-wing fascism as it was the decision whether to become politically committed and socially active at all. The division in English intellectual life was not between the communist intellectual and the fascist intellectual, or between the Stalinist intellectual and the Trotskyite intellectual, as it was in France and America, but rather between the politically detached and politically committed, between those who took politics seriously and those who were preoccupied with narrower intellectual pursuits. Once the decision was made to take politics seriously, then the natural inclination for all but a few younger members of the English intellectual class was toward the left, a move "forward from liberalism," toward a general radical revolutionary leftism vaguely identified with such ideas as socialism, communism, artistic responsibility, and political commitment.

There were four more or less distinct phases of English intellectual involvement in left politics in the thirties, each reacting to different stimuli, each raising distinct problems about the relationship of the intellectual and political commitment, and each represented by different organizations and institutions established to focus the new political consciousness. These four periods were:

I. *1926–33:* the development of left intellectuals during the early years of the economic depression and the rise of fascism in Germany. This was the period best represented by the more famous of the left intellectuals, W. H. Auden, Stephen Spender, Christopher Isherwood, C. Day Lewis, and other members of the "Left Poets" group.

II. *1932–35:* the drive toward political commitment associated most directly with the rise of fascism and the increasing threat of war. This was the period of the establishment of anti-fascist, anti-war cultural associations organized by university undergraduates, artists, writers, theatre people, and film makers.

III. *1935–38:* the organization of a Popular Front intellectual left focused primarily on the Spanish Civil War and best represented by the various cultural institutions set up to mobilize the intellectuals' concern with that struggle.

IV. *1938–40:* the disillusionment of the intellectual left; the period of the defeat of Republican Spain, the recognition of the inevitability of war, the final disenchantment with the Soviet experiment, and the general disappointment with the effectiveness of intellectuals' involvement in political issues.

I. THE MAKING OF THE AUDEN GROUP: 1926–33

Oxford has been renowned as the home of lost causes, thus it is perhaps appropriate that the history of the English left intelligentsia should begin among the spires and gardens of this famous city. In the period 1924–30 the most eminent members of what became known as the "Left Poets"—W. H. Auden, Stephen Spender, and C. Day Lewis—were at Oxford. But their activities and interests while at university give little hint of the socially conscious and politically active individuals they were to become. Their actions were distinctly apolitical and often blatantly anti-political. They were rebels but not revolutionaries, manifesting their hatred of English society in a wholesale attack on the bastions of middle-class culture, public school discipline, and the vestiges of Victorian morality imposed upon them by their parents and social milieu. All of them were born during the first decade of this century; consequently their recollections of the First World War were necessarily vague and often rather confused. For the better part of the fighting they had been sequestered in their prep schools where the war, if it meant anything, as Day Lewis remembered, meant only worse food and funny large maps.

Products of the comfortable middle-class society that flourished in the early twenties; sons of clergymen (Day Lewis), journalists (Spender), doctors (Auden), and army officers (Isherwood), they followed the traditional educational pattern of their class: prep school to public school to Oxford or Cambridge.

At university, the initial attraction of Auden, Isherwood, Day Lewis, Spender, and MacNeice to one another was not due to a common political or even cultural interest, but to similar social backgrounds and a common circle of friends. By 1928 a coherent group existed, centering around the personality of Auden. Called interchangeably the "gang," "the Happy Few," the "Lads of the Earth," the group included Auden, Spender, Isherwood, Day Lewis, and their close friends. Day Lewis brought in his room-mate, novelist Rex Warner; Auden introduced his friends, Gabriel Carritt, son of an Oxford philosophy don; Derek Kahn; historian A. J. P. Taylor; Hugh Gaitskell, and Louis MacNeice; Spender added Isaiah Berlin, painter Robert Medley, poet Richard Goodman, and Harold Acton. From Cambridge came Isherwood and his friend Edward Upward. Around this extraordinary collection of undergraduates could be found such Oxford dons as C. M. Bowra, Nevill Coghill, Richard Crossman, and Patrick Gordon-Walker. One of the more obvious aspects of the group was a strong element of undergraduate homosexuality.

Their most representative collective expression was the publication of a periodical called *Oxford Outlook,* edited at different times by Spender, Kahn, Berlin, and Crossman. Their most directly literary outlet was the yearly collection of *Oxford Poetry,* edited in different years by Auden, Day Lewis, and Spender.[1]

During the late twenties Oxford undergraduates were divided between what were termed the "athletes" and the "aesthetes," the "hearties" and the "arties." The "hearties" constituted the overwhelming majority of students and have been characterized as those undergraduates who "played games, ransacked rooms, were sexually successful and generally brutal, devoting themselves to rowing or rugger, beer-drinking, back-slapping, furtive love affairs, and a duly dutiful attempt to get through their 'schools' and then take some job for which they were not entirely unqualified."[2]

The "aesthetes" were conspicuous not for their number but for their eccentricity, their dress, their manner of speaking, and their intellectual preoccupations. The Auden "gang" made little attempt to hide their aesthetic inclinations. Day Lewis read poetry perched on a huge copper-beech tree in Wadham College gardens. Spender wore a red tie, cared "passionately" for the paintings and letters of Van Gogh and the stories and poems of D. H. Lawrence. MacNeice walked around Oxford in a black cape and wore long sideburns and raised the pitch of his voice whenever his opinions were unpopular. Auden worked by artificial light, wore outrageous hats, and carried a loaded starting pistol, especially when taking long rambling walks past his favorite Oxford spot, the gas works and municipal rubbish dump. For

---

[1] Cambridge had a similar grouping of promising young undergraduates in John Lehmann, William Empson, Julian Bell, Anthony Blunt, Charles Madge, and J. Bronowski. Their work was centered around two Cambridge publications, *Experiment* and *Venture.*

[2] Stephen Spender, *World Within World* (London, 1951), p. 185.

Auden and his friends, Oxford was a sort of "convenient hotel" where one stayed and was able to read books and entertain one's friends; a

> time to wear odd clothing
> behave with panache
> and talk nonsense
> ambling in Oxford's
> potamic meadows with friends.[3]

While the Auden group was at Oxford, their lives and work were devoid of political or social concerns. Auden, for example, never read a newspaper until 1930. The "group's" poetic ideas were dominated by T. S. Eliot, and their attitude toward man resembled that of D. H. Lawrence. Their image of society became "the wasteland," their intellectual symbol the ivory tower, and their goal in life artistic self-fulfillment.

Literature was not to be for the masses; it was sprinkled with private jokes, erudite sayings, and subtle allusions and was addressed to a well-educated and limited audience—their friends. Consciously, they attempted to narrow the stream of cultural communication. Poetry, for Auden, was to concern itself with shapes and volumes. Form alone was considered significant. The subject of a poem was only "a peg on which to hang the poetry," and a poet was a kind of chemist who mixed his poems out of words, while remaining detached from his own feelings.[4] Spender recalled Auden's literary canon as set down for the Oxford poets in the late 1920s: "A poet must have no opinion, no decided view which he seeks to put across in his poetry"; "above all, poetry must in no way be concerned with politics"; "a poet must be clinical, dispassionate about life"; "the poet feels less strongly about things than do other people."[5] The highest intellectual virtues were extreme individualism, aesthetic

[3] Taken from "To Professor Nevill Coghill upon his retirement in A.D. 1966," in John Lawlor and W. H. Auden, eds., *To Nevill Coghill from Friends* (London, 1966), p. 154, and reprinted with the permission of Faber & Faber Ltd. of London, and Random House, Inc., of New York.
[4] Christopher Isherwood, "Some Notes on Auden's Early Poetry," *New Verse*, Nos. 26–27 (November 1937), p. 9.
[5] Stephen Spender, "The Life of Literature," *Partisan Review*, Vol. XV (1948), p. 1317.

self-consciousness, literary experimentation, and political and social detachment.

A clear indication of the apolitical or anti-political inclination of the Auden "group" while at university is seen in their reaction to the General Strike in 1926. The British Trades Union Congress on May 3 called for a general strike of all union labor except those engaged in public health services. The government countered with an appeal for volunteers to maintain necessary supplies like transportation. This call was answered enthusiastically by volunteers from the universities. For most undergraduates at Oxford and Cambridge the strike was a lark, a chance to conduct a tram and run a train or take time off from their dreary studies. To many it was a rallying point for adventure. But its effect in arousing the political involvement of undergraduate intellectuals was practically nil. Isherwood recalls that he didn't even know why the men had struck, he could only shudder with fear and hatred: hatred of both sides. After a miserable week of doubts and self-reproach, he sneaked around to Chelsea town hall in London and volunteered for duty. But before he could be called up the strike, which lasted nine days, had ended. Day Lewis spent the period of the strike in Oxford helping socialist don G. D. H. Cole and running off cyclostyled reports of the negotiations between the government and the strikers. His only real sacrifice was that he ruined his best suit by spilling ink on it. Auden acted as a courier but spent most of the strike moving a disabled car four miles from Old Marston to Oxford.[6]

The first hesitant steps toward political consciousness by the members of the Auden "group" were not taken in England but rather in Germany. Auden, Isherwood, Spender, John Lehmann from Cambridge, Edward Upward, among others,[7] all spent a

[6] Christopher Isherwood, *Lions and Shadows* (London, 1938), p. 109; C. Day Lewis, *A Buried Day* (New York, 1960), p. 171; and A. J. P. Taylor, "Confusion of the Left," in John Raymond, ed., *The Baldwin Age* (London, 1960), p. 72.

[7] Other intellectuals who went to Germany between 1928 and 1932 and who first began to take an active interest in social and political questions due to their experiences there are: Alan Bush, Felicia Browne, Naomi Mitchison, Arthur Calder-Marshall, Rupert Doone, David Guest, Gonorys Rees, and Michael Davidson.

considerable time in Germany, especially Berlin, in the period 1928–32. Auden went in early 1929, after graduating with a disappointing third. Isherwood followed in March, and Spender spent time there in 1930.

Those members of the Auden "group" who went to Germany went without any political intentions; the appeal of late Weimar Berlin was not political—it was intellectual and social. To young English university graduates it represented all that was missing in the stuffy middle-class English atmosphere. Identified with youth, nudism, pleasure, avant-gardism in art, loose sexual mores, Berlin became the "Left Bank" of the late twenties. Moreover, its appeal was greatly enhanced, in the period of Germany's economic depression, by becoming, particularly for foreigners, a very cheap place to live. This city offered all the various amenities and "forbidden pleasures" a rebel could desire. Here was a society where personal rebellion was a common thing; where homosexuality was generally accepted and even encouraged; where intellectual experimentation was given its proper recognition and rewards.

The Auden "group," however, not only found the pleasures that they had sought, but also soon discovered that the society, which symbolized all that they desired, was on the verge of total anarchy, of social conflict. Spender recalled that "one began by noticing symptoms of decadence, suffering and unemployment; one looked further and saw beneath the decay of the liberal state, the virulent reaction of the Nazis and the struggle for a new life of the Communists."[8]

Moreover, for the first time these young English intellectuals experienced poverty and revolution first hand. In their street-walking, bar-hopping, café-sitting, in the people they met, the experiences they had, and the events they witnessed, they were brought face to face with the brutal reality of poverty, suffering, despair, and misery—a confrontation they could have avoided, or at least viewed with detachment, had they remained in England.

The people they tended to associate with were workers, proletarians. In his *Berlin Stories* Isherwood sympathized not so

[8] S. Spender, "Oxford to Communism," *New Verse*, Nos. 26–27 (November 1937), p. 10; and Christopher Isherwood, *Berlin Stories* (London, 1954).

much with the middle-class world of Mr. Norris as with the down-to-earth working-class philosophy of Otto. Spender spoke of Germans who

> Walk home remembering the straining red flags
> And with pennons of song still fluttering in their blood
> They speak of the world state
> With the towns like brain-centers and its pulsating arteries.

Auden described his experiences in the Berlin streets, where

> All this time was anxiety at night
> Shooting and barricade in street
> Walking home late I listened to a friend
> Talking excitedly of final war
> Of proletariat against police.[9]

In England, for these sensitive young intellectuals, economic decay, poverty, misery were recognized and acknowledged, although not experienced. But because these social ills were present in Germany, and because, in a more acute form, revolution or a sense of doom and disaster pervaded the whole society, these English intellectuals reconsidered many of their original assumptions about the relationship of the artist to society and the intellectual to politics. What was the real cause of the crisis? Could it be analyzed, primarily, as they had done previously, in psychological terms, or worked out in a disinterested pursuit of a poetic ideal? Was personal rebellion enough?

As fascism became a greater threat, Auden, Spender, Upward, Lehmann, and Isherwood left Germany and arrived back in England during the height of the economic slump, the period of widespread unemployment. Forced to maintain themselves, they took jobs as journalists, publishers, schoolmasters, private tutors. But their experiences in Germany, reinforced by what they found to be the state of society on their return to England, had re-

[9] The first four lines of poetry are from "The Funeral" in Stephen Spender, *Poems* (London, 1933), and are reprinted with the permission of Faber & Faber Ltd. of London and Random House, Inc., of New York. The next four lines are from "Poem XVI" in W. H. Auden, *Poems* (London, 1930), p. 62, and are reprinted with the permission of Faber & Faber Ltd. of London and Random House, Inc., of New York.

directed many of their concerns, had sensitized them to new problems and new approaches to life. Their attitude toward the proper role of poetry was changing; their assessment of the expected role of the intellectual, the desired relationship between the artist and his society, were all undergoing violent alteration.

The first indication of this changed attitude was the publication in September 1930 of Auden's *Poems*. The underlying theme was a "society where nobody was well," the failure of civilization, of a decaying landscape, of disease and death, of a society approaching the point of social conflict. But the analysis was still assessed in psychological terms and the corresponding revolt was in the form of a sort of social buffoonery, boy-scout rebelliousness, or undergraduate pranks. But Auden's clarion call to his generation was clear:

> Shut up talking, charming in the best suits to be
> had in town
> Lecturing on navigation while the ship is going down.
> Drop those priggish ways for ever, stop behaving like
> a stone:
> Throw the bath-chairs right away, and learn to leave
> ourselves alone.
> If we really want to live, we'd better start at once
> to try;
> If we don't it doesn't matter, but we'd better start to die.[10]

The first real literary landmark, symbolizing the moral-political revolt of these young intellectuals, was a little anthology, edited by Michael Roberts and printed in September 1932 by the publishing arm of Bloomsbury, Hogarth Press, entitled *New Signatures*. This publication marked the first time that Auden, Spender, and Day Lewis appeared together in print.

New Signatures was more a literary than a political manifesto. It expressed, according to Roberts, a new attitude toward poetry, a new consciousness of the need for a closer relationship between the writer and his society, the artist and his audience. Roberts saw in the poetry of Auden, Spender, Day Lewis, and

[10] Taken from "Poem XXII," in Auden, op. cit., and reprinted with the permission of Faber & Faber Ltd. of London and Random House, Inc., of New York.

Lehmann a concerted reaction against the poetic rural agrarian-
ism of the Georgians and against the ivory-tower exclusivism of
the Eliots and Sitwells, and a call for a celebration of a new
urban poetry, a "poetry of the machine age." These poets, he
felt, marked a shift away from the poets of the twenties who
were "unwilling to accept the responsibility of leadership," who
were "detached and pessimistic observers of the democratic process," whose poetry was addressed to a select educated minority
which could appreciate their frivolously decorative or elaborately
erudite passages, and a move toward a new attitude that envisioned the poet as a "leader," a person of unusual sensibility,
whose poetry, if it were to be effective, "must first be comprehensible."[11] Roberts asserted that the anthology marked a "clear
reaction against esoteric poetry," a shift away from poetry for the
private coterie toward the production of poetry for the public
group. He affirmed the belief, illustrated in the poems antholo-
gized, that hitherto such "unpoetic" things as pylons, internal-
combustion engines, airplanes, gas works, decaying wharves were
proper material for poetry. A poem, Roberts demanded, must
be about something "real"; "real" implying that it was contemporary, and in the context of the thirties, contemporary increasingly meant politics. A poet must have a message, written in
the most direct and simple manner possible.[12]

If the "new signature" of the group was a revolt against introspective and esoteric poetry, what was its new message? The
critique was aimed at bourgeois English society. Auden and his
generation were brought up on "fashionable despair"; they were
"weaned on the Wasteland," and, like Eliot, charted the decay of
civilization.[13] Unlike Eliot, however, they offered a way out, a
prospect of healing. The symptoms were economic decay, of the
"gradual ruin spreading like a stain," of a wasteland that was not
a symbolic myth but a geographical reality. The cure was a
major psychological operation for a social malady; a call for
heroes and healers to lead a revolutionary rebirth, of "change
of heart/new style of architecture," of "death of the old gang"—

[11] Michael Roberts, ed., *New Signatures* (London, 1932), pp. 7–20.
[12] Ibid.
[13] Dilys Powell, *Descent from Parnassus* (London, 1934), p. 178.

the selfless bourgeoisie. Progress was illusory, but they believed the "game worth playing."

They do not so much preach a "new life" as assail the old. Their poetry is a poetry of anger and, following one of their culture heroes, Wilfred Owen, a poetry of pity; anger over the evils produced by the economic system and pity for the victims of that system—the fleeing refugees of Germany and the proletarian unemployed in England.

In 1933 the moral-poetic revolt of the *New Signatures* group was fortified by the publication of Spender's *Poems,* Day Lewis' *Magnetic Mountain,* and a second, more socially conscious edition of Auden's 1930 *Poems.* But the transition from this moral indictment of English society to a more openly political outlook was signaled by the second literary landmark of the thirties generation, another anthology edited by Roberts and published in 1933, called *New Country.*

The shift in emphasis is illustrated in the change of title. The Auden "group" was concerned no longer with a purely aesthetic approach, with finding a new signature, a new moral code, but with discovering a new country, a new social order. The tone of this anthology, which included prose works, was definitely political; the position advocated, distinctly revolutionary. The call was for a revolutionary social change, not just a "change of heart," a shift away from a poetry expressing a nagging social conscience to a prose advocating a deep-seated political commitment; from a poetry of pity to a prose of propaganda.

Roberts set the tone in his introduction. "We do not need a new moral code," he said, "we do not need new standards of criticism—we need a new social system." "Prepare the way," he asserted, "for an English Lenin." It is too late "for a letter to *The Times.*" Finally, he asked, "What is the use of isolated protests?"[14]

The enemy became much easier to recognize. Satire turned to invective. The targets aimed at in the selections were the established fortresses of English society, not the recognized canons of poetic taste. The enemies were singled out: the press lords, the bankers, the "proprietors of Guinness, the Gaumont Palaces,

[14] Michael Roberts, ed., *New Country* (London, 1933), pp. 12–13.

Harrods and the *Daily Mail"; the inept politicians, the "golf-playing, church-going, tea-drinking Boy Scoutish eccentric middle classes"; the older intellectuals with their "pettifogging squabbles in Bloomsbury drawing rooms"; the literary recluses "in country houses at the end of drives."[15] It amounted to an attack on the philistinism of their parents and of their society.

Roberts issued a call for intellectuals to get involved in politics. He concluded that "only a revolution can save intellectual standards," that one could "no longer remain aloof from politics," that intellectuals must make up their minds to tie themselves to a revolutionary party and use their "technical ability as organizers and propagandists" for the benefit of the party.[16]

The Auden "group" openly identified themselves with a revolutionary communist position. But it was a quite distinctive kind of Marxism or communism, a "Marxism of the heart." Their attitude toward the proletarian working class, for example, was more romantic than revolutionary. They were more interested in the personality of the proletarian than in his ideology.

The desire to expiate their own feelings of guilt through their attitudes toward the working class is a continual theme in the writings of Auden, Isherwood, Spender, and Day Lewis. Spender when in Germany felt he was purging himself of the "sin" of being part of a wealthier, more privileged class by letting himself be cheated and exploited by the unemployed. Isherwood drank vile tea and ate enormous quantities of chocolates to ruin his teeth, a malady he identified with the working classes. Auden wore corduroy trousers and a worker's cap and dropped his aitches and ate peas with a knife to prove his sincerity. His Oxford friend, Gabriel Carritt, joined the Communist Party and changed his name to "Bill."

While trying to identify with the working-class man in actions, they also idolized him in their poems and stories. The working man became the new social hero, often romantically symbolized, especially by Day Lewis, mounted on a magnificent tractor chugging steadily toward the dawn of a new country. In general, "Comrade" became a more tender word than "lover."

---

[15] Ibid.; and W. H. Auden, *Paid on Both Sides* (London, 1932), p. 10.
[16] Roberts, *New Country*, pp. 12–13.

The "Marxists of the Heart" saw the classless society as an ethical necessity based on love, justice, and human dignity. They had an optimistic view of human nature, but a pessimistic assessment of modern society. Marxism or communism came to mean a philosophy of personal action, a moral force for good. They espoused the communist position because it was presently the repository for justice and freedom. These men came to Marxism through a compassion for the suppressed and suffering humanity. They wanted a revolution, but one that included the establishment of their most cherished moral values. Believing in the necessity of a moral view of society, the Auden "group" became increasingly convinced that this attitude could not be held without a concern for social action: that a moral position had to be stated in political terms.[17]

However, the "group" was not prepared to sacrifice censorship or suppression of individual liberty to the discipline of the Communist Party. They rejected any entanglement with Party discipline or Party bureaucracy. Communism seemed the only valid alternative, but the British Communist Party at this time was distinctly unappealing.

Discussions about the appeal of communism or Marxism to English intellectuals in this period have almost exclusively concentrated on psychological explanations, diagnosing the attraction in terms of a powerful dream, a personal revolt, a romantic episode, or a sublimation or perversion of a religious instinct. The acceptance of Marxism by English intellectuals has been considered merely as an escape for the sick, the frustrated, and the isolated. Orwell described it as a revolt of the "deracinated"; Crossman viewed it merely in terms of a "God that failed"; others saw it as a function of an unhappy childhood, friendly persuasion, public school revolt, or a mother complex.[18] One cannot deny that these explanations can be applied to the attraction of many English intellectuals of the thirties toward these

---

[17] See Stephen Spender, *The Destructive Element* (London, 1935).
[18] See Neal Wood, *Communism and British Intellectuals* (London, 1959); Julian Symons, *The Thirties* (London, 1956); R. H. S. Crossman, ed., *The God That Failed* (New York, 1954); Hugh D. Ford, *A Poet's War: British Poets and the Spanish Civil War* (Philadelphia, 1965); Peter Stansky and William Abrahams, *Journey to the Frontier* (Boston, 1966); and George Orwell, *Inside the Whale and Other Essays* (London, 1940).

new doctrines. Many did join the Party or accept Marxism as an act of public conscience. But for others, and for many of the Auden "group," the simple explanation seems closest to the truth; that is, Marxism and communism made sense of the times. It was a moral code as well as a social prophecy. Marxism gave a feeling of intellectual security in a period of baffling flux. It provided the answers to the rise of fascism, the failure of liberalism and socialism in England and Europe; it forecast the world-wide economic depression and explained the reasons for the rising unemployment. It provided direction, purpose, certainty in a time of social confusion and economic despair. These intellectuals turned in part to Marxism not in any attempt to solve their own aesthetic or philosophical problems, but rather as a way of making sense out of the external world about which they were becoming more and more concerned.

Moreover, the Marxism they were attracted to, or what they took to be Marxism, was a distinctly thirties product. The English Marxist intellectuals of the thirties went back to the Marx of 1845, the Marx of the thesis on Feuerbach, just as the Marxists of the fifties have gone back to the Marx of 1844, the Marx of the *Economic and Philosophical Manuscripts*. The thirties model of Marxism in England was not the traditionally conceived deterministic doctrine with the belief that men are purely products of circumstances, reacting automatically to changing economic conditions, but rather the idea that there was an interaction between man and his environment, to which man contributes an active, striving force. The revolutionary motto of the English left intelligentsia in the thirties was that philosophers have interpreted the world, our job is to change it.[19]

In explaining the political commitment of the Auden "group," one must add to the attraction of Marxism the initial experience in Berlin, 1928–32, and the reinforcing occurrence of coming to maturity during the early years of the economic depression, a deep-seated feeling that as intellectuals they were being stifled in English society. Part of this disgust and bias against England can be explained by the nature of the intellectual community at the time. In the early thirties there was no intellectual establish-

[19] See John Strachey, *The Coming Struggle for Power* (London, 1932) and *The Theory and Practice of Socialism* (London, 1936).

ment. The depression had helped dry up the existing private patronage system, and, as yet, the government had not stepped in to form an "official" patronage system. There were no institutions and agencies like the present-day Arts Council, BBC third program, generous publishers' advances, or paid articles for periodicals, through which the intellectual could earn a living. The economic depression closed many doors to the newly graduating middle-class intellectuals. They were forced to take positions as schoolmasters, private tutors, journalists, office clerks, film cutters, and salesmen. Auden, addressing Byron, recorded the plight of the intellectuals of his generation:

> The only thing you never turned your head to
> Was teaching English in a boarding school.
> Today it's a profession that seems grand to
> Those whose alternative's an office stool
> More, it's a job, and jobs today, are rare
> All the ideals in the world won't feed us.[20]

This situation engendered a sense of intellectual isolation and heightened the belief that, under capitalism, the intellectual did not get a fair deal. Moreover, with the increasing reports of Soviet cultural advances in the films, drama, and the Russian's appreciation and idolization of his intellectuals, the English intellectual like Auden and Spender became convinced that in the Soviet Union and under socialism the intellectual was accorded due respect and given proper recognition and received adequate rewards. To the members of the Auden "group," the appeal of Soviet Russia was first as an alternative to a decaying capitalist order, and second, and more important, as a model of a desirable intellectually appreciative society.

By 1933 the Auden "group," although politically committed, were not forced to maintain an intellectual position outside their creative work. They manifested their concern for politics in a general moral outrage rather than in the espousal of a specific political platform. They illustrated their political commitment

[20] Taken from "Letter to Lord Byron" in W. H. Auden and Louis MacNeice, *Letters from Iceland* (New York, 1937), pp. 210–11, and reprinted with the permission of Curtis Brown Ltd. of London and Random House, Inc., of New York.

through the written word, not through a Party card. They were more concerned with a professional devotion to poetry than with an amateur involvement in politics. Their work expressed a general sense of indignation, a genuine outpouring of outraged conscience. What they were not faced with was a choice between the desires of private creative experience and the demands of public political action. Political themes and Marxian ideology could be absorbed into their work without being concerned with its effect on political events. The potential conflict between political commitment and moral engagement, although recognized, had yet to raise its inconvenient head.

II. THE ENGLISH LEFT INTELLIGENTSIA, 1932–35

After 1933 the intellectuals' movement to the left became much more widespread, the intensity of commitment deepened, the manifestations of revolt became more overt and the political implications more direct.

Roberts ended his introduction to *New Country* by suggesting that it would be to "younger men" that one would look for an "acceptance of a newer outlook." These "younger men" were to be found at the universities of Oxford, Cambridge, and London in the early thirties.

A. THE UNIVERSITIES AND THE SCHOOLS

The politicalization of the universities, especially Oxford and Cambridge, began in late 1932 and early 1933: the years of the highest number of unemployed in England, the time that Hitler came to power in Germany, and the period when there was increasing talk of the possibility of war. Consequently, undergraduate involvement in politics amounted to a broad-based attack on war, fascism, and the economic ills of a dying capitalist system.

Oxford in the early thirties ceased to be a home of lost causes and became a nursery for new ones. Students organized campaigns against war. They published magazines, featuring not esoteric articles about Baudelaire but serious political polemics on fascism and unemployment. *Oxford Outlook,* the magazine of the Auden "group," was resurrected, renamed *New Oxford Outlook,* and filled its pages with articles on political and discussions of social questions. New, exclusively left-wing political magazines, like *This Unrest,* found their way into student studies. *Daily Workers* were ordered for undergraduate common rooms. At the Oxford Union, the university's debating society, a new tone of political involvement by students was struck, displayed most famously by the February 1933 debate at which students voted 275 to 153 that "under no circumstances would they fight for King and Country." Other similar resolutions were passed, like the less famous but more revolutionary one that "this House recognizes no flag but the Red flag." During this period Philip Toynbee, son of Arnold Toynbee, was elected the Union's first and only communist president.

In contrast to the activities of undergraduates in 1926, the Oxford students of the thirties, instead of breaking strikes, often helped organize and win them. In many colleges and societies, study circles were organized to discuss the political situation, read the works of Marx and Lenin, and learn about the new civilization emerging in Soviet Russia. Students could be heard singing "Stalin Is My Darling," proclaiming the "fiery spirit of Karl Marx," and seen sprouting beards à la Lenin. In place of the aesthetic outfits of the twenties, undergraduate rebels were more often attired in a new outfit of stained corduroy trousers, black shirt, ragged raincoat, and red tie. Undergraduates at Oxford enjoyed their new interest, looked forward to spending a weekend visiting the unemployed in the Rhondda, of marching with the strikers along the High, of shouting revolutionary slogans up Park Lane, of attending innumerable conferences and meetings to decide on the next tactic, of discussing the latest "line" and planning the next attack.[21]

For many students the most profoundly moving experience, the one that, more than any other event, helped to sensitize them to an overtly political position, was the Hunger Marches. In 1932 and in 1934 the unemployed organized national marches

[21] See Philip Toynbee, *Friends Apart* (London, 1954), Chapter V.

to London to highlight their plight. These marches passed through the university towns, and for many undergraduates who went to greet the unemployed, to help feed them, talk to them, march with them, it marked the first real experience with the working classes. In the summer students helped organize camps for the unemployed and during the term joined newly created political clubs to manifest their conversion to political action.

The largest political club created at Oxford in the early thirties was the communist-dominated October Club, around which the history of Oxford undergraduate radicalism is centered. In December 1931 a group of students established this organization with the object of studying "Communism in its world, social, economic and cultural aspects." Membership quickly rose to 150 and by January 1933 to 300. Not all its members were Party cardholders. Many still held key posts in the University Labour Club, the undergraduate socialist organization tied to the British Labour Party. But the undergraduate Party members who had founded the club managed to keep control of its activities, making the organization the new focal point for student revolutionary activities.

In October 1933 the October Club with other student left-wing societies formed a committee to coordinate anti-war activities at the university. This committee held a meeting in November to protest the inclusion of Officers Training Corps (hereinafter referred to as O.T.C.) as an established part of the university system. The university authorities banned the meeting. As a result, the October Club, with other political left-wing societies, organized themselves into a new committee, called the Free Speech Committee. This group approached the university authorities for permission to hold a public meeting to discuss the ban. The authorities refused. At this point the October Club announced its own public meeting, unauthorized by the university, which was attended by 300 undergraduates. University officials retaliated by officially banning the October Club from the university.

Deprived of their own organization, the new aim of Party undergraduates was to infiltrate other student groups, especially the University Labour Club, and even the small, moribund university fascist organization. In 1934 communists gained complete control of the Labour Club, signaling the capture by the hanging of a gigantic picture of Lenin at the club's meetinghouse. By 1935 the Labour Club had 600 members. Its Friday evening meetings were packed, its Wednesday lunches overflowing, its clubroom, its library, its Sunday study groups jammed with eager, politically minded undergraduates searching for some outlet to focus their political commitment. At the center of the agitation were the most active of the University Labour Club undergraduates, the estimated 200 members who held Communist Party cards.

At Cambridge, like Oxford, the concern for poetry and aesthetics that had been a keystone of undergraduate conversation in the twenties turned in the early thirties to politics and for many toward the Communist Party.

Left-wing political activities at Cambridge were more serious, better organized, less frivolous, and more effective than at Oxford. Cambridge had a number of communist dons, like the economist, Maurice Dobb, and the biochemist, "Doggy" Wolf. In the period before 1933 a small number of undergraduates had already joined the Party. These students, led by undergraduate intellectuals David Guest, Maurice Cornforth, and poet Charles Madge, held to well-defined political objectives, most of which necessitated an isolation from university life and a complete identification with the local Communist Party cell. They gave most of their time, not to university activities, but to organizing unemployed protests in town, recruiting workers in trade unions, and taking courses on Marxism-Leninism.

After 1933 the political involvement of Cambridge students was more directed toward university activities. The new direction of politically active undergraduates was to put politics on the university map and build an extensive anti-war and anti-fascist movement among students.

For most students at Cambridge, the real beginnings of political involvement started in Armistice Week, 1933, with the picketing of a war movie at a local theatre and a large anti-war demonstration at the town war memorial. This was followed by other activities like the greeting of the Hunger Marches in February 1934; a "No More War" exhibition; the publication of new radical student magazines like *Cambridge Red Front, The Outpost,* and *Cambridge Left;* student agitation on behalf of college servants for higher wages; organization of a strike for lower student rents; plus the normal daily routine of a politically active undergraduate—distributing leaflets, selling *Daily Workers,* working in local elections, and attending endless committee meetings, demonstrations, and rallies. The center of communist activity was Trinity College, and its leaders were James Klugmann and John Cornford.[22]

Cambridge communists did not establish a political club parallel to Oxford's October Club. They were content with capturing control of the already existing Cambridge Socialist Society. In 1934 those members of the Socialist Society who felt that the society was becoming too radical broke away, leaving the communists in complete control, with John Cornford as leader. By 1935 the society had amassed a total of 500 members, among which were 150 actual Party members.

In London the student communist movement centered around the London School of Economics (hereinafter referred to as L.S.E.), which in 1931 had formed a Marxist Society. In the period 1932–34 the most active communist undergraduate at L.S.E. was an American Rhodes Scholar named Frank Meyer, who had helped organize the October Club before leaving Oxford to attend L.S.E. At L.S.E. student radical politics centered around the Student Union, of which Meyer was elected chairman. But in 1934, owing to some militant activity that the university authorities declared illegal, Meyer was expelled and eventually deported by the British government.[23]

The organization of student communist activities in London was hampered until 1935. Before 1935, a student who joined the Party was registered with the branch in the area in which he lived, and his duties were dictated by that branch. This meant, especially in a city like London where most students live at home or in the suburbs, that there was little time to develop Party work at one's college or among one's fellow undergraduates. But in 1935, as part of a far-reaching reorganization of student political activities, the Party work of undergraduates was put on a new basis. Student branches were organized in the univer-

---

[22] See Stansky and Abrahams, *Journey to the Frontier,* pp. 201–46.
[23] Frank Meyer is presently in America, where he is a senior editor of *The National Review.*

sity and communist students could dedicate their full time to undergraduate activities.

As the political involvement of students in radical activities developed, it was natural that a national link between all the various socialist and communist university societies would be forged. There already existed a national student organization in the form of the University Labour Federation (U.L.F.). But this association, established after 1917, was tied directly to the Labour Party.

In 1933 the leaders of the Oxford, Cambridge, and London communist societies decided to establish their own organization and disaffiliate their respective groups from the U.L.F. The new organization, called the Federation of Socialist Societies (F.S.S.), soon dominated student politics. By the end of 1934 the F.S.S. had become more politically militant than the U.L.F., being led by such hard-working communist leaders as John Cornford. The organization published its own periodical, *Student Vanguard,* which it circulated to its fifteen affiliated societies and to its national membership of 1,500 students.

The English public schools also had their own brand of undergraduate radicalism, centered around the exploits of Esmond and Giles Romilly, nephews of Winston Churchill, and their scandalous periodical, *Out of Bounds. Out of Bounds* labeled itself an anti-fascist, anti-war, and anti-public school magazine. The first issue, published in April 1934, was banned in many public schools, but in spite or because of this, it sold 850 copies in 23 schools. Largely through the urgings of the Romillys, the "Out of Bounds" movement mounted a campaign in the schools against the semicompulsory nature of the O.T.C.; the reactionary propagandist teaching in history classes; the fetish of games worship; the old-fashioned attitude to sex and personal freedom; and the suppression, so common at the time, of left-wing opinion in the schools. They recommended the introduction of Marxism into the school curriculum. Some members of the movement actually set up unemployment centers, which usually consisted of a hut where the unemployed could sit by a fire and partake of tea and buns while talking to the rebellious public schoolers.[24]

[24] See Toynbee, *Friends Apart,* Chapter II; and Giles Romilly and Esmond Romilly, *Out of Bounds* (London, 1935).

In the state secondary schools the political interest was best displayed not by students but by a small group of teachers who in May 1932 organized a Teachers' Anti-War Movement. The movement called for a de-emphasis of militarism in the schools; a revision of textbooks, expunging war propaganda; and through its journal, *The Ploughshare,* edited by Edward Upward, it attempted to organize effectively its 1,000 secondary-school teacher members to work actively for peace and against fascism.

B. ARTISTS

Paralleling the politicalization of university undergraduates, public school children, and secondary-school teachers was the development of political consciousness of middle-class intellectuals in the arts, literature, and the theatre. One of the first organized political associations of professional intellectuals was among artists, architects, and designers, who established in September 1933 an Artists' International (A.I.) organization.

The inspiration for the organization came from Clifford Rowe, an impoverished painter, who went to Moscow in 1929 as many other unemployed Western intellectuals did, to seek employment and a better life. He secured a job as an illustrator for a Soviet English-language publicity organization. While in Moscow he participated in an international exhibition of class-struggle revolutionary art, representing England. He left Russia to return to England in early 1933, and on the boat he met Pearl Binder, an English communist artist. They discussed the possibility of gathering English artists together to form a link with other already flourishing revolutionary art movements. In September 1933 a group of seven assembled in the apartment of industrial designer and political activist Mischa Black. They all agreed that a group should be formed, that it should be anti-fascist and should help artists to engage more effectively in political activities. Disagreement arose over whether to limit the group to political artists, or to open it to all. A compromise was reached by making the organization broad but politically oriented.

At first the A.I., which had 32 members, consisted almost exclusively of Party artists. Its leaders were Rowe, Binder, Black, and political cartoonists James Boswell, James Fitton, and James Holland.

Members of the A.I. offered their services as artists to the working-class political movement. In the period 1933–35, the A.I.'s aim was to organize the skills of the political artist in resisting war and fascist propaganda by the production of revolutionary counterpropaganda. The organization's constitution defined its purpose as an association of "artists against imperialist war on the Soviet Union, Fascism, and Colonial Oppression." Its goal was to unite "all artists in Great Britain sympathetic with their aims into working units ready to execute posters, illustrations, cartoons, book-jackets, banners, tableaux, stage decorations; to spread propaganda by means of exhibitions, the press, lectures and meetings."[25]

The A.I.'s first exhibition, held in 1934, was called "The Social Scene" and was composed largely of paintings depicting the hardships of the proletariat, the brutality of the police, and the display of armed force against street orators. There were pictures of starving children, slum conditions, simple workmen, and scenes of pleasant domestic working-class life. In general, like most of the activities of the A.I. in this period, the exhibition resembled a political demonstration more than a gallery showing.

C. WRITERS

As early as 1930, the central committee of the International Union of Revolutionary Writers in Moscow urged British communists to establish an organization of left writers in England and to start a magazine of revolutionary literature. At that time all attempts to establish such an organization had died in the discussion stage, although a few magazines of left literature, like *Storm* and *Viewpoint,* did receive some financial support from the Party. It was not until February 1934 that a group of communist intellectuals, following the lead of French intellectuals who had established L'Association des Ecrivains et Artistes Revolutionnaries (A.E.A.R.) in March 1933, set up a British section

[25] *International Literature,* Vol. I, No. 7 (1934), p. 151.

of the Writers' International (W.I.). This organization became affiliated with the A.E.A.R., the John Reed Clubs in America, and with the largest national writers' group against war and fascism, the Union of Revolutionary Writers in Moscow.

The leaders of the British group were Communist Party middle-class intellectuals Ralph Fox, Tom Wintringham, Montagu Slater, and Edgell Rickword. Included on its executive committee was England's leading communist economic theorist, John Strachey, and his sister, Annabel Williams-Ellis. The headquarters of the W.I. was in a small left-wing bookshop in central London where it held its infrequent general meetings for its 250 predominantly non-Communist members.

The principal preoccupation of the W.I. in the years 1934 and 1935 was with its monthly periodical, *Left Review,* which started publishing in October 1934. *Left Review* led an attack "for militant Communism and against individualism and metaphysics in the arts." Its aim was to expand the public knowledge of Marxism; to urge its authors to write in defense of the Soviet Union; to aid in the struggle of the working classes for a new society; and to help devise a Marxist theory of culture—in short, to spread the communist doctrine of the arts among the middle-class intelligentsia. The editors and leaders of the W.I. did not, however, lose sight of the necessity to encourage taxi drivers, miners, and dockers to submit "real" proletarian poems, plays, and stories to the journal.[26]

The W.I., besides publishing *Left Review,* also sent delegates to the First All-Union Congress of Soviet Writers in August 1934, and to the First Annual Meeting in Paris in June 1935 of the International Association of Writers for the Defence of Culture. After this meeting, the W.I. changed its name to the British Association of Writers for the Defence of Culture.

D. DRAMA

The history of the English revolutionary theatre movement dates back to the 1920s. In 1924 a small number of Communist

[26] "Editorial," *Left Review,* Vol. I (October 1934), p. 38.

Party members and some left-wing supporters of the Independent Labour Party formed a Council of Proletarian Art, which, owing to lack of support, soon collapsed. In July 1926 a remnant of this group, a small dramatic section, reorganized itself as the Workers' Theatre Movement (W.T.M.).

The W.T.M. was hampered in its early years by not having any original material and little genuine support. At first it came under the influence of the German Workers' Theatre League and the German-dominated International Workers' Dramatic Union (I.W.D.U.), which stressed the need for agitprop dramatic productions. In the period 1926–32 the W.T.M. was little more than a federation (30 groups) of small bands of revolutionary workers who performed short agitprop political skits from backs of trucks, in trade union meetings at street corners, consisting of about two minutes of rhythmic gestures, choral singing, and shouting of slogans through megaphones. All the actors in the W.T.M. troupes were Party members. Their aim was not so much to develop working-class drama as to win members to the Party. All their skits were performed in working-class districts. The troupes disdained "spotlights, lime-lights, stars" and other trappings of the bourgeois theatre. "Our only spotlight," its leader, Tom Thomas, wrote in the movement's journal, *Red Stage,* "is a Worker's Britain; our only star—the five pointed badge of the Soviet State."[27]

The tendency to broaden communist cultural activity to include left-wing middle-class intellectuals, as illustrated by the development of the A.I. and the W.I., also had its echo in the W.T.M. The German-dominated I.W.D.U. in 1931 moved its headquarters to Moscow, marking the transition of power in the organization from the agitprop-oriented German theatre movement to the more professionally oriented Russian drama group. In 1932 the I.W.D.U. called for an international competition of workers' theatres, to be entitled the First International Workers' Olympiad. It was planned for October 1932, the fifteenth anniversary of the Revolution, but was postponed until March 1933 because of inadequate preparation by some of the participants.

The W.T.M. sent two of its groups: Red Player and Red

[27] *Red Stage,* Vol. I (November 1931), p. 1.

Front. In Moscow these groups were given assistance by two professionals: Andre van Gyseghem, a left-wing English West End producer attending the Olympiad, and Herbert Marshall, an Englishman who was in Moscow studying the films and theatre with Eisenstein.

The English group performed before a combined jury of the Olympiad and was severely criticized for poor material, over-simplification of presentation, and disregard for professional technique. The jury suggested that the English W.T.M. take stock of its aims and purposes and devise a means to become more effective. A division of opinion developed within the W.T.M. Some members wanted to get away from street corner agitprop productions and develop a more professional theatre, with some bourgeois elements, in particular, a proper curtained theatre. Other members continued to believe in the desirability of agit-prop and were concerned only with raising the technical and artistic level of the groups.

The desire for a more traditional revolutionary theatre movement gained ground. On the urging of the Olympiad jury, Van Gyseghem agreed to work with a special group, comprising the best talent from the London groups. This became the Rebel Players. It included, for the first time, a W.T.M. group with non-Party members. On July 2, 1933, the Rebel Players passed a resolution that, while still paying lip service to the necessity of agitprop theatre in working-class districts, stressed the need "to draw elements in the professional theatre into the Movement to assist workers with their technical skills," and talked in terms of building "a mass revolutionary permanent theatre" with "groups of workers performing plays written for the curtained stage."[28]

In 1935 the Rebel Players were still without a permanent theatre or an economically secure foundation. Later that year, however, the Players began presenting Clifford Odets' *Waiting for Lefty,* which proved to be such a great success that on Christmas Eve, 1935, a Roman Catholic priest offered the Rebel Players a disused hall in central London for their productions. The Rebel Players called together the existing W.T.M. troupes

[28] "The Workers' Theatre Movement" (unpublished report, 1936).

in London, and all agreed to establish one theatre group, which they named the Unity Theatre Club. Volunteers set to work on the hall, and in two months had cleaned, painted it, and installed a stage and chairs for a hundred people. On February 19, 1936, London's first premanent left-wing theatre, with a starting active membership of 30 and an associate membership of 300, opened its doors, appropriately with a production of *Waiting for Lefty*. A new phase of intellectual involvement in politics was to begin. Another cultural institution was added to growing numbers of intellectual associations created to struggle against war, fascism, and economic depression.

Unity Theatre was an amateur group. Its actors and helpers were usually political activists who also happened to be interested in the drama as a vehicle for political expression. Van Gyseghem, one of Unity's leaders, felt, however, that London should also have a permanent repertory company of left-wing professional actors and actresses. In January 1934, Van Gyseghem, with a group of Party activists and some left-wing theatre people, established the Left Theatre. This organization gave Sunday evening performances in the West End of plays that expressed the life and struggle of the workers (i.e., Gorky's *Mother*, Slater's *Easter, 1916, Miner*), which during the week they took down to working-class districts to perform free of charge. The hope of the founders was to tie this left-wing professional repertory theatre to a trade organization and set up a working-class cultural center. Their plans never materialized.

In the period immediately following the rise of Hitler to power in January 1933, an entire series of politically oriented cultural organizations was established, many of which were tied closely to the Communist Party and composed of newly converted Party members. The Workers' Bookshops were organized to distribute the large number of Marxian classics turned out on the presses of Modern Books, the official publishers of Lenin in England, and Martin Lawrence Ltd., the official Party publishers. A working-class evening and Sunday afternoon school, Marx House, with classes in literature, science, and economics, was founded in 1933. Kino, a film-distributing organization set up in early 1933, showed Soviet classic silent films of Eisenstein and Pudovkin. In 1934 the film-making section of Kino, called the Film and

Photo League, established its own production unit and made short 16-mm. films on such subjects as the means test, unemployment, and anti-fascist rallies.

All the above organizations of undergraduates, writers, artists, theatre people, and film makers became politically active among the middle-class intelligentsia after 1932. Their primary concern was with altering the society in which they existed, through criticism, political action, and propaganda. They were all closely tied to a particular political movement—communism—and all concentrated their activities on the workers' struggle against economic exploitation and the menacing threat of emergent fascism.

Alongside these anti-fascist, communist-oriented cultural organizations there existed less overtly political but nevertheless genuinely socially conscious cultural organizations, whose main concern was with reasserting the social function of the intellectual and with bridging the gap between the intellectual and his society, rather than with the production of political propaganda.

Whereas Unity Theatre and Left Theatre were more concerned with using the drama as political weapon, another theatre organization, called Group Theatre, established in 1932, althought politically left wing, was more interested in using drama as a vehicle to expose the problems of modern society. In February 1932 a group of young actors and dancers, led by Rupert Doone, the last English male dancer to work for the great Diaghilev, moved by a common dissatisfaction and impatience with the existing West End theatre, formed themselves into a small repertory company that put on Sunday afternoon performances of contemporary plays with social content. The Group Theatre's motto was that "art should serve life"; its aim was to make the theatre a social force free from the dependence of commercial or purely popular considerations, and not a political weapon tied to a political doctrine.

Doone and his company of artists included Auden, Spender, MacNeice, Isherwood as writers, John Piper, Robert Medley, and Henry Moore as artists, a young composer named Benjamin Britten, and a group of young actors including Alec Guinness. They wanted to restore the idea of collective theatre to the British stage, with the actors and the audience cooperating actively to form a play. In some productions the audience was seated on the stage, actors were placed in the middle of the audience; discussions were conducted after each performance. Auden's play, *Dance of Death,* written especially for the Group Theatre, for example, ended with a crowd of "Bolsheviks" coming from the audience singing the Internationale and waving an enormous Red flag.

In 1934 the Group Theatre underwent debate on its relationship to the political movement in England. Some of its early members tried to steer the Theatre into the Communist Party orbit. This attempt was successfully sidetracked by Doone, and the small Party cell within the Group Theatre was asked to leave the organization.

Most of the plays produced by the Group Theatre were written especially for it by Auden, Isherwood, MacNeice, and Spender. Auden's *Dance of Death,* performed in February 1934, was the first big event for the Theatre. This was later followed by a production of less politically overt plays like T. S. Eliot's *Sweeney Agonistes,* and then in the period 1935–38 by more directly political satires like Auden's and Isherwood's *Dog Beneath the Skin, The Ascent of F6, On the Frontier,* and Spender's *Trial of a Judge.*

Some of the people associated with the Group Theatre participated in another venture designed to bridge the gap between the artist and the audience—the making of documentary films under the auspices of the Government Post Office (G.P.O.) Film Unit. Auden, Britten, Medley all worked in the production of documentary films. The G.P.O. Film Unit was an outgrowth of an earlier film unit established in 1929 by the Empire Marketing Board (E.M.B.), a government agency to make short silent films to promote the marketing of Empire-made products in Britain. Led by John Grierson, the leader of the English documentary film movement, the E.M.B. film unit produced films like *Industrial Britain,* which, although leaving the social and political implications unstated, attempted to bring to the screen in cinematic realism, for the first time, the English working man as a serious and vital figure. Among the hundred silent films produced by the E.M.B. unit, the largest number dealt with the working-class laborer and the skilled craftsman at his job.

In July 1933, after the disbanding of the E.M.B., the film unit, led by Grierson, was reorganized under the auspices of the G.P.O., with the object of producing sound films that depicted the communications services between Britain and the Commonwealth. Under this new government agency, the Film Unit felt it was no longer possible merely to describe and dramatize the working man and his products, but found it necessary to explore through the film such social problems as housing (i.e., *Face of Britain*), health (i.e., *Smoke Menace*), unemployment (i.e., *We Live in Two Worlds*), the evils of nationalism, and the benefits of manual labor.

Some film producers who trained with the G.P.O. Film Unit, men like Paul Rotha and Arthur Elton, wanted to make more openly political films. Unable to attempt this under the G.P.O., they sought support from private concerns and produced, in the middle thirties, films like *Housing Problem,* on the evils of urban housing, and *Peace of Britain,* a film made overnight in response to crises over Ethiopia and the League of Nations.

The English documentary film unit led by Grierson produced under government agencies like the E.M.B. and the G.P.O., and with the support of private commercial concerns, over two hundred movies. These films fulfilled Grierson's own aim to use the "cinema as a pulpit, and exploit it as a propagandist." He wanted to make the film a potent medium of public persuasion, not just a public toy for amusement and relaxation, as in the commercial cinema, or just a device for propaganda about the Soviet Union, as in Kino. Grierson and his staff gave the film a genuine social function.[29]

Painters and professional artists were also concerned with making their creative products more responsive to social needs. Artists were among the groups hit most directly by the economic depression. Many young painters couldn't sell their work. By 1933 the market for new, virtually unknown painters had dried up. Part of their problem the young artists blamed on the exclusiveness of artistic expression identified most closely with the formalistic art theories of Clive Bell and Roger Fry. Art, like literature and the drama, had become the preserve of a very

[29] See Forsyth Hardy, ed., *Grierson on Documentary* (London, 1966).

small coterie of highly specialized minds and sensibilities. In the twenties English painters, following the canons of taste laid down by the Continental art movements of post-impressionism, cubism, dada, and surrealism, regarded the seen world as only a starting point to explore the artist's own inner feelings, or as something to transform into an ideal shape, or as something to escape from into a world of images and personal symbols.

In the thirties the young artists, growing up during the depression, called for a new realism, desiring to make art a serious public activity in direct contact with the most important social problems of the time. Art was no longer to be viewed as separate from society.

The leading socially conscious art critic of the thirties was Anthony Blunt, who led the battle for artistic realism in his reviews and essays in the *Spectator*. Blunt championed, for example, the work of the Hungarian refugee sculptor, Ladislaw Peri, who worked in concrete and executed group sculpture for public buildings to be viewed by all, and not for private gardens for the appreciation of a select few. Blunt also heaped praise on Lord Hastings, a student of Mexican communist painter Diego Rivera, who became England's only political mural painter.

The triumph of realism in the British art world did not occur until 1937, when a group of socially conscious and politically aware young painters established the Euston Road School of Painting, which taught its pupils to paint the world they saw around them—the slums, the urban dwellings, the unemployed, and the Hunger Marches.

The most blatantly political and didactic art work in the thirties was done not by oil painters but by political cartoonists. Political cartoons were England's answer to Russia's socialist realism. Cartoons, especially the more communist-inspired ones of the three Jameses of the A.I.—James Boswell, James Fitton, James Holland—were ideally suited to the rapidly changing political and economic situation of the thirties. They could be dashed off in quick response to a particular political event without losing any artistic effectiveness or dramatic impact. In fact, the most effective intellectual products of the thirties—the political cartoon, the dramatic satirical review, the mass declamation poem, the short documentary film—all share the characteristic of being able to respond quickly to a specific political event without sacrificing artistic, literary, or dramatic effectiveness.

The move toward realism is also apparent in the literature produced in the thirties. The introspective self-analysis, so typical of the literary products of the twenties, gave way to the journalistic, socially conscious novels of the thirties. As drama became more didactic, poems easier to read, and painting more representational, novels became shorter and less esoteric. The language of the novel became simple, the images less erudite, the themes more common. For the novelist of the thirties, external reality, not internal drives, became the subject; social realism, not stream of consciousness, became the method; Marx, not Freud, became the culture hero; heroic action, not passive contemplation, became the central preoccupation of the novelist and his characters. In the novel, political themes superseded previous concentration upon sexual problems; a stress on class struggle replaced a concern with sibling rivalry. Novels were not about the internal struggles of the mind and soul, but rather were concerned with the external struggle against poverty, death, and economic misery.

Literature, especially poetry, became a public act. One didn't read poems in drawing rooms to a small coterie of friends, or study them assiduously over one's writing desk; instead, one declaimed them from the plinth of Nelson's column, chanted them in working-class pubs, printed them on broadsheets, or handed them out at factory gates.

The new canons of literary criticism, asserted by Spender in *The Destructive Element,* Day Lewis in *A Hope for Poetry,* by the editors of *Left Review,* and by the contributors to a symposium entitled *The Mind in Chains,* stressed the idea that every work of literature was a product of the social condition of the writer, and that the success of the work depended on the degree to which the author had become aware of the social conditions around him. Literature was viewed as a social product and evaluated on its social function. Changes in the form and content of literature were not due to the whims of accidental aesthetic fashion, or to racial, national, or genetic traits, but were determined by the changes in the economic structure of society. Literature was a form of social consciousness, a reflection of social reality, and a revolutionary agent for the transformation of that reality.

New periodicals were established to publish the new socially realistic literature. *New Verse,* founded in January 1933 by Geoffrey Grigson, printed poems that dealt with contemporary issues and championed the approach to poetry outlined by the *New Signatures* and *New Country* group. *New Writing,* founded and edited by John Lehmann, aimed at a broad anti-fascist front, but limited its selections of short stories and prose to works on "realism"—stories about ordinary men and women in simple, direct prose. It published the best samples of "proletarian" writing done in England and presented, for the first time in English, works of prominent European left intellectual realists like Anna Seghers, Ignazio Silone, Bert Brecht, Jean-Paul Sartre, Boris Pasternak, and Michael Sholokhov.

By 1935 few young, sensitive English intellectuals could avoid becoming either involved in one of the various intellectual organizations established to mobilize an attack on fascism, economic depression, and war, or convinced of the necessity of making their intellectual products reflect the social crises of the period and serve a genuine social function. Artists became socially aware, poets socially conscious, writers more didactic, and young intellectuals, in general, more politically involved.

III. THE POPULAR FRONT LEFT INTELLIGENTSIA, 1935–38

With the outbreak of the Spanish Civil War in 1936, the movement of socially conscious and politically active intellectuals found a central force and a cohesive symbol. Support for Republican Spain became a rallying point for all on the left. It brought into the anti-fascist cultural movement intellectuals with half-formulated political ideas, sustained by vague humanitarian hopes. It offered the English intellectual who was becoming more sensitive to the social and political scene around him a time and a place where a legitimate cause that represented a greater degree of freedom and justice was resisting a thoroughly reactionary one. Spain lifted the intellectual anti-fascist cause into a crusade for justice. It widened the intellectual front against fascism and war to a more Popular Front support for justice and civilization.

Already existing anti-fascist cultural organizations broadened their appeal. They became less concerned with ideological exclusiveness and more with getting as many politically conscious intellectuals within their fold.

A. UNIVERSITY

In the universities the communist societies linked up with the old Labour groups they had originally split from. In September 1935 the F.S.S. approached the U.L.F. to create a united federation of students. A new, popular front student organization, renamed the Student Labour Federation, was formed in February 1936, with two vice-presidents, one representing the less revolutionary U.L.F. and the other, John Cornford, representing the communist-controlled F.S.S. This new student radical movement reached its acme in 1938 with over 3,000 students in 35 affiliated sections. This increase in membership reflected the fact that undergraduate involvement in left-wing politics had extended far beyond the Oxford-Cambridge-London student axis to the more working-class red brick universities.

The communist-controlled Socialist Society at Cambridge and the Oxford Labour Club concentrated their activities after 1936 on the struggle in Spain. Some students, like Cornford, volunteered to join the International Brigades and fight, and in Cornford's case to die, in Spain. But most students stayed at home, organizing collections, attending rallies for Spain, partaking in austerity lunches, paying 1s. 6d. for bread, cheese, and a speech, with the profits sent to Spanish medical aid. Where in 1934 undergraduates marched with the unemployed, they now begged for the Basque children.

B. ARTISTS

By 1935 the leaders of the Artists' International found that only a few artists were prepared to accept the more militant outlook of the organization. In accordance with the general trend toward united front intellectual activities, the A.I. broadened its appeal by declaring that it was "for the Unity of Artists against Fascism and war and the suppression of culture." The leaders affirmed that the organization was concerned primarily with "cultural progress and Expansion, Freedom of Speech and expression," and not with the mobilization of artistic talent for propagandistic exploitation. The organization signaled its shift in outlook by changing its name from the Artists' International to the Artists' International Association (A.I.A.).

The A.I.A.'s activities became less directly propagandistic and more educational. It organized meetings and activities of artists *on* political issues, instead of mobilizing groups of artists for the production of political propaganda. Popular Front Exhibitions against fascism and war were substituted for the production of banners and posters for the Communist Party. The new aim was not to perform the functions of a political sign-painting association or establish a common approach to art, but to organize a large enough artists' pressure group to fight fascism, avoid war, and mobilize public opinion in support of the Republican forces in Spain. Political consciousness among artists, not a political attitude toward painting, became the critical criterion for A.I.A. membership. One could become politically conscious without becoming a social realist.

Within the organization, however, there still existed a hard core of artists, mainly the original founding members, who wanted to work out a political approach to their art. But these people found their creative outlet, after 1934, by forming an artists' discussion group within the Communist Party, called the Hogarth Group. All of its members were active in the A.I.A., but the only official joint activity between the two groups was a cricket match played to raise money for the International Brigades.

By 1936 the A.I.A. had established an artistic popular front within its 1,000-member association, by enlisting the active participation of a number of prominent surrealists, constructivists, cubists, academy traditionalists, as well as social realists. This new broad-based approach was best illustrated by the Second Exhibition of the association, held in November 1935.

The 1934 exhibition was organized around a thematic unity of art in support of the working class. The 1935 exhibition concentrated not on the attempt to make art a weapon in the class struggle but on organizing artists, irrespective of their conception of the role of art in society, as a protest against war and fascism.

This A.I.A. exhibition, as well as the 1937 exhibition of artists for "Peace, Democracy and Cultural Development," included all forms of political commitment on the left, from vague liberals to dedicated communists, as well as all artistic expressions, from the Post-Impressionism of Duncan Grant, the abstractionism of Ben Nicolson, the surrealism of Roland Penrose, to the socialist realism of Clifford Rowe.

The A.I.A. organized artists for peace, forming a Peace Publicity Bureau in June 1936 and becoming affiliated to the International Peace Campaign in September 1936. But the central focus of A.I.A. members after 1936 was with the war in Spain. The first English person killed in Spain was an A.I.A. member, artist Felicia Browne, and the association held an exhibition of her drawings and raised money to buy an ambulance for the International Brigades. Other A.I.A. activities in aid of the Spanish Republicans consisted of some artists like Jacob Epstein, Henry Moore, and Picasso donating works of art to be auctioned off for money sent to Spain. Its members painted appeals for Spanish relief on London buildings. Augustus John and other prominent artists would go to Trafalgar Square on Sundays and paint "Portraits for Spain," donating the money they collected, £600, to the Spanish cause.

C. THEATRE

In 1935 the Unity Theatre Club was still producing short one-act plays of political propaganda with some dramatic content, like *Waiting for Lefty*. But in the period 1936–39 the Theatre Club broadened its activities to include full-length realistic dramas. The shift was signaled by the acquisition of a new theatre with a modern lighting system and a proper, curtained stage. From an organization with a small theatre performing short sketches twice a week for a predominantly working-class audience, Unity became a first-rate dramatic society, located in a newly converted theatre, performing full-length plays six nights a week to a mixed working-class, middle-class audience. Under the leadership of professional directors, it performed such works as Pogodin's *Aristocrats,* Irwin Shaw's anti-war drama, *Bury the Dead,* the first British production of a Brecht play, *Señor Carrar's Rifles,* and Spender's *Trial of a Judge.* Unity established a theatre school, under the direction of Marshall, based on Stanislavsky's acting method, and a play clinic designed to produce original plays by Unity members. One group of Unity, led by Marshall, even wanted to go so far as to make the Theatre Club into a professional repertory company, performing plays to West End audiences. But this proposition was overridden by the votes of those Club members who wanted to assert the political aspects of the organization.

During this period Unity was tied directly to the Communist Party. There was a large Party cell within the club, which, in practice, controlled everything, its administration, its finances, its general policy, as well as the choice of its plays. With at least one third of the 300 active members of Unity holding Party cards, the Club became one of the best recruiting organizations for the Party. Many Unity members performed the routine tasks of Party members, of selling *Daily Workers,* doing door-to-door recruiting, going on slogan-chalking expeditions, participating in local demonstrations and poster parades, selling pamphlets, distributing leaflets, arguing with strangers. Many members recognized that efficient propaganda did not necessarily go with effective theatre and that the primary aim of the organization should not be to produce better plays but to use drama to focus the attention of the audience as well as the actors on the struggle against fascism, war, and the battle in Spain.

D. WRITERS

The Writers' International in the period 1936–39, like its Artists' International counterpart, broadened its activities and changed its name to the British Section of the International

Association of Writers for the Defence of Culture. Under the chairmanship of Day Lewis, who had joined the Communist Party in 1936, the Association set up a number of committees to investigate the feasibility of creating a writers' trade union; to suggest changes in the libel laws; and, after 1936, to disseminate information about the cultural work of the Spanish Republican government. It sent delegates to the International Conference of Writers against War and Fascism held in Paris in 1935 and Valencia in 1937, and organized the Second International Conference of Writers, held in London in 1936. *Left Review,* the journal of the Association, shifted its policy to concentrate on organizing a widespread movement of writers against fascism. Stephen Spender and Day Lewis were coopted onto the editorial board, and the journal became less concerned with developing a coherent Marxist theory of culture and more interested in organizing and mobilizing an effective number of middle-class intellectuals to speak out against fascism and war.

In its most famous attempt to mobilize the English writers and poets in support of the Republican cause, the Association circulated a questionnaire on the War to English intellectuals. The questions were:

> Are you for, or against, the legal Government
> and the People of Republican Spain?
> Are you for, or against, Franco and Fascism?

The results were published in a pamphlet entitled *Authors Take Sides on the Spanish War,* with 127 for the Republic, 17 neutral, and only 5 against the Spanish government. Because of such an overwhelming response, the Association decided to organize a giant Writers Against Fascism meeting in June 1938. It was the largest meeting of writers against war and fascism held during the decade, and the audience of 3,000 passed a resolution, with two dissenters, that "this meeting declares its abhorrence of the aims and methods of Fascism."

In January 1938 the Association of Writers recognized that it was duplicating much of the same work being done by a newly established broad-based intellectual organization called For Intellectual Liberty (F.I.L.). So in January the British Section of the International Association of Writers for the Defence of Culture became affiliated with the F.I.L., as an autonomous section, and changed its name to the Association of Writers for Intellectual Liberty. All the Association members became members of the F.I.L., but they were able to pursue their separate but similar activities.

The F.I.L. was founded in 1936 as a coordinating center for intellectuals who "felt the condition of the world called for the active defence of peace, liberty, and culture." The inspiration for the organization came from an appeal from the French Comité de Vigilance des Intellectuels Anti-fascistes, which in January 1936 called a conference in Paris at which time it was decided to form an International Federation of Intellectual Workers. After this meeting, which some English intellectuals had attended, a group of some fifty English intellectuals decided to follow the suggestion of the Paris conference and formed an association called For Intellectual Liberty. Its leaders represented a curious amalgam of old, established liberal intellectuals like Leonard Woolf and Kingsley Martin; remnants of the elite of Bloomsbury, E. M. Forster, Adrian Stephen; politically active scientists J. D. Bernal, C. P. Snow, and Hyman Levy; celebrated artists like Henry Moore; old-line Labour intellectuals like R. H. Tawney; as well as C. Day Lewis and members of the old Writers' International. The whole organization was presided over by Aldous Huxley, and its spiritual home was in fashionable Hampstead.

F.I.L. served as a Popular Front intellectual organization, working with all "progressive" political groups in England, especially with the National Council for Civil Liberties, Spanish Aid Committee, and the Committee for Fascist Refugees. However, unlike the Writers' International, or other anti-fascist cultural organizations, F.I.L. did not contemplate formulating a "definite political creed." It existed basically as a potential body of names and people who could be organized quickly on a particular issue of critical importance for intellectuals. The assumption behind the organization was that intellectuals as "eminent people" could influence public policy if they acted in concert. A council was set up which drew up statements on problems of immediate national or international significance. These draft manifestos were sent to a list of "influential members" to gain signatures. Thus, within hours of an event like the execution of a Nobel Prize scientist or an arrest of a Spanish intellectual, a manifesto with an illustrious list of names could be sent to *The Times* or a local paper, or to the appropriate government offices. F.I.L. sent a note of thanks to F. D. Roosevelt for pushing peace; a letter of admiration to President Schuschnigg on the Austrian plebiscite; initiated the now common practice of sending letters to national newspapers with a statement on a particular issue signed by a large number of prominent personages.

The F.I.L. also organized deputations to M.P.s as well as to foreign embassies. This organization illustrates the manner in which many intellectuals could manifest their protest in the thirties, not through their own creative work, but through organized public opinion as intellectuals on specific topics. A sort of left-wing P.E.N. Club, its aim was to mobilize and educate public opinion through collective letters to the editors, petitions, and deputations to important officials.

Only one organization established in the 1930s was able to gather up the scattered efforts of intellectual activity in the theatre, films, literature, art, and music; that was the Left Book Club (L.B.C.). The L.B.C. was as close as England got to an intellectual popular front. The Club canalized anti-fascist opinion and became the most active and largest organized body in Britain working for a popular front. Established on the eve of the Spanish Civil War by publisher Victor Gollancz, with the assistance of political theorist Harold Laski and John Strachey, the L.B.C. was a left-wing book-of-the-month club. Members could receive for 2s. 6d. (about 60¢ in 1936) a "Left Book of the Month," and the Club's monthly periodical, *Left Book News* (later called *Left News*). The response to the scheme was overwhelming. By 1939 it had 57,000 members. It quickly developed numerous supplementary activities and auxiliary organizations: discussion groups, weekend seminars, and political rallies were held; overseas groups, Russian-language classes, and Left Book Club centers were organized. The affiliated organizations encompassed theatre, poetry, music, travel, and film.

An L.B.C. poets' and writers' group included most of the active members of the left-wing literary organizations of the period. Membership in the poets' group approached 200; its activities included poetry reading, mass recitations, and heated literary discussions. It tried to revive the broadsheet ballad, discuss the folk tradition in art, and devise declamatory verse for mass meetings and revolutionary songs that could be sung in pubs. The group even founded its own periodical, *Poetry and the People,* which reached a circulation of over 1,000.

The most successful of the special intellectual organizations established under the auspices of the L.B.C. was the L.B.C. Theatre Guild. Created in April 1937, it sought to help express through the theatre the same interpretation of life and politics that Club publications expressed through the printed word. By September 1938 there were over 250 amateur Theatre Guild groups in existence, publishing left-wing drama, putting on topical skits at local political gatherings, and performing one-act plays. Under the leadership of its paid organizer, John Allen, and in close cooperation with Unity Theatre, the Theatre Guild became the coordinating center and information bureau for all left-wing amateur theatre in Britain. Through its groups it helped develop an active left-wing provincial theatre movement. The Guild published a monthly review of its local activities called *New Theatre.*

In the films, Kino and the Film and Photo League both became affiliated to the L.B.C. Together they published a bulletin, *Left Film Front,* urging film makers and film workers to use the film to aid in the battle against war and fascism.

An L.B.C. Musicians' Group, led by communist composer Alan Bush, had over 100 members and cooperated with the newly established Workers' Music Association (W.M.A.), founded by Bush. The W.M.A. organized musical pageants and festivals of music, which amounted to a musical Marxian interpretation of English working-class history. Bush and the various choral unions associated with the W.M.A. provided entertainment during many of the anti-fascist, pro-Spain rallies of the period.

The L.B.C. and its various affiliated organizations based their activities on a faith in the efficacy of reason, the power of public opinion, and the magic of rational argument. It was assumed that if people were sufficiently rational and intelligent, given the "facts," they would act accordingly. There was a belief that all one had to do was persuade people what were the right things to have done, and they would do them, that knowledge of an evil was the first step toward its eradication.[30]

The hope of the politically conscious intellectuals of the period was centered on the struggle in Spain. "On that arid square," Auden asserted,

> that fragment ripped off from hot Africa,
> Soldered so crudely to inventive Europe: On that tableland
> Scored by rivers, Our thoughts have bodies.
> The menacing shapes of our fever
> Are precise and alive.[31]

The issues in Spain were clear-cut. Republican Spain was the legal, democratically elected government. Franco represented fascist aggression. Republican Spain conjured up images of a flourishing culture, a country of social justice, reason, a people with tenacious courage, of workers and peasants. It meant freedom, justice, and democracy. Franco, on the other hand, was identified with obscurantist religion, brutish nationalism, "gangsterism," slavery of workers, degradation of women, economic reaction, runaway royalism, and rapacious landlords. He stood for barbarism and destruction of culture.

The struggle in Spain helped to alleviate the politically conscious intellectual's problem of how to express his political commitment without compromising his artistic integrity. Intellectuals spent most of their time fighting by proxy; gazing at a map of Spain; marching in anti-fascist parades; taking up collections for Spanish medical relief; working for the L.B.C. or the F.I.L.; helping the Committee of Spanish Relief; composing poems on events read about in newspapers; painting portraits to collect money for an ambulance for the Society of Friends; abstaining from "port" or Rheinwein in protest against supporters of Franco. Being a left intellectual almost became a career in itself.

But for the more thoroughly committed intellectual, the Span-

[30] For a fuller discussion of the L.B.C., see my article, "The Left Book Club," *Journal of Contemporary History,* Vol. I (April 1966), pp. 65–86.
[31] Taken from "Spain 1937" in W. H. Auden, *Spain* (London, 1937), p. 10, and reprinted with the permission of Faber & Faber Ltd. of London and Random House, Inc., of New York.

ish Civil War presented a deeper and more agonizing problem. Was it enough to limit one's activities to collecting money, addressing meetings, and attending mass rallies? Wasn't there something concrete that could be done, some gesture to signal a more politically positive position? For many intellectuals the solution was in joining the Communist Party, which from 1936 to 1938 was simply another way of showing that one supported the Republic and opposed fascism. For many, like Spender, the transition from a non-Party intellectual to a Party member scarcely altered one's outlook.

In 1930 there were only 1,376 members in the Communist Party of Great Britain, almost all of working-class origin, while in 1938 there were 15,570. The rising membership was due in no small measure to the many middle-class intellectuals who became politically conscious in the middle thirties and streamed into the Party ranks. But until 1933 the Party actively discouraged or simply ignored middle-class intellectual recruitment. The cultural activities engaged in by the Party were aimed, until 1933, exclusively at the working class, like the Workers' Theatre Movement or the small Workers' Film Society established in 1929.

This attitude changed in 1934, with a concerted effort by the Party to encourage bourgeois, middle-class participants in communist-dominated, anti-fascist cultural organizations like Unity Theatre, Kino, Artists' International, and Writers' International. In 1935 the Party set up a supervisory section within the Agitprop Department, led by Emile Burns and assisted by Ralph Fox, and organized along professional lines the theatre, films, journalism, artists, writers, musicians to coordinate intellectual involvement in anti-fascist activities. Communist members of these various organizations established informal discussion groups within the Party to decide upon direct action. These groups were guided by a generally inactive and very tolerant Agitprop Department, which permitted a great deal of ideological freedom. There was no particular effort to stress dogma or disseminate accepted rules of intellectual behavior; for the Party leadership, desiring not to alienate any possible intellectual support, deemphasized adherence to the texts of Marxist-Leninism. Between 1934 and 1938 there was little external evidence of the rigid sectarianism that characterized the Party's intellectual front in the late 1920s and the early 1930s.[32]

As the influx of middle-class intellectuals into the Party, especially after the outbreak of the Spanish Civil War, became great and as the anti-fascist cultural organizations multiplied, the small Agitprop Department was found to be quite inadequate to meet the demands of the Party intellectuals. In 1937 the Party formed a Cultural Committee of about twenty members, representing various left intellectual cultural organizations, which met monthly and during crisis periods at weekly or sometimes nightly intervals to coordinate Communist Party intellectual activities. The formation of the Cultural Committee, headed by Emile Burns, allowed the cultural activities of Party members to be free from all other Party activities. It recognized that different rules of behavior could be applied to middle-class intellectuals than to working-class members. In 1938 the Party officially recognized the importance of "work amongst the middle class and professional sections," and signified the need to "mobilize the middle class and professional people on the basis of their professional interests. . . ."[33]

Some English intellectuals learned to serve the Party as citizens but didn't feel it necessary to serve it as intellectuals. They were unwilling to accept the "marching orders of the proletarian general staff," no matter how unsectarian these happened to be. They believed agitation was necessary, but intellectual propaganda intolerable. Their goal was not to become blank-verse propagandists, or create poems out of rhymed Marxian economics, or sprinkle their work liberally with proletarian jargon or revolutionary slogans, but to do something that mattered. As Spender asked,

> [I] who live under the shadows of war
> What can I do that matters?[34]

[32] See L. J. MacFarlane, *The British Communist Party* (London, 1966).
[33] Communist Party of Great Britain, *Report of the Central Committee: 1st Party Congress, September 16–19, 1938*, p. 43.
[34] Taken from Stephen Spender's poem in *New Signatures,* Michael Roberts, ed., p. 91, and reprinted with the permission of the Hogarth Press of London and Random House, Inc., of New York.

Joining the Communist Party became one of the accepted ways to signal one's willingness to act.

Some Communist Party intellectuals wanted to do more than just join the Party. Edgell Rickword, Edward Upward, Ralph Fox, among others, gave up personal creative writing for total political action. During the Spanish Civil War a few intellectuals, who believed they were living under the lengthening shadow of fascism, felt it was not enough to produce efficient propaganda or perform the tasks of an active Party worker. They wanted to lay their lives down for the cause, to go out and fight in Spain.

Those intellectuals who joined the International Brigades, organized to allow foreign volunteers to fight in Spain, went for different reasons: some, no doubt, looking for adventure; others because they were frustrated with their position in English society; still others, notably Cornford and Bell, were persuaded to go by considered action motivated by emotional indignation. Others fought because they were told to go by the Party, and some because they were dedicated fighters for freedom. Some saw the struggle in terms of a romantic journey, others as a propaganda holiday, still others as an anti-fascist crusade.

IV. THE PERIOD OF DISILLUSIONMENT, 1938–40

The potential conflict between those thoroughly committed communist intellectuals giving their services as intellectuals to the Party or acting as Party functionaries, and those intellectuals who were willing to lend their names to the Party or volunteer their services for a crusade of anti-fascism, but believed that the creative intellectual should never engage in any activity for the cause of peace and the fight against fascism to the extent of abandoning or seriously curtailing, for any length of time, his activity as a creative artist—this conflict, never far below the surface, emerged more clearly in the period after 1938.

In the period 1935–38 the question of political and social consciousness was taken for granted. What was in doubt in the period after 1938 was the way in which one manifested this commitment. Was it enough just to "reflect" the social crises of the time in your work? Was it sufficient just to assert the social function of the intellectual? Wasn't it necessary for the intellectual, as a thinking, sensitive instrument, to take a stand on political issues? How far could one join private feeling with public action, with being bourgeois by birth and proletarian by sympathy? How was one to relate a public passion for politics with a private concern for a personal vision, between the necessity of political commitment and the desire for artistic creation? How easy would it be to mingle private sentiments with public slogans, political efficiency with poetic virtue? To what extent should intellectuals use their talent for propagandistic purposes? How could one engage in political sloganeering without sacrificing individual integrity? How far could a bourgeois intellectual disown his own class values? These questions and dilemmas preoccupied the intellectuals during the period 1936–38, the time of the Spanish Civil War, and haunted them in the period after 1938. They represented the dilemma Spender called the problem of the "divided generation"—not divided between a loyalty to the past and the demands of the present, or even the appeal of the left and the attraction of the right, but rather between the desire to engage in action, be committed, and the impulse to remain artistically detached; between the fulfilling of a literary vocation and the urge to save the world from fascism and war.[35]

The struggle in Spain forced many English intellectuals to make a decision on the nature of their commitment to politics. For if Spain marked the high point of the left intellectuals' involvement in the political struggle, it also marked the point at which the commitment was seriously questioned. This shift in the intensity of commitment was due less to a change of intellectual outlook on questions of policy than to a reappraisal of the international situation and a reassessment of the avenues open for effective action by intellectuals.

Those who left to fight in or visit Spain felt, at first, a great sense of personal completion, a great enthusiasm for what they saw, a feeling that they were finally doing something of significance. They were visibly excited by the activity in the streets of Barcelona, the harbors of San Sebastian, the heroic defense of Madrid, the flood of waving banners. But this feeling, for all

[35] Stephen Spender, *World Within World*, p. 202.

but the most dedicated or the most disciplined, soon faded. The harsh reality of the situation soon made itself apparent—the unbelievable disorganization of the Brigades, the harsh mutual criticism, the disgraceful retreats, the "rumors" of internal dissension, the often cold, uncongenial company. For those who went to Spain, in general, there was a fading of romance.[36]

For some of the most committed intellectuals it was a physical disaster. Ralph Fox, dedicated Party member since 1921 and leading Party intellectual, was killed in January 1937. John Cornford, David Guest, two leaders of the university communist movement, and Christopher Caudwell, England's foremost Marxian cultural theorist, were all killed. After their deaths the Party actively prevented any other prominent intellectuals from going to fight in Spain.

At home, in England, rumblings of doubt about the purity of the cause to which intellectuals had committed themselves began to find their way into print. There was the case of André Gide, with his sudden reversal of his favorable opinion on Russia, and then the Communists' sudden reversal on Gide. There was concern over the Soviet trials in 1937 and the doubts and questions raised about their authenticity. But in England, which had an almost non-existent Trotskyist movement, the trials were easily explained away. Reports about the fierce internal fighting between Communists and Trotskyists found their way into more and more newspaper columns. But since the English left intellectuals were not as tied to a pro-Soviet commitment as they were to an anti-war, anti-fascist position, the doubts and questions concerning Russia were not necessarily final and disillusioning. They did, however, produce a sense of uneasiness about what was happening in Russia and Spain. They sensitized the left intellectual, put him in a questioning mood.

At about the same time as these doubts were being raised about the purity of the cause, the Communist Party leaders, in an effort to maintain control over a larger and growing number of Party intellectuals, decided to impose a stricter doctrinal position on the intellectual organizations connected with the Party. In late 1937 the Party decided to make *Left Review* a more

[36] Toynbee, *Friends Apart*, p. 92.

popular, less narrowly intellectual periodical, in order to aim at a wider, more working-class audience. The Party took complete control of the journal in 1938, even deciding on such small items as its size and shape. As a result, by June 1938, *Left Review,* owing to lack of Party funds and gradual disenchantment on the part of some of its most dedicated supporters, had ceased publication.

The Cultural Committee of the Party, led by Douglas Garman, imposed a tighter discipline on other communist-dominated organizations. Gollancz was forever trying to sidetrack efforts by communist activists to draw the L.B.C. into the open political arena. A political commissar was sent to Unity Theatre to keep an eye on the "political purity" of its members, which resulted in an open clash between those who wanted Unity to produce more effective drama and those who wanted to maintain Unity as an efficient political organization. Some of the less politically active members of the A.I.A., angered over the position of the communist artists within the organization, tried unsuccessfully to excise the political clause from the A.I.A. constitution. The Party established a more doctrinaire periodical, *Modern Quarterly,* to establish a clearer Marxian position in the arts, music, history, and science.

The attempt by the Party to set down a "Party Line" on culture and the arts had the effect of bringing out the divisions of opinion among intellectuals on the relationship of creative activity to political commitment. Anti-fascist cultural organizations found that they were spending more time debating among themselves than in organizing campaigns to fight fascism and war. Many intellectuals drifted away from further active participation. Party memberships were permitted to lapse. A general feeling of disenchantment had begun to make itself known among the left intelligentsia.

But this process of disillusionment came less from one event or from a change in Communist Party strategy than from a widespread feeling among intellectuals of ineffectiveness, of an overwhelming sense of defeat, of fatalism, especially after 1938, of the inevitability of another World War.

Political events in the thirties took on a sense of high melodrama. More than anything else, the constant political crises of the decade kept the enthusiasm and fervor of left intellectual activity at a high pitch. The compelling motivation behind the whole movement of left intellectuals was the persistent and powerful belief that one more push, one more *Daily Worker* sold, one more giant rally of intellectuals against fascism, one more letter to *The Times,* one more political poem—would be the critical act that could swing the balance in favor of peace. If the most typical work of the twenties was *The Wasteland,* its thirties counterpart was *L'Espoir* (*Man's Hope*). Fascism provided a target, Russian success an inspiration, Spain a cause, the economic depression and constant political crises a constant nagging reality.

Intellectuals believed that the Marxist diagnosis of dying capitalism was accurate, that history was on their side. There was a sense of purpose, of excitement, of exhilaration in their commitment to politics. They felt they were on the offensive—against war, fascism, and economic exploitation.

But in 1938, as the news from Spain became worse, as Franco seemed to be gaining the upper hand, as the questions about Russia remained unanswered, as the economic situation became brighter, there was an increasing assumption of a defensive attitude on the part of left intellectuals. The apparent defeat in Spain disillusioned as many people, dampened as much enthusiasm, as the outbreak of Civil War engendered in 1936. The belief that you were living *entre deux guerres* became more real, the forebodings of a coming war more apparent. The protests over Vienna in 1934, Abyssinia in 1935, China, and Spain all failed.

The event that seemed to seal the doom for many left intellectuals was the signing of the Munich Pact with Hitler in September 1938. During the period leading up to the Pact, war became the dominating topic. Intellectuals were constantly buying newspapers, waiting for the latest headlines. Trenches were being built in Hyde Park, food tins were hoarded. There were intermittent days of optimism, of rallies and marches, distribution of leaflets, which seemed useful only to gather strength for the next fit of despair. The signing of the Pact by Chamberlain showed many intellectuals that, no matter what one did, no matter how many names one accumulated on a petition, no matter how many "influential" people one could gather to march—these actions could have little effect on changing the minds of the political decision makers. War under these circumstances seemed inevitable.

As Day Lewis said:

> We were the prophets of a changeable morning,
> We hoped for much but saw the clouds forewarning,
> Spain was a death to us, Munich a mourning.[37]

After Munich, writers, poets, artists began once again to ask themselves if their political interests were not obstructing their artistic responsibilities. The choice was between writing good propaganda or honest poetry, between being politically effective or poetically false. Life *seemed* to be more and more controlled by a public fate that was beyond human control. Many less thoroughly committed intellectuals drifted out of the movement.

With the signing of the Nazi-Soviet Pact in August 1939, for all but the most dedicated, final hopes were dashed. For a generation of intellectuals fed on a strict diet of anti-fascism and pro-communism, where Russia symbolized all that was good, rational, and humane, and Germany exemplified all that was evil, irrational, and inhumane, the Nazi-Soviet Pact undermined most of the intellectual pronouncements of the decade. The political slogans and public activity all became out of date, all startlingly inadequate.

The outbreak of war in September 1939 came to many committed intellectuals as a form of relief. Anti-fascist activities were no longer a choice of commitment but a sign of patriotism. With the coming of conscript armies and government anti-Nazi propaganda, anti-fascism became a professional game. Day Lewis summed it up best in answering the question: Where are the war poets now?

---

[37] Taken from the poem, "Dedicatory Stanzas to Stephen Spender," in C. D. Lewis' translation of Virgil's *Georgics* (London, 1940), p. 9, and reprinted with the permission of Jonathan Cape of London and Harold Matson Company, Inc., of New York.

They who in folly or mere greed
Enslaved religion, markets, laws,
Borrow our language now and bid
Us to speak up in freedom's cause.

It is the logic of the times,
No subject for immortal verse,
That we who lived by honest dreams
Defend the bad against the worse.[38]

"The fight against Fascism," said Cyril Connolly, "is in the hands of the General Staff and there is no further use for the minor prophet."[39]

This picture of the process of disillusionment, however, pertains only to those intellectuals who fell out of the movement, who felt they had been living, as Auden said, in a "low dishonest decade." There were also intellectual remnants of the left, those who remained committed, who stayed in the Communist Party, or those who joined it late in the thirties or during the war. For these people there was also a feeling of disenchantment, but they failed to break with the Party, refused to question their fundamental commitment to politics. They took the twists and turns of Party policy in stride. The Party and its various affiliated groups had become for these intellectuals a way of life. Party publishers printed their work. Party papers favorably reviewed them. One's circle of friends found its locus in the Party. These intellectuals became socially and economically dependent on the Party. To cut their ties by denouncing political involvement as a swindle meant ostracization by friends and deprivation of a small but steady income from one's creative efforts.

Moreover, toward the end of the decade a group of new intellectual recruits came into the Party ranks, men who were more preoccupied with working out a Marxian approach to history, literature, science, and culture than in mobilizing intellectual protest on current political events.

[38] Taken from "Where Are the War Poets?" in C. Day Lewis, *Collected Poems* (London, 1954), p. 228, and reprinted with the permission of Jonathan Cape and the Hogarth Press of London and Harold Matson Company, Inc., of New York.
[39] Cyril Connolly, "The Ivory Shelter," *Horizon*, Vol. I (October 1939), p. 2.

But to the large majority of the left intellectuals who became politically committed during the thirties the war facilitated a return to the fold. Some escaped completely from the wasteland—Auden, Isherwood, MacNeice went to America—but most became fighters and firemen for God, King, and Country. For if the remnants of the left intelligentsia stayed within the Party to form a sort of "Communist Establishment," the disillusioned managed to find a new home in a new "Establishment"—an official governmental one. From 1938, with the establishment of the British Council to the formation during the war of the Ministry of Information film unit, C.E.M.A., the BBC third program, the Fire Brigade, A.B.C.A. lectures, and Artists for War, a new intellectual patronage system peopled by many of those intellectuals who were the most virulent critics of English society in the thirties came into existence. The disillusioned left intelligentsia, many of whom were shocked and horrified by Auden's acceptance of the King's Medal for Poetry in 1936, found a new intellectual home under government patronage and are today proud holders of M.B.E.s, O.B.E.s, life peerages, and university chairs of poetry.

But members of both "Establishments" retrospectively viewed the thirties with some misgivings. The clarion call for intellectual involvement in politics sounded by Auden in the early thirties had subsided, to be replaced by the sounding of the call of retreat by Eric Blair, better known by his pen name, George Orwell, who wrote the epitaph of a generation he was in but never part of, of a movement he toyed with but never joined.

> Progress and reaction [he said] have both turned out to be swindles. Seemingly, there is nothing left but quietism. . . . Get inside the Whale . . . give yourself over to the world process, stop fighting against it or pretending that you control it; simply accept it, endure it, record it.[40]

Thus the detachment of intellectuals of the twenties had given way to political commitment in the thirties, and this in turn was giving way to the disenchantment that was to characterize English intellectual life in the forties.

[40] Orwell, *Inside the Whale, and Other Essays,* pp. 48–49 (Penguin edition).

PLAN OF THE SCIENTIFIC OPERATIONS NECESSARY FOR REORGANIZING SOCIETY

Auguste Comte

Introduction

OUR SOCIAL ANARCHY AND ITS SOURCES

A social system in its decline, a new system arrived at maturity and approaching its completion—such is the fundamental character which the general progress of civilization has assigned to the present epoch. In conformity with this state of things, two movements, differing in their nature, agitate society; one a movement of disorganization, the other of reorganization. By the former, considered apart, society is hurried towards a profound moral and political anarchy which appears to menace it with a near and inevitable dissolution. By the latter it is guided to the definitive social conditions of the human race, that best suited to its nature, and in which all progressive movements should receive their completest development and most direct application. In the co-existence of these two opposed tendencies consists the grand crisis now experienced by the most civilized nations; and this can only be understood when viewed under both aspects.

From the moment when this crisis began to show itself to the present time the tendency of the ancient system to disorganization has predominated, or rather it alone is still plainly manifested. It was in the nature of things that the crisis should begin thus, so that the old system might be sufficiently modified to permit the direct formation of the new social system.

But now that this condition has been fully satisfied and the Catholico-Feudal system has lost its power, as far as is possible, until the new system has been inaugurated, the preponderance still maintained by the negative tendency constitutes the greatest obstacle to the progress of civilization and even to the abolition of the ancient system. Its persistence forms the first cause of those terrible and continually renewed shocks by which the crisis is accompanied.

The only way of ending this stormy situation, of staying the anarchy which day by day invades society, in a word of reducing the crisis to a simple moral movement, consists in inducing the civilized nations to abandon the negative and to adopt an organic attitude; turning all their efforts towards the formation of the New Social System as the definitive object of the crisis and that for the attainment of which everything hitherto accomplished is only a preparation. . . .

LIBERTY OF CONSCIENCE AND SOVEREIGNTY OF THE PEOPLE

Under spiritual aspects the principle pervading the popular aim is the dogma of unlimited Liberty of Conscience. Considered in the sense which it originally had, that is to say, in reference to a negative destination, this dogma is nothing but the extension of a great general fact, the decline of theological beliefs.

Itself the result of such decline, this doctrine has, by a necessary reaction, powerfully contributed to accelerate and propagate it; but by the nature of things its influence stopped there. Regarded simply as a means of combating the theological system the dogma in question favours the progress of the human mind. But it ceases to do so and loses all its value when conceived as a basis for the great social reorganization reserved for our epoch. It then becomes just as injurious as before it was useful, since it constitutes an obstacle to reorganization.

Proclaiming the sovereignty of each individual reason, this doctrine in fact essentially tends to hinder the uniform establishment of any system of general ideas, without which nevertheless society cannot exist. For let the mass of men become as highly instructed as is possible, it is evident that the greater part of the general conceptions currently received can only be accepted by them on trust and not as the result of demonstration. Thus such a dogma is, by its very nature, only applicable to ideas destined to vanish and therefore regarded with indifference; and in point of fact it has only been applied to such at the moment of their decline and in order to hasten their fall.

To apply this doctrine to the new as well as to the old system, still more to see in it an organic principle, is to fall into the strangest contradiction. If such an error could last, the reorganization of society would be forever impossible.

In astronomy, physics, chemistry and physiology there is no such thing as liberty of conscience; that is to say everyone would deem it absurd not to place confidence in the principles established for these sciences by competent thinkers. If the case is different in politics, this arises from the circumstance that, the old principles having been abandoned while the new are yet unformed, established principles during this interregnum do not in a just sense exist. But to convert this transitory fact into an absolute and eternal dogma and treat it as a fundamental principle, evidently amounts to a proclamation that society should always continue deprived of any general doctrinal basis. It must be admitted that such a notion justly deserves the charge of anarchy brought against it by the ablest defenders of the theological system.

Under the temporal aspect the dogma of the Sovereignty of the People corresponds to the dogma just considered of which it is only the political application. It was created as a means of combating the principle of Divine Right, itself the general political basis of the ancient system, shortly after the dogma of liberty of conscience had been formed to destroy the theological ideas on which this principle was founded.

What has been said for one applies therefore to the other. The anti-feudal, like the anti-theological dogma, having effected its negative aim, has reached the natural term of its career. The former can no more furnish the political basis of the social reorganization than the latter its moral basis. Both, being devised for purposes of destruction, are equally unfitted for construction.

One of these doctrines, far from furnishing an organic principle, merely substitutes individual for papal infallibility; the other only replaces the arbitrary power of kings by that of the people, or rather of individuals. The 'sovereignty of the people' tends to dismember the body politic by placing power in the least capable hands; while the 'right of private judgment' tends to the complete isolation of thinkers by investing the least enlightened men with an absolute right of control over the system of ideas conceived by superior intellects for the guidance of society.

The criticism just developed as to the two fundamental doctrines can be easily applied to all the more special notions which constitute the popular philosophy. The result will always be the same. It will be seen that all of these, like the two principal ones, are merely the formal expression of corresponding historical facts relative to the decline of the feudal and theological system. It will also be seen that all alike have a simply negative destination, which constitutes their only value, and renders them wholly unfitted for reorganizing society. . . .

The destination of society now come to maturity is neither to inhabit forever the old and miserable hut which its infancy erected, as kings suppose; nor to live eternally without shelter after having left it, as the people imagined. Its destiny is rather this, that, aided by acquired experience, it should with all the accumulated materials construct an edifice fitted for its needs and enjoyments. Such is the great and noble enterprise reserved for the present generation. . . .

THEORY AND PRACTICE MUST BE SEPARATED

Endeavouring then to ascertain in what precise way the nature of this work has been misconceived, we find that the error consists in regarding an enterprise which is essentially theoretical, as purely practical.

The formation of any plan for social organization necessarily embraces two series of works as distinct in their objects as in the intellectual efforts they demand. One, Theoretical or spiritual, aims at developing the leading conception of the plan—that is to say the new principle destined to co-ordinate social relations—and at forming the system of general ideas, fitted to guide society. The other, Practical or temporal, decides upon the distribution of authority and the combination of administrative institutions best adapted to the spirit of the system already determined by the theoretical labours. Since the second series reposes on the first, of which it is only the result and realization, the general enterprise must of necessity begin by the former. It constitutes its soul and, although merely preliminary, forms its most important and difficult portion.

In consequence of their having overlooked this fundamental distinction or, in other words, of having exclusively fixed their attention on the practical side, the People have naturally been led to conceive Social Reorganization in accordance with the defective doctrine which we have examined in the previous chapter. All their errors flow from this profound original aberration; and their derivation from it is easily shown. . . .

A society, however numerous it may be, can, just as an individual, propose it itself only one of two possible active aims. These are a violent action upon the rest of the human race, that is to say conquest; and an action upon nature modifying it for the advantage of man, or production. Every society which is not definitely organized for one or other of these aims, must be mongrel and devoid of character. The military aim characterized the ancient, while the industrial aim characterizes the modern system.

The first step needed for social reorganization was therefore to proclaim this new aim. Since this was not done, we have not abandoned the ancient system even when seeming to diverge from it most widely. Now, this strange deficiency in our so-called constitutions has, clearly, sprung from the desire to organize a system in detail, before the ensemble had been conceived. In other words it was the consequence of having directed attention exclusively to the practical side of the reorganization without having first decided on the theoretical part or even thought of constituting it. . . .

In our day society is disorganized under both spiritual and temporal aspects. Spiritual anarchy has preceded and engendered temporal anarchy. In the present epoch the social malady depends much more on the first than on the second cause. On the other hand an attentive study of the progress of civilization proves that the spiritual is now more completely prepared than the temporal reorganization of society. Thus our first efforts to terminate the revolutionary epoch should aim at reorganizing the spiritual power; yet hitherto attention has only been fixed upon the renovation of the temporal power. . . .

The nature of the works to be executed, of itself sufficiently indicates the class on which their execution must devolve. Since these works are theoretical, it is clear that those whose professed aim it is to form theoretical combinations, in other words *Savants* occupied with the study of the sciences of observation, are the only men whose capacity and intellectual culture fulfill the necessary conditions. It would be evidently abnormal when the most urgent social needs call for a general work of the highest order of importance and difficulty, to entrust this work to any but the greatest intellectual forces we can command and to men who pursue a method of which the superiority is universally recognized. Doubtless in other branches of society men may be found equal and even superior in theoretical capacity to that of the majority of savants, for the effective classification of individuals is far from conforming universally to the natural or physiological classification. But in a work so essential we must consider classes and not individuals. Besides, even as regards such exceptional instances, education, that is to say, the system of intellectual habits which results from the study of the sciences of observation, can alone develop their natural theoretical capacity. In a word whenever society requires theoretical work of any given sort, it is conceded that this must be confided to the corresponding class of savants. Hence it devolves on the ensemble of the scientific corps to guide the general theoretical work the necessity for which has been demonstrated.

Besides, the nature of the case forbids any mistake on this head; since liberty of choice is absolutely interdicted for several reasons which point to the class of savants as the only one qualified to execute the theoretical labour of social reorganization.

In the system to be constituted the spiritual power will be confided to the hands of savants, while the temporal power will belong to the heads of industrial works. These two powers then should naturally proceed to the formation of this system; just as they will when it is established undertake its daily application; due allowance being made for the superior importance of the work now to be executed. This work embraces a spiritual portion which ought to be treated first and a temporal portion which will follow. Accordingly on the savants devolves the task of undertaking the first series of works and on the leaders of industry that of organizing, on the bases thus established, the administrative system. Such is the simple course indicated by the nature of things, which teaches us that the very classes which form the elements of the powers of a new system and must one day be placed at its head, can alone create it because they alone are capable of truly apprehending its spirit, and impelled in this direction by the combined force of their habits and their interests.

Another consideration places in a still clearer light the necessity for confiding to the cultivators of Positive Science the theoretical labour of reorganizing society.

In the preceding chapter it has been remarked that the negative doctrine encourages in most minds, and increasingly strengthens, the habit of setting themselves up as the supreme judges of general political conceptions. This anarchical state of intellect, when erected into a fundamental principle, is a manifest obstacle to the reorganization of society. The intellects really competent to construct the true organic doctrine destined to end the existing crisis would therefore labour in vain unless from their antecedent position their authority was in fact recognized. Deprived of this condition and subjected to the capricious control of a policy of inspiration their work could never be uniformly adopted. Now casting our eye over society we shall soon perceive that this spiritual influence in our day lies exclusively in the hands of the savants. They alone as regards theory exercise an uncontested authority. Thus, apart from their being alone competent to form the new organic doctrine, they are exclusively invested with the moral force essential to secure its recognition. The obstacles to such recognition presented by the negative prejudice which attributes a moral sovereignty to each individual as his inborn right would be insurmountable by any other than that class. They possess the only leverage capable of overthrowing this prejudice, in the habit gradually contracted by society since the foundation of the positive sciences of submitting to the decisions of the savants as regards to all special theoretical ideas. This habit the savants will easily extend to general theoretical conceptions as soon as they undertake their coordination.

Thus the savants in our day possess, to the exclusion of all other classes, the two fundamental elements of spiritual government, Capacity and Authority in matters of theory.

Lastly, one other essential characteristic, which like the above exclusively belongs to scientific power, calls for notice.

The existing crisis is manifestly common to the several nations of Western Europe although all do not participate in it to the same degree. Nevertheless it is treated by each of them as if it were purely national. Yet it is evident that a European crisis demands a European treatment. . . .

It is clear that scientific men alone constitute a really compact and active body, all of whose members throughout Europe have a mutual understanding and communicate easily and continuously among themselves. This springs from the fact that they alone, in our day, possess common ideas, a uniform language, a general and permanent aim. No other class possesses these powerful advantages, because no other fulfills the above conditions in their integrity. The industrial classes, even, so eminently disposed to union by the character of their labours and habits, are still too much influenced by the hostile inspirations of a savage patriotism to allow of their establishing as yet a real European alliance among themselves. Such a result is reserved for the active labours of scientific men.

It is doubtless superfluous to demonstrate that the existing relations of scientific men must acquire a far greater intensity when they direct their general efforts towards the formation of the new social doctrine. This result must follow since the force of the social tie is necessarily proportionate to the importance of the aim sought by association. . . .

To resume then; the necessity for confiding to Scientific Men the preliminary theoretical labours recognized as indispensable for reorganizing society is solidly based upon four distinct con-

siderations, each of which would have sufficed to establish it:
1) scientific men are by the character of their intellectual capacity
and cultivation alone competent to execute these works; 2) from
the nature of the case, this office is reserved for them as constituting the spiritual power of the system to be organized; 3) they,
exclusively, possess the moral authority requisite in our day to
determine the adoption of the new organic doctrine when formed;
4) and finally, of all the social forces in existence, that of scientific
men is alone European. Such a combination of proofs should,
without doubt, place the great theoretic mission of scientific men
beyond question and controversy.

From all that precedes it follows that the fundamental errors
committed by the People in their mode of conceiving the Reorganization of Society are in the first instance referable to the
mistaken course which they have adopted for attaining this end;
that the error of this course consists in treating social reorganization as a purely practical operation, though it is essentially
theoretical; that the nature of things and the experience of history
demonstrate the absolute necessity of dividing the entire work of
reorganization into two series, one theoretic the other practical of
which the former should be first executed and serve as basis to
the latter; that the preliminary execution of the theoretical works
demands the exertion of a new social force distinct from those
which have hitherto occupied the scene but have become entirely
inadequate finally that for various decisive reasons this new
force should appertain to scientific men devoted to the sciences of
observation.

SAVANTS MUST RENDER POLITICS SCIENTIFIC

The ensemble of these views may be regarded as intended to
lead reflecting minds to that elevated point of view whence
both the vices of the course hitherto followed for the reorganization of society and the character of that which should, in our
day, be adopted may be embraced at a single glance. In the last
resort all resolves itself into establishing, through the combined
efforts of European savants, a positive theory in politics distinct

from practice, and one which shall bring our social system into harmony with the present state of knowledge. Pursuing this course of reflection, we shall perceive that the above conclusions may be resumed in a single conception: scientific men ought in our day to elevate politics to the rank of a science of observation. . . .

LAW OF THE THREE STATES

From the nature of the human intellect each branch of knowledge in its development is necessarily obliged to pass through three different theoretical states: the Theological or fictitious state; the Metaphysical or abstract state; lastly the Scientific or positive state.

In the first state supernatural ideas serve to bind the small number of isolated observations which then constitute science. In other words the facts observed are explained, that is to say, conceived *a priori*, by means of invented facts. Such is the necessary state of all knowledge in its infancy. With all its imperfections this forms the only mode of connecting facts possible at that epoch. It furnishes, therefore, the only instrument by means of which we can reason on facts, thus sustaining our intellectual activity which above all requires a rallying point. In a word this state is indispensable as a condition of further progress.

The second state is simply destined to serve as a means of transition from the first to the third. It has a mongrel nature, connecting facts by ideas which are no longer entirely supernatural and have not yet become completely natural. In a word these ideas are personified abstractions, which the mind can at will regard as the mystic name for a supernatural cause, or the abstract statement of a mere series of phenomena, according as it approximates more nearly to the theological or the scientific state. This metaphysical state presupposes that facts, multiplied in number have at the same time become more closely connected by more extended comparisons.

The third is the definitive state of all knowledge whatsoever; the two first having been destined to prepare it gradually. Then facts become connected by general ideas or laws of a completely

positive kind, suggested or confirmed by the very facts, which
are themselves frequently only simple facts sufficiently general to
be elevated to the rank of principles. We constantly endeavour to
reduce these to the smallest possible number, yet without propos-
ing any hypothesis incapable of being sooner or later verified,
and always regarding these principles simply as a general mode
of stating the phenomena.

Men familiar with the progress of the sciences can easily verify
the truth of this general historical résumé in reference to the four
fundamental sciences already rendered positive, Astronomy,
Physics, Chemistry, and Physiology, as well as their dependent
sciences. Those even who have only considered the sciences in
their present state can make this verification as to physiology
which, although it has at last become as positive as the other
sciences, still subsists under the three states in different classes of
intelligence. This fact is particularly evident in reference to the
phenomena specially called moral: for these are conceived by
some as the result of a continuous supernatural action; by others
as incomprehensible results of the action of an abstract entity;
and lastly by others as connected with organic conditions susceptible of demonstration and beyond which it is impossible to go.

Considering Politics as a science and applying to it the preceding remarks, we find that it has already passed through the two
first states and is now on the point of reaching the third.

The doctrine of Kings represents the theological state of politics.
In the last result, this is in truth based on theological ideas. It
exhibits social relations as resting on the supernatural idea of
Divine Right. It explains the successive political changes of the
human race by an immediate supernatural guidance, exercized
continuously from the first man to the present day. In this way
alone was political science conceived, until the ancient system
began to decline.

The doctrine of the People expresses the metaphysical condition of politics. It is wholly founded on the abstract and metaphysical hypothesis of a primitive Social Contract antecedent to
all development of the human faculties by civilization. The instrument of reasoning which it habitually employs are 'rights',
regarded as natural and common to all men in the same degree
and guaranteed by this contract. Such is the primitive negative

doctrine, originally drawn from theology as a means of warfare against the ancient system and which has been subsequently erected into an organic idea. Rousseau was its chief systematizer, in a work which served and still serves as the basis of the ordinary reflections upon social organization.

Lastly the Scientific Doctrine of politics considers the social state in which the human race has always been found by observers as the necessary effect of its organization. It conceives the scope of this social state as determined by the rank which man holds in the natural scale, the result of facts which are not themselves susceptible of explanation. It perceives in truth that from this fundamental relation results the constant tendency of man to act upon nature in order to modify it for his own advantage. It then considers the social order as aiming at a collective development of this natural tendency, so as to give the highest possible efficiency to this useful action. This being settled, it endeavors, by direct observations on the collective development of the race, to deduce from the fundamental laws of the human organization the evolution it has undergone and the intermediate states to which it has been subjected before reaching its definitive state. Guided by this series of observations this doctrine regards the improvements reserved for each epoch as necessitated, without resorting to any hypothesis, by the stage of development which the human race has reached. Thus, in reference to each degree of civilization, it views political combinations as merely intended to facilitate natural tendencies when these have been sufficiently ascertained.

Such is the spirit of the positive doctrine which it is important to establish in our day, applying it to the present state of civilized man and considering antecedent states only so far as may be necessary in order to establish the fundamental laws of the science.

It is easy to explain at once why politics could not sooner become a positive science and why at the present time they are destined to become one.

Two fundamental conditions, distinct yet inseparable, were indispensable for that object.

In the first place, it was essential that all the Special Sciences should have successively become positive, for the ensemble could not acquire that character so long as the elements were devoid of it. This condition is now fulfilled.

CLASSIFICATION OF THE SCIENCES

The sciences have become positive, one after the other in the natural order of effecting this revolution. This order is that of the greater or less degree of complication in their phenomena, or, in other words, of their more or less intimate connection with man. Thus at first astronomical phenomena, as the simplest, and then in succession, physics, chemistry and physiology have been reduced to positive theories; the last of these only quite recently. The same reform could not be accomplished for politics until it had been effected for the other phenomena, since political phenomena depend upon these and are the most complicated of all. But if this renovation could not be effected sooner, its realization now has become an evident necessity.

In the second place, it was essential that the Preparatory Social System during which action upon nature was only the indirect object of society should have reached its last stage.

On one hand, the just theory could not arise until then, because it would have been too far in advance of practice. The former being destined to guide the latter, could not precede it too long. On the other hand it could not earlier have obtained a sufficient experimental basis. It was requisite that a social order should have been founded and accepted by a very large population, embracing several considerable nations, and lasting as long as possible, before a theory could be founded upon this vast experiment.

The second of these conditions is now satisfied no less than the first. The theological system, destined to prepare the human intellect for the scientific system, has closed its career. This is undeniable since the metaphysical system, the only object of which is to subvert the theological system, has, generally speaking, obtained a preponderance among the nations. A Scientific Polity must therefore arise, for some theory being indispensable, we should otherwise be driven to assume the reconstitution of a theological polity; the metaphysical polity being, to speak correctly, not a true theory but a negative doctrine suitable only for a transition.

To resume, no moral revolution ever existed at once more inevitable, more ripe, and more urgent than that required to elevate politics to the rank of the natural sciences, through the combined efforts of European savants. This revolution can alone introduce into the great crisis of our day a really preponderating force, capable of preserving society from the terrible explosions of anarchy which threaten it, by putting it on the track of that improved social system which the state of our knowledge demands.

In order to set in motion with the utmost possible promptitude the scientific forces destined to fulfill this salutary mission, it was essential to lay down the general prospectus of the theoretical works required for the reorganization of society, by raising politics to the rank of the natural sciences. I have ventured to conceive this plan which I now solemnly submit to the savants of Europe.

Profoundly convinced that, whenever this discussion commences, my plan be it adopted or rejected, will necessarily lead to the formation of the definitive plan; I do not hesitate in the interests of society now threatened with long and terrible convulsions which their intervention can alone avert, to adjure all the European savants to express, freely and publicly, their well-considered judgment upon the general scheme of constructive operations which I submit to them.

This prospectus embraces three series of works.

The first series aims at forming a System of Historical Observations upon the general progress of the human intellect destined to become the basis of a positive polity, thus wholly freeing it from a theological and metaphysical character and impressing on them a scientific character.

The second series seeks to establish a complete system of Positive Education adapted to a regenerated society constituted with a view to action upon nature; in other words it aims at perfecting such action so far as this depends upon the faculties of the agent.

Lastly, the third series embraces a general exposition of the Collective Action which civilized men, in the present state of their knowledge, can exercize over Nature so as to modify it for their own advantage, directing their entire forces to this end and regarding social combinations only as means of attaining it. . . .

THE METHOD OF THE SCIENCE OF POSITIVE POLITICS

The fundamental datum and positive starting point of general practical politics consists therefore in a determination of the real tendency of civilization. By ascertaining this we can harmonize political action with it and render as mild, and as short as possible, the crisis which the human race inevitably undergoes during its successive passages through the different stages of civilization.

Persons who, though intelligent, are unfamiliar with the method which suits the human mind, and even those who see that a knowledge of the laws which regulate the progress of civilization can alone furnish a solid and positive basis for political combinations, may suppose that this historic investigation need not be pushed back to the origin of civilized society, but that it will suffice to consider its present condition. Such a view is natural, having regard to the narrow way in which politics are now regarded. But its delusive character is easily shown.

Experience has proved that, so long as the human mind advances in a positive direction, there are many advantages and no inconveniences in rising to the highest degree of generality, because it is far easier to descend than to ascend the scale. In the infancy of positive Physiology it was supposed that the human organization could be understood by studying man alone; an error completely analogous to that now under discussion. It has been since recognized that the formation of clear and large conceptions of the human organization requires us to consider man as forming the limit of the animal series; and even, in a still more general point of view, as forming part of the system of organized bodies. Physiology has only received its definitive constitution since the comparison of the different classes of living beings has been carried out on a large scale, and systematically employed in the study of man.

In Politics the various states of civilization correspond to the different organizations on Physiology. But, the reasons which compel us to consider all the epochs of civilization are still more imperative than those which have induced physiologists to institute a comparison of all organizations.

Doubtless a study of the present condition of civilization, considered apart, and independently of the states which have preceded it, may furnish very useful materials for the formation of a positive polity, provided the facts are observed in a philosophical spirit. Nay it is certain that, by studies of this kind, true Statesmen have hitherto been enabled to modify the conjectural doctrines which guided their efforts, so as to rendér these less discordant with the real wants of society. But it is not the less evident that such a study is totally inadequate to form a true positive polity. It can furnish nothing but materials. In a word, the observation of the present state of civilization, considered by itself, can no more determine the actual tendencies of society than the study of any other isolated epoch can do.

The reason for this is that the existence of a law cannot be established by a single term. Three terms, at least, are needed, in order that the connection ascertained by comparing the two first are verified by the third, may serve to reveal the following ones. Such prevision is the practical object of every law.

When, in tracing an institution and a social idea, or a system of institutions and a complete doctrine, from their birth to their present stage, we find that, from a given epoch, their influence has always been either diminishing or increasing, we can foretell with complete certainty the destiny which awaits them. In the first case, it is proved that their tendency is at variance with that of civilization, and hence their final disappearance may be predicted. In the second case, on the contrary, we may conclude that they will ultimately predominate. The period of their fall or triumph may even be calculated, within narrow limits, from the extent and rapidity of the variations observed. Manifestly therefore such a study is a fruitful source of positive knowledge.

But what can we learn from the observation of a single State where we must embrace, at one view, doctrines, institutions, and classes, both growing and declining, without reckoning the ephemeral action which only depends on the routine of the moment? What human sagacity could avoid confounding these opposed and heterogeneous elements? How could we discover the realities which make so little noise amid the phantoms which hurry over the stage? It is clear that, amid such confusion the observer could only advance if guided by a knowledge of the past, for this alone can teach him to direct his view so as to see things as they really exist.

The chronological order of historic epochs is not their philosophical order. In place of saying: the past, the present, and the future, we should say the past, the future, and the present. In truth it is only when we have conceived the future by the aid of the past that we can with advantage revert to the present so as to seize its true character.

CONFLICT OF SOCIAL SYSTEMS

These considerations, though applicable to every epoch, are so, in a still higher degree, to the present. In our day three different Systems co-exist in the heart of Society: the theologico-feudal system, the scientific-industrial system, and lastly the mongrel and transitional system of metaphysicians, and lawyers. In the midst of such confusion it is entirely beyond the grasp of the human mind to make a clear and exact analysis, or to frame real and precise statistics of the body politic, unless it be enlightened by the past. It is demonstrable that sound intellects, which if better guided would have risen to a truly positive polity, have continued in a metaphysical state because they considered the present condition of affairs apart from their antecedents, and even because they did not go back far enough in the series of observations.

We therefore are bound to study, as profoundly and completely as possible, all the states through which civilization has passed, from its origin to the present time. We must consider their coordination and connection and how they can be combined under general heads capable of furnishing principles; making manifest the natural laws of the development of civilization, and exhibiting the philosophic picture of the social future as deduced from the past, in other words determining the general plan of reorganization destined for the present epoch. Lastly we need the application of these results to the present state of things so as to determine the direction which ought to be impressed on political action with a view to facilitate the definitive transition to the new social state. Such are the operations essential for giving to political theory a positive basis adequate to the best and urgent needs of society.

The above constitutes the first series of theoretic problems, for the solution of which I venture to invoke the combined forces of European savants. . . .

In order to establish a new Social System, just conceptions will not suffice. It is necessary that the mass of society should feel attracted by it. This condition is not merely indispensable to overcome the obstacles, more or less serious, which this system must encounter among the classes who are losing their ascendancy. It is needed above all for the satisfaction of the moral craving for enthusiasm inherent in man when he enters upon a new career. Without such enthusiasm he could neither overcome his natural inertness nor shake off the powerful yoke of ancient habits; without which it is impossible to secure the free and full development of all his faculties in their new occupation. Since this necessity always manifests itself even in the least complicated cases, its absence would involve a contradiction in the most complete and important changes, in those which must most deeply modify human existence. Accordingly all history testifies in favor of this truth. . . .

Here then we find a sort of work in which the Imagination should perform the principal part. Its activity can produce no bad effect, since this will be exerted in the direction pointed out by scientific labors; and it will aim, not at inventing a new system, but at spreading one which has been determined by positive polity. Thus set in motion the imagination ought to be entirely left to itself. The more open and free its attitude, the more complete and salutary will be its indispensable activity.

Such is the part specially reserved for the Fine Arts in the general work of social reorganization. Thus this vast enterprise will obtain the cooperation of all the positive forces; that of the savants to determine the plan of the new system; that of the artists to cause its universal adoption; that of the industrial chiefs to put it into immediate execution by establishing the needful practical institutions. These three great forces will lend each other a mutual support in founding the new system, as they will do to ensure its daily application, when established.

In determining, then, the social system suitable to the present epoch, the positive polity invests observation with the supremacy now accorded to imagination. At the same time it confides to the imagination a new and more perfect office than that which the theologico-metaphysical polity assigned to it; for since the human race has advanced near the positive state the imaginative faculty, though supreme, has revolved in a circle of obsolete ideas and monotonous pictures. . . .

LAW OF THE THREE STATES

In the preceding chapter I have submitted, though under the spiritual aspect only, a general view which as it seems to me, fulfills, the conditions above stated for effecting the primary co-ordination of the past. It constitutes the first result of a philosophic study of the ensemble of the history of civilization.

I believe that this history may be divided into three grand epochs, or states of civilization, each possessing a distinct character spiritual and temporal. They embrace civilization at once in its elements and its ensemble, which, as above pointed out, evidently constitutes an indispensable condition of success.

Of these the first is the Theological and Military epoch.

In this state of society, all theoretical conceptions, whether general or special, bear a supernatural impress. The imagination completely predominates over the observing faculty to which all right of inquiry is denied.

In like manner, all the social relations, whether special or general, are avowedly and exclusively military. Society makes conquest its one permanent aim. Industrial pursuits are carried on only so far as is necessary for the support of the human race. Slavery, pure and simple, of the producers is the principal institution.

Such is the first great social system produced by the material progress of civilization. It existed in an elementary shape from the very commencement of regular and permanent societies. In its entirety it becomes completely established only after a long series of generations.

The second epoch is Metaphysical and Juridical. Its general character is that of possessing no well-defined characteristics. It forms a link and is mongrel and transitional.

Under spiritual aspects it has been already characterized in the preceding chapter. Observation is still kept subordinate to imagination, but the former is, within certain limits, allowed to modify the latter. These limits are gradually enlarged until, in the end, observation conquers the right of examining in every direction. At first it obtains this right in reference to all special theoretical conceptions, and gradually, by force of exercise, as to general theoretic ideas, which constitutes the natural termination of the transition. This period is one of criticism and argument.

Under temporal aspects industry in this second epoch becomes more extended, without as yet acquiring the upper hand. Consequently society is no longer frankly military and yet has not become frankly industrial, either in its elements or in its ensemble. The special social relations are modified. Industrial slavery is no longer direct; the producer, still a slave, begins to obtain some rights in his relations with the military. Industry makes fresh advances which finally issue in the total abolition of individual slavery. After this enfranchisement, the producers still remain subject to a collective arbitrary authority. Nevertheless, the general social relations soon undergo a modification. The two aims of activity, conquest and production, advance *pari passu*. Industry is at first favoured and protected as a military resource. Later its importance augments; and finally war is regarded and systematically pursued as a means of favouring industry: which is the last term of the intermediate regime.

Lastly, the third epoch is that of Science and Industry. All special theoretic conceptions have become positive and the general conceptions tend to become so. As regard the former observation predominates over imagination; while in reference to the latter observation has dethroned the imagination, without having as yet taken its place.

Under temporal aspects industry has become predominant. All

the special relations have gradually established themselves upon industrial bases. Society, taken collectively, tends to organize itself in the same manner, by making production its only and constant aim.

To resume, the last epoch has ended as regards the elements and is commencing as regards the ensemble. Its direct point of departure dates from the introduction of the Positive Sciences into Europe by the Arabs, and the enfranchisement of the Commons, that is to say, from about the eleventh century.

In order to prevent all confusion in applying this general view, we should never lose sight of the fact that civilization necessarily progressed in reference to the spiritual and temporal elements of the social state, before advancing in regard to their ensemble. Consequently the three great and successive phases were inevitably inaugurated as to their elements before they commenced as to the ensemble, a circumstance which might occasion some confusion if we did not make a large allowance for this unavoidable difference.

Such then are the principal characteristics of the three epochs into which we can divide the entire history of civilization, from the period when the social state began to acquire real solidity until the present time. I venture to submit to savants this primary division of the past; which appears to me to fulfill the essential conditions of a good classification of the ensemble of political facts. . . .

THE POLITICAL HISTORY OF SAVANTS HARMONIZES WITH THE LAW OF THE THREE STATES

This general résumé presents the social existence of men of science under a point of view which departs from ordinary ideas. It remains then to develop it in order to take a complete grasp of the great moral revolution that now tends to realize itself in the human race.

The political history of savants, regarded as a whole, presents three great epochs which correspond exactly to the triple condition—theological, metaphysical and positive—of human philosophy that forms the subject of our first article. I must here confine myself to a summary exposition of this new series of general facts.

THE THEOCRACIES

The first social system under which the human mind was enabled to achieve real and lasting progress, was fundamentally characterized by the confusion of the temporal with the spiritual power; or, more accurately, by the complete subordination of the one to the other. To speak with still greater precision, it essentially consisted in the general and absolute preponderance of a Philosophic Caste, organized under the influence of theological philosophy.

Every primitive society, so far as its development is indigenous and spontaneous, manifests a natural tendency towards such an organization. But this regime could not establish itself completely and acquire a great consistency in any countries but those where, by a favourable conjunction of climate and position—which this is not the place to explain—the theological philosophy was enabled soon to attain its complete development, and in consequence to gain an irresistible ascendancy over the other parts of the social system. These conditions were fulfilled in Egypt, in Chaldea, in Hindustan, in Tibet, in China, and in Japan, to which we may add Peru and probably Mexico, some generations before the discovery of America.

Considering this state of society merely from an abstract point of view, one is especially struck by this profound character of unity and interdependence, which then so entirely predominated in the intellectual system. Never, since this period, did the esprit d'ensemble manifest itself to the same extent; and it can never again be realized except by the direct construction of the positive philosophy.

The primary cause of this absolute systematization doubtless lay in the homogeneity of human conceptions, then uniformly theological. But this cause, though operating universally, did not everywhere produce the same effect, at least not in so eminent a degree. An organization of the scientific body peculiar to this social state was also requisite.

By the mere existence of a Philosophic Caste it may be said that a regular and permanent division had been established between theory and practice. But in the first place, this division was incomplete in one very important respect, since it did not extend to social combinations; in the second place, there existed no precise distribution of labour within the theoretical domain. Such is the special nature of this primitive scientific organization.

That universality of knowledge, which is now so justly regarded as an ambitious chimera, then, on the contrary, constituted the dominant character of the members of the spiritual corporation. In the upper ranks of the hierarchy each minister of worship was at once astronomer (or rather astrologer), physicist, doctor, even engineer, and also a legislator and statesman. In a word the names of Priest, Philosopher, and Savant, which have since acquired such different significations, were then exact synonyms. The combination of these three characters is well marked in the person of Moses, whom we may consider as the best-known type of this primitive condition of the human intellect.

It is easy to explain this pretension to universal knowledge, since it directly depends upon the same causes which produced the preponderance of the learned caste, and it is at least as inevitable. Granting that a given combination of physical causes has permitted human conceptions to attain, in certain countries, a development sufficiently rapid to allow of their being quickly systematized under theological inspiration, it manifestly resulted from this very rapidity that at the period of coordination the different branches of knowledge were not sufficiently extensive to demand or to admit of a real and stable division.

But this universality of work is not only coincident and necessarily connected with the social supremacy of the learned caste, it also forms its strongest support. The credit obtained by the Priests as astronomers, doctors, and engineers was the basis of their political authority; and vice versa the power they enjoyed was an indispensable condition for the development of their scientific speculations.

We must seek in the nature itself of this spiritual organization the true and fundamental explanation of the admirable vigour and consistency always so characteristic of this primitive social system, as compared with all societies that have since existed. In a society whose elements are so closely connected that no portion can be impaired without shaking the ensemble ought we to be astonished at the energy of resistance which has hitherto triumphed over all known forces? Accordingly this social state should be considered as the glorious epoch of the theological system. However real may have been its subsequent influence we may say, without exaggeration, that after this period it continually declined. To this point therefore must the human race recede, if retrogradation were possible.

While recognizing that the theocratic regime was at once the necessary consequence and the indispensable condition of the earliest advances of the human intellect, we cannot disguise from ourselves the fact that this system, by its nature, tended to become a permanent and almost invincible obstacle to more extended progress. Whether there be a necessary incompatibility between the complete consolidation of the social system and its perfectibility, or whether, rather, the combination of these two qualities was merely a task which exceeded the means then accessible to man, it is certain that the most strongly organized nations became at last almost stationary. This happened in all countries when the theocracy was able to establish itself completely. The explanation is easy.

Without division of labour, the perfecting of the human intellect is not possible. Intellectually the theocratic system had no value, except as furnishing the means of organizing, on a regular and stable basis, the germ of the separation between theory and practice. But this primary division which, once fixed, became by the very nature of the system, unalterable, required to be pushed much farther in order to allow of an indefinite development of the human faculties. Such was the radical vice of this primitive system.

The different classes of our conceptions cannot develop themselves with equal rapidity. I have already pointed out the necessary succession which their development invariably manifests. From this we may perceive that the scientific organization in question, by virtue of which all the various theories are cultivated at once by the same intellects, cannot long exist without becoming strongly opposed to the perfecting of our knowledge, since it admits only of such advances as can be simultaneously made in all parts of the intellectual system.

This view is much strengthened, when we combine with the purely philosophical point of view, the political stand-point, characteristic of this first social epoch, the fusion of the temporal with the spiritual power. For this condition, by itself, renders impossible every great improvement of human theories, as tending to the total and immediate overthrow of the political order. How could any important progress by expected under a regime which converted every great discovery, not only into an act of impiety, but into a revolt. The theological philosophy was, in those primitive times, and has since continued to be the only sort fitted to guide society. Accordingly so long as the temporal power was merely a derivation from the spiritual power; nay further so long as physical theories and social doctrines were not entirely separated, the former could not advance beyond the theological state without destroying the bases of society.

If then the progress of the human intellect was, at first, only rendered possible by means of an elementary stage in the division of labour regulated by the theocratic regime, it is evident that its subsequent advance demanded, no less imperatively, a much greater subdivision, but one that could only be effected under a totally different regime. Above all, it was essential that the culture of the human mind should become independent of the immediate guidance of society, in order that the division and perfecting of our knowledge might take place without compromising the existence of the political order.

The natural development of the various theories would doubtless, in the end, have spontaneously determined this separation, even in the theocracies, although from the causes above indicated such a change would in them have been much retarded. In fact it would seem impossible but that, however slow might be the progress, at the end of a certain time, the ever-increasing difficulty of comprehending the totality of human ideas, must lead to a continual increase in specialization. We may even observe in the learned castes of the different theocracies some beginnings of a perfected division. But the course of events did not allow any theocracy to enjoy an existence sufficiently prolonged to allow of our observing the development of such a revolution. Happily for human civilization, the new scientific organization established itself in a much more rapid manner. . . .

What remains to be done by men of science in order to raise them, in their turn, into a New Spiritual Power, no less powerful in its way than the old power? It is necessary to complete the system of positive knowledge, by creating Social Physics, and so, at last, to construct Positive Philosophy. Thus and only in this way can the sciences, investing themselves with complete generality, replace theology become powerless for the moral government of society.

POSITIVE REORGANIZATION OF SAVANTS

This conception of the future of the sciences leads us to consider the third organization of the scientific body which corresponds to the positive state of philosophy, as did the Greek organization to its metaphysical, and the Egyptian or Asiatic to its theological state. Savants, having at last constructed their appropriate philosophy, will incorporate themselves anew with society in order to assume, once more, its spiritual guidance, but in a way completely different from the theocratic method. . . .

Simultaneously with the formation of this new class of savants, an important subdivision should also be effected in the scientific body, indispensable to the exactness of its philosophic character and consequently to the efficiency of its political action. It consists in a new and final improvement in the general division between Theory and Practice. This division is still incomplete inasmuch as the office of Engineer has always been, more or less, mixed up with that of the Savant, on which, even in our day, it exerts a very prejudicial influence. In the early history of natural theories this confusion was, doubtless, inevitable; as it was also indispensable, in order to make their value appreciated by minds too gross to understand the utility of theories which do not allow of immediate applications. But, now, this direct and permanent relation is no longer needed. Henceforward the sciences should be judged above all by their philosophic value.

Accordingly men of science, far from being bound to place limits on their sentiments of theoretic dignity, should firmly resist every attempt, inspired by the exaggerated practical tendencies of our age, to reduce them to mere engineers. But an appropriate system of doctrines constitutes the best way of definitively extinguishing pretensions which will necessarily continue and be, to a certain extent, legitimate, until the relations between theory and practice have been organized by the aid of conceptions specially adapted to this end. Scientific men can alone construct this system, since it must flow from their positive knowledge of the relations that subsist between the external world and man. This great operation is indispensable in order to constitute the class of Engineers into a distinct corporation, serving as a permanent and regular communication between the Savants and Industrialists in reference to all special works.

Such then, speaking generally, are the different doctrines essential for completing the modern organization of the scientific body, and previously shown to be indispensable for completing the intellectual system adapted to the new condition of the human mind. Doubtless these works will not be executed by living savants, whose faculties are irrevocably engaged in important researches, the interruption of which would be absurd and injurious. They could, however, be usefully undertaken only by minds educated under the influence of the various positive methods, familiar with the chief results of all the physical sciences, and subject to the direct and continued sanction of the existing scientific body. On the formation, more or less rapid, of this new class of savants must depend the development of these complementary labours, destined at last to invest the positive system with that spiritual supremacy assigned to it by the invariable law of progress of the human race.

As soon as these various works shall have attained sufficient maturity to acquire an unmistakable character, we shall see the education of society fall, spontaneously and forever, into the hands of the savants. Already every preparation is made for this great revolution. The natural sciences have at last, in the eyes of all men, and must more and more, become the principal object of instruction. Where the regular system of public education does not sufficiently supply this pressing need of existing minds, they seek its independent satisfaction and succeed in finding it. Governments, assisting, as they have done from the commencement, this special movement, create a multitude of special establishments. From the highest branches of theoretical instruction to the simplest rudiments destined for the least cultivated intellects, they endeavor by every means in their power, to impress a positive character on all minds. In a word the political measures which can really hasten this regeneration, are already essentially developed. Nothing is wanting except the great philosophical condition, without which all these partial efforts, however efficiently pursued, could produce no very important result—the formation, as above pointed out, of generalized positive conceptions.

The views submitted in this essay may be regarded as a first sketch of the problem of the Spiritual Power, treated merely from the philosophical point of view. Having thus laid down the principles of our discussion, we can now directly and thoroughly examine this great question, the most momentous of our time. This shall form the subject of a new investigation. . . .

SCIENTIFIC FAITH THE TRUE BASIS OF ACTIVITY

Neither individuals nor the human race are destined to consume their life in a course of sterile reasoning, continually disserting on the conduct they ought to observe. The mass of the human race is essentially called to action, except an imperceptible fraction only, who, by their nature, are chiefly devoted to contemplation. Nevertheless, every sort of action presupposes directing Principles already ascertained, which individuals and the masses have, in most cases, neither capacity nor time to establish, or even to verify, otherwise than by their results. Such, intellectually considered, is the fundamental consideration that decisively justified the existence of a class absorbed by speculative labours, constantly and exclusively occupied in furnishing all the rest with the general rules of conduct, which they can no more dispense with than create; and which, once admitted, allow the masses to employ their faculties in applying them to practice, only asking for the assistance of the contemplative class, when deduction or interpretation presents too many difficulties.

SPIRITUAL GUIDANCE NEEDED FOR PERSONAL AND SOCIAL MORALITY

This necessity for Spiritual Guidance manifests itself, no less clearly, if man is considered, not merely as an intelligent, but as a moral being. For, even admitting that each individual or collective being could by his unaided faculties form the plan of action best adapted to his own welfare, or to the harmony of the ensemble, it is certain that this doctrine, being generally opposed, more or less, to the most energetic impulses of human nature, would by itself, exert hardly any influence on real life. It therefore needs to be, so to speak, vivified by a moral force, regularly organized, which, continually recalling it to the remembrance of each in the interest of all, can impart the energy that results from such universal adhesion, and is alone capable of overcoming, or even adequately counterbalancing, the force of the anti-social dispositions naturally preponderant in human nature.

However great the progress of civilization may be it must ever remain true that if the social state is, in certain respects, a continuous state of individual satisfaction, it is also, under other not less necessary aspects, a continuous state of sacrifice. To speak more precisely, each person, in every personal act, must experience a certain degree of satisfaction without which society could not exist; and a certain degree of sacrifice without which it could not maintain itself, having regard to the opposition of individual tendencies which is, in some degree, absolutely inevitable. The relative intensity of the former kind of feelings may doubtless increase, and, in fact, it does constantly increase, thus creating a progressive amelioration of the human condition. But the latter necessity also always exists and its absolute strength even augments continually, through that increasing warmth of desire which our organization invariably connects with the augmentation of our enjoyments, as an inevitable compensation and an indispensable corrective.

The highest attainable state of social perfection would manifestly consist in the fulfillment by each person of the particular office for which he is best adapted in the general system. Now even in such a state of things—itself, purely ideal, though capable of being indefinitely approached—men would need a moral government, because no one could of his own accord confine his personal dispositions within limits suitable to his condition. For nature and society will, by common accord, ever assign to different persons, functions which afford satisfaction in very various degrees. Natural aptitudes and social positions present an infinite variety as regards both kind and intensity. On the contrary the instincts that habitually predominate are nearly the same under both aspects in all men, or at least they exist in all with sufficient energy to inspire a wish for the enjoyments that others have, let their positions differ as they may. Hence the necessity for developing, by a special influence, the natural morality of man, in order, as much as possible, to bring the impulses of all within the limits required for the general harmony, by habituating them from childhood to a voluntary subordination of their personal interest to the common interest, and by constantly producing in active life, with necessary emphasis, the consideration of the social point of view. Without this salutary influence, which extinguishes the evil in its source, society, being constantly obliged to act on individuals, either by violent means or by interest, in order to repress the results of tendencies allowed to develop themselves freely, the maintenance of order would become impossible, even did this temporal discipline reach its utmost limits. But happily, from the nature of things, the absolute notion of such a mode of government, at once barbarous and illusory, is, and can only be, a mere supposition. In truth temporal repression never has been, and never will be, anything but the complement of spiritual repression, which, at no time, can wholly suffice for social necessities. If, by the natural progress of civilization, the former unceasingly diminishes, this diminution unavoidably presupposes a proportional increase of the latter.

Thus, both under intellectual and moral aspects, it is proved that, in every established society, the notions of good or evil intended for guidance of each person in his various social relations (and even in his purely individual life as far as it can influence these relations), are reducible to prescriptions or prohibitions, founded and maintained by Spiritual Authority properly organized, and which, as a whole, constitute the guiding social doctrine. In this way, we can explain that ancient estimate of human nature, systemized by Catholic philosophy, in accordance with the profound, though necessarily empirical, knowledge of our nature, so eminently characteristic of it. It directly sets forth as a fundamental virtue, the immutable and necessary basis of private and public happiness, faith: that is to say, the disposition to place confidence, spontaneously and without previous demonstration, in doctrines proclaimed by a competent authority. This, in fact, constitutes the general and indispensable condition on which depends the establishment and maintenance of a true intellectual and moral communion.

INDIVIDUAL FREEDOM RESIDES IN THE
APPLICATION OF ASCERTAINED PRINCIPLES

In principle, the influence exerted by the individual upon the regulating doctrine is, normally, limited to deducing the practical rule applicable to each special case; the spiritual organ being consulted in all doubtful cases. But as regards the construction of the doctrine, under every possible aspect, no one possesses any legitimate right beyond that of suggesting its partial rectification, when experience has proved that it fails, in any respect, to fulfill its practical end. To the spiritual power, thus warned, it naturally belongs to make suitable changes in the doctrine, after verifying the necessity for them. Such at least is the normal state of things. On any other hypothesis society must be considered as being, more or less, in a truly revolutionary state. This state, necessary also at certain determinate epochs, although always transitional, is subjected to special rules of a wholly different nature, with which I need not occupy myself in this place since I am only prescribing for the normal state.

The two classes of general considerations above pointed out have a special application to the social state towards which modern nations tend. For in this new state, characterized as it is by a more complete and ever increasing separation of the various functions, each person, whatever may be his capacity, can, unaided, grasp but a very small portion of the doctrine which he needs for his guidance, either industrially or socially. On the other hand his personal interest, having been narrowed, naturally tends to deviate from the common interest more frequently, though to a less degree.

The evident tendency of modern societies towards an essentially industrial state, and, consequently towards a political order in which the temporal power shall regularly belong to the preponderating industrial forces, begins to be generally felt in our day, and the natural course of events will manifest it more and more. The sway unavoidably exercised by the sentiment of a truth, so important though partial, disposes men to overlook or neglect the moral reorganization of society. It tends to keep up the habit, engendered by the critical doctrine, and specially encouraged by political economy, of assigning the first place to a purely material point of view in social considerations. By looking too exclusively at the immense moral and political advantages which incontestably belong to the industrial state, these are exaggerated so far as to suppose that they dispense with a true spiritual reorganization; or at least, that this will only possess a secondary importance, when social relations have become purely industrial and are no longer deteriorated, as is still the case, by institutions and habits derived from the military antecedents of society.

We, who should consider this great fact not aesthetically, as artists attracted by its power over the human imagination, but as observers who, neither admiring nor reprobating, admit its existence as a fundamental datum in all speculations on modern politics, ought, as much as possible, to study it under every aspect. In this attitude we can easily perceive that the regulating and directing influence of the spiritual power is not less necessary for industrial than for military relations, although not exactly in the same way. On this subject I limit myself to some general indications, reserving their complete development for another occasion should the question demand it.

On the supposition, which moreover is impossible, that the

temporal order corresponding to this new state of society can establish itself completely, without the intervention of any spiritual power, it is certain that in the absence of this conservative influence, such a social order could not maintain itself. If, besides those general sources of disorder inherent in every society which render a moral government necessary, the military system presents some peculiar to itself, the same undoubtedly holds true for the purely industrial system; but the special causes are not the same for both and consequently do not attain the same degree of intensity.

It is no doubt much easier to reconcile individual interests in the modern than in the ancient mode of existence. But this happy characteristic which renders the moral rule easier to establish in no degree dispenses with it, since the antagonism, while less intense, has not disappeared, nay, has become more extensive, by reason of the multiplied points of contact. Thus, to choose the most important example, although hostility between the chiefs of industry and the workmen is socially preferable to that which existed between the warriors and the slaves, it is no less real. We should hope in vain to destroy it by temporal institutions, which uniting the material interests of these two classes more intimately, might reduce the arbitrary power they mutually exercize. No stable social state can ever be firmly based on mere physical antagonism, the only sort which such institutions can regularize. Although useful, no doubt, these will always be inadequate; because they necessarily allow the chiefs to entertain the desire, and even to exercize the power, of abusing their position, in order to reduce wages and work, and permit the workmen to obtain by violence what a life of labour cannot procure them. The solution of this grave difficulty necessarily demands the continuing influence of a *moral doctrine,* which shall impose upon both chiefs and workmen mutual duties in conformity with their mutual relations. Now it is evident that this doctrine can only be founded and maintained by a spiritual authority, placed at a point of view sufficiently general to include the entire [range] of these relations, and at the same time sufficiently disinterested in reference to the practical movement to be above suspicion of partiality from either of the two hostile classes between which it should intervene. Similar remarks may be made as to the other great industrial relations, such as those of agriculturalists and manufacturers, of either class with merchants, and of all with bankers. It is evident that in all these respects, interests if left completely to their own guidance, without any regulation but such as springs from their antagonism, must always end in direct opposition. Hence the absolute necessity for a moral rule, and, consequently, for a spiritual authority, indispensable for retaining interests within those limits, where, instead of being antagonistic, they converge, yet from which they constantly endeavour to escape. Moreover it would be easy to show that this moral action, considered under both its aspects, must play an indispensable and leading part in establishing temporal institutions destined to complete this regulation of social relations.

We should attach too great importance to the demonstrations of political economy which prove the necessary harmony of the various industrial interests, were we to hope that this conformity could ever suffice for their discipline. Allowing even, to these demonstrations the complete logical extent, much exaggerated in truth, which economists assign to them, it is certain that man does not act only, or even mainly, from calculation, and secondly, that he is not always, or even generally, capable of calculating wisely. The physiology of the nineteenth century, confirming, or rather explaining universal experience, has demonstrated the worthlessness of the metaphysical theories which represent man in the light of a calculating machine, solely impelled by self-interest.

Morality, private or public, will therefore, of necessity, be fluctuating and feeble, so long as the exclusive consideration of personal utility is taken as the point of departure for each individual or class. Yet the industrial spirit naturally leads in that direction, as does every other kind of purely temporal influence, when this appears by itself, and without having undergone that regulative moral action, which can only proceed from a spiritual power rightly organized. Even could we conceive a society entirely and exclusively abandoned to the direct impulse of a purely temporal activity, the new political order, (if this name could be given to it) would have no other real advantage over the old one, (considered likewise under the same abstract hypothesis) than that of substituting monopoly for conquest, and a despotism founded on the right of the wealthiest for a despotism founded on the right of the strongest. Such would be the extreme, yet inevitable, consequences of a purely temporal organization, could such an hypothesis ever be realized. Happily, however mistaken may be our political views, the nature of things preserves society from the unmitigated influence of its own aberrations, and the final order which arises spontaneously is always superior to that which human combinations had, by anticipation, constructed.

The necessity for a spiritual order in the new social state, manifests itself not alone as regards the relations of individuals or classes, but in reference to merely personal morality. In the first place a general consideration, derived from the study of human nature, and pointed out by nearly all philosophers in every age, shows that the most solid basis of the social virtues is to be found in the habit of the personal virtues, since in this way man can test most severely his power of resisting the vicious impulses of his natural dispositions. But, apart from this universal ground, the inevitable influence which a simply individual activity indirectly exerts over society in any system of social relations, reveals itself specially in the modern system, and, consequently, furnishes a new motive for the moral regulation of society. To cite only one example: since the appearance of Mr. Malthus' works, it is generally admitted, that the continual tendency of population to increase more rapidly than the means of subsistence, a tendency which is especially developed in industrial societies, demands a certain degree of permanent repression as regards the most energetic of human impulses. Now such repression, it is evident, cannot be adequately effected by any but a moral authority, whatever may be the incontestable influence of temporal measures in restraining this instinct within proper limits. . . .

PROJECT CAMELOT:
An Autopsy
Robert A. Nisbet

Project Camelot may well have been the worst single scientific project since King Canute dealt with the tides: the worst conceived, worst advised, worst designed, and worst executed. But this much has to be said for it. Never has one project in the social sciences aroused interest so broad, so diverse, and in such high places of the national government. More important, never has one project produced, or at least stimulated, results so momentous (and possibly beneficial) in the long run to government policy with respect to the social sciences.

What was Project Camelot, and why the fuss?[1] Reading

[1] The bare details of Project Camelot are as follows: the Project was conceived in late 1963 by some officers in the Army's Office of Research and Development. Detailed planning was turned over to American University's Special Operations Research Office (SORO), an organization that had been established a number of years before under Army funding for the express purpose of conducting social science research for the Army. The objectives of Camelot were declared to be (1) the systematic identification of the symptoms of the breakdown of society and (2) the identification of actions that might forestall breakdown. The major national areas of Camelot research interest were chosen from countries in Latin America, the Middle East, the Far East, Western Europe, and Africa. Project Camelot was activated in late 1964 by SORO with a special group of social scientists under the direction of the late Rex Hopper, a sociologist with Latin American interests. Advising the Project, with varying degrees of directness and continuity, were some thirty-three consultants, many of them among the most distinguished behavioral scientists in the United

through the multitude of reactions and comments aroused by Project Camelot one is reminded irresistibly of the ancient tale of the three blind men and their individual descriptions of an elephant. For the *Washington Evening Star,* whose political reporter, Walter Pincus, first broke the story, Camelot was another episode in the unending conflict between the Departments of Defense and State. For the United States Army, under whose auspices Camelot had been conceived, it was a research project concerned with conditions of social unrest, riots, and insurrection, that would, in the words of General Dick, "help us to predict potential use of the American Army in any number of cases where the situation might break out." For more than a few Chileans, in whose country Camelot first came to international light, it was a flagrant and odious intervention in the domestic affairs of a country with which the United States was at peace. Secretary Rusk saw Camelot as a less than brilliant intrusion by the Army into the always delicate sphere of Latin American foreign relations. Most members of the House Subcommittee on International Organizations and Movements saw Project Camelot as a sad consequence of the dispersed, unfocused, and inadequate role of the behavioral sciences in the Federal government. This last view, as we shall see, comes perhaps the closest to revealing the whole elephant.

For many social scientists, the most conspicuous feature of Camelot was its summary cancellation by the Army, an act widely held to unfold yet another chapter in the government's discrimination against the behavioral sciences. (This view, as we shall also see, was perhaps the most self-serving, the least founded in reality.) For some university administrators across the country, and also a few behavioral-science project tycoons, the reaction to Camelot was, or might have been: "There but for the grace of God. . . ." For American social scientists at work in the field abroad, especially in those political areas where national patriotisms tend normally to be on trigger, Camelot was dynamite that might easily spell disaster for future foreign area research. And so it went.

States. Project Camelot was terminated in July, 1965, by order of Defense Secretary McNamara, following a chain of events described briefly in this article.

THE OUTSIDERS MOVE IN

There was one other reaction to Project Camelot that we must mark for the sake of the record: the reaction of many liberals and non-Establishment social scientists. What they learned from Camelot, others have learned elsewhere: the wages of sin is death. One of the most ironic—let us say, Camelotian—aspects of the Project was the utter absence from its operational staff of those social scientists who are most commonly the targets today of the Outsiders: those for whom the sesquipedalian "Establishment" has come to replace all four-letter words in the lexicon of Outsider profanity. Think of it! Here was a huge behavioral science project sponsored and financed by that most establishmentarian and hoary of all Establishment agencies, the Army; a project created—to cite the words of the high chief of Camelotians, Dr. Theodore Vallance, Director of American University's Special Operations Research Office (SORO)—as "an outgrowth of continuing interest in the Government in fostering orderly growth and development in the newer countries in the world," an Establishment objective if there ever was one. Add to all this the fact that Project Camelot was probably the most richly endowed (up to six million dollars had been allocated) single project in the history of the behavioral sciences. And, *Gloria in Excelsis Deo,* it was a project at long last in which Outsiders were Insiders—most of the social scientists involved were, to one degree or another, on the liberal-left of the political spectrum, and it is not likely there was a single supporter of the Viet Nam war among them. Across the River Styx, the shades of Plato and all his descendants down to C. Wright Mills must have danced in joy at the sight of this final ascent of the pure in heart to the very citadel of modern power.

What were the incentives that attracted and the motives that inspired such social scientists to a project, the official nature of which was a kind of unclassified intelligence enterprise to permit the U. S. Army easier tactical footing? Irving Louis Horowitz, who had no part in Camelot but whose article is the most informed and the most clarifying of all that have appeared, tells us that a glittering range of motives was to be found among Camelot's participants. The following is drawn in paraphrase from Professor Horowitz's "collective self-portrait of Camelot as the social scientists who directed it perceived it."

First, there was the joy of being able to do something Big in social science, something to wipe out memory of the picayune, to obliterate the remembered tedium of what C. Wright Mills had once called "abstracted empiricism." Second was the intoxicating sense of freedom that came with a position at the pinnacle of power; this in contrast to the unfreedom of ordinary academic existence where peers could examine one's work for merit and substance. Third, there was the Platonic prospect of educating an elite, of moulding the minds of that most ancient and reactionary of ruling groups, the generals, and of perhaps endowing the Army, for the first time in history, with peaceful and constructive aims. Fourth was the hope of accelerating man's ascent to perfectibility through the humanization, if not immediate capture, of military power: a dream that had heretofore been confined to utopians in history but was now part and parcel of the newest men of power, the behavioral scientists. Fifth was the intoxicating sense of living dangerously while other poor behavioral scientists remained within university cocoons.

These are a few of the motives that Professor Horowitz was able to uncover in his investigation of Camelot. From them it is easy to conclude that a sense of millennial excitement must have seized the minds of Camelotians during the stirring days of 1964–65; a sense of excitement generated by the realization that minds incorruptible and imperishably humanitarian were in the halls of power, at the ramparts indeed, able to look down upon those lesser social scientists, the Establishmentarians, who had sold their souls too early and too cheaply.

Then all hell broke loose. After months of Camelotian response, of contemplation, of thought and planning, of endless cost-plus consultation with the favored, months in which dreams were dreamed and then coded and punched, the whole thing (oh, cursed spite!) had to end. End not with a bang but a whimper. It happened this way.

DISASTER IN CHILE

One of the Camelot consultants, an assistant professor of anthropology, of Chilean birth but American citizenship, who was on his way to Chile for the summer on personal business, offered —for a fee, of course—to sound out Chilean social scientists on their possible enthusiasm for a project in which the United States Army, working through behavioral scientists, would undertake— in a strictly basic science sort of way, naturally, and with only the highest of motives—to investigate the conditions of social unrest, of insurgency, and means of counterinsurgency, in foreign countries; not necessarily in Chile, understand, but in other Latin American and foreign countries. This seemed like a dandy idea to the Chief Camelotians in Washington, and off went the, if not very first, the very last of Camelot's Intrepids.

The rest is history. Chilean social scientists, for some reason, did not take kindly to the thought of their country or any other being investigated by behavioral scientists who, however pure in heart and in methodological design, and however many echelons removed from tanks and flamethrowers, were nevertheless inescapably acting as agents of the United States Army on foreign ground. We are informed in the Chilean Select Committee Report to the Chamber of Deputies that the initial slight interest of a few Chilean social scientists in the project came from their having been assured in writing that such study as Camelot envisaged was sponsored by private or civil agencies and that it was not until they began reflecting on the implications of the use of a code name and, even more revealing, had received a full and documentary account of what Project Camelot was in fact from another of its consultants—a man of pacifist inclination unable to bear longer the weight of guilt—that they were able to respond in ways appropriate to the occasion.

One of the ways was to turn the whole thing over to a left-wing newspaper which, after months of the usual dreary leftist copy, had, for a change, something of Stop Press significance. It is not difficult to imagine the theme: American diplomacy, after a century of working through banana royalists had now turned to behavioral science royalists, that is, from industrial to academic tycoons, etc. etc. In any event, the news of Camelot was out—in Chile at least. Domestic uproar was predictably immediate and substantial, reaching the Chamber of Deputies which, as I have indicated, saw fit to receive a report on the whole matter from a special committee. All things considered, the Chilean report is remarkable for its temperateness, but it spares few details of Camelot, its operating structure, personnel, contacts with Chileans, and so on. In these respects it is a more useful document than the report on Camelot of our own House Subcommittee on International Organizations and Movements which protects the identity of Camelot scientists and the nature of all the details of the project—in a way that would probably not have been allowed had Camelot involved business or government figures rather than academics.

But if the Chilean Select Committee report was relatively moderate in temper, public and governmental opinion was not. The backlash produced by Camelot caught at least one American social scientist that I know of, leading to his summary eviction from Chile, with months of important research left dangling. He was indeed a victim, hardly qualifying as a bystander, for he was not only unconnected in any way with Camelot but totally ignorant of its existence. His protests were unavailing. The odium of Camelot was inclusive so far as American social scientists were concerned.

It was not, however, Chilean but Washington reaction to Camelot that proved decisive and of great long run significance to the behavioral sciences. Our Ambassador to Chile, Ralph Dungan, stung by his ignorance of something that (given U. S. Army sponsorship) understandably seemed part of his proper business, sent a sharp cable to Rusk after reading the details of Camelot in Chilean newspapers. Rusk went to LBJ, LBJ went to McNamara, McNamara went down gracefully (and gratefully, no doubt), and out of it—in one of the fastest actions ever recorded in official Washington—came a Presidential directive prohibiting Government-sponsored foreign area research that in the opinion of the Secretary of State would adversely affect United States foreign relations. Without the loss of measurable instant, Defense put Camelot to rest; or, to stay within the lovely imagery of it all, sentenced its inhabitants to return to the world of reality.

And the saddest of all the sad little ironies in the whole story is that, as one of the principals was to say, almost plaintively, Chile had not even been marked for Camelot study, had not been brainstormed, programmed, coded or punched! Of such, alas, is the city of man.

But Camelot's memory lingers on. Its real importance in the history of the social sciences begins indeed with its death. As nothing in the life of Charles I of England was said to have become him as did his manner of ending it, so nothing in Camelot's life was as fertile to the social sciences, as pregnant with issue, as its corpse; the corpse that was ordered exhumed for Congressional autopsy almost before its last breath. From the hearing conducted on Camelot by the House Subcommittee on International Organizations and Movements came a report, and I can think of nothing more edifying for social scientists than a reading of this two-hundred-page document; edifying and flattering. If any further medicine is needed to wash away the minority-group syndrome that still characterizes the self-evaluation of so many of us in the social sciences, that still leads us to feel despised, discriminated against, and disliked by society and government, it is to be found, free, in this report. Let it be trumpeted far and wide: the Federal government, starting with the Subcommittee whose job it was to look into Camelot's coffin, and going all the way across town to Secretaries Rusk and McNamara, loves the behavioral sciences.

In fact, one discovers, as he reads through the text of the Report, that the behavioral sciences are miraculously found free of sin. The Military's *use* of the behavioral sciences is not free of sin, but that, as we shall see, is a different story. Twice only could I find, in comments of individual members of the Subcommittee on the behavioral sciences, undercurrents of the ironic, but these were prompted by testimony on the behavioral sciences that has to be read to be believed. Let me cite the two instances. At one point, the Director of SORO (the administrative structure within which Camelot was hatched) was explaining to Subcommittee members the importance of American behavioral science "know-how" being exported to the underdeveloped nations; his illustration is the account given him by a friend who, while traveling in Africa, had once seen an automobile on an African highway stopped because of a flat tire, with its occupants standing about helplessly, as it seemed. To this one of the Subcommittee members could only gently recommend that the Director drive down any American highway. The second example was offered by a representative of the Military. He pointed, when pressed by the Subcommittee, to behavioral science's "discovery" that the Viet Cong frequently travel in village groups, with women and children along, and that they eat their meals at fixed times of the day. This intelligence, he noted, has made possible easier exterminatory actions by the American forces. One of the Subcommittee members, patience by now somewhat tried, wondered why batteries of behavioral scientists were required to discover what presumably would be within the powers of any scouting detail, something that Julius Caesar had found out through simple legionaries in his Germanic campaigns.

But these, I emphasize, are the only such examples I can find in the Subcommittee Report, and their real butt was not the behavioral sciences but, rather, the Military and its use of them. Reading the Report one finds himself, as a social scientist, almost literally holding his breath as he progresses through the testimony, for if ever a single behavioral science project lay exposed—in professional judgment, in design, in execution, quite apart from heavy expenditure of money (several hundred thousands of dollars had already gone into it)—to the possibility of merciless caricature by a Congressional committee, it was Project Camelot. But, far from caricature or hostility, there is only respect, courtesy, and seriousness of interest in the contributions of the behavioral sciences and in their proper status in the Federal government. After all, where else in a Congressional document (or professional document, for that matter) can one find the behavioral sciences characterized as "one of the vital tools in the arsenal of the free societies," with concluding recommendation made that funds for their subvention be greatly increased and their official status honored by inclusion in the Executive Office of the President as well as in a national foundation?

Not once in the Subcommittee hearing was the matter of professional ethics raised with respect to the behavioral scientist participants of Project Camelot. It was, however, in Chile, where apparently a different standard of conduct is expected of academic scholars. Reading the Chilean Select Committee report and some of the expressions of opinion in Chilean newspapers, one finds little if any of the censure of the American military that our own Subcommittee confined itself to, for in Chile, as in Latin America generally, nothing but the worst is usually expected from the military. What bothered, and still bothers, Chilean social scientists is, first, the fact that American academics could have allowed themselves to become involved in something like Camelot and, second, that no acts of censure toward Camelot social scientists have been taken, or even voiced, by American social science organizations. From a Chilean perspective it seemed incredible that social scientists could have given themselves, in the first instance, to a project under the auspices of the United States Army involving research into "the most intimate details" of Latin American institutions and personal lives; equally incredible that in their earliest communication with Chilean social scientists American social scientists had camouflaged Army sponsorship by referring vaguely to private foundation and National Science Foundation support. To this day there are Chilean and other Latin American social scientists who believe it the responsibility of American academic professional organizations to render apology in some form; even to register censure for the conduct of the Americans. But anyone who knows the reluctance of American professions, medical, legal, or academic, to voice censure of their own kind knows that the Chileans will wait a long time.

The ethical aspects of Camelot have received some attention by American social scientists, but it has been chiefly in the form of letters to the editor of one or another journal, and these seem, on the whole, superficial and tangential, frequently self-serving, with the Military and State Departments made the scapegoats, and are largely concerned with the question whether or not the behavioral sciences have any business working for the Military. The last seems to me a baseless question, except on grounds of personal ideology. I happen to believe that there was a major ethical responsibility that Camelot's technicians flouted by acceptance in the first place of *the nature of this assignment*. But that has nothing to do with what would appear to me to be the unquestionable, the almost axiomatic, propriety of the behavioral sciences entering into *certain kinds* of professional engagements with the Military.

If the behavioral sciences are what their prime representatives say they are—non-ideological, objective bodies of hypothesis and conclusion drawn from dispassionate and controlled study of human behavior—then there is nothing intrinsically wrong with their conclusions being used by, or given to, the Army. Why should not the behavioral sciences contribute to military and foreign policy as they contribute to community organization, urban renewal, race-relations, and other areas of society? Whether behavioral scientists make this contribution to the military directly —as employees on a military-designed project—or through quasi-autonomous foundations or universities is, as I shall emphasize below, a matter of profound operational and organizational significance. But it is hardly an ethical matter.

The right of the individual, whether he be a sociologist, chemist, or engineer, to hold back from the Military, to the best of his abilities, the efforts and contributions he has made as a scientist is, I should suppose, incontestable, however vain and illusory it might be. But the grounds for this have nothing to do with the nature of the sciences and everything to do with personal moral values. I do not see how we can argue on the one hand that the behavioral sciences are *sciences*—that is, bodies of knowledge which reach beyond individual caprice and moral preference to the level of empirically validated conclusions—but that on the other hand their principles should not be given to the military or some other established, recognized part of American society and government.

THEIRS NOT TO REASON WHY

Where the issue of professional ethics entered most significantly in Project Camelot, it seems to me, was in the initial acceptance of the mission of the project by social scientists *acting in their role as social scientists.* Let us, for sake of emphasis of this one point, dismiss the feelings of the Chilean social scientists and others who felt put upon by the Americans; it is always difficult to prove who said what, when. Let us, for the same reason, dismiss the ethical matter of the motives Professor Horowitz's interviews uncovered among principals of Camelot—motives which, I have to confess, shock in me what I had thought was an unshockable sense of propriety; for, motives, after all, are elusive, tenuous, and probably irrelevant. But what cannot be overlooked is the fact that a group of American social scientists, acting as social scientists, allowed the American military to believe there was nothing *scientifically* wrong in an American social science project, under American Army sponsorship, entering the historically sensitive areas of Latin America for the express purpose of discovering, through every possible penetration of culture and mind, the conditions of social unrest, conflict, and insurgency.

Here is a cross-cultural consideration that one might justifiably assume to be understood by every sophomore in an introductory sociology or anthropology course, one that might occur to any lay American who has been reading the news over the past decade or two. Was there no one in the administrative organization of SORO, no one among the social scientists who were appointed as *professional* men, not as simple technicians, to say in effect to Lt. General William Dick, Chief of Research and Development, Army: "Your objective is your business and no doubt admirable from the point of view of the Army; as behavioral scientists we desire to be of such help as we can; *but everything we know as behavioral scientists suggests the monumental, possibly catastrophic, unwisdom of such a project.*"

Not five minutes would have been required to acquaint the good general with the most elementary aspects of Latin American ethno-centrism, especially when the American military is involved. Was not the raising of such a question necessary and fundamental? I do not mean "ideologically" fundamental, but *professionally, scientifically,* fundamental. Is not the physician *as physician* professionally bound to refuse the order of a patient to prepare a compound that medical knowledge tells the physician is injurious? Does any sociologist believe that the physician can properly take refuge in the implicit statement: I am a behavioral scientist and if my sponsor orders it, it is not mine to reason why?

To say that the social scientists have no right, as scientists, to question a mission, even to refuse (still as scientists) cooperation, is not only to miss the nature of professional ethics but also to be blind to the view that has come to prevail in the larger scientific community today, where the scientist's duty to pronounce on matters of research policy, to pronounce as a scientist on the feasibility, economy, and wisdom of research policy, is not only unquestioned but, as Don K. Price has documented in admirable detail in his *The Scientific Estate,* is a matter on which Congressional and Executive opinion has come to depend.

But this, from all I have been able to read, was not a consideration in the minds of the behavioral scientists of Camelot or their consultants. Theirs not to reason why, theirs but to do or die—an epitaph more fitting, however, for cavalrymen than for professional scientists from whom judgment of feasibility is recognized part of any contract.

But if the behavioral scientists and the Military never saw the underlying, constitutive question, the members of the House subcommittee assuredly did. Over and over during the hearing, the question was raised by one or another member as to the wisdom of the Military undertaking the kind of research contained in Camelot's objective. No one asked the question more tersely and pointedly than Representative Roybal: "Wouldn't the mere fact that the Army was heading the Project itself create a problem in many countries?" That is indeed the question: How does the military get into this act? To which General Dick replied that, when American soldiers go into a foreign area, it is useful for them to know about the mores, customs, and also possible internal conflicts of that area; hence the Army's long-standing custom of issuing handbooks to its entering troops. But this was hardly an answer to the real question which pertained, not to handbooks issued soldiers in areas in which the United States maintained troops, but to the multi-million dollar "basic science" project that was Camelot. Representative Fraser conceded the necessity of handbooks in Viet Nam or Korea. "But," he went on, "when you try to create a model of a developing society for purposes of predicting what is going to happen in that society, for purposes of trying to figure out what kinds of things can be done to affect decision making, and the social processes, I do not see the Army in the game."

Nor would a good many other persons, but so far as one can infer from a reading of the transcript, neither Dr. Vallance, representing Camelot's behavioral scientists, nor General Dick and Mr. Seymour Deitchman, representing the Army, ever got it into his head that some gross stupidity or—looking at the matter "methodology-wise"—some scientific anomaly lay in the U. S. Army having commissioned behavioral scientists to go into Latin American countries like Chile. It was not a behavioral scientist connected with Camelot but, once again, Congressman Fraser who uttered the following words—this time following some rather pious testimony from Dr. Vallance:

"[T]here is throughout your whole presentation a kind of—an implicit attitude or relationship that this country bears to the rest of the world which, if I were not an American, I would find perhaps most highly offensive, but it suggests somehow we are the ones to find out the dynamisms that are at work in these countries for the benefit of our Military Establishment. If I were a Latin American, I wouldn't find this a particularly happy arrangement."

With Camelot to spur them, Subcommittee members could have entered into the record that just as war has long been held too important a matter to be left in the hands of the generals, the behavioral sciences are too important to be left in the hands of project titans. But the Subcommittee didn't. With the kind of luck that, as Arthur Guiterman described it many years ago in his famous jingle, God grants to children, fools, drunkards, and citizens of the United States of America, the behavioral sciences emerged from this potentially devastating hearing with their luster untarnished, their prestige, if anything, higher, having been treated to the always joyous spectacle of the military being spanked, and the clear prospect ahead of Federal organization and funding of the social sciences beyond anything that might realistically have been dreamed of once the Pandora's box of Camelot had been opened.

STATE DEPARTMENT VS. THE ACADEMICS

Nor was this all! We are treated also in the Subcommittee report to something that social scientists can rejoice in almost to the degree of their pleasure in seeing the military made the scapegoat. This is the spectacle of the State Department being told by the Subcommittee to commence making more use of the behavioral sciences in the formulation of foreign policy. In some ways, this is the most Camelotian byproduct of the whole weird enterprise, for if ever there was a time for the State Department to shore-up its traditional dislike of the behavioral sciences, this was it.

It is an old story that between State Department policy sections and the American academic community there is, and for long has been, distrust founded upon the State Department's lack of confidence in the concrete results of social science research and the academic community's belief—best expressed by Professor Gabriel Almond to a reporter for *Science*—that the State Department is a "conservative institution dominated by a foreign service which is trained largely in the law, in history, in the humanistic disciplines. They believe in making policy through some kind of intuitive and antenna-like process." According to official estimates gained by *Science,* of the $25.3 million spent by government agencies on social science research abroad during fiscal 1966, the State Department spent only $200,000. The Defense Department spent $12.5 millions or half the total.

Despite his generally candid and impressive testimony before the Subcommittee, Secretary Rusk did not appear eager to go into reasons for this disproportion. When pressed by Representative Frelinghuysen as to why, given the large amount of money that Defense got from Congress for behavioral science research, State received, and asked for, only pennies, and, more to the point, why such research as that represented by Camelot was not in State's hands rather than the military's, Rusk indicated only that he preferred not to get into the "question of criteria by which one or another Department might accept responsibility for certain types of research." To be sure, Secretary Rusk did, at this juncture, make the important point that such research "might be better left even to private agencies." I shall return to this in the final section of my article, for it is probably vital to the future of foreign area research by American scholars.

But if Secretary Rusk did not choose to explain the gulf between the State Department and the academic community, others with equal experience in both the foreign service and the universities have. Louis J. Halle, writing in *The Virginia Quarterly Review* (Winter, 1964), has put the matter illuminatingly. "There was a period after the [Second World] War when various departments of the Government tried to marry themselves to the universities. This worked in the case of the Pentagon and the faculties of science and technology, a wartime precedent having already been established at Oak Ridge and Los Alamos. In the case of the State Department it did not work. Professors of diplomatic history, professors of Latin American history, professors of economics and of sociology were brought to Washington for meetings at which the men in the State Department tried to explain their troubles. But the gulf could not be bridged. The professors tended to confine themselves to the general nature of the problems that the officials hopefully set before them, often speaking about the need to maintain the traditional idealism of our international conduct. When confronted by the direct question, 'What shall we *do?*', they fell silent. They could answer every question up to that last, but that last was the one question for which the men in the State Department had to have an answer. The experiment, abandoned at last, left the State Department men in a mood of disenchantment tinged with bitterness, such as often follows a frustrated courtship or a broken engagement."

One guesses, however, that in the future the State Department, under the prodding of the Subcommittee (formal prodding, contained in its official recommendations), will engage more actively in research partnered with social scientists. Not the kind that is expected to produce an answer to each *ad hoc* question that crosses a desk during a State Department day, but a kind that, when carried on long enough, and, hopefully, with a degree of discimination lacking in Camelot, could be the context or seedbed of decisions of policy.

We cannot conclude discussion of Camelot's impact on the State Department without reference to one development that for awhile led to considerable agitation in the social science world. This was the memorandum for President Johnson, hard on the heels of Camelot's exposure in Chile, directing the Secretary of State henceforth to screen all Government-sponsored foreign area research for its possible adverse effects upon United States foreign relations. Heaven knows, given the blunders of Camelot, there was every good reason for such a directive. But the first response of social scientists, including those who had been involved in Camelot, was to cry "censorship." By what right, it was asked, did one department of government take to itself the function of scrutinizing research projects sponsored by other Government departments in which American social scientists were participating?

The answer could have been stated simply: by the same right under which today, though still imperfectly, the State Department screens "projects" of American industry that involve entry into Latin American countries. The once odious spectacle of American businessmen entering the banana republics of Central America and then calling for the Marines when the going got difficult should not be repeated, it would appear obvious, when it is large-scale social science projects that are involved. Despite the myth of Immaculate Conception that obtains among American behavioral scientists—under which the most aggressively intimate forays into human privacy are held miraculously pure—the rape of national dignity by American academic enterprise is as repugnant to foreign feeling as rape by American business or government. The Chilean Select Committee Report makes this very plain indeed! On a hot day one can chill himself by reflecting on what might have happened in Chile—or any of the countries marked by Camelot for invasion—had the project had "good" luck; had it been "successful"; had unforeseen exposure not led to premature death. Several regiments of Marines would have been necessary to salvage American research capital and protect American researchers' lives.

The blessed wonder is, given all the considerations of national dignity involved, considerations that, as the Select Committe Report specifically emphasized, could not be waived "under the pretext of the scientific character of Camelot," that the President's directive did not include *all* foreign-area research. For what can be more important than preservation of good feeling in Latin America, good feeling that for years was jeopardized by American commercial arrogance and that American academic arrogance jeopardized in 1965? But the President's memorandum did not make this mistake. It properly confined itself to *Government-sponsored research*. It excludes altogether from its scope private research—of universities, foundations, and individuals. Secretary Rusk made this emphatic in his testimony before the Subcommittee. Almost equally important, the Foreign Affairs Research Council that was established by the State Department to give effect to the President's memorandum, has, in practice, excluded also from its jurisdiction domestic grants of the National Science Foundation, the National Institutes of Health, the National Defense Education Act, and the Fulbright program. The Council's range thus is restricted to Federal departments—Defense, Commerce, Treasury, etc.—in the more customary sense. Finally, in the year's experience with the new procedure, it would appear that nothing of legitimate concern to the social sciences has arisen in the Council's actual administration of its responsibility. It is difficult to understand what the executive officer of the American Psychological Association had in mind when, according to *Science* (8 July), he declared that the new risk review procedures "have eroded confidence in the government's understanding of how science goes about its business. . . . You would prefer that your peers look at your work. This is the way science is advanced, by having your critical colleagues look over your shoulder."

Such words are as irrelevant as they are pious. Returning to Camelot, it may be assumed that dozens of scientific consultants looked over the shoulders of dozens of Camelot principals. But if there is any record of their having looked critically enough to get at the core of this monumental blunder, I have been unable to find it. To talk serenely about the holy ground of science in the aftermath of Camelot, a project that, above anything that has ever happened, has weakened the confidence of Latin American intellectuals *in the American academic and scholarly community,* is a little like talking about the rights of free private enterprise in the predatory contexts of dollar diplomacy.

As I indicated above, the members of the Chilean Select Committee were unmoved by the "scientific" objectives of Camelot. It is useful to quote the words of the Committee report: "We wish to say that this foreign intervention in our internal affairs may not be defended on the pretext that the social investigation which was proposed has a scientific character." I shall have more to say below of the mounting implications to American foreign policy of large scale, corporate research in search of foreign areas. Here it suffices to emphasize only that when a major Federal department—be it Defense, State, or Commerce —sponsors a scientific project, even one composed of dues-paying psychologists and sociologists, it is elementary that not even the elixir of scientific method is sufficient to wipe away the fact of sponsorship.

We come now to what are surely the most far-reaching episodes in the aftermath of Camelot: the Congressional hearings and bills which, if approved, will result in a National Social Sciences Foundation and an Office of the Behavioral Sciences in the Executive Office of the President—not to mention a White House Conference on the Behavioral Sciences.

I do not mean to imply that Camelot was the sole cause of these momentous events. After all, proposals along their line have been in the minds of social scientists for years. There was, moreover, the effect on academic and government consciousness of disclosure that Michigan State University had had for some years a project, under Federal financing, for the training of police in South Viet Nam, a project in which individuals were employed "who had background in intelligence work for the United States," according to President John Hannah. It was charged that CIA under-cover agents were among these individuals, and although President Hannah declared that none "was known by the University or its representatives to have affiliations with the Central Intelligence Agency," such a statement, with all respect to its maker, is a little hard to assess. In the nature of things the University *wouldn't* have known, wouldn't have been permitted to know, officially at least, if some of those "with background in intelligence work" were agents of the CIA.

But the Michigan State affair was only a tempest—with rather limited consequences, a few being cancellation of some potentially sensitive university projects around the country with CIA and other agencies of the American military apparatus. Camelot, on the other hand—in terms not only of ensuing governmental action but also of ethical, intellectual, and academic issues— was, by comparison, an earthquake, one whose repercussions will continue for a long time. Let us examine a few of these.

SOCIAL SCIENCE AND PUBLIC POLICY

There is, in the first place, the vital matter of Federal policy with respect to the social and behavioral sciences. As I noted above, the House subcommittee, in its autopsy of Camelot, made strongly evident its dislike of military sponsorship of foreign area research. This is explicit in the Subcommittee's official recommendations. And while there was an inclination among Subcommittee members to see such research under the State Department, the most significant recommendation (with but one member dissenting) was toward the establishment of a separate agency in the Federal government for sponsorship of the social sciences. The official recommendation of the Subcommittee did not go beyond an Office of Behavioral Science Advisor in the White House. Subsequently, however (in June, 1966), the Chairman of the Subcommittee, Dante B. Fascell of Florida, introduced bills in the House to give formal effect, not only to this recommendation, but also to the establishment of a White House Conference on the Behavioral Sciences and, most important, to the establishment of a National Social Sciences Foundation. At the present time (August, 1966), the Senate Government Research Subcommittee under Senator Fred R. Harris of Oklahoma, is holding hearings on these and related matters. The preponderance (though by no means all) of academic testimony has been in favor of such a foundation, and we are told that Senator Harris' own sentiments in the matter are favorable. Still another hearing on the social sciences and their use by the Government is currently being held by the House Research and Technical Programs Subcommittee (of the House Committee on Government Operations), under the chairmanship of Representative Henry S. Reuss of Wisconsin. Again, of Camelot, one can only say reverently, never have so few so unintentionally earned the gratitude of so many!

Whether a National Social Sciences Foundation, not to mention an Office of Behavioral Sciences Advisor in the White House, is desirable at this juncture in the history of the social sciences is a difficult question even for those of us whose immediate interest is the welfare and prosperity of the social sciences. There is no doubt much to be said for both agencies. Some embarrassments and difficulties might be obviated. But there are others that, far from being obviated, might easily be created by such agencies. I am surely not alone in my belief that formal and heralded establishment of these agencies could well lead to a burden of expectation by government and public opinion that the social sciences are ill-prepared to shoulder. I say this not from belief that nothing or little of scientific character exists in the social sciences. Far from it. There are areas in the social sciences today where work of more genuinely scientific nature (using the word in its strict and hard-core meaning) exists than in certain areas of the biological and, for all I know, the physical sciences. This is not in question. The major difficulty would come, I believe, from the heavy likelihood that the Federal government—which already tends to be largely and increasingly "mission-oriented" in its conception of science—would place upon such a Federally-sanctioned office responsibility for massive *policy* questions and problems that the social sciences neither can, nor should, be expected to answer.

Over the past generation, the social sciences have made contributions of considerable value to society and to social policy. This is incontestable. That, given current tendencies, they will make even greater contributions in the future is almost certain. But this is not the essence of the problem. The essence is whether, given the monumental policy *expectations* of the social sciences that would be created by establishment of such agencies as those envisioned in Representative Fascell's bills, the social sciences (or, for that matter, *any* sciences) could meet them in a way not leaving a gulf between expectation and reality so wide as to promote disillusionment in government and society. Stating the matter briefly, one can say the danger consists in the ever present temptation of government to see the social scientists as *physicians* —called upon to answer *ad hoc* questions today, yesterday if possible—when they are, at their best, *physiologists,* still concerned with vital matters of the nature of human behavior.

BUREAUCRATIC SHADOWS

There is another disturbing aspect. The social sciences contain today a great diversity of not merely *kind* of work done, but, equally important, of conceptions of kind of work that *should* be done. Beneath the crust of apparent unity in the phrase "the social sciences" lie fissures of extraordinary depth in self-conceptions by social scientists. Orientations here vary much more greatly than among natural scientists. The almost inevitable effect, it would seem, of the establishment of a social sciences foundation would be to create an all too visible hand in the eventual resolution of their conflicts. A national foundation means a powerful director, not to mention vast funds. Everything we know as social scientists about bureaucracy and about the informal but potent pressures on bureaucracy, from inside and out, suggests the prospect of an external shaping of the development of the social sciences that one cannot contemplate with equanimity.

There is, finally, and from the strict point of view of social science research the most important of all considerations, the inevitably fragmenting, not to say segregating, effect that such a foundation would have upon the science of human behavior. The root is still man, and one of the most fascinating and encouraging of all tendencies today in the behavioral sciences is the synthesizing of strains of social, psychological, and physiological (and, who knows, physical in the next generation) research in the study of man. If there is anything that makes the elusive term "behavioral science" different from the "social sciences," it is the closer concentration, it would seem, upon *human behavior,* as the rigorous point of departure, in contrast to the plethora of problems, issues, values, and ideologies that the long history of moral philosophy and the social sciences have bequeathed to us. There are vital problems that are neither social nor biological in character but both—problems on which important research is now being conducted. To seek, in effect, through separate funding and design of problems, to disengage the social from the biological would be to reverse present healthy trends.

It seems to me that it would be far better to widen, through appropriate legislation, the present social science area of the National Sciences Foundation. (A bill now before Congress proposes exactly this.) Experience of recent years with this agency has certainly been encouraging from the viewpoint of the social sciences. Having for years protested, as many of us have, the arbitrary distinction the public makes between "science" and "social science," why, now, seek to institutionalize this distinction, risk perpetuating it forever, through establishment of a separate foundation?

Important as it is, the matter of a new foundation may be of less vital relevance than still another question—one also dramatized by Camelot—and that is the continued usefulness of the whole "project system" that has been in vogue in the Federal government's relation to the sciences ever since the years just following the Second World War, when a group of outstanding scientists in Washington were able to give it the wise guidance and control that the project system so plainly needs. But such wisdom cannot be taken for granted. The opportunities, on the one hand, for bureaucratic direction and misdirection of scientific research and, on the other, for political (I mean intra-scientific politics as much as other) considerations to govern, are all too rife. There is much to be said for the abandonment, or at least sharp cutback, of a system which not only permits, but encourages scientists to go to Washington as individuals or in small groups and receive grants for projects with scrutiny too hurried and too much governed by pecking-order considerations. The system, moreover, promotes disaffection within the universities.

Dr. Frederick Seitz, President of the National Academy of Science, has uttered some recent, important words to this effect. "I think that the whole process of supporting academic research with federal funds would be improved substantially if a larger fraction of the money granted by the government came to universities in the form of institutional grants that were handled on the basis of decisions made jointly by university administration and faculty."

Dr. Seitz makes clear that one of the primary reasons for his recommendation of this change in policy is that of restoring strength to the inner governments of universities—to department chairmen, to deans, but also to constituted faculty committees and councils; strength they have lost under a project system in which they are either bypassed altogether or reduced to mere clerical or clearing-house status by individual scientists whose own power and mobility are guaranteed by the independence of their project from the university in which their primary identity (and tenure, and high salary, and perquisites) are rooted. As Dr. Seitz emphasizes, such independence helps explain the kind of disintegration of academic community on a campus that Berkeley experienced two years ago.

The second reason Dr. Seitz gives for his recommendation is the fatal affinity that seems to lie between the project system and the *size* of projects that take residence on university campuses. No bureaucracy likes to administer funds for an infinity of small, individual projects. It is so much easier to grant one distinguished man large sums of money in a single project. Knowing this, scientists make application accordingly. Add to this the fact that Congress can most easily be pleased, on the occasions of its examination of how funds for science have been spent, by projects that are "mission-oriented," that have a high degree of applied flavor. The result of this is to encourage proliferation of types of scientific project of a practical or applied nature that could as easily be handled by non-university bodies—Federal, state, or private—and a subtle but puissant down-grading of appeal of those smaller, more open-ended, even amorphous "projects" that fall in the basic or theoretical areas of science.

THE PROBLEM OF SPONSORSHIP

There would be, it is clear, still another gain, and that is to the steadily enlarging field of American foreign-area research. If

Project Camelot teaches anything, it is the crucial importance of *sponsorship* when a team of American social scientists goes abroad to conduct inquiries into social structure, culture, and values which, by their very nature, run the risk of offending foreign sensibilities. There is, among many foreign scholars— quite apart from government officials and citizens—a certain suspicion of, not only the United States government and its agencies, but of government agencies in general: a suspicion founded upon frequent conflicts between their own governments and the intellectual communities in these countries—especially in the new and underdeveloped areas. Research projects which go abroad from the United States under the aegis of a governmental department, even departments as generally "clean" as AID or NSF or NIH, will increasingly encounter suspicion of, or will at least be subject to partisan political charges of, clandestine military penetration.

Universities, on the other hand, would appear much less susceptible to such suspicion or charges, especially when their research enterprises abroad are based, from the start, upon full cooperation with universities in the areas to be studied. In almost all countries of the world, the university is, and is most likely of all institutions to remain, trusted. One need think only of the large numbers of scholars, scientists, and public servants in the Latin American, Asian, and African countries whose higher educations have been gained in whole or part in American universities—quite apart from a generally distinguished record of American university scholars in these foreign areas.

It can be said, of course, that Camelot is evidence of the contrary. After all, this project was conceived within SORO which is itself administratively connected with American University. But from all one can gather, SORO has virtually independent status; it would appear to be only nominally a part of the University, in it but not really of it; its ties with the Army come closer to being those of RAND's to the Air Force. It is, in fact, a research center of the Army that, for various reasons which must once have seemed good to officials of American University, is housed there instead of in the Pentagon.

This is surely a very different thing from university-sponsorship as we generally and rightly understand it. And if Latin

American scholars were, unhappily for us all, justified in placing some of the odium on a university in the United States, sober analysis nevertheless requires the differentiation I am making. But there is a hard lesson, nevertheless, in Camelot. If the system of block-grants to universities should be adopted by Government foundations, in preference to the present project system, then much is properly owing these Government foundations by the universities in the way of *guaranteed administrative machinery* within the universities through which all such block-grants will be handled. Federal foundations should insist upon, at a minimum, proper academic-administrative bodies of review within the universities, composed of faculty members, as well as of administrators, which would have something of the same overall responsibility for research conducted under these block-grants that faculty-administrative councils and committees have immemorially had over curriculum, courses, and over internally-financed research in the universities.

Let us make no mistake. Such a system, replacing the twenty-year old project system in this country, will have its bitter enemies among scientists themselves; among those, at least, by now well accustomed to the free-wheeling possibilities, the independence, the sense of titanship, that go with the project system. Nevertheless, both for the reasons given by Dr. Seitz and for reasons inherent in the special nature of the social sciences—especially inherent in the nature of foreign-area research —I think the block-grant system, making the universities rather than Federal agencies acting through *ad hoc* projects the true principals, will work to the long run enhancement of research. There will be, I should think, far less probability of a Project Camelot again occurring. But this will be true only if a bona fide university "infrastructure" for the allocation and handling of these funds within the university exists. To turn such vital matters over to an agency like SORO, where university ties are only nominal and those between it and the Army (or any other Federal department) are decisive, could be ruinous.

But no matter what the "infrastructure" of American foreign-area research, it would be naïve to suppose that the future can be made free of the threat of impact upon foreign relations that

Camelot represented in so egregious a way. Even if Camelot had never happened, there would still be what Camelot assuredly intensified: the problem of retaining (not to mention increasing) the hospitality of foreign nations toward American research in the behavioral sciences. Granted that Chileans, Nigerians, Ceylonese, English, French, and Germans would be more hospitable to a project of Camelot's general type emanating from Harvard University than from the Department of Defense, the question remains: how favorable? For we are dealing with research orientations in today's behavioral sciences in the United States of a mass, and of a type, that increasingly pose problems of potential conflict with foreign sensibility.

It is well to be reminded that some of the animus toward Camelot found in the Chilean Select Committee Report has to do with the basic type of problem that was buried beneath the Project's more manifestly absurd pretensions. From the Chilean point of view, there was gross impropriety in the fact that, irrespective of Army sponsorship, Project Camelot proposed (I am quoting almost verbatim here) to investigate not only isolated and innocuous aspects of Chilean life, but to make an X-ray of the nation, including the most intimate aspects of human beings: what they think, feel, believe, or hope. And all of this without the consent of or authorization of either the Chilean government or the Chilean universities.

It is a fact worth stressing that personal and institutional privacy is still taken more seriously in Latin American and many other countries in the world than it is in the United States, where Gallup and Roper Polls, Kinsey reports, behavioral science and/or FBI bugging of juries, class rooms, offices and conference halls, not to mention the oceans of questionnaires that go forth daily from social science centers, industrial personnel offices, and civil service agencies, inquiring into every intimate and sensitive aspect of one's political, sexual, financial, and dream life have, over a period of a quarter of a century, made Americans the most nakedly exposed—and in this vital sense, perhaps, unfree —people in history. Even under the military dictatorships of Latin America, a freedom of individuality and of personal privacy is known and cherished that we in the United States may be beginning to forget.

BREACHES OF CONFIDENCE

There is a further reason for possible distrust among intellectuals and social scientists abroad of American foreign-area projects. That is the slightly uneven record of preservation of research confidence by individual American social scientists. There have been instances, as is well known, in which full entry into a community, a sect, a club or gang, or a file of documents was granted a social science project *only* under the guarantee of absolute confidentiality and anonymity of respondents: confidentiality and anonymity which were ruthlessly violated by one or more individuals of the self-same projects acting, despite the best efforts of the principals to restrain such violation, under the cloak of individual academic freedom to publish the truth, however gained. The recent cancellation, by the U. S. Air Force, of a project funded by the Air Force Office of Scientific Research, but administered at the University of Wisconsin, is possibly a case in point. Although the Air Force gave no official excuse for cancellation, there is reason to believe that when some of the detailed and intimate questions that were to be asked of selected Air Force officers were examined, the conclusion was reached that such a questionnaire would be inimical to service morale, given the ever-present possibility of future leaks of community-, group-, or individual-identity.

Here again, as with so many of the issues raised by Camelot, the immediate, instinctive reaction of the academic-research community is a curious one, to say the least. We find one professor declaring that the prime lesson to be learned from the Air Force cancellation is that we, the social scientists, must educate the public to understand that the same kind of personal intimacy of question is to be expected and accepted from social scientists as has long been accepted from physicians and lawyers. But at least two aspects of the matter render this comparison decidedly suspect. In the first place, the physician's "intimacy" stems solely from diagnosis designed to cure. Intimacy of the social scientist stems from research designed for publication. There is, second, the matter of responsibility and sanctions. A physician found guilty of broadcasting or leaking the identity of a patient with, say, a venereal disease or an advanced case of alcoholism or nymphomania would be broken professionally. There are no such sanctions in the academic profession. It is possible, indeed, to be promoted and to draw excellent royalties in the behavioral sciences for actions that would lead to suspension from the legal or medical professions.

This may seem a tangential matter. I am suggesting, however, that what is an increasingly complex and uneasy matter for American conscience is bound to be, given the less than perfect record that the behavioral sciences have for preservation of confidentiality, a matter of considerable moment when the subjects are Chilean or French instead of American. As I noted above, one of the responses of the Latin American academic and intellectual community to Camelot has been precisely that of asking what acts of censure have been taken by American social science associations toward the individuals involved in Camelot.

THE IMPERIALIST PHASE OF SURVEY RESEARCH

More important, however, to the future of American foreign-area research than type of research project and question is its potential volume. Here we have something that can, not inexactly, be put in Malthusian terms. The number of foreign research areas will increase (through dropping of barriers) *arithmetically,* but the population of American behavioral scientists with questions to ask of foreign areas will increase *geometrically.* Where once American foreign area research was confined to a tiny handful of anthropologists and geographers who learned, the hard way, the exceeding importance of tact, trust, honesty, and limits to questions when dealing with foreign peoples, and who went in as individuals, not as members of formidable projects, such research now, as we know, engulfs all the behavioral sciences. Given its rising popularity among social scientists who once could not have found their way to a passport office; given the shrinking (in the sense of yielding diminishing returns) domestic supply of political attitudes, religious beliefs, social aspirations, dreams, orgasms, etc., against the voracious requests of domestic behavioral science titans for ever enlarging masses of subjects; and given, finally, the hordes of graduate students writing dissertations, junior professors on the make, senior professors in struggle for project titanship, not to mention the tens, the hundreds of millions of dollars for such research that will inevitably come from formalized Federal assistance—given all this, it could hardly be a matter for wonder if more and more foreign governments (and also foreign academic communities) began to take the hostile stance toward American social scientists that was once reserved for American businessmen. The bland and righteous belief among American academics that any degree of invasion of privacy, any degree of public exposure of the human psyche, is justified so long as it is in the name of science rather than, say, the TV industry, is no more likely to win popularity in the long run than did the medieval Inquisition when it defended *its* invasions in the name of piety and protection of the faithful. To assume that all will be well if only investigation of natives abroad is done by an American NSSF or a university is, I fear, naive. There will be, all too certainly, other considerations—of foreign relations, national policy and so on—when the American knowledge industry really gets tooled up for foreign markets, and its production rolling.

Does such language offend? We had better get used to it. The relevant model of behavioral science research is fast ceasing to be the scholar—he of "furrowed brow in bookish corner"—and fast becoming the brisk executive, at home, equally, in institute, business, and government. We still use the beguiling image of the scholar and his natural right to freedom of inquiry. It is to today's large-scale, corporate research what the image of the small individual businessman and his natural right to profit is to corporate industry: a compound of honest nostalgia, guilty conscience, and camouflage. The structure, the incentives, and even the language of contemporary large-scale research have more in common with business than with the academy. And it matters little, substantively, whether we have reference here to "academic" or "nonacademic" research.

It is possible, I think, to apply to today's knowledge industry what Berle and Means wrote thirty years ago of the modern corporation. "Just what motives are effective today, in so far as control is concerned, must be a matter of conjecture. But it is probable that more could be learned regarding them by studying the motives of an Alexander the Great, seeking new worlds to conquer, than by considering the motives of a petty tradesman of the days of Adam Smith." Substitute "petty scholar" for "petty tradesman" in the foregoing words, and the relevance is immediate.

Foreign-area research is bound to become massive and, potentially, invasionary. If one were a Marxist-Leninist he could say that the American research industry is just beginning to enter its imperialist phase. Diminishing returns, a falling rate of profit, are encountered in the American market. Smalltown, Midcity, Big City have been entered too often; the middle, upper, and lower classes are beginning to be sucked dry. New worlds are needed for conquest if the already frenzied competition for returns within the United States is not to result in civil war. (A sometime business executive, now financial vice-president of a great university, said recently: "Nothing I saw in fifteen years of business compares with the gut competition, the dog eat dog, that I see in the university. God help the natives abroad when the academics get at them in full force.") There must be, at this moment, literally tens of thousands of American behavioral scientists— Ph.D. aspirants in search of dissertations, professors of all ranks, not to mention the hordes of nonacademic researchers in business and government—poised, computers oiled and at the ready for the Big Leap across all oceans, once long-dreamed-of capital is available.

L'ENVOI

The time is 1984. Dispatches from the Latin American country, Bralivia, have just been received, reporting thundering headlines and editorials in Bralivian newspapers, riots in the streets, and the government in mortal danger of collapse. The American Embassy and consul offices are being stoned. A vast Project Shangri-La in Bralivia has just been discovered; funded by the United States Foundation for the Behavioral Sciences and led by eminent American behavioral scientists in secret cooperation with Bralivian scientists under American salary. Confidential permission of access had earlier been given by the Bralivian government in return for an 87 percent administrative override, payable in dollars, the going rate in American universities for projects Federally funded. Project Shangri-La, according to Bralivian newspapers, had been organized years earlier—immediately after the mistakes of Project Camelot had been counted and assessed—for the objective of Saturation Inquiry of an unsuspecting (and, hence, research-pure) foreign population. With the permission of the Bralivian government and the aid of Bralivian scientists, Bralivian confessional boxes, juries, schoolrooms, household kitchens, and brothels had been bugged. Through recently discovered computer techniques of Simultaneous-Total Assault, all Bralivian institutions—church, family, political party, local community, trade union, school, mental asylums, infant nurseries, business enterprise, and bureaucracy—had been engaged. Depth interviews of new intimacy had been made possible through psychodelic techniques that destroyed all possibility of suspicion on the part of the Bralivian subject. Project Shangri-La, it is learned, has been in existence in Bralivia for more than three years. Although no American behavioral scientist could be found who professed knowledge of Project Shangri-La, a member of the Project administrative staff made the following statement: "Shangri-La was only a feasibility study; we were not really interested in Bralivia at all; it was not among the 24 countries marked for intensive study. The tragedy is that we were just on the verge of the greatest methodological breakthrough in the history of science. Now it is all for nothing." It is understood that exposure of Project Shangri-La came from a leak by one of the American consultants when he learned that the results of Shangri-La would be made available to the Department of Commerce.

THE CASE OF DR OPPENHEIMER
Philip Rieff

It has become a habit among thoughtful Americans to see the handwriting on the wall. What indeed suggests nothing but mean times ahead is not so much the events themselves as the official explanation of them. Thus the case of J. Robert Oppenheimer has been judged entirely on the basis of his character and social conduct. Psychology has masked politics, victories and defeats essential to the future course of American history have gone largely unremarked in the general curiosity over twists in Dr Oppenheimer's character and over questions of his behaviour. These are important enough; Dr Oppenheimer's soul was searched for its deceits, its contradictions, its dubious soul-mates, and a goodly number were found. But even granting that the scientist, like the poet, is uniquely neurotic, and that therefore he must be judged more leniently than ordinary men (as some of his defenders have foolishly urged) the position held on the hard issues of American politics by Dr Oppenheimer cannot be collapsed into his character or even into his associations. His position, his place and influence in the political order, were rarely touched in the thousands of pages of published testimony and opinions. In the end, after an inquiry dating from December 23rd, 1953, to June 30th, 1954, he was condemned in an appellate decision by the Atomic Energy Commission (A E C) for 'fundamental defects of character' and for social relations with Communists extending 'far beyond the tolerable limits of prudence and self-restraint.'

Dr Oppenheimer's soul being searched and his private conduct surveyed, the findings were reviewed by two separate boards of inquiry—the Personnel Security Board and the parent Atomic Energy Commission. In both decisions, with only the one scientific member of each panel dissenting, it was found that his personality was too 'complex' to carry the responsibilities his scientific position and access to restricted data inevitably entailed. He lied in order to protect friends, and some of his lies were so elaborate and unnecessary that they alarmed the normal people by whom he was judged; above all, he dined with the translator Haakon Chevalier in Paris, in December 1953—the very man who once approached him with a treasonable proposition. The entire case was a triumph of psychological over straight old-fashioned political warfare. The charge sustained in the first decision by Gordon Gray[1] and Thomas J. Morgan,[2] as the majority members of the Personnel Security Board, that Dr Oppenheimer showed a notable lack of 'enthusiasm' during the early stages of hydrogen bomb research, was carefully excluded from the appellate decision. Oppenheimer, the man, the neurotic scientist who did not have sense enough to know that M. Chevalier might well have acted for Soviet agents who would spirit him away to the Soviet Union, was tried. Oppenheimer the spokesman for an alternative military and political policy for the United States never once emerged for public judgment.

The decisions of the Gray Board and the A E C merit careful examination. It is something of a landmark in American political history that a man can be officially condemned for his private associations. But behind this inquiry into the character and conduct of one man lay a long battle over the facts of American military strategy. It was Oppenheimer's misfortune that he had lost the battle many months before; his lost case was a public parody of his lost battle. The open decision on his char-

[1] Subsequently, President of the University of North Carolina, formerly a Cabinet member in the Truman Administration.
[2] A Southerner; once President of United Negro College Funds; retired head of Sperry Gyroscope, a company contributing greatly to the American arsenal.

acter masked the hidden decision on his policy; his exclusion from 'restricted data,' whatever the fears about his past associations, was, objectively, a savage act of revenge for the long fight he waged against established American military policy.

The public was never allowed to look at the real issues. When the Government chose to make a public examination (the release of the decisions and testimony amounted to that) of Dr Oppenheimer's character, his political role was already thwarted and with this the persistent effort of his profession to gain a voice in the councils of state. The bitter five-year struggle between science and military politics in the United States was carried on mainly in the privacy of bureaucratic offices and in the secrecy of research laboratories. And the official version of the case, as involving simply the character and personal conduct of Dr Oppenheimer, was the way in which modern victors in the secret wars of state rewrite history. Losing sides never get their position written clearly into the record; they are forced to argue on grounds chosen by the winners, and the issue is staged for public edification after the real battle is over. It is like an internecine party struggle, of which the rank and file knows nothing until the defeated leader is brought before some tribunes of the people, his person condemned and his great contributions to the cause expunged from the official histories.

Dr Oppenheimer's contribution to American history is in no danger of being forgotten or denied. If only he had remained within the ambience of scientific research and organization the entire case might never have been aired, although it is unclear how Senator McCarthy could have been kept from airing it. But the line between science and politics has grown very shadowy. Neither Dr Oppenheimer nor his fellow-scientists knew, after they had by their inventions added another long arm to the body of the state, how to remain within the limits of their technical capacities. The scientist has, since World War I, achieved a new place in the political order—a place that has given him enormous public prestige and involved him in the most serious decisions of government. The Oppenheimer case signals not merely the personal defeat of a leading scientist, but the removal of the American scientists as a group from their high place in the political order. Dr Oppenheimer's personal humiliation covers the failure of American scientists as a more or less corporate body to play a role in shaping an American military policy they themselves have made possible.

Between the first and second world wars, the relation of science and politics in America entirely changed. Newton Baker, Secretary of War in Wilson's Cabinet, found *one* chemist adequate to the needs of the military forces. Charles Wilson, Secretary of Defence ('War' is an unsophisticated word) in the mid-fifties, had an Under-Secretary in charge of research. From 1941 to 1954 the Government spent some eighteen billion dollars for mainly military research and development. Of 155,000 persons who might be classed as natural or physical scientists in the United States (about two thirds of 1 per cent of the working population of sixty-three millions) some 32,000 work for the Government, and many of the remainder are indirectly dependent upon the Government through industrial and university research on official projects. The importance of the scientists' connection with the Government cannot, however, be rightly measured by their involvement in such work, although this is in itself of great significance; above all there is the fact that the scientific élite creates the weapons of offence and defence upon which the political and military élites depend. Along with the concentration of control over the material apparatus of society, as described by Marx and later by Max Weber, has come the concentration of scientific skills. Science has forged great new weapons and therefore the scientific élite is absolutely necessary, especially at the creative stages, to the political élite—the military and the high policy planners. This brings the scientists directly into politics, for the planning and execution of new elements in the arms race is inseparable from other parts of the political process. And as the scared rabbits of the arms race, the scientists are continually urged to provide a lead that the military can follow to new advantage in the struggle for power within and between nations.

Élite politics characterize all mass societies, totalitarian and democratic alike; indeed, the élites may have greater importance in democratic societies. Thus the real decisions in the United States tend to hang in the balance between the competing aims and skills of small groups. Into this sort of politics, demagogues such as Senator Joseph McCarthy may intrude as representatives of popular forces, breaking through the matrix of élite formations and capturing some measure of power by the public intimidation of one or another group. Nevertheless, despite these intrusions, the élites, or *service classes,* usually make, or fail to make, history without benefit of much public discussion or awareness—which is why their increased dominance is a threat to the liberal principles of democratic politics. Thus, the United States was on the verge of unlimited intervention in Indo-China, but the public knew almost nothing about it; there was not even a spurious debate on intervention, such as that preceding Pearl Harbour. Until the recent counter-development from below of street politics, the American public might wake one morning to hear over the car-radio that the nation was in yet another conflict, and immediately accept the *fait accompli* as the necessary logic of higher powers.

With the explosions over Hiroshima and Nagasaki, the physical scientist had made an auspicious entry into élite status. Willingly or no, the scientists found themselves beyond the realm of technique and in politics; they responded with that balanced concern for both the nation and the world that is the special virtue of the scientific morality and, in their special knowledge of the atomic bomb, with the almost Messianic fervour of men who had seen hell and wanted to do something to save the rest of us from it. The nuclear scientists organized themselves into regional and national groups, and set up a lobby in Washington. The Federation of Atomic Scientists, with advisors from among America's most astute and sophisticated social scientists, was an unprecedented political organization of American scientists, concerned not only with the protection of the scientist in his new political environment, but with the larger disposition of atomic energy, the great new transformation of nature that could affect the social order for good or evil.

Tension between the scientific élite, on the one side, and the military on the other, began almost immediately. Some tension between such different personality types and levels of intellection was inevitable, but the issues ran deeper than psychological difference. Some early battles (1945–46) were won by the scientists; the McMahon bill setting up a civilian commission (the

Atomic Energy Commission, which ruled Dr Oppenheimer a
'security risk') was their victory, against the May-Johnson (Administration) bill which would have continued military control
of the atomic energy project after the war. This was no personal
victory for J. Robert Oppenheimer, who in fact supported the
May-Johnson bill. Nevertheless, in the immediate post-war period
his authority and prestige increased. From being merely scientific
head of the Manhattan District and director in the construction
of the bomb at Los Alamos, Oppenheimer became a symbol of
the new status of science in American society. His thin handsome
face and figure replaced Einstein's as the public image of genius.
Less charismatic, although equally important figures among the
atomic-researchers took lesser parts in the new pantheon. Behind this scene, in the bureaucratic labyrinth of Washington, Dr
Oppenheimer's importance was greater than his public image
showed. He had actually become the priest-scientist of the
Comtean vision, transforming history as well as nature. His
place as advisor in the State Department on matters of atomic
strategy during the tenure of Dean Acheson was bound to bring
him further into contact with the makers of policy. He began to
play a leading role, perhaps the first scientist in American history
to achieve so great an influence in government. The Acheson-
Lilienthal[3] plan for international control of atomic energy, which
the Russians rejected, was largely his work.

Dr Oppenheimer's hope was for some sort of *modus vivendi*
with the Russians, to avert an atomic catastrophe. But as the
cold war grew hotter and the Russians proved intransigent, the
post-war flutter of public campaigns to reach diplomatic agreement was stilled. World government organizations of all sorts lost
motion; the American public had in any case maintained its
vigorous disinterest in international proclamations, including those
by the atomic scientists. The latter's efforts to play a role in
deciding American policy shifted out of public view to the operations of the élites themselves. Struggles over the future course
of American strategy were to take place, for two decades, over
the heads of the public, and any shots that were fired in the
open were aimed deliberately high, so that only the instructed
reader could understand. A major dispute arose within the scien-

[3] David Lilienthal, first chairman of the A E C and former head of T V A.

tific group itself, over the problem of constructing a hydrogen bomb. Edward Teller, a Hungarian-born scientist, had proposed as early as 1945 a theoretical solution that would permit the construction of an H-bomb. Oppenheimer, and men such as Conant, DuBridge, Rabi, Bethe—great names in science—disagreed for technical reasons, although plainly they also considered the construction of the H-bomb a political and moral error. But in 1947, in a seminar at Los Alamos incidentally attended by Klaus Fuchs, Dr Teller came within one final step of working out the theoretical mechanics of exploding an H-bomb; the theory of the fusion of hydrogen atoms, worked out by Hans Bethe, had been long accepted. Lewis Strauss,[4] then a member of the A E C and afterward its chairman, decided with Senator McMahon to push construction of the H-bomb. Lilienthal, then chairman, opposed it, as did almost all the leading scientists on the advisory council. H-bomb research dragged for various reasons, none of which can be laid at Oppenheimer's door. The Air Force wanted it, because it would mean a greater slice of appropriations, although they had no clear idea of its special usefulness. Not only were there technical and moral doubts, but the problem of recruiting personnel without injuring other atomic bomb work presented itself. Finally the Air Force, then under the Secretaryship of Thomas K. Finletter, a liberal lawyer, forced the A E C to establish Dr Teller in his own laboratory (by 1952) and the production of thermonuclear weapons, having proved feasible, began in earnest.

The decision to go ahead with the H-bomb marked the official adoption of a new military policy built around the Strategic Air Command (S A C) of the Air Force—a policy of immediate and massive retaliation from the American stockpile of atomic and super-atomic weapons as a deterrent against any Soviet aggression. As the vehicle of delivery, S A C, commanded by General Curtis Le May, became the essential unit of American strategy. As stated to a Los Angeles Chamber of Commerce meeting in October of 1953 by Gordon Dean, a former member of the

[4] Admiral Lewis Strauss, investment banker, devout Jew, Taft Republican, former Secretary to Herbert Hoover, and valuable naval bureaucrat.

Atomic Energy Commission personally friendly to Dr Oppenheimer, the United States' policy takes on the therapeutic value of a shock treatment:

> The time has come . . . to make Russia understand that if she moves in any quarter of the globe, she will be struck and struck hard, not simply at the front line of her aggressive troops but at every element which supplies these troops. Let's make it plain that if Russia moves directly or indirectly . . . we not only will, but we must, destroy the vitals of such a movement—every marshalling yard, every supply depot, every contributory industrial population.

The established policy[5] of immediate and massive retaliation—hard to distinguish in theory or practice from the doctrine of preventive war—was necessarily total, for every population in modern warfare contributes something to the war effort. Against this conception, embodied in the perpetual readiness of the S A C to strike at targets from one end of the Soviet Union to the other, or anywhere else in the world, Dr Oppenheimer raised the possibility of a tight defensive ring around the American continent. Thus his opposition to the H-bomb reflected his feeling about the futility of the arms race as such, if it was not balanced with an equal concentration on defence. The sporting belief of Americans that 'the only good defence is a good offence' (a phrase popular in every sport, and essential to understanding the American style of play and politics) militated against the Oppenheimer conception as 'Maginot Line' and as the defeatist psychology of a hand-wringing scientist, perhaps even of a neutralist with no stomach for fighting Russia. As against him, the official school held that

> the surest way to prevent bombs from falling on American cities is to destroy those bombs, and particularly the enemy carriers designed to take them to their objectives, before they leave their bases. Offensive air power, to strike against enemy atomic facilities and stockpiles, and particularly against enemy airfields and submarine bases, is the first element of sound air defence.

[5] The missiles program is a further development of the same strategy.

Yet the position taken by Dr Oppenheimer was not a clear-cut 'defensive versus offensive' strategy, but aimed at greater emphasis on defence. Dr Oppenheimer argued that in order for the United States to negotiate from strength a far more elaborate continental defence system than the offensive-mindedness of established strategy allowed was needed. He further argued that the major problems of defence against total attack in a democracy needed the participation and understanding of the public, and that this was impossible to achieve under the heavy cloak of secrecy wrapped around all military strategy. The basic Air Force argument was that no adequate defence against atomic attack was foreseeable. The late General Vandenberg, when head of the Air Forces, thought that American air defence might bring down 20 or 30 per cent. of an attacking force. But even if by 1957, after a substantial national investment, the air defence system should be able to bring down 50 per cent. of a Russian force, the damage from the other half that got through could cripple America's industrial capacity for war and produce millions of casualties; night attack would cause even larger havoc. It should be noted that, when the argument between the scientists and the air officers was at its height, it was assumed that a Russian attack with 100 atomic weapons would destroy well over a third of American industrial power and cause about 13 million casualties. The defence apparatus of the U S against air attack at the time consisted mainly of interceptors and anti-aircraft artillery, with some World War II style radar coverage along the continental approaches. The anti-aircraft batteries, consisting predominantly of World War II batteries of 120 mm. guns and other types, were token weapons, ineffective above twenty thousand feet. In darkness the interceptor wings would lose much of their accuracy, few of them at that time being equipped with radar devices. A comparable study by the British authorities of their air defences forecast that an all-out attack on the British Isles would take a toll of two million lives.

Both sides used these grisly figures for their own purposes: the military to demonstrate the need to keep the S A C's retaliatory weapon always sharp and enlarging, the scientists to demonstrate the futility of the entire arms struggle and the need for a greater scientific and financial expenditure on defence research. The scientists' argument was really a technical elaboration of George Kennan's 'containment' thesis, which affirmed that the democracies must hold the line and wait for disintegrating forces to operate within the Soviet sphere. A greater emphasis on defence, however, cannot be called static any more than the policy of containment; and plainly a retaliatory thesis must veer ever closer to a preventive war thesis, which was abandoned at least by the executive arm of the Government. In any event, the scientific élite moved to test their own defence theories. In 1951 the scientists of Project Vista, who had been recruited by the Air Force to study tactical and field use of atomic weapons, came up with a report that supported the Oppenheimer thesis. Contradicting the Air Force conception of a huge heavy atomic stock-pile carried by inter-continental bombers, Project Vista concluded that short-range tactical air forces with small atomic weapons, in addition to a small ground force, could check the Red Army in Europe. The struggle over atomic strategy soon involved General Eisenhower, who as an old ground soldier showed some inclinations toward the scientists' view when the Project Vista report was presented to him in Paris during the last period of his N A T O command. But General Norstad, then head of the N A T O air forces, opposed the report with its underlying thesis of a 'mutual forswearing of strategic air war', and it never received serious consideration. The argument then shifted to the strategy of air defence, which appeared to the scientists to leave the American continent virtually open to inter-continental attack. An actual increase in the American capacity to negotiate with the Russians was predicted if the United States could build a defence network that would also act as a deterrent to aggression. The Air Force strategy counted on the instinct of self-preservation among the Soviet leadership, the rational recognition on the part of the potential enemy that the retaliatory price of atomic attack on the United States would be too high. Clinging to a policy originally adopted before the Russians had developed in their own atomic stockpile weapons between four and five times more powerful than those used at Hiroshima and Nagasaki eight years before, the Air Force continued to concentrate on offensive weapons immune from annihilation, rather than on defensive networks.

As if again to demonstrate the feasibility of their own conception of defence, the scientific *élite* gathered a remarkable task force, drawn from the leading university centres of research. The controversial Lincoln Summer Study group of thirty scientists played war games for three months in 1952 at the Massachusetts Institute of Technology and demonstrated, to their own satisfaction at least, that with an early warning system of interlocking radar stations, guided missiles, 'mother' aircraft launching smaller interceptor wings, Russian bomber penetration could be reduced to mere 'leakage'. Of course the retaliatory striking force would continue to be shielded; thus the present retaliatory-deterrent strategy would not be scrapped, but in the scientists' view actually increased in effect. The novelty of these proposals lay in plans for the defence of the ten thousand miles of American frontier available to the Russians. Existing radar equipment could not keep such a territory under accurate surveillance. The Summer Study group, organized by friends and disciples of Dr Oppenheimer, advocated a new system of radar surveillance along the Arctic circle as close to the Soviet frontiers as possible, increasing the margin of warning from an hour or less in the present system to four and perhaps six hours. The Air Force objected to the cost of such a warning system, to its drainage effect on the remainder of the air budget, and its consequent effect on American striking power, which still seemed the primary weapon of defence. Technical doubts also arose and some resentment at the aura of originality around the scientists' proposals.

The Summer Study had its effect in sharpening the conflict between the scientists and the military. Faced with a good motion, the standard riposte of the politician is to shelve it and get the entire problem reviewed; shelving has the value of a clinch in boxing—a chance to recover from a blow, study the opposition and learn how to meet it. The Summer Study findings did not reach a formal stage of discussion in the National Security Council (the President, Secretary of State and Chiefs of Staff), which is now the body ultimately responsible for the strategy of the United States. But it did push the argument into such a state of intense controversy during the final months of the Truman Administration that a new special committee of investigation (under Mervin Kelly, vice-president of the Bell Laboratories) was appointed to review the entire problem of vulnerability. The Kelly Report substantially confirmed the established military thesis that the best defence was the retaliatory-deterrent theory of offence. In direct criticism of Dr Oppenheimer's attempt to alter the pattern of American military strategy, the Kelly Report

> expressed concern . . . about the recent public advocacy of a programme which would purportedly give nearly perfect protection against air attack. . . . Any such level of protection is unattainable and . . . completely impractical, economically and technically, in the face of expected advances in [Russian] capabilities.

In rebuttal to the Summer Study, the report urged 'continued development of a powerful United States atomic offensive capability, reasonably invulnerable to initial attack'. The deeply ingrained American view of offense as the best defense remained invulnerable to the complicated alternative suggested by the scientists.

The Oppenheimer affair involved far more than uncertainty about the political and personal attitude of a leading scientist; in fact the whole complex of American military strategy in the atomic age was involved. The first full-length journalistic account of the scientists' efforts and the position of the military was given in an article in *Fortune* magazine, May 1953, headlined 'The Hidden Struggle for the H-bomb: the Story of Dr Oppenheimer's Persistent Campaign to Reverse U. S. Military Strategy'. The writer fairly reports the history of the struggle, despite his clear animus against Oppenheimer and the scientists for their meddling in military affairs. The last sentence formulates concisely, from the military point of view, the present tension between science and politics in America: 'There is a serious question of the propriety of scientists trying to settle grave national issues alone, inasmuch as they bear no responsibility for the successful execution of war plans.'

Dr Oppenheimer's own position was best summed up in his famous article in the quarterly *Foreign Affairs* of July 1953, a rewriting of a speech he delivered before the Council on Foreign Relations, which in turn grew out of his State Department dis-

armament report. Here he reviewed his challenge to the foundation of American strategy: the 'rather rigid commitment to use
(atomic weapons) in a very massive unremitting strategic assault
on the enemy'. The Air Force strategy depended on maintaining
a larger stock of weapons than the Russians. But 'the very least
we can conclude is that our twenty-thousandth bomb . . . will
not in any deep strategic sense affect their two thousandth'. The
futility of stockpiling and retaliation as the basis of American
strategy was accented by the 'relatively little done to secure our
defence against the atom'. There was also the unsolved question of how we would defend our Allies, and behind this the
agonizing logic of the present strategy which would make it
necessary for the United States to atomize the cities of Western
Europe if they came under Soviet control early in the next
world war. As a final—technical—point against the stockpiling-
retaliatory strategy, Dr Oppenheimer foresaw a 'time when . . .
the art of delivery and the art of defence will have a much higher
military relevance than supremacy in the atomic munitions field
itself'. This restated the conclusions of the Summer Study group.

But perhaps the major point Dr Oppenheimer had to make
was not technical but political. At the end of his article he suggested a reform in official behaviour, in order to make 'available
to ourselves, in this tough time, the inherent resources of a
country like ours and a government like ours.' Especially, in
view of the alarming tendency of the Air Defence command to
concentrate on the protection of the nation's striking arm rather
than on the protection of the country itself, Oppenheimer was
worried about what he called the 'political vitality' of America.
Of one source of political vitality—'the interplay, the conflict
of opinion and debate, in many diverse and complex agencies,
legislative and executive, which contribute to the making of
policy'—he had seen a great deal. But the other resource—a
'public opinion which is based on confidence that it knows the
truth'—was 'not available to-day'. Public opinion was the great
factor which the Government had by-passed. In the field of
atomic strategy 'public opinion cannot exist'. Secrecy veiled the
'important conditions'. For the survival of democracy, for the
preservation of its will to fight in the unparalleled tests to come,
Dr Oppenheimer recommended 'candour' as the first reform to

which the new Republican Administration should attend. Against this, the military insisted that only the Russians could possibly benefit from candour, that the American people could not understand the technicalities, and that to frighten them was dangerous from the perspective of morale.

Certainly one *Foreign Affairs* article by Oppenheimer, and the rebuttal of Oppenheimer's position in *Fortune,* was not enough to bring the struggle into the arena of public debate. And even in the open, the military and governmental élites would have held a profound advantage. Air Force strategy was deeply rooted in the American ethos. The 'fortress' or 'Maginot Line' strategy could never have evoked the same appeal; it was a complicated argument, led by a 'complicated' man. In the press, only the Alsop brothers (in the New York *Herald Tribune*) carried the Oppenheimer position to their readers, and even their perceptive and sometimes hair-raising frankness failed to develop any public pressure on the scientists. The issues seemed too strategic, not moralistic enough to attract a sufficient number of do-gooders. The aloofness of the scientist from even the educated and liberal portions of the public is evident in America, for this public tends to moralize a great deal about the 'ethical failure' of science, as well as about all other ethical failures. The humanist intellectual in the United States has been retreating at a remarkable pace from his earlier interest in politics and science. This increasing isolation of the scientific élite is an important factor in the crisis of culture that has overtaken liberal democratic society in America. The main fact of political life in America during the fifties was that an Oppenheimer could never operate in the open with any expectation of significant public support. Not only was there no party that might conceivably have supported him, but no constellation of public opinion could form near him. The autonomous cosmopolitan community of science is necessarily alienated from the American public and gains no advantage in taking an argument before it. The distance between the scientist with a liberal ethic and even the educated public is perhaps greater now than in the Protestant era of American culture, when 'science' was more popular and the educated classes could more easily confront it. No significant segment of American public opinion exists to appraise or even interest itself in 'technical' problems. The ignorance of the public no longer keeps it away from politics, but it does keep it away from science. In a technologically mysterious culture even the educated take the magic of their electric toasters and their atomic strategy for granted; they are more helpless before it than the primitive before the unorganized powers of nature, for modern man has no magic to exert. The magic is left to the scientist, and therefore in a technologically recondite age more and more issues become magical and are considered outside the orbit of public competence. This is a problem of democratic life which no argument for candour can easily turn.

It was cruelly appropriate that a battle fought so secretly should end not with private dismissal but with public humiliation. For the basis of attack was not the one still unknown to the American public, but the one familiar now through years of public investigation by Congressional committees. Dr Oppenheimer was accused not for the policy to which he had bent his science, but for his past and his associations which remain unmendable—all family 'relations' being in the official definition 'associations'.

Dr Oppenheimer's past was well known to the Government: a number of friends, a dead sweetheart, his wife's first husband, his wife, his brother, his brother's wife—all at one time or another Communists. Nevertheless in 1942 he was asked to organize atomic bomb research. The same past could be again in question, not because new evidence had been offered, but because a conspiratorial tedium had settled even more heavily upon American institutional and élite life than upon the public. The Administration could not decline to compete with Senator McCarthy in the art of demonstrating its fixation on the past. Such fixations—like the revived spy charges made against Harry Dexter White, who died in 1948—provided the nation with relief from the frustrations of the present. Dr Oppenheimer's former military superior, General Groves, pin-pointed the paranoid tendencies of the security drive—ironically, as I think—when he replied to a question about Dr Oppenheimer's trustworthiness: 'I don't know. How can you always tell if your own husband or wife is trustworthy?'

Dr Oppenheimer's past had permitted the Government to display all sorts of cleverness in catching him out, not only in the final cross-examinations but in the earlier investigations. He was exposed not so much in the few obvious lies he told to protect friends, but in the more subtle possibilities of treason. A dialectic the more resembling that of the Communists in the very fervour of opposing them had seeped into the American official mind. In the 1951 report of the California State Senate Fact-Finding Commission used by the A E C to prepare its original charges against Dr Oppenheimer, this dialectic is marvellously strung together out of gossamer inference. Since it was discovered that he was classified in secret Communist Party communications as unsympathetic to Communism, the California report suggested that the Party was really counting on Dr Oppenheimer and that his known antipathy to them might well be a 'deliberate ruse'. Starting from this plausibility, American secuirty forces found the facts 'quite plain that [Russian agents] were unanimous in picking Dr J. Robert Oppenheimer as the most suitable man to contact.' They judged him as a 'potential traitor'.

The case broke on March 4th, 1954, when Oppenheimer released to the Press his reply to a letter of charges from Major-General Nichols, general manager of the A E C. It was then made known that since the previous summer, on the personal order of the President, a 'blank wall' had been placed between Dr Oppenheimer and all 'restricted data'. For almost a year he had been barred from Government work and consultations. The letter listed an unsorted number of charges, most of them held over from the previous investigations of Dr Oppenheimer in 1946 and 1948. The only new accusation, that of opposing the hydrogen bomb, seemed the most ominous.

But this was not the charge singled out as decisive in Dr Oppenheimer's reply. He did not choose to defend his policies but his past and person—the old charges on which he had already been cleared. His letter to the Atomic Energy Commission (March 4) avoided the homiletics on 'the god that failed' we have come to expect in such cases, for he was never a believer but only a friend and relative of believers. Nevertheless, if he did not indulge in any theoretic recantations, Dr Oppenheimer did in another sense exceed the limits of defensiveness.

His response to the rehash of his past in the changed climate of America was if anything too appropriate to the pattern of attack. Dr Oppenheimer did not discuss the objective political argument which was responsible for his present humiliation. The effect of his language was to transform his case into a case history, as if a clinical understanding was the best one he could reach with his accusers (and the public). Read against the nasty brief-like letter from the Atomic Energy Commission, Dr Oppenheimer's reply was too long and too intimate for a political accounting. Such a letter is in itself an act of penance, for the total man can never be innocent. In modern politics it is not resistance but the fullness of revelation that is the standard act of guilt. A chilling sense of confession could easily be read into the letter.

Dr Oppenheimer exercised the intellectual's right of introspection in coming up against power. But the self-portrait he drew was uncomfortably general, a portrait not of an individual but of a stock academic American. When not suspect, the professor in America is invariably located a little outside the main realities. Piano-players in the brothels of Storyville (New Orleans), where jazz was born, were for their fine art and eunuchal functions honoured with the title 'Professor', a considered opinion of the few relatively sexless males at the gate to the plenitude sexuality. The mass media are full of mad professors. The academies are full of men who, despite the ruthlssness of university politics, are convinced that they could not survive in the 'real' world outside. Many of them accept even now, despite student instruction to the contrary, the popular definition of reality as practically anywhere outside the academy, and Dr Oppenheimer could not be expected to escape the air he breathed. It was inevitable that his self-criticism should appeal to our sense of comedy. His letter reports how friends 'chided' him with being too much of a 'highbrow', and how his fault was the fault of the world in which he moved, for his friends were 'mostly faculty people . . . and artists.' Thus he studied and read Sanskrit; 'Led Abnormal Life', ran some newspaper headlines when the case first broke. Forwarded to clarify 'the context of my life and my work' by the self-examination of 'character' as well as 'associations and loyalty', Dr Oppenheimer's letter even hinted at some sort of hereditary highbrowism. Although his father was a successful businessman, his mother 'before her marriage was an artist and teacher of art.' One is left to wonder what his mother's premarital talents had to do with the case, unless it is part of the case-history.

There is also a more specialized cliché evoked by Dr Oppenheimer's defence. Although he identified himself as an intellectual (poetry and protest), in another sense he removed himself from membership of the cultured classes in general. It is not simply the joke about the absent-minded professor to which his letter appealed, but specifically the popular image of theoretical physicists confused by a short circuit in the basement, of mathematicians helpless before this week's grocery bill. Dr Oppenheimer stood finally as the practitioner of what used to be an unpolitical science. He reports that he

read very widely, but mostly classics, novels, plays, and poetry; and . . . something of other parts of science. I was not interested in and did not read about economics or politics. I was almost wholly divorced from the contemporary scene in this country. I never read a newspaper or a current magazine like *Time* or *Harper's;* I had no radio, no telephone; I learned of the stock market crash in the fall of 1929 only long after the event; the first time I ever voted was in the Presidential election of 1936.

The familiar plea of innocence by dissociation marred Dr Oppenheimer's defence. The highbrow—especially the physical scientist —breathing only the rare realities available at his heights, develops a special brand of political innocence. It is from the abstractedness of his perspective that Dr Oppenheimer denominated his past. Such an account seems to request that the physical scientist, dealing in nature not history, should be treated with a special clemency. *Nolo episcopari.* But this logic makes life a little harder for those less specialized intellectuals who always did read papers and political magazines (perhaps other than *Time* and *Harper's*), installed telephones, knew all about the stock market crash, and yet also—as Dr Oppenheimer did— sympathized with the Popular Front against the rise of Fascism in Spain and elsewhere.

To understand why Dr Oppenheimer's defence was so accommodating to the means of attack chosen by his political enemies, one must understand the deep and broad acceptance of psychology in America. The popular myth of the treason of the intellectuals is now widely reinforced by the myth of the special neuroticism of the 'scientist,' as well as the artist. Dr Oppenheimer was thus at once condemned and condoned as too 'complex' a personality. After all those years of great responsibility, he had been washed out of Government service, like a young officer candidate in training school, for showing unstable tendencies. This test of character, as distinct from 'association', in American politics indicates to some extent how the idea of the neurotic has been fused, in the official as well as in the popular mind, with the idea of the treasonably inclined. Sickness and health are fast becoming political categories, as once they were religious categories. 'Security' is after all a significantly psychological term, and by the awful weight of psychological accusation one's opposition can be crushed even more thoroughly in public encounters than in private.

The viciousness of the psychological accusation does not of course discount the real problem which is today compromised and manipulated by the language of 'security'. The tightening anxieties expressed in the Oppenheimer opinions have to be understood against the background of shock among many of the nation's leaders at the size and depth of Communist infiltration. In response to the incomprehensible challenge of ideological betrayal, the honourable and old-fashioned men at the head of American affairs reacted with renewed and calculated suspicion of those within the nation who appear so different in their habits of thought and in the range of their loyalties. Fear of the scientist, as of the politically cultured, becomes more understandable as a reaction to the strange new political culture in which old-line American political and military leaders find they must operate. Since it has been discovered that there are strange creatures without and within who have no price, make no deals, and talk a language of morals and tactics foreign to the popular culture which the leadership shares, Red-hunting easily incorporates highbrow-hunting. The attack upon radicals as intellectuals, and upon intellectuals as radicals, is a standard item of popular resentment since the Dreyfus case; and anti-intellectualism appears especially ominous when it is compounded with psychological investigation. Nevertheless, no criticism of the rhetoric of the attack, either in its simple-minded or vicious forms, argues away the closeness of belief and action, nor the traumatic betrayals already known.

These considerations have not yet, I think, been taken seriously enough by liberals. Despite Dr Oppenheimer's somewhat over-cooperative admissions of political ignorance and the allusions to neurotic braininess, there was some optimism about the outcome of the case. Since Dr Oppenheimer's past associations had always been known to the Government, many did not expect to see condoned, even in the fifties' climate of 'hysteria', such 'a breach of faith on the part of the Government' (the words of a May, 1954, editorial in the *Bulletin of Atomic Scientists*)[6] that calls upon a man 'to assume such heavy responsibilities in full knowledge of his life history and then, after he has demonstrably done his best and given the most valuable services to the nation . . . uses facts which were substantially known all the time to cast aspersions on his integrity'. Some defenders of Dr Oppenheimer privately considered it a pity that his case was tried long after that of Alger Hiss. If only Oppenheimer, and not Hiss, had represented them when their generation was put on trial, liberals might have felt less guilty. Yet the Oppenheimer case portended something more sinister than that of Hiss. If Hiss was condemned for his acts and admired for his strong character (set off against the neurotic Chambers who had accused him), Oppenheimer was condemned for his character and praised for his actions. The latter may stand in history as a form of condemnation far more dangerous to liberal society than any straightforward condemnation for acts of treason.

The decision of the Gray Committee was issued on June 1, 1954. Its members had met for eight weeks and heard 500,000 words (992 pages in fine print) of testimony; of the forty witnesses who testified, the majority (including Gordon Dean, former chairman of the A E C in 1950–53, James B. Conant, and Vannevar Bush, director of the Office of Scientific Research and Development during World War II) were favourable to

[6] The Editorial Board, "Editorial: The Oppenheimer Case," *Bulletin of the Atomic Scientists,* Vol. 10, No. 5 (May 1954), p. 173.

Oppenheimer. The decision was in the light of the later appellate decision of the A E C, a heavily qualified one. Gray noted that if they had been able to use common sense rather than the harsh requirements of 'security', the decision might have been different. Oppenheimer's 'loyalty' was reaffirmed, but in the light of his associations and his opposition to the hydrogen bomb, he was judged a 'security risk' and denied renewal of access to 'classified material'. The decision of the A E C board made public four weeks later, on June 29, presented a more formidable majority (4–1 instead of 2–1) against Oppenheimer and a more severe and consistent verdict, solely on the basis of his character and associations. In a separate concurring opinion, one member of the commission, Thomas E. Murray,[7] found Dr Oppenheimer 'disloyal' for failing to show 'exact fidelity' and 'obedience' to the Government's security regulations. As the editorial in one major newspaper ran, Dr Oppenheimer

> can clear himself. To do so he will have to forsake suspect companions. He will have to work independently in his chosen field. He must prove that he can learn under this painful pressure, that he can be discreet in his friendships.

Thus while Dr Oppenheimer was not asked to change his mind, he was encouraged to change his heart. Perhaps this is a more insidious demand than any the State could make upon his mind. It is a demand higher than any but recent totalitarianisms have yet made. There is already a touch of this in the original verdict, in the place where the Gray Report congratulates itself on its human tenderness and psychological delicacy. 'We believe', wrote Gray and Thomas J. Morgan, representing the majority, 'that it has been demonstrated that the Government can search . . . the soul of an individual whose relationship to his Government is in question.' Not his scientific decisions but his lack of the proper spirit made of Dr Oppenheimer a political danger. For these reasons he was denied further access to secret information and his

[7] The majority voters of the A E C, aside from Admiral Strauss and Mr. Murray, were Eugene M. Zuckert, a former Assistant Secretary of the Air Force, and Joseph Campbell, former vice-president and treasurer of Columbia University. Strauss and Campbell were Republicans, Murray and Zukert Democrats.

role as adviser to the Government terminated. Although there was no question of his having committed any act prejudicial to national interest, Dr Oppenheimer did not have properly fervent emotions about his Communist relatives and friends.

The case for special restrictions on the life and habits of certain classes of the skilled and informed within a garrison state was brilliantly developed in the concurring opinion of A E C Commissioner Murray. 'The American citizen in private life, the man who is not engaged in Governmental service, is not bound by the requirements of the security system.' Only certain persons are subject to this 'special system of law'. A man in Dr Oppenheimer's position should 'relinquish the right to the complete freedom of association that would be his in other circumstances.' It is not a matter of action or even omission contrary to the national interest. 'What is incompatible with obedience to the laws of security is the associations themselves, however innocent in fact.' Thus the friend-enemy relationship (chiefly the dinner meeting with M. Chevalier) is the key to the Oppenheimer decision. Dr Oppenheimer cannot have for a friend anyone who can, by any stretch of the imagination, be considered an enemy of the State. No relation is unpolitical, no level of dining politeness can continue between the Oppenheimers and the Chevaliers, even if all they did together was to go and see M. André Malraux. As a Government scientist, Oppenheimer would have to live under special restrictions and must observe the friend-enemy relationship in his personal life. In his case the tragic impossibility of this demand on his person is obvious: he would have had to deny his brother (whose career in physics was then ruined and who turned to ranching in the West) and divorce his wife.

Among the scientists there was a great public outcry against the Oppenheimer decision. From the beginning they cried 'Shame' and 'Ingratitude' at the excommunication of so great a figure among them. In both hearings the dissenting opinion came from a representative of science on each board, the chemist, Evans, on the three-man Gray Commission and the physicist, Smyth, on the five-man Atomic Energy Commission sitting as an appellate board. Yet within the scientific élite there was much the same fear, mutual suspicion, whispering, shamming, and discarding of powerful leaders, once they are beaten, as besets other elite formations in modern politics. Although the scientists know each other intimately and have great corporate feelings, in the atmosphere of American culture during the fifties they were rent by a variety of schisms and hatreds caused by their new relation to political power.

Particularly among the younger scientists there were many who found it agreeable to combine their technical functions with a technical morality, and for whom the Oppenheimer policy wars were simply intrusions on their established honorific relation to the political order. Actually the Oppenheimer case marked an end to the unique and necessary theoretical work related to atomic weapons. Oppenheimer's services were no longer indispensable, and the fulsome thanks he got with his kicks only made the cries of 'Ingratitude' the more bitter. Another element in the scientific élite, the engineers, who are more tractable than the theorists, increased in value as the arms race neared a saturation level in point of destructive capacity. Reacting to this trend, some theorists, unwilling to submit to the aims of policy, advocated retreat from Government service. If, between the established Soviet reality and the American reaction to it, there then appeared to many scientists a shrinking difference, retreat from direct or indirect Government employment takes on prudent as well as moral aspects. This position was advanced by the celebrated founder of cybernetics, Prof. Norbert Wiener. Immediately after Oppenheimer was put on his long trial, Wiener wrote an editorial for *The Nation* asking the rhetorical question whether those who play with fire ought not to expect to get their fingers burnt. No doubt it was as a man of high moral as well as intellectual qualities that Oppenheimer could not submit to policy as a technician does. And with his figure the urgent alternatives of doom or grace were bound up in a way sensible to Americans otherwise even more indifferent to ultimate urgencies. Oppenheimer spoke for 'science'; as the American inheritor of the mantle of Einstein no one else could have played this role and hoped somehow to reach public opinion. Before the emergence of the militant blacks, the prophetic thunder, so far as in America it sounds at all, sounded from the scientist agonizing over his entrapment in a final politics. The design on the cover of the monthly *Bulletin of Atomic Scientists* (Dr Oppenheimer was the chairman of its board of directors) is a clock whose hands pointed some minutes to midnight. It is the scientist who has consistently prophesied, in however small and censored a voice, the real probabilities of Judgment Day. To have such a prevision is not calculated to make a scientist with keen moral sensibilities comfortable in his connection with any régime. Modern régimes in particular do not take suggestions of the Apocalypse seriously and, with perfect political rationality, seek to translate them into logistical terms or terror propaganda.

In the liberal vision, science carried along with it belief in progress (through science) toward the apotheosis of humanity. It was, no doubt, this liberal vision that brought Dr Oppenheimer into some sympathy with the Communist movement, as he understood it, in the 'thirties. The scientist's confidence in his capacity to transform nature fitted in perfectly with the Marxist confidence in a new political capacity to transform society. Sophisticated scientists could thus become naïve Marxists, for there appears little transfer of training from scientific to political skills. But nowadays, for reasons inherent in the logic of science as well as in the logic of politics, the scientist is troubled by a decline of optimism concerning the consequences of scientific knowledge. A loss of that confidence which is an inseparable part of the priest-scientist role has made it far more difficult for the contemporary scientist to assume a position in relation to politics more positive than alarm. Science appeared not to remake the world, but to be remade by it. Men like Oppenheimer did indeed hold the keys to the arms race—thereby becoming figures of immense political relevance. But when they tried to enlarge their function and influence policy, with only fragments of the old progressivist scientific faith upon which to fall back, they were left peculiarly vulnerable to attack and internally divided. Plainly, Oppenheimer had none of the self-confidence of the Communist that comes with the convergence of personal and movement identity. No doubt qualities of personal impatience did offend a number of the highly intelligent administrators with whom he dealt, but the scientists' criticism of American strategy was never offered by Oppenheimer with any theoretic arrogance that he held the secret of victory and peace. It was advanced hesitantly and with careful qualification, as befits the condition of the modern liberal who has shed any residual Marxist certainties. The immediate postwar calls of the American atomic scientists for world government were nostalgic evocations of an earlier optimism, now held in trust by dwindling numbers of liberals. As the realities of living in a world that includes Russia and China impressed themselves on the scientists, such grand solutions to the world's ills were rapidly dropped.

Nevertheless, despite a loss of surety, the faith of the scientist remains liberal. The liberal conception of intellectual and political life depends on assuming the virtue of an 'antagonism of influences'[8] in which no defeat is total; decisions should emerge out of a never-ending discussion in which, soon or late, all would have their say. It was the duty of participants in such an ongoing discussion to revive those positions which they noticed had been neglected for any considerable time, so that all the truths could be available in the public market place. Not Dr Oppenheimer's certainty that he had a correct answer, but his liberal impulse to have an alternative so as to clarify the issues in public (for the public and by the public) motivated the preliminary argument for 'candour', beyond which he never got. The surprise and disappointment among the scientists at the rough treatment of Oppenheimer reflects their illusion that they still lived in a liberal society. The scientific élite never dreamed that it would be so defeated and humiliated publicly. The gratuitous raising of ten-year-old issues in the Oppenheimer case confirms their sense of shock that the rules of fair play by which controversy in a liberal society is governed were scrapped. But the shock was too great to be accepted and there was great emphasis laid on the fairness of the entire procedure.

So far as this liberal conception of politics and culture emergent from an antagonism of influences persists, it has led to a newly trivial social role for the intellectual, who becomes the perpetual minority member moralizing for lost causes. In scholarship especially the tendency is well established: whole fields are

[8] The summary notion of society as a "balance of countervailing forces" by Professor Galbraith, of Harvard University, is a recent and no doubt unconscious rendering of Mill's phrase.

preoccupied with marginal or safely empirical problems that cannot be taken seriously, nor leave any serious impression even on the academic world. The present revival of interest in the theory and practice of religious heresy, for example, is not a symptom of intellectualized revolt but simply an intellectual safety valve, for history has fossilized heresy and orthodoxy together. It is therefore safe to make great play with protecting 'heresy', for it has no political relevance. Dare the 'heresy' become political, the game turns vicious. Still liberated in their civic pride, the scientific élite did not foresee that they would be defeated in such a way that they would no longer be able to argue their case—indeed, in such a way that their case could never be presented.

It is tragic that the American scientists did not have a passion more positive than horror from which to elaborate their opposition to the drift, not only of military policy, but of American politics in general. When the warfare was chiefly between science and theology a more positive emotion was easier to develop. Theology took special pains to keep science from developing along its own logic, and science resisted this in the name of freedom and progress. Now that warfare is ended. A subtler enemy faces science: for the State is without any dogma it cannot abandon overnight to catch the shifts of power. The freedom and progress of science are not necessarily interfered with by the state. On the contrary, the State is zealous for the most advanced scientific knowledge and for its practical application. The scientist is free to work, urged to work, recruited, honoured. But the opinions of the scientist may interfere with the prosecution of policy. The scientist and his élite may go into opposition to the other élites. Neither science nor the scientist, when they serve the State, can be expected to stop short of exact obedience without inviting investigation and reprisal. What was heresy when science was under theology becomes disloyalty when it is under politics. Scientists have never held power anywhere; they have never been able to command. But as a reward for their skill and conscientiousness they thought to reserve the right to advise, persuade, withdraw, suffer defeat, and stay on. The Oppenheimer case signified that these rights were no longer theirs. Scientific opinion cannot claim that immunity from political discipline won for it by 19th century liberalism.

The social ambition of science was based on quite another image of the technological society, with the scientists as masters, not as the magicians of new masters. In a scientific age, scientists were to have duties like those of priests in the old society—duties superior to those of the warriors. By the twentieth century it was expected that in the scientist the Greek prophecy of society governed by philosopher-kings would at last be fulfilled. But something went astray, even while the expectation was at its highest in the mid-nineteenth century. With the Oppenheimer case the modern relation between science and politics in America was painfully revealed. Great social consequences are bound to follow from this revelation. Such an interference with the scientific élite, thwarting their free associations with undesirable social and political types, may alter the social conditions of its development. The élite is transformed into a service class, technically still supremely competent and much rewarded, but no longer so attractive to the most creative minds of the succeeding generations.

INDEX

Acheson, Dean, 319
Acton, Harold, 199
Adorno, Theodor, 103n., 111n.
Akhnaton, 32
Alcuin, 31
Allen, John, 236
Almond, Gabriel, 296
Althusser, Louis, 91, 104n.
America. *See* United States
Anti-intellectual tradition of order, 43, 47
Apocalyptic tradition, 43, 45–46
Applied science
  increasing importance of, 20–21
  and pure, conflict between, 16–18
Aquinas, Thomas, 10
Arendt, Hannah, 110n.
Aretino, Pietro, 62n.
Aristarchus of Samos, 65
Aristotle, 31
Aron, Raymond, 103n.
Asoka, 32
Auden, Wystan Hugh, 197–212, 223, 224, 237, 246, 247
Aurelius, Marcus, 32
Authority, intellectual and, 47–52
  See also Dissent

Bacon, Roger, 11
Baker, Newton, 317

Bakunin, Michael, 141, 158
Barbarism, in United States history, 167–95
Barber, 57n.
Barrès, Maurice, 87n.
Barzun, Jacques, 70n.
Bataille, Georges, 92
Bauer, Bruno, 131, 133, 141
Behavioral sciences, federal government and, 283–313
Bell, Clive, 225
Bell, Daniel, 23
Bell, Julian, 199n., 240
Benda, Julien, 61n.
Ben-David, Joseph, 15n.
Berger, John, 108n.
Berger, Peter L., 76n.
Berle, Adolph A., 311–12
Berlin, Isaiah, 110n., 199, 125–66
Bernal, J. D., 234
Bidwell, Charles, 63n.
Binder, Pearl, 217
Bismarck, Otto von, 50, 51
Black, Mischa, 217
Blok, Alexander, 88
Blunt, Anthony, 199n., 226
Boswell, James, 218, 226
Bowra, C. M., 199
Bramson, Leon, 110n.
Britten, Benjamin, 223

Bronowski, J., 199n.
Browne, Felicia, 201n., 231
Burisch, Wolfram, 60n.
Burke, Kenneth, 23
Burns, Emile, 238, 239
Bush, Alan, 201n., 236
Bush, Vannevar, 333
Bushnell, Horace, 167–95
Byron, George Gordon (Lord), 196

Cabet, Etienne, 141, 142
Calder-Marshall, Arthur, 201n.
Calvin, John, 10
Capitalism, 56–57
Carritt, Gabriel, 198, 207
Caudwell, Christopher, 242
Caute, David, 91n.
Chevalier, Haakon, 315
China, 7–9, 106
Chomsky, Noam, 117n.
Class. See Social class
Clausen, John A., 16n.
Clemenceau, Georges, 87n.
Coghill, Nevill, 199, 200n.
Cohen, Israel, 160n.
Cole, G. D. H., 201
Communism, 125–66 passim
  in England during 1930s, 196–247
  passim
  See also Marxism; Union of So-
    viet Socialist Republics
Comte, Auguste, 47, 67, 99, 130,
  248–82
Conant, James B., 333
Connolly, Cyril, 246
Cooper, D. E., 92
Copernicus, Nikolaus, 65
Cornford, John, 215, 216, 229, 240,
  242
Cornforth, Maurice, 214
Cornu, Auguste, 163n.
Coser, Lewis A., 54n., 57n., 61n.,
  62n., 74n., 92n., 112n.
Creative arts
  politics and, 196–247
  universities and, 18

Crosland, Maurice, 73n.
Crossman, Richard, 199, 208
Cultural evolution process, 5–7
Cultural innovation, systematization
  of, 19, 21
  See also Innovation
Cultural specialization, historical de-
  velopment of, 3–24
Cultural systems and social systems,
  analytical independence of, 3–7

Dahrendorf, Ralf, 49–52, 62n., 103
Davidson, Michael, 201n.
Davies, R. W., 96n.
Dean, Gordon, 320–21, 333
Debray, Régis, 105, 108
Deitchman, Seymour, 295
Dick, William, 284, 293–95
Dinerstein, Herbert S., 122n.
Disraeli, Benjamin, 32
Dissent, 30–33, 42–43, 66–122, 314–
  40
Dobb, Maurice, 214
Doone, Rupert, 201n., 223, 224
Dostoevsky, Feodor, 132n.
Dumazedier, Joffre, 100n.
Dungan, Ralph, 288
Durkheim, Emile, 4n.

"Eggheadism," 18
Ehrenzweig, Anton, 65n.
Eliot, George, 160
Eliot, T. S., 200, 205, 224
Elton, Arthur, 225
Empson, William, 199n.
Engels, Friedrich, 132–43 passim,
  161, 163
England, 74
  1930s left-wing intelligentsia, 196–
    247
Enzensberger, Hans Magnus, 107n.
Epstein, Jacob, 231

Fadeev, Alexander, 119n.
Fascell, Dante B., 301, 302

Fascism, English intellectuals and, 196–247 *passim*
Feuerbach, Ludwig A., 131, 133
Fichte, I. H., 128, 129, 160, 165
Finletter, Thomas K., 320
Fischer, Ernst, 103n.
Fitton, James, 218, 226
Ford, Hugh D., 208n.
Forster, E. M., 234
Fourier, François, 128, 133, 141
Fox, Ralph, 219, 238, 240, 242
France, 88–93
Fraser, Representative, 294–95
Frelinghuysen, Representative, 296
French Revolution, 71–74, 82–83, 87
Freud, Sigmund, 70, 75–76, 104n.
Fromm, Erich, 109, 110n.
Fry, Roger, 225
Fuchs, Klaus, 320

Gaitskell, Hugh, 198
Galbraith, John Kenneth, 338n.
Ganz, Herbert J., 111n.
Garman, Douglas, 243
Geiger, Abraham, 159
Genet, Jean, 92
Gide, André, 242
Gillespie, C. C., 68n.
Gladstone, William, 32
Glazer, Nathan, 107n.
Goitein, I., 163n.
Gollancz, Victor, 235, 243
Gombrowicz, Witold, 92n.
Goodman, Richard, 199
Gordon-Walker, Patrick, 199
Gorky, Maxim, 95–97
Gould, Julius, 107n.
Graetz, Heinrich, 153
Grant, Duncan, 231
Gray, Gordon, 315
Gray Committee, 333
Grazia, Alfred de, 59n., 67n.
Grazia, Sebastian de, 110n.
Greece, 6–9
Grierson, John, 224–25

Grigson, Geoffrey, 228
Groves, Leslie, General, 328
Grün, Karl, 133, 141
Guest, David, 201n., 214, 242
Guinness, Alec, 223
Guizot, F. M., 32
Gurvitch, Georges, 60

Habermas, Jurgen, 103n.
Halle, Louis J., 297
Hannah, John, 300
Hanson, N. R., 57n.
Harris, Fred R., 301
Hastings, Lord, 226
Heath, T. L., 65n.
Hegel, Georg Wilhelm Friedrich, 77–78, 80, 128, 130–44 *passim*, 156, 159
Heidegger, Martin, 80
Helvétius, Madame, 72
Hess, Moses, 125–66
Heuss, Theodor, 51
Hirsch, Helmut, 161n.
Hiss, Alger, 333
History, three states of (Comte), 266–68
Hobbes, Thomas, 14, 31, 47
Hobshawm, Eric, 110n.
Hofstadter, Richard, 61n., 69n.
Hölderlin, Friedrich, 80, 81n.
Holland, James, 218, 226
Holton, Gerald, 69n.
Hopper, Rex, 283n.
Horowitz, Irving Louis, 285–86, 293
Howe, Irving, 113n.
Hughes, H. Stuart, 113n.
Huizinga, John, 62n.
Humanities and sciences, conflict between, 16, 64
Husserl, Edmund, 80
Huszar, E. B. de, 54n.
Huxley, Aldous, 234

Ideas
  classification of, 62–80
  society's receptivity to, 58–59

Ideology, 22–24
India, 6–7, 9
Individual freedom, 278–82
Industrialization, 83–122 *passim*
Innovation, 19, 21, 58–59, 84–86
Institutionalization, 36–38, 55–57, 71–80, 89–90, 113–17
Intellectual
   analysis of, problems in, 53–62 *passim*
   and bourgeois society, 56–57
   as a collectivity, 58–61
   as a role type, 3–24, 61–62
   as articulator of cultural values, 3–24 *passim*, 54
   community, structure of, 33–39
   cultural vs. social considerations by, 4
   definition of, 55–83
   functions of, 26–33, 49–52
   historical antecedents of, 34–36
   ideal, pursuit of, 32
   intersocietal models provided by, 29–30
   in business, 31
   intra-intellectual alienation, 30–31
   nature of, 25–26
   origin of term, 87n.
   socio-structural problem, 56–59
   traditions, 39–47
   See also specific entries
Intellectual training, social importance of, 18–21
Intelligentsia, origin of term, 87–88
Isherwood, Christopher, 197–203 *passim*, 207, 223, 224
Israel, 6–9
   See also Zionism

Jacobs, Norman, 111n.
Jews, 125–66
John, Augustus, 231
Johnson, Lyndon Baines, 288, 299

Kahn, Derek, 198, 199
Kalischer, Hirsch, 154, 160

Kapitsa, P. L., 96n., 97n.
Kaplan, Norman, 96n.
Kaverin, Venyamin, 119n.
Kelley, Mervin, 325
Kennan, George, 323
Keynes, J. M., 31
Kierkegaard, Sören, 90
Kling, Merle, 113n.
Kluckhohn, Clyde, 5n.
Klugmann, James, 215
Knowledge, three states of (Comte), 257–60
Koestler, Arthur, 65n.
Kornhauser, William, 111n.
Kraus, Karl, 101n.
Kraus, Wolfgang, 121n.
Kroeber, Alfred Louis, 19n.
Kuhn, Thomas S., 58n., 63n., 68–69

Lacan, Jacques, 104n.
Lafleur, Laurence, 67n.
Laharanne, Ernest, 154
Laing, R. D., 92
Lane, Robert E., 116n.
Lasch, Christopher, 117n.
Laski, Harold, 235
Lassalle, Ferdinand, 140n., 143–44, 157
Lasswell, Harold D., 108n.
Lawrence, D. H., 200
Lehmann, John, 199n., 201, 203, 205, 228
Levy, Hyman, 234
Lewes, George Henry, 160
Lewis, Cecil Day, 197–99, 201, 204, 206, 207, 227, 233, 234, 245–46
Liberty of conscience, dogma of, 249–50
Lichtheim, George, 91, 99n.
Lilienthal, David, 319, 320
Lipset, Seymour Martin, 82, 97, 112
Li-Ssu, 47
Lukács, Georg, 78, 100, 163n.
Luther, Martin, 10

McCarthy, Joseph, 316, 318, 328
McLuhan, Marshall, 110n., 118n.
McNamara, Robert, 284n., 288, 289
MacNeice, Louis, 198, 199, 223, 224, 247
Madge, Charles, 199n., 214
Maistre, Joseph de, 47
Malthus, Thomas, 282
Mannheim, Karl, 60, 62n., 84–85, 111n.
Marcuse, Herbert, 103n., 109, 110n.
Marshall, Herbert, 221, 232
Martin, Kingsley, 234
Marxism, 45–46, 60n., 67, 70, 76–78, 85–86, 93–99, 103–4n., 105, 111, 127, 130–44 passim, 156–66 passim, 207–12
Masaryk, Thomas, 32
Mass society concept, 110–11
Mazzola, Michel, 93n.
Medley, Robert, 199, 223
Mendelssohn, Moses, 151, 152, 158
Merton, R. K., 17, 57n., 61n., 68n., 85, 102n.
Meyer, Frank, 215
Military, intellectual and, 282–340 passim
Millenarian tradition, 43, 45–46
Mills, C. Wright, 114, 285, 286
Milton, John, 31, 196
Mitchison, Naomi, 201n.
Montagu, Slater, 219
Montesquieu, Charles de, 98
Moore, Henry, 223, 231, 234
Moore, J. Barrington, Jr., 58n.
Morality, 276–78
Morgan, Thomas J., 315
Morin, Edgar, 81
Mornet, Daniel, 72n.
Morris, William, 196
Murray, Thomas E., 334

Natonek, Rabbi, 155
Nehru, Jawaharlal, 32
Nettl, J. P., 53–122
Nichols, Kenneth, General, 329
Nicolson, Ben, 231

Nietzsche, Friedrich Wilhelm, 90
Nisbet, Robert A., 98n., 283–313
Norstad, Lauris, General, 323
Novalis (Friedrich von Hardenberg), 80

Odets, Clifford, 221
Oliphant, Laurence, 160
Oppenheimer, Robert, 115–16, 314–40
Order, anti-intellectual tradition of, 43, 47
Orwell, George, 80–81, 208, 247
Owen, Wilfred, 206

Parsons, Talcott, 3–24, 54, 57n., 60n., 79, 97, 112, 113
Penrose, Roland, 231
Peri, Ladislaw, 226
Pestel, Paul, 160
Philosophic breakthrough, 5–7
Picasso, Pablo, 231
Piper, John, 223
Pipes, Richard, 94n.
Plato, 31, 47, 59
Pluralism, 23
Politics, intellectual and, 21, 30–33, 42–43, 49–52, 82, 86–122 passim
Populistic tradition, 43, 46–47
Positivism. See Comte, Auguste
Price, Don K., 294
Printing, development of, 34
Project Camelot, 101n., 283–313
Proudhon, Pierre, 141, 142, 158
Pure science, 37
  and applied, conflict between, 16–18

Rees, Gonorys, 201n.
Reformation, the, 71, 83–86
Religion, 12, 41–43, 45, 167–95
  historic role of, 9–11
  pure and applied functions of, 4–5
Renaissance, the, 10–11
Reuss, Henry S., 302
Rickword, Edgell, 219, 240

Rieff, Philip, 76n., 78n., 116n., 314–40

Roberts, Michael, 204–7, 211

Robertson, Roland, 122n.

Roman Empire, 9

Romanism, in United States history, 169–94 passim

Romantic tradition, 43–45

Romilly, Edmund and Giles, 216

Rostow, W. W., 21n.

Rotha, Paul, 225

Rothe, Wolfgang, 101

Rowe, Clifford, 217, 231

Ruge, Arnold, 132, 133, 137

Rusk, Dean, 284, 288, 289, 296–99

Saint-Simon, Claude Henri de, 47, 98, 128, 133, 141

Salvador, Joseph, 160

Samuels, Stuart, 196–247

Sartre, Jean-Paul, 92, 104n.

Schelling, Friedrich Wilhelm von, 128–30

Schelsky, Helmut, 103

Schumpeter, Joseph, 56–57, 62n.

Sciences
  applied, increasing importance of, 20–21
  applied vs. pure, 16–18
  classification of, 260–62
  politics and, 283–340
  positive reorganization of (Comte), 273–75
  pure, 37

Scientism, tradition of, 43, 44

Scientist, dissent by, 115–17, 314–40

Sears, David, 116n.

Seitz, Frederick, 304–5, 307

Seton-Watson, Hugh, 121n.

Shaw, George Bernard, 196

Shelley, Percy Bysshe, 196

Shils, Edward, 25–48, 81n., 82, 111–12

Silberner, E., 127n., 133n., 140n., 145n.

Smith, Robertson, 5

Snow, C. P., 112n., 234

Social class, intellectual and, 13–16

Social disorganization and reorganization, 248–82

Socialism, 125–66 passim
  See also Marxism

Social structure
  and diffusion of ideas, 65
  intellectual and, 56–59

Social systems
  conflict of, 264–66
  and cultural systems, analytical independence of, 3–7

Society, intellectual and, 25–52 passim, 102–4

Sociology, 53–64 passim, 98, 108–19
  federal government involvement with, 283–313
  ideology and, 23–24

Sontag, Susan, 106

Sontheimer, Kurt, 107n., 109n.

Sovereignty of the people, dogma of, 250–51

Soviet Union. See Union of Soviet Socialist Republics

Spanish Civil War, English intellectuals and, 228–47

Spender, Stephen, 197–210 passim, 223, 224, 227, 233, 238, 239, 241, 247

Spinoza, B., 128, 129, 133

Stansky, Peter, 208n.

Stein, Lorenz, 137

Steiner, George, 118n.

Steinschneider, Moritz, 159

Stephen, Adrian, 234

Stirner, Max, 141

Strachey, John, 219, 235

Strauss, David Friedrich, 131

Strauss, Lewis, 320

Strauss, Robert, 16n.

Structuralism, 103–4n.

Student activism, 115, 122, 104–8

Symons, Julian, 208n.

Taine, Hippolyte, 47, 73n.

Tannenbaum, Frank, 14n., 24
Taubes, Jacob, 54n., 86n.
Tawney, R. H., 234
Taylor, A. J. P., 198, 201n.
Teaching, historical function of, 8–9
Teller, Edward, 320
Theocracies, 269–73
Theory and practice, separation of, 251–56
Thierry, Augustin, 148
Thomas, Tom, 220
Thornton, T. P., 122n.
Tocqueville, Alexis de, 82–83
Tomkins, Sylvan S., 69n.
Totalitarianism, 100–1
   See also Fascism
Toynbee, Arnold, 130, 212
Toynbee, Philip, 212

Union of Soviet Socialist Republics, 87–88, 93–98, 118–21, 122
United States, barbarism in, historical, 167–95
University, 17–21, 65, 71–80, 113–17, 211–17, 311–12
   and creative arts, 18
   development of, 14–15, 36
   nationality, idea of, and, 36 37
   as sponsor of social science projects, 306–7
Upward, Edward, 199, 201, 203, 217, 240

Vallance, Theodore, 285, 295
Vandenberg, Hoyt Sanford, 322
Van Duzen, Charles H., 73n.
Van Gyseghem, Andre, 221, 222
Velikovsky, Immanuel, 59n., 67n.
Verne, Jules, 55
Violence, in American society, 167–95 passim

Warner, Rex, 198
Weber, Adolf, 100
Weber, Max, 7n., 100
White, Harry Dexter, 328
White, Winston, 24n.
Wiener, Norbert, 336
Wiener, Jerome, 21n.
Williams, Robin M., 109n.
Williams-Ellis, Annabel, 219
Wilson, Woodrow, 32
Wilson, Charles, 317
Wintringham, Tom, 219
Wittgenstein, Ludwig, 75
Wolf, "Doggy," 214
Wood, Neal, 208n.
Woolf, Leonard, 234
Written language, 5–6, 34

Yevtushenko, Yevgeny, 88, 119

Zionism, 125–66 passim
Zlocisti, Theodor, 161n.
Znaniecki, Florian, 59n., 62n., 63n.

K27